= Doubling the Point

Essays and Interviews

J. M. Coetzee

Edited by David Attwell

Harvard University Press
Cambridge, Massachusetts
London, England
1992

This book is printed on acid-free paper, and its binding materials have been chosen for strength and durability.

Library of Congress Cataloging-in-Publication Data

Coetzee, J. M., 1940–
    Doubling the point : essays and interviews / J. M. Coetzee ; edited by David Attwell.
        p.   cm.
    Includes index.
    ISBN 0-674-21517-6 (acid-free paper) (cloth)
    ISBN 0-674-21518-4 (paper)
    1. Coetzee, J. M., 1940–   —Interviews. 2. Authors, South
African—20th century—Interviews. 3. Literature, Modern—History
and criticism. 4. South Africa—Civilization. I. Attwell, David.
II. Title.
 PR9369.3.C58Z464   1992
 823—dc20   91-34251
                CIP

= Doubling the Point

Contents

Author's Note

David Attwell and I set out on this project in 1989 and completed the last interview in early 1991. Regarding the essays, we agreed that he would select and edit them, and that where I revised them I would do so with a light hand, since they were to be seen as part of a larger autobiographical text.

Save for the essay on the revisions of Beckett's *Watt*, from which only an excerpt is given, and the reviews of Musil's stories and the film *The Guest*, from which a few inconsequential paragraphs have been cut, the pieces are accordingly reprinted in full. In three cases—"Samuel Beckett and the Temptations of Style," "Into the Dark Chamber," and "Remembering Texas"—cuts made by earlier editors have been restored.

While trying to respect the character of the originals, I have, in the interest of clarity, done a fair amount of local revision. Style and content are not separable: it would be disingenuous for me to claim that my revisions have not touched the substance of the originals. I have also updated some references, thereby creating anachronisms in one or two of the endnotes.

My thanks to Lindsay Waters for his share in the conception and shaping of this book, to Ann Hawthorne for her scrupulous copyediting, to Dorothy Driver for assistance with proofreading, to Tim James for preparing the diagrams, and to the University of Cape Town for the material support it has given me in my research and writing.

J. M. COETZEE

= Doubling the Point

Editor's Introduction

I
n August 1973 the *New York Times Book Review* devoted its
regular column "The Last Word" to a report which had appeared shortly before in *Scientific American*.[1] It concerned an
experiment conducted at the University of Cape Town, in which
someone had produced a computer-assisted reading of a short
work by Samuel Beckett called *Lessness* (*Sans*, 1969).[2] Using a
Univac 1106, the analyst had gone to certain lengths to identify
the rules of construction in Beckett's text (a structure of repetitions, in which all the phrases appearing in the first half of the
work are repeated in a different order in the second). Exasperated
by what seemed mere pedantry—"Ah, Beckett! Ah, Cape Town!"—
the columnist ended with a quotation from Günter Grass: "'Our
listeners' ears have grown to tunnels . . . not a single word sticks.'"

The scholar in question was J. M. Coetzee. A decade later, Coetzee would appear in a different guise altogether, that of an internationally respected novelist. By the late 1970s, his reputation had
been established in South Africa. With the appearance of his third
novel, *Waiting for the Barbarians* (1980), a wider readership began
to develop, first in the United Kingdom and then in the United
States. Today, he is regarded as being in the foremost rank of
contemporary writers of fiction.[3] Indeed, Coetzee brings to his
work a unique combination of intellectual power, stylistic poise,
historical vision, and ethical penetration. Was the columnist for
the *New York Times*, with his seemingly urbane dismissal, simply
mistaken? Not entirely: Coetzee did spend several years from the
late 1960s to the early 1970s pursuing what turned out to be the
relatively unrewarding, technical branch of modern stylistics. But
what the columnist missed, what he could not have foreseen, was
what was at stake in those early wanderings: a rigorous inquiry
into the ontology of fictional discourse, and an attempt to locate

a position from which Coetzee himself might one day begin to speak.

Doubling the Point explores the relations between Coetzee's critical writing from 1970 to 1990, and his fiction, an oeuvre of six novels which have appeared regularly every three to four years since 1974. More than an anthology of critical essays, this book establishes the connections between the different elements of Coetzee's literary activity. Readers may have encountered Coetzee as critic previously through his essays on colonial and early twentieth-century South African literature, collected in *White Writing* (1988) or through his reviews in the *New York Times* and the *New York Review of Books*. But the present volume represents the full range of Coetzee's nonfiction, showing him as linguist and stylistician, critic of metropolitan and modern South African literatures, translator, essayist in popular culture, reviewer, polemicist, and autobiographer. Whatever his achievements in these fields, the intensity and accomplishment of Coetzee's life in literature and scholarship are borne out finally in the novels. The interviews which tie this collection together show the interplay of fiction and scholarship: conducted over a period of two years, they fashion the selection into the shape of a writer's intellectual autobiography.

The notion of "doubling the point" relates, in the first instance, to the kind of autobiography the collection represents. The relevant illustration is from Coetzee's *Foe* (1986). As the bearer of literary authority, Foe (Daniel Defoe's original patronym) is advising Susan Barton—a would-be autobiographer—on the subject of selfhood and its relation to language:

> In a life of writing books, I have often, believe me, been lost in the maze of doubting. The trick I have learned is to plant a sign or marker in the ground where I stand, so that in my future wanderings I shall have something to return to, and not get worse lost than I am. Having planted it, I press on; the more often I come back to the mark (which is a sign to myself of my blindness and incapacity), the more certainly I know I am lost, yet the more I am heartened too, to have found my way back.[4]

Foe plants a sign as a marker. Coetzee's writings on literature, rhetoric, popular culture, and censorship are his personal markers; taken together, they provide a retrospective itinerary. Just as Foe's markers remind him of what he does not know, so these essays and reviews provide Coetzee with occasions for further reflection in the interviews. There can be no final guarantees, of course, but the strategy strengthens the possibility that Coetzee's "doubling back" will involve more than mere repetition. The decision to turn to dialogue as the appropriate medium makes this principle explicit, even as it increases the risk of failure. And there are limits to the enterprise. It is true, as Coetzee says here, that all writing is autobiographical; but for a novelist the two genres cannot be on the same footing: autobiography is secondary to fiction—hence the element of redundancy in the title. Readers will find in these dialogues, therefore, a desire, on one hand, to conduct a conscientious inquiry in which Coetzee is not installed as final authority, and, on the other, a desire not to supplant the novels themselves.

"Doubling the point" refers, more broadly, to the reflexive self-consciousness which characterizes all Coetzee's work. This particular turn in Coetzee is not simply the usual reminder of the constitutive functions of language that has become so familiar a trademark of contemporary fiction. For although Coetzee might well be described as working within the culture of postmodernism, he certainly does not do so in the spirit of abandonment that seems to typify much of what goes under the name. Rather, reflexivity here is a mode of self-consciousness which, informed by Coetzee's learning, is directed at understanding the conditions—linguistic, formal, historical, and political—governing the writing of fiction in contemporary South Africa. This volume, therefore, intimating the history (since early mercantile expansionism) of "rounding the Cape," implicitly reflects on an encounter in which the legacies of European modernism and modern linguistics enter the turbulent waters of colonialism and apartheid. It is this that makes Coetzee's work particularly illuminating today: a form of postcoloniality felt on the bone, it brings its metropolitan heritage into a charged and complex relationship with the historical crisis in which it finds itself.

There are marked variations of register in Coetzee's nonfiction. Since *Doubling the Point* is organized along biographical rather than thematic lines, it necessarily reflects that diversity. Furthermore, the selection is broadly but not rigorously chronological: the composition of each chapter allows for areas of concentration which stand out in the record. The interviews define these contours clearly enough; for newcomers to Coetzee, however, or for readers familiar with the novels who need points of entry into the relations between the fiction and scholarship, the following pages offer a narrative of significant developments in Coetzee's intellectual biography.[5]

Coetzee's principal concern from *Life & Times of Michael K* (1983) to his most recent novel, *Age of Iron* (1990), is the nature and crisis of fiction-writing in South Africa today, the South Africa of what Nadine Gordimer has called "the interregnum."[6] The argument—less a "position" than a condition of Coetzee's work—is that the discursive-political consequences of the country's protracted trauma *militate against* fictionality. For what kind of authority can the novel muster if it is to speak in terms commensurable with the times? What form of address is possible under such conditions? Questions such as these bring into focus the more representative crisis of postmodernism and its so-called paralysis before history, but Coetzee's achievement is to have found the means, within fiction, to interrogate this paralysis—indeed, not only to interrogate it but to move beyond it to a reconstructed position in which fiction begins to speak to the political on its own terms. This Coetzee manages both by drawing into his fiction the skepticism and symptomatic sensitivity of poststructuralism, and by searching for ways in which the novel might recover an ethical basis, in full appreciation of the political context.

Needless to say, there is a great deal of struggle in this enterprise, which is why Coetzee musters his scholarly resources behind him: his readings of the later modernists (Kafka, Musil, Beckett, Nabokov); his knowledge of modern linguistics (generative grammar, stylistics, rhetoric, continental structuralism and semiotics); his command of the history and development of the novel, from Cervantes through Defoe and Sterne to the Russian realists; and his appreciation of poststructuralism, in particular, his strategic affinities with Lacan, Foucault, and Derrida.

In these essays and interviews, then, one sees the point of Coetzee's mode of reflexive narrative more clearly. One also witnesses its emergence. Obviously, it comes from the modernists and from linguistics, but it was anticipated, curiously enough, by mathematics. For mathematics—Coetzee's professional pursuit before his decision in the mid-1960s to return to literature—prepared the way for the later interest in the rule-conditioned character of discourse. Over several years, Coetzee's absorption in technical stylistics (whose high-water point was a doctoral dissertation on Beckett) involved to some extent an attempt to integrate these elements. Academically, he was perhaps never entirely successful, but the consequences of his academic work for his novel-writing were significant. From the beginning, the novels have included an element of metafictional commentary on the conventions and the politics of form. The entrance of politics, or more strictly, of *power*, into this configuration is the result of Coetzee's immediate context: the linguistic foundations of his relationship with narrative were laid in Texas during the worst years of the war in Vietnam. The connection Coetzee was making at this time between South Africa and the United States was not so much literary as experiential and ethical: he could scarcely avoid associating the spectacle of the bombing of Vietnam with the legacy he was trying to shake off as a South African. As he explains in his memoir on the Texas experience, Noam Chomsky and the universal grammarians had already rendered problematic his youthful, unquestioned affiliation to high modernism (Pound, Eliot). But the war in Vietnam and its domestic consequences, and Coetzee's rediscovery in that moment of his own South African heritage, were decisive in shaping his point of departure in fiction.

It is in this matrix that the first novel, *Dusklands* (1974), was formed. It is a parody juxtaposing Eugene Dawn (one of Chomsky's "backroom boys"), who is writing a report on propaganda methods for the American Department of Defense, and Jacobus Coetzee, an eighteenth-century frontiersman (historically, one of Coetzee's own ancestors) who ventures up the west coast of Southern Africa in search of ivory and produces a deposition to the authorities at the Cape on his return. *Dusklands* is an explosive, even aggressive work which replays some of the dominating, rationalistic discourses of the West in an attempt to understand the forces, both violent and epistemic, which were determining Coetzee's own historical experience and social identity. Although it was begun in

Buffalo, New York, *Dusklands* was completed in South Africa. The decision to return to his country of origin was more or less forced on Coetzee: his application for permanent residence in the United States was repeatedly denied, partly because the terms of his visa required him to return, but possibly, too, because he had been arrested during an antiwar imbroglio on the Buffalo campus (a common enough experience at the time, but less consequential for many others). Coetzee had lived as a cultural émigré for nearly ten years; now, *place* was beginning to reassert itself (as *history* had already done in the spectacle of the war). Coetzee's second novel, *In the Heart of the Country* (1977), tests the limits of a late modernist consciousness—now influenced by the *nouveau roman* and its equivalent in film—in the "savage torpor" of settler-colonialism.

Magda, the narrator of *In the Heart of the Country*, struggles both with the legacy of the political father and with the pathological master-servant relations of the family farm. She is unable, finally, to satisy her desire for association and community, and the novel ends with Magda constructing stone icons addressed to chimerical sky-gods. Hegel's master-slave dialectic lies behind much of Coetzee's ethics and epistemology in this novel, as it had informed parts of *Dusklands*. This is Coetzee's small contribution to the Hegelian-existential critique of colonialism which had been prominent in the 1960s, although its roots go back to Sartre's essay of 1948, *Black Orpheus*, which introduced the *négritude* poets to metropolitan France.[7] Composed as a series of numbered paragraphs, *In the Heart of the Country*, however, also displays its own fictiveness, to the point that Magda begins asking what kind of life she might have led in a domestic metropolitan novel, where she might have "atoned for physical shortcomings with ten nimble fingers on the pianoforte keys and an album full of sonnets."[8] The metafictional commentary here turns on the literature of colonial pastoralism in South Africa, and on the liberal-Romantic novel of isolation, which can be traced back to Olive Schreiner's *The Story of an African Farm* (1883).

But Coetzee is skeptical about what he calls "the impasse of anti-illusionism." Once it has shaken off the tyranny of the real, radical metafiction has few options: it can simply bequeath a record of failed attempts at transcendence, or, in defiance, it can try to turn paralysis into a virtue by appealing to notions of play, though only at the risk of calling up the ghosts of Romanticism. Coetzee shows his discomfort with this position in his translation and commentary on Gerrit Achterberg's "Ballade van de gasfitter." He is concerned here with person as a grammatical category, particularly the relationship between *I* and *You*. He refers to the continental and Prague School structuralists (Emile Benveniste and Roman Jakobson) on pronouns and "shifters" and discusses several traditions of theological, post-Romantic, and existential reflection that depend on the semantics of person. Magda in *In the Heart of the Country* does not speak the monologic discourse of criticism, linguistics, or philosophy, but she dramatizes the vicissitudes of the *I–You* relation, showing its implications for the subject in a deeply divided society where a language of equal exchange seems to be unavailable. The shorter, Barthesian pieces grouped with the Achterberg essay are skirmishes of another kind into the conventions and politics of formal self-consciousness. They draw attention, especially, to the authorial self-positioning and putative class relations encoded in novelistic conventions. In his Jerusalem Prize acceptance speech, delivered some years after these essays, Coetzee returns to the problem of reciprocity, speaking directly of the colonizer's failure of love in South Africa—that is, his valorization of land above people and polity. In this very personal statement, one sees the ethical underpinnings of Coetzee's absorption in the linguistic conditions of reciprocity.

Coetzee's linguistics also enables him to see the continuities between the lowbrow and the highbrow. This is apparent in the attention he gives to film, comic strips, and advertising in the essays grouped together under the rubric of popular culture. There has been less of this kind of work from Coetzee in recent years. He explains this by saying that what engages him more is the construction of and experimentation with rules, rather than the kind of critical demystification to which studies of popular culture are inclined. But these pieces stand as a record of Coetzee's critique of form at every level of culture. The essay on Captain America, especially, is a playful contribution to the concerns of the generation Coetzee had left to its own devices on returning to his native country. It illustrates the mixed appeal of American national myths, and the romantic American rejection (with Marcuse) of technological reason—ideas which also found their way into *Dusklands*.

Toward the end of the 1970s, the scope of Coetzee's stylistics broadened to accommodate more-traditional forms of rhetorical analysis. The essays on passivization enact this shift: concerned though they still are with what Coetzee calls "microenvironments," these essays nevertheless engage the semantic, metaphoric, and rhetorical dimensions of eighteenth-century prose with greater flexibility than in the earlier studies. What prompted the change of emphasis is not immediately obvious: stylistics was at the time abandoning its mechanistic armory (a trend hastened by the rise of deconstruction), but by this stage Coetzee had also spent eight years in South Africa, where such traditions are relatively alien, or at least where Leavisite humanism provided an unreceptive environment for what was a rather scientific formalism. Although Coetzee resists too immediate a connection, the new studies seem to coincide with changes taking place in the fiction. In the earlier essays he had been drawn to the notion that specific linguistic structures could somehow be related to specific epistemologies (Benjamin Whorf had provided the most tempting account of this theory in his work on the Hopi); later, Coetzee began to raise questions of strategy, asking whether there are not signs of discontinuity in the relation of form and content which would reveal symptomatically a writer's attempts to push at the limits of available discourses. This is evident especially in the essay on Newton, where Coetzee discovers that a Whorfian prediction about Newton's prose—that it ought to reflect a mechanistic epistemology—is inadequate to Newton's struggle literally to find the right words with which to account for gravitational force.

This scholarly development, in which language is conceived less as an imprisoning structure than as a field of contestation, has its literary fruit in *Waiting for the Barbarians* (1980). The novel deals with that moment of suspension when an empire imagines itself besieged and plots a final reckoning with its enemies. In the poem by C. P. Cavafy which gives Coetzee his title, these nervous pleasures quickly turn into anxiety when the barbarians fail to materialize at the city gates: "Those people were some sort of solution," says Cavafy.[9] Coetzee's novel stages this dependency, dramatizing the terroristic drive of the imperial state to achieve mastery. (It is difficult not to associate this with the South African government's policy of "total strategy," which was developed in the late

1970s to counter growing insurrection and international isolation.) The novel's writerliness, its determination to establish its own, fictive manipulation of history, lies not only in its formal stability (when measured against the earlier novels) but also in its attention to questions of signification and closure: for instance, in the magistrate-narrator's attempts to read the body of the tortured barbarian girl, to decipher the remains of a barbarian script recovered from his archaeological diggings, or to write a history of imperial settlement. The magistrate fails in each of these projects, providing disconfirmation at every turn of what Foucault in the introduction to *The Archaeology of Knowledge* called "the sovereignty and transcendence of the subject" of historical discourse.[10] Indeed, History emerges in this novel as the informing myth of empire itself: "What has made it impossible for us to live in time like fish in water, like birds in air, like children? It is the fault of Empire! Empire has created the time of history."[11] The moment is an empowering one because from this point on in Coetzee, the question of history becomes a question of *living in historical culture;* instead of being the ambivalent medium of a reaction to historical givens, fiction has become an arena in which historical discourse and fictionality begin to compete for authority.

Coetzee's return to Kafka, after *Barbarians*, is therefore a logical development. The essay on verb tenses in "The Burrow" follows Kafka into a syntactic labyrinth where one witnesses the act of writing as a mode of self-preservation in a highly politicized culture. The novel which resembles this project most closely is, of course, *Life & Times of Michael K.* Coetzee's K is a prodigious survivor in a South Africa of the near future as it marches into a corrosive civil war. The novel's minutely observed scenario of social conditions, however, only creates a framework of quasi-realism in which K's resilience and elusiveness appear all the more miraculous. A municipal gardener in Cape Town, K journeys to the Karoo with his dying mother to return her to the farm where she spent part of her youth in a family of servants. She dies en route, but K continues, burying her ashes on what seems to be the farm, and planting pumpkins and melons. He declines to join the rebels and escapes internment several times. Marked with a harelip, K remains outside human intercourse and, by extension, outside the culture's various forms of entrapment. As the well-meaning medical officer puts it, maddened by K's resistance to all attempts to rehabilitate him: "Your stay in the camp was merely an allegory, if you know that word. It was an allegory—speaking at the highest level—of how scandalously, how outrageously a meaning can take up residence within a system without becoming a term in it."[12] "K" is therefore Coetzee's muted affirmation of the freedom to narrate, to textualize; the narratological equivalent, in a sense, of the Derridean trace. However, Coetzee's is a precarious affirmation whose pertinence comes from a precise and clear-eyed recognition of a general hostility which continually threatens textuality's eclipse.

In *Foe* (1986), Coetzee turns directly to the situation of marginality from which he speaks. This shift, from an affirmation of textual freedom to an analysis of marginality, involves a characteristic turn of self-qualification. In what is perhaps his most allegorical work, Coetzee replays *Robinson Crusoe* as an account of the relations between the institution of letters (Foe), the colonial storyteller seeking authorization through the metropolis (Susan Barton), and the silenced voice of the colonized subject (Friday). The narration belongs, in the main, to Barton, who seeks out Foe in an effort to get the story of her sojourn on Cruso's island told; but the true authority, indeed potency, of the tale belongs to Friday, whose tongue has been severed in an unspecified act of mutilation and who therefore cannot speak or articulate that authority. Friday's watchful presence as what Gayatri Chakravorty Spivak calls the "wholly other"[13] closes down the narrative in an act of authorial deference or abnegation, on Coetzee's part. In a final sequence, an unnamed narrator enters the scene of writing, a shipwreck in which paraphernalia of the Crusoe tradition— including Barton's own narrative—lies buried. The only sign of life comes from Friday, but Friday's home is "a place where bodies are their own signs." Friday's breath overwhelms the narrator, flowing "up through his body and out upon me; it passes through the cabin, through the wreck; washing the cliffs and shores of the island, it runs northward and southward to the ends of the earth."[14] Coetzee's deference is to a form of truth-telling which the novel itself cannot possess, a truth-telling which neutralizes textuality the closer it approaches full consciousness of its own conditions of possibility.

Coetzee seems to prepare for this conclusion in what is perhaps the most challenging and substantial of the essays collected here, the study of confession in Rousseau, Tolstoy, and Dostoevsky. The principle elaborated here is that truth in confession cannot be arrived at by introspection alone, no matter how rigorous, that the endless story of the self will be brought to finality only at the point where it is most unaware; release comes with an affirmation or imposition of truth—alternatively, from grace. This is not an easy lesson for a secular, critical postmodernism to absorb, but it is one that enables Coetzee to address more directly the crucial problem of narrative authority. This question had been surfacing ever since *Life & Times of Michael K*, of course, although one could go back still further, to Coetzee's use of gender since *In the Heart of the Country* to dramatize power relations as they affect speech and discourse. But if we read the later fiction in relation to the essay on confession, we can see that Coetzee's address to the problem of authority depends on two unstated propositions: first (and more obviously), the brute facticity of power can halt the endlessness of textuality; but second, if authority *is* ultimately a function of power, then it ought to be possible, through the rediscovery of fiction's capacity to reconfigure the rules of discourse, to find a position *outside* current power relations from which to speak. This is the sense in which Coetzee speaks, in these interviews, of the imperative to "imagine the unimaginable."

Age of Iron (1990) rests on similar principles. Elizabeth Curren, a retired lecturer in classics at the University of Cape Town, is dying of cancer in a society infected with other kinds of malignancy. She has little or no authority: her death is a private one, and her canon is largely ignored. However, her very marginality frees her, paradoxically, to speak with extraordinary candor. Thus she tells Thabane, who tries to get her to understand the uncompromising, "iron" logic of the township comrades:

> "I fear I know comradeship all too well. The Germans had comradeship, and the Japanese, and the Spartans. Shaka's impis too, I'm sure. Comradeship is nothing but a mystique of death, of killing and dying, masquerading as what you call a bond (a bond of what? Love? I doubt it). I have no sympathy with this comradeship. You are wrong, you and Florence and everyone else, to be taken in by it and, worse, to encourage it in children. It is just

another of those icy, exclusive, death-driven male constructions. That is my opinion."[15]

She and Thabane "agree to differ." In the novel's climax, which involves a chilling police assassination of a young activist in the servants' quarters of her own backyard, Elizabeth is reminded yet again that the corruption starts with the criminality of apartheid. In the novel, then, Elizabeth's opinions seem to count for little. But why is it that they strike the reader with such force? Does Elizabeth really have no authority? Far from this being an attempt, on Coetzee's part, to retrieve an unreconstructed liberal-humanism—which has been compromised, like Elizabeth, by complicity—Elizabeth seems to project us forward to a society in which judgment is once again *possible*, a society in which ethical consciousness is not hamstrung by interestedness. In his brief essay on the representation of torture in South African literature, "Into the Dark Chamber," Coetzee speaks of the ethical vision he finds in Gordimer's *Burger's Daughter*, a novel which anticipates a time when "human acts . . . are returned to the ambit of moral judgment," when it will "once again be *meaningful* for the gaze of the author . . . to be turned upon scenes of torture." The vision is no less a feature of Coetzee's own work. What is distinctive in Coetzee, however, is that he broaches the possibility of ethical reconstruction in a movement which begins with abnegation, with the recognition of unbridgeable historical constraints. It is a scrupulous position: more than conscious of the limits of its authority, it nevertheless anticipates a properly ethical reciprocity at some as-yet-unimagined historical moment. One is reminded of Theodor Adorno's essay on commitment, in which he says (appropriately, for the present context, with reference to Kafka and Beckett): "As eminently constructed and produced objects, works of art, including literary ones, point to a practice from which they abstain: the creation of a just life."[16]

Doubling the Point shows that although Coetzee's intellectual affiliations are largely metropolitan, the pressures to which his fiction responds are local and national. Indeed, in its dramatization of what it means to narrate-in-history, in the story it tells of a struggle with the dynamics of authorial agency, Coetzee's work makes visible the connections between narrativity and nationhood in his particular situation. South Africa seems poised before a new phase of history: the legalization of oppositional activity, the release of numbers of political prisoners, and the repeal of racially discriminatory legislation, have, since February 1990, created conditions in which a different conception of the nation-state seems to be emerging, in which, at least, a debate between the chief antagonists over the meaning of nationhood has begun to develop. In this context, Coetzee's achievement seems to be a timely one. His struggle with the problem of agency is exemplary in bringing to light the *positionality* which underlies any attempt to imagine the collective. Moreover, in Coetzee both narrativity and nationhood are shown to be fragile structures: the fragmentation, the susceptibilities, are revealed through the essentially ethical prism of an ideal of equality and reciprocity. This achievement could have come about, however, only through Coetzee's almost relentless skepticism, and an unwavering commitment to the exigencies of his artistic practice. While the fruits of his labor are in the novels themselves, the story of Coetzee's determination to follow his subject, wherever it leads, is the story of these pages.

= Beckett

=

Interview

DA: I would like to begin at the beginning, by raising the question of autobiography. There are few contemporary writers whose work enjoins us quite as rigorously as yours to examine the authenticity and authority of the speaking subject. The question is implicit in each novel from *Dusklands* on, and it is explicitly handled in *Foe;* in criticism, you have looked closely at autobiographical "truth" and confessional writing in Tolstoy, Rousseau, and Dostoevsky. In view of the prominence given to this question in your work, it is not surprising that you have written so little autobiographical prose, in the ordinary sense. What is it, then, that enables you to speak about the relationship between your critical activity and your fiction?

JMC: Let me treat this as a question about telling the truth rather than as a question about autobiography. Because in a larger sense all writing is autobiography: everything that you write, including criticism and fiction, writes you as you write it. The real question is: This massive autobiographical writing-enterprise that fills a life, this enterprise of self-construction (shades of *Tristram Shandy!*)—does it yield only fictions? Or rather, among the fictions of the self, the versions of the self, that it yields, are there any that are truer than others? How do I know when I have the truth about myself?

My first response is that we should distinguish two kinds of truth, the first truth to fact, the second something beyond that; and that, in the present context, we should take truth to fact for granted and concentrate on the more vexing question of a "higher" truth.

But what is truth to fact? You tell the story of your life by selecting from a reservoir of memories, and in the process of selecting you leave things out. To omit to say that you tortured flies as a child is, logically speaking, as much an infraction of truth to fact as to say that you tortured flies when in fact you didn't. So to call autobiography—or indeed history—true as long as it does not lie invokes a fairly vacuous idea of truth.

Therefore, instead of trying to distinguish between kinds of truth, let me come at the question from a different angle.

As you write—I am speaking of any kind of writing—you have a feel of whether you are getting closer to "it" or not. You have a sensing mechanism, a feedback loop of some kind; without that mechanism you could not write. It is naive to think that writing is a simple two-stage process: first you decide what you want to say, then you say it. On the contrary, as all of us know, you write because you do not know what you want to say. Writing reveals to you what you wanted to say in the first place. In fact, it sometimes constructs what you want or wanted to say. What it reveals (or asserts) may be quite different from what you thought (or half-thought) you wanted to say in the first place. That is the sense in which one can say that writing writes us. Writing shows or creates (and we are not always sure we can tell one from the other) what our desire was, a moment ago.

Writing, then, involves an interplay between the push into the future that takes you to the blank page in the first place, and a resistance. Part of that resistance is psychic, but part is also an automatism built into language: the tendency of words to call up other words, to fall into patterns that keep propagating themselves. Out of that interplay there emerges, if you are lucky, what you recognize or hope to recognize as the true.

I don't see that "straight" autobiographical writing is any different *in kind* from what I have been describing. Truth is something that comes in the process of writing, or comes from the process of writing.

So we return to the question of elementary lies. I am tempted to try out the following definition of autobiography: that it is a kind of self-writing in which you are constrained to respect the facts of your history. But which facts? All the facts? No. All the facts are too many facts. You choose the facts insofar as they fall in with your evolving purpose. What is that purpose in the present case? Tentatively I propose: to understand the desire that drove me to write what I wrote from 1970 to 1990—not the novels, which are well enough equipped to perform their own interrogations, but everything else, the critical essays, the reviews, and so forth—pieces whose genre does not usually give them room to reflect on themselves.

Is that my true purpose? The truth is, at this stage of our interchange I probably know as little about my purpose, which lies in the present, as about the drives and desires, lying in the past, that I am now returning to. Desire and purpose are on the same level: one does not command the other. Perhaps that is why I have turned to the mode of dialogue: as a way of getting around the impasse of my own monologue.

DA: Can we go back to the period before 1970? Before you began writing in earnest you served different apprenticeships, not all of them literary. You turned to fiction only after pursuing three different academic specialisms—mathematics (later, computer science), literary studies, and linguistics—and after taking your philological interests to the doctoral stage. Aside from the poetry and other work you produced as a student at the University of Cape Town, it was well over ten years before you committed yourself to fiction. To what extent was this preparation, and to what extent paralysis?

JMC: It is true, I wrote nothing of substance before I was thirty. I am not sure this was wholly a bad thing. How many men in their twenties write novels worth reading? But of course I did not see it like that, at the time. I did not say to myself, "Wait, you are not yet thirty . . ." On the contrary, as I remember those days, it was with a continual feeling of self-betrayal that I did not write. Was it paralysis? Paralysis is not quite the word. It was more like nausea: the nausea of facing the empty page, the nausea of writing without conviction, without desire. I think I knew what beginning would be like, and balked at it. I knew that once I had truly begun, I would have to go through with the thing to the end. Like an execution: one cannot walk away, leaving the victim dangling at the end of a rope, kicking and choking, still alive. One has to go all the way. (I could have used a metaphor of birth, I realize, but let it stand as it is.) I hesitated through the 1960s because I suspected, rightly, that I would not be able to carry the project through. But the materials for *Dusklands* had begun to be assembled a long way back. William Burchell, for instance, I had been reading and making notes from as early as 1962, knowing that they would go into some such book as *Dusklands* turned out to be.

DA: Can we turn to your introduction to the novel? While living in London in 1962–63, you wrote a master's thesis (300-odd pages) for the University of Cape Town on Ford Madox Ford. Later, in Texas, in 1967–68, you wrote your doctoral dissertation on stylistic analysis, concentrating on Beckett's English fiction. How did you come to be involved with these authors in particular, and what did they—or the kind of fiction they wrote—represent to you?

JMC: I had read Ford Madox Ford as an undergraduate and been much attracted to him: to the Tietjens tetralogy in the first place, then to *The Good Soldier.* I had come to Ford via Pound, who thought him the finest prose stylist of his day. The kind of aestheticism Ford stood for struck a chord in me: good prose was a matter of cutting away, of paring down (though Ford actually wrote voluminously); novel-writing was a craft as well as a vocation; and so forth. But I now suspect that there was more to the attraction than that. Ford gives the impression of writing from inside the English governing class, but in fact he wrote as an outsider, and as a somewhat yearning outsider at that. His father was an anglicized German, and his mother was born into the Pre-Raphaelite circle—bohemians of a kind. Ford's social aspirations drove him to become in many ways *plus anglais que les anglaises.* He cultivated a kind of gruff stoicism, which he thought of as Tory (old-fashioned Tory, of course) and embodied in his hero Christopher Tietjens. I now suspect that what attracted me to Ford was as much the ethics of Tietjens as the aesthetics of *le mot juste.*

Which is not to say that when I myself write I do not quite laboriously search out the right word. I do believe in spareness—more spareness than Ford practiced. Spare prose and a spare, thrifty world: it's an unattractive part of my makeup that has exasperated people who have had to share their lives with me. On the other hand, I was reading George Bourne the other day, on rural England pre-1914. The key word for Bourne, a complex, value-laden word with a long history, is *thrift:* the culture of the western European peasantry was a culture of thrift. My family roots lie in that peasant culture, transplanted from Europe to Africa. So I am quite deeply ambivalent about disparaging thrift.

As for Beckett, I had read *Waiting for Godot* in the 1950s when it was a talking-point all over the world, but the encounter that meant more to me was with *Watt,* and after that with *Molloy* and, to a lesser extent, the other novels. Beckett's prose, up to and including *The Unnamable,* has given me a sensuous delight that hasn't dimmed over the years. The critical work I did on Beckett originated in that sensuous response, and was a grasping after ways in which to talk about it: to talk about delight.

DA: You worked as a computer programmer in England for four years (1962–1965) before going back into English studies. In Texas, your mathematical and literary interests seem to have come together, under the umbrella of stylistics and stylostatistics (although a few years earlier you had experimented with computer-generated poetry, and were to do so again). Let me put to you some observations about this aspect of your work.

Interest in the quantitative branch of stylistics has waned over the years. Roman Jakobson's essays on verbal patterning, for instance, seem to have proved less influential than much of his other work. But your relationship with the field, even at the time, was complicated and even somewhat contradictory. On one hand, you seem to have been drawn to its positivism, perhaps its promise of objectivity (in your doctoral dissertation you distance yourself from the more intuitive features of New Criticism); on the other hand, you were suspicious of some of the results and consequences of stylistics (the dissertation is also radically self-reflective, even skeptical, about some of its own methods).

Another example of this ambivalence: your earliest published essay (1969) sought to refine the measure of prose "difficulty" developed by the German stylostatistician Wilhelm Fucks,[1] but not long afterward (1971) you published a review of Fucks's *Nach allen Regeln der Kunst* in which you refer to positivism as a "mythology" and mention ironically its assumption, which I assume is a Hegelian one, of an "ascending consciousness."[2] (In your fiction, certainly in *Dusklands,* this ambivalence is resolved in a critique, via Eugene Dawn, of scientific positivism in the service of imperial power.)

In two essays from this period, you brought computer programming into stylistics with results which are interesting in hindsight (though perhaps still rather arcane for many readers). Beckett's *Lessness* consists of 1,538 words; words 770–1,538 repeat words 1–769 in a different order. For this essay (1973) you ran a program which mapped repetitions occurring at different levels—the phrase, the sentence, and the paragraph.[3] In the interpretation you argue that what is most important in the work is not "the final disposition of the fragments but the motions of the consciousness that disposes them" and conclude by saying, "This endless enterprise of splitting and recombining is language, and it offers not the promise of the charm, the ever-awaited magical combination that will bring wealth or salvation, but the solace of the game, the killing of time."

There are games of evasion, games of self-preservation in Beckett's *Watt,* as there are in *Dusklands* (in the second narrative, during Jacobus Coetzee's solitary journey back to the Cape after his encounter with the Namaquas). In the essay, your comments on Beckett seem to resonate not only to the activity of plotting the repetitions, but also to your fiction (and I see that *Dusklands* and the *Lessness* essay were published in the same year).

The second essay in which you used computer programming is "Surreal Metaphors and Random Processes," published much later (1979).[4] Here, having entered a lexicon drawn from translations of Pablo Neruda, you used a random-number generator to produce simple sentences, which you then sifted for properly surreal metaphoric effects—such as "the nude with the haggard fingernail disdains the schoolboy of splendour." You then discuss this process in relation to Breton's poetics. (Incidentally, was the strange poem, "Hero and Bad Mother in Epic," published in *Staffrider* in 1978, a spinoff from this exercise?) This essay is, I think, more immediately illuminating than the one on *Lessness* because in this case the mechanical procedure, by demystifying the element of chance, brings into sharp focus the Romantic and utopian aspirations of surrealism.

What does your absorption in quantitative stylistics mean to you today, as you look back on it? Would it be correct to say that in Beckett, in particular—with his mathematical metaphors and technical obsessions—this trend achieved a working relationship with your other interests, one which was superseded for the most part by structuralism?

JMC: To answer your parenthetical question first: Yes, the poem you mention came out of my interest in, and experiments with, phrase-generation by computer. It's a piece I'm quite fond of, although there is a big hole in it toward the end.

As for the main question, I would distinguish between statistical stylistics and generative stylistics, simply because the mathematics behind the two enterprises are so completely different. They are two distinct fields in which I immersed myself for a long while and from which I emerged with rather little to show for the experience. Why did I do it? A wrong turning, I suppose, a false trail both in my career and in the history of stylistics. It didn't lead anywhere interesting. As stylistics gave up on the ideal of mathematical formalization that at one time inspired it, and started looking to more pragmatic models, I lost interest in it.

Beckett's prose, which is highly rhetorical in its own way, lent itself to formal analysis. I should add that Beckett's later short fictions have never really held my attention. They are, quite literally, disembodied. *Molloy* was still a very embodied work. Beckett's first after-death book was *The Unnamable*. But the after-death voice there still has body, and in that sense was only halfway to what he must have been feeling his way toward. The late pieces speak in post-mortem voices. I am not there yet. I am still interested in how the voice moves the body, moves in the body. (This isn't quite an answer to your question, but it does say something of what matters and does not matter to me in Beckett.)

As for structuralism, the line that intrigued me most was Vladimir Propp's analysis, followed by its structuralist extensions, of how stories (folktales, in Propp's case) are put together. I did experiments with my students in putting together synthetic stories—constructions built up out of common story elements—and then seeing which worked and which didn't work, and so coming to ask what a *nonstory* might be. A common curiosity in postmodern times, don't you think?

DA: I am going to stay with structuralism for a moment. If the actual analytic projects of structuralism, with the possible exception of Propp's work on folktales, did not hold your attention for very long, then is it not the case that what did engage you more fully was the *promise* of structuralism, the confidence with which it claimed to reveal the *langue*, the rule-governedness of things? (This is the connection I am making between structuralism and mathematics.) The emphasis in your fiction—and also in *White Writing*—on myth and epistemic frames seems to share in this aspect of structuralism.

In the mid- to late 1960s, when you were at Texas, the power in American linguistics was shifting from the American structuralism associated with Leonard Bloomfield to generative-transformational grammar. (Before Noam Chomsky, Benjamin Whorf had left his mark on the popularization of linguistics as the basis of a social vision.) At some point during this period, perhaps shortly after, you began reading continental structuralism, not only Roland Barthes but also Claude Lévi-Strauss. In other words, your linguistic studies coincided, quite dramatically it seems, with the emergent moment of linguistics in the West, both as method and as a model for the analysis of culture.

You have commented, in the Texas memoir, on some of these influences; you mention in particular their democratizing effects, and the disquiet that comes with the suspicion "that languages spoke people or at the very least spoke through them." Could you take this further? I am interested in how your linguistic reading might have conditioned not only the obvious preference in your work for nonrealist narrative modes, but also your developing sense of how writing was achieved. How does an interest in the systemic logic of culture become transposed into the business of producing fiction?

JMC: Yes, the actual productions of structuralist analysis—Jakobson's readings of short poems, Lévi-Strauss's readings of myths—though meant to show the creative mind at work, never provided me or any other writer, I believe, with a model or even a suggestion of how to write. In that sense structuralism remained a firmly academic movement. Barthes's phantasies disguised as science were far more valuable.

What structuralism did do for me—and here I have in mind anthropological structuralism and Jakobson's work on folk poetry—was to collapse dramatically the distance between high European culture and so-called primitive cultures. It became clear that fully as much *thinking* went into the productions of primitive cultures. Human culture was human culture, unchanging, more or less, beneath the changing forms of its expression. An old lesson, I suppose; but I had to learn it in my own way.

So, although the heyday of French structuralism, as it touched me in the United States, didn't necessarily have a democratizing effect (your word, about which I'm cautious here—*kratis* is power, after all), it certainly broadened the horizons of someone who had grown up in a European enclave in Africa, who disliked travel, who preferred books to life.

It makes a great deal of sense to assimilate Chomskyan linguistics to structuralism, as you suggest, if only because of the similar weight the two enterprises give to innate structures. I did immerse myself in generative grammar, at quite a technical level. I turned—as one has to if one's interests stretch beyond the grammars of individual languages to questions of universal grammar—to non–Indo-European languages. It was this immersion—shallow enough if one is talking about real command of detail—that gave the biggest jolt to a Western colonial whose imaginary identity had been sewn together (how thinly, and with how many rents!) from the tatters passed down to him by high modernist art.

But the nub of your question is about how these preoccupations relate to the business of producing fiction, and the answer must be, I suppose, that it is hard to see how they do. Nothing one picks up from generative linguistics or from other forms of structuralism helps one to put together a novel. What remained from those studies was probably no more than a very general residue: respect for other cultures, respect for ordinary speakers, for the unconscious knowledge we carry, each of us.

DA: A related question. Your essay "Samuel Beckett and the Temptations of Style" brings together several themes falling under the heading of doubt, formal and conceptual, that you were drawn to in your Beckett studies. I say formal and conceptual: more strictly, you treat these things as inseparable. What are the implications of your search for the underlying matrix of Beckett's prose?

JMC: I think I have already hinted at an answer. Beckett has meant a great deal to me in my own writing—that must be obvious. He is a clear influence on my prose. Most writers absorb influence through their skin. With me there has also been a more conscious process of absorption. Or shall I say, my linguistic training enabled me to see the effects I was undergoing with a degree of consciousness. The essays I wrote on Beckett's style aren't only academic exercises, in the colloquial sense of that word. They are also attempts to get closer to a secret, a secret of Beckett's that I wanted to make my own. And discard, eventually, as it is with influences.

DA: What drew you to the Beckett manuscripts?

JMC: The Beckett manuscripts were in Texas, and I was there. A coincidence. I didn't know they were there before I arrived. But I became quite absorbed in them, particularly in the *Watt* papers. It was heartening to see from what unpromising beginnings a book could grow: to see the false starts, the scratched-out banalities, the evidences of less than furious possession by the Muse.

DA: Let me ask you then: What drew you to Texas?

JMC: In 1964 I was living in England, working in a computer research laboratory. I was going nowhere; I needed to change direction. There seemed to be something in the air, a possibility that linguistics, mathematics, and textual analysis might be brought together in some way (the vague name under which I thought of this synthesis at the time was general morphology). My academic record wasn't good enough to open up major fellowships to me. I wrote to a number of U.S. universities, got a handful of positive responses, chose Texas. They offered $2,100 a year and a reduction in fees, as I remember it, for studying half-time and teaching freshman composition half-time. It was a reasonable stipend, for those days, for that kind of work. Aside from the facts that the University of Texas had a good reputation in linguistics and a big manuscript collection, I knew little about it.

DA: The Texas memoir begins by invoking the immigrant experience, but did you have something more specific in mind here?

JMC: I would not have had the confidence to make that first foray into autobiography without some more solid text to resonate against. I took as my sounding board the prose of *The Education of Henry Adams,* and particularly its affectless irony. I suspect the memoir works only if you have Adams at the back of your mind.

DA: There is a philosophical dimension to Beckett that is somewhat muted in these essays. Hugh Kenner, whose work on Beckett and early modernism you admired, described the Beckett trilogy of *Molloy, Malone Dies,* and *The Unnamable* as undertaking the disintegration of the *cogito,* "[reducing] to essential terms the three centuries during which those ambitious processes of which Descartes is the symbol and progenitor . . . accomplished the dehumanization of man."[5] Kenner also asked whether Descartes, like The Unnamable, was "spoken through by a Committee of the *Zeitgeist.*" Your first two novels address similar issues: in the context of colonialism, speaking within and on behalf of an obsessive rationality (with due regard for the way it coheres with dominance and violence), your narrators play out the failure of the Cartesian self to reach transcendence. Was it indeed Beckett who set you thinking in this direction?

JMC: Not Beckett specifically. There was a confluence of interests. But it is unlikely that Beckett would have gripped me if there hadn't been in him that unbroken concern with rationality, that string of leading men savagely or crazily pushing reason beyond its limits. Nevertheless, *Dusk-*

lands didn't emerge from a reading of Beckett. What was more immediately behind it was the spectacle of what was going on in Vietnam and my gathering sense, as I read back in South African history but more particularly in the annals of the exploration of southern Africa, of what had been going on there.

DA: In several of the essays on Beckett—notably the one on *Murphy*—you discuss the question of formal reflexivity, of fiction displaying its own conventions. However, although what you call the "anti-illusionism" of reflexive consciousness is a position you are comfortable with, you also refer to it as an "impasse." What do you mean here?

JMC: Illusionism is, of course, a word I use for what is usually called realism. The most accomplished illusionism yields the most convincing realist effects. Anti-illusionism—displaying the tricks you are using instead of hiding them—is a common ploy of postmodernism. But in the end there is only so much mileage to be got out of the ploy. Anti-illusionism is, I suspect, only a marking of time, a phase of recuperation, in the history of the novel. The question is, what next?

DA: In addition to Beckett, Nabokov was an important, though lesser, influence on your early fiction. In "Nabokov's *Pale Fire* and the Primacy of Art" (1974)[6] you contrast the reflexive consciousness of the two writers, arguing that whereas Beckett pushes it as far as it is humanly possible to go, Nabokov stops short and even negotiates a way out, finding in reflexivity the post-Romantic supports of irony, high art, and the imagination. You also argue that Nabokov's version is a preemptive attempt, and one that fails, to escape history ("history-as-exegesis") by incorporating interpretation into the fiction. Despite your reserve about his resolutions and evasions, though, you seem sympathetic with Nabokov's nostalgic playfulness about the past, fictionalized in *Pale Fire* as "the child's kingdom of Zembla." You quote a letter by Rilke which explicates this aspect of Nabokov, a passage worth repeating:

> It is our task to imprint this provisional, perishable earth so deeply, so patiently and passionately in ourselves that its reality shall arise in us again "invisibly." *We are the bees of the invisible* . . . And this activity is curiously supported and urged on by the even more rapid fading away of so much of the visible that will no longer be replaced. Even for

our grandparents a "house," a "well," a familiar tower, their very clothes, their coat: were infinitely more, infinitely more intimate; almost everything a vessel in which they found the human and added to the store of the human. Now, from America, empty indifferent things are pouring across, sham things, *dummy life* . . . A house, in the American sense, an American apple or a grapevine over there, has *nothing* in common with the house, the fruit, the grape into which went the hopes and reflections of our forefathers . . . Live things, things lived and conscient of us, are running out and can no longer be replaced. *We are perhaps the last still to have known such things.*[7]

Dusklands is structurally indebted to *Pale Fire*. It deals, moreover, with your own situation, both your experience of America in the late 1960s, and features of your ancestry in South Africa, but it does so ironically and parodically, using the doubling effects of metafiction. The influence seems strong. What account would you give of your relation to Nabokov today?

JMC: If I had to be brief, I would say I have no relation with Nabokov left. Nabokov loved Russia in a way that (one is told) non-Russians cannot understand. He was also proud of his family and his family history. His childhood in Russia was clearly a time of unforgettable happiness. His love and his longing for that departed world are plain in his work; they are what is most engaging in him. But I am not sure he approached the reality that took Russia away from him in a responsible way, in a way that did justice to his native gifts; indeed, he sometimes approached it in a quite childish way, as though the Bolsheviks were to blame for robbing him of his childhood (wouldn't he have grown up anyway?).

Underneath the surface, in Nabokov, there are real pain and real loss. He said he loved America, but how could he have, really? He was grateful to America, he was amused and intrigued by America, he became an expert on America, but his heart (as I read his heart) was as much with the Old World as Rilke's was.

There is more of the tragedy of the loss of that world in Rilke's wonderful letter than there is in all of Nabokov. That is, I think, why I have lost interest in Nabokov: because he balked at facing the nature of his loss in its historical fullness.

DA: Historical fullness is a paradoxical notion here: the more complete and irreversible the loss, the more searching will be—or ought to be—

the writing that comes in its wake? What does this mean to you, as a South African?

JMC: Yes, the more searching it ought to be. I too had a childhood that—in parts—seems ever more entrancing and miraculous as I grow older. Perhaps that is how most of us come to see our childhood selves: with a gathering sense of wonder that there could once have been such an innocent world, and that we ourselves could have been at the heart of that innocence. It's a good thing that we should grow fond of the selves we once were—I wouldn't want to denounce that for a moment. The child is father to the man: we should not be too strict with our child selves, we should have the grace to forgive them for setting us on the paths that led us to become the people we are. Nevertheless, we can't wallow in comfortable wonderment at our past. We must see what the child, still befuddled from his travels, still trailing his clouds of glory, could not see. We—or at least some of us, enough of us—must look at the past with a cruel enough eye to see what it was that made that joy and innocence possible. Forgivingness but also unflinchingness: that is the mixture I have in mind, if it is attainable. First the unflinchingness, then the forgivingness.

DA: The Nabokov essay quotes Lacan in the context of a discussion about aggressivity, the aggressivity of Nabokov's characters toward attempts to explicate them (which mirrors that of the patient before the analyst). The source of discomfort is the recognition that any construct of the self in language is a form of dispossession, because the self is being represented like another, for another. My question is not about Nabokov, but about Lacan. The first major work of criticism on your fiction, by Teresa Dovey, has as its central thesis that the novels are allegories of the Lacanian subject, attempting to realize itself, unsuccessfully, in the linguistic conditions provided by colonialism and "the South African tradition." The thesis will stand or fall on its own terms, but would you comment on the place that Lacan has occupied in your thinking?

JMC: Lacan is a seminal thinker. I haven't [November 1990] read Dovey's book, so I don't have a sense of what might already have been said about Lacan and myself, to respond to. But let me observe that some of Lacan's most inspired remarks have been about speaking from a position of ignorance. He finds his justification not only in the practice of analysis, where the patient seems to speak most truly when he is, so to speak, making a mistake, but in poetry. When one is getting as close to the center of one's own endeavor as this question takes one—where am I when I write?—it may be best to be Lacanian and not to bother too much about what one means (can I interchange "one" and "I" in this context?); and that would entail not knowing too much about where one stands in relation to the advice—Lacan's—that one can afford to speak without "thought."

The Comedy of Point of View
in Beckett's *Murphy* (1970)

S amuel Beckett's *Murphy* (1934) presents itself as, among other things, a sequence of some 3,500 sentences, written down by an author who is not entirely identifiable with a fictional narrator or scribe who in some sense "knew" Murphy and his friends in Dublin and London and now records their adventures. As author, Beckett (or "Beckett") lends his authority to these sentences by printing them under his name; he also delegates this authority to his narrator, who on occasion delegates it in turn to various of the characters. He accomplishes this last by quoting their words (dialogue) or by retiring from the page and allowing them to take over his narrative authority. For the reader to assign an authority to each sentence is thus a potentially complex task. But as writers and readers of fiction we have come to agree, it seems, on a largely unambiguous tacit code, and we manipulate that code well enough to be able to draw fine distinctions between, say, the veracity and the truth of an authoritative narration: we are capable of such feats as reading F. M. Ford's *The Good Soldier* as the comedy of a self-deceiving narrator, and we perceive at once the lack of authority of the Ph.D. who writes ("writes") the preface to Nabokov's *Lolita*.

Sometimes, however, what poses as a problem for the reader of choosing rationally among authorities may be a false problem, a problem designed to yield no solution, or only arbitrary solutions. Consider the following passage from *Murphy*.

He [Murphy] closed his eyes and fell back. It was not his habit to make out cases for himself. An atheist chipping the deity was not more senseless than Murphy defending his courses of inaction, as he did not require to be told.[1]

The first two of these three sentences are in two of the habitual composite narrative modes of the novel. In the first, the author's preterite fiction of "seeing" "Murphy" close his eyes and fall back is coextensive with the fictive narrator's "recollection" of the sight of Murphy closing his eyes and falling back, and with the same narrator's all-knowing translation into words of the unending inner commentary of Murphy's consciousness, "I close my eyes and fall back." Our fictional code suggests that we should grant the authority for this sentence to the narrator. (In fact it makes no difference to whom we grant it.) The second sentence is (a) the author's preterite fiction of the habits of "Murphy"; (b) the narrator's judicious estimate, on the basis of his recollections, of Murphy's habits, as well as (c) his bald translation of Murphy's unspoken reflection, "It is not my habit to make out cases for myself"; and (d) the author-amanuensis' record of Murphy's reflection ditto. Our code tells us to ascribe the sentence to (c), the narrator in the second of his roles: there is little to choose among (b), (c), and (d), but the principles of simplicity and consistency with the whole of the text tell us to exclude (b) and (d).

The third sentence is more puzzling. Up to the word "inaction," it is open to the same analysis as the second sentence. But what of the sentence modifier "as he did not require to be told"? Concealed within it is a passive that complicates the ascription of the sentence to any of the four authorities proposed above. By whom does Murphy not require to be told? In the underlying deep structure—to use the terms of transformational grammar—lies the sentence S, "X tells something to Murphy," which subsequently undergoes embedding in "Murphy requires (S)," followed by passive and negative transformations. Who is X? Author? Narrator? Murphy? Anyone in Murphy's London? Either of the first two answers implies—in terms of the fictive convention—that the Word can pass not only from Murphy, will-he, nill-he, to his puppet-master(s), but also in the other, conventionally proscribed, direction. "If thou lookest, uncle Toby, in search of this mote one moment longer— thou art undone," warns the autobiographer Tristram Shandy (VIII, xxiv), but in Tristram's fiction Uncle Toby cannot hear. Murphy, it is implied, can. As for the third answer—Murphy himself—it implies that there are not one but two incessantly chattering voices in Murphy's inner commentary, two voices because there exists the possibility of disagreement: "An atheist chipping the deity is not more senseless than me [you] defending my [your] courses of inaction."—"As I [you] don't require to be told by you [me]." And the fourth answer—anyone in Murphy's London—is unreal because only Celia is in the room with Murphy and she is in a huff. (Note that the modifier is *not* "as he would not have required to be told [if he had been in a position to be told by anyone in London]," which is a different story.) "As he did not require to be told" thus implies the presence of a concealed dialogue: between the fiction "Murphy" and his creator or his amanuensis, or between Murphy and the narrator recording his own opinions or Murphy's thoughts, or between Murphy's self and alter ego. The modifier is multiply ambiguous, a joke on the conventions of point of view.

How important is this play with point of view to the whole of *Murphy?* First, note that the sentence above is not a solitary *jeu.* Consider the following:

> Regress [a play on progress] in these togs was slow and Murphy was well advised to abandon hope for the day shortly after lunch and set off on the long climb home.   (73)

If the sentence read ". . . and Murphy was correct/intelligent to abandon hope for the day . . ." or " . . . and Murphy would have been well advised to abandon hope for the day, as he did . . . ," its meaning would be different. As it stands, it contains in its deep structure the sentence "X advises Murphy well." The identity of X is again a riddle. In the second alternative version I supply, the riddle is insignificant, reading in expanded paraphrase, "Murphy would have been well advised by X, if he had been advised by X, to abandon hope for the day, as he did": X is here a grammatical fiction killed off in the conditional clause.

Far from being oddities picked out from the text of *Murphy* after careful scrutiny, the two sentences discussed above belong to a sample of 100 drawn by a process of random selection from the 3,500 or so in the text. The randomness of the selection procedure allows us to suggest with some conviction, and without subjecting the text to grammatical microscopy, that there is a fair probability that quite often bland passives conceal play on the code of point of view.[2]

What other varieties of play do we find in this sample of 100 sentences? Here is a brief catalogue:

Type 1: foregrounding of the narrator. The following are the first and last (fifth) sentences of a paragraph.

> But Miss Counihan did not know when she was beaten, or, if she did, her way of showing it was unusual . . . No, Miss Counihan did not know when she was beaten. (209)

By repeating his words, the narrator foregrounds his act of narration, thereby thrusting himself from decent obscurity on to the stage as head-shaking chorus.

Type 2: foregrounding of the author.

> Celia, thank God for a Christian name at last, dragged her tattered bust back into the room, the old boy's. (229)

The author at his desk expresses relief at a momentary respite from the stream of surnames that, invented by him, become his *pensum* to inscribe on paper. (Alternatively, the narrator sighs with relief at the respite allowed him by his author. The result is the same.)

Type 3: foregrounding of anomalies created by a convention of a preterite narration of an imaginary history. Of Murphy and his five biscuits we read:

> He always ate the first-named last, because he liked it best, and the anonymous first, because he thought it very likely the least palatable. (96)

The biscuits come in a standard five-pack (Ginger, Osborne, Digestive, Petit Beurre, anonymous). Murphy has been eating such packs for many days and so knows the taste of "the anonymous" well. The expansion "He always ate the first-named last, because he always liked it best, and always ate the anonymous first, because he always thought it very likely the least palatable" is therefore self-contradictory: a statement of probability implies that the unexpected is possible, and there can be nothing unexpected in a world of habit. On the other hand, "He always ate . . ." does describe habitual action, and we know that Murphy does in fact always eat the anonymous first. There is no way of reconciling grammar with reality here: the sentence is pure anarchic play with the temporal code of narration, a conflation of the narrator's authoritative summary of Murphy's habits with Murphy's thought, weeks old, "This one is very likely the least palatable."

Type 4: interplay between narrator and character in authorial roles.

> "You don't know what you are saying," said Murphy . . . "Close the door."
> Celia closed the door but kept her hand on the handle.   (39)

The last sentence quoted is the narrator's report of Celia's action, but its form is conditioned by the form of Murphy's command: "'Close the door.' Celia closed the door." The independence of the form of his utterance is impinged on by the utterance of a being nominally insulated from him by the lens of his camera eye. Another example:

> When he awoke the fug was thick. He got up and opened the skylight to see what stars he commanded, but closed it again at once, there being no stars. He lit the tall thick candle from the radiator and went down to the w.c. to shut off the flow. What was the etymology of gas?   (175)

The first sentence belongs to the narrator's summary report, which constitutes the bulk of the novel. The fourth comes straight from Murphy's consciousness: the narrator becomes amanuensis, his self totally submerged. The second and third sentences are the narrator's but prepare for the fourth in two ways: by slowing down the pace of the narrative (that is, the reader's time) relative to the events described (from summary we move to the opening and the closing of the skylight, discrete, consecutive phenomena, appropriately concatenated); and by miming, at the end of each sentence, a movement from external act (closing the skylight, going down to the w.c.) to internal cause within Murphy (because there are no stars, because he wants to shut off the flow). The form of the fourth sentence, Murphy's, thus casts its shadow over the form of the third.

Type 5: interplay between narrator and author.

> Cooper's account, expurgated, accelerated, improved and reduced . . . gives the following.
>
> . . . As he burst out of the door the most beautiful young woman he had ever seen slipped in.   (119, 121)

The second sentence derives from a hypothetical intermediate version something like "He said that as he had burst out of the door the most beautiful young woman he had ever seen had slipped in," which derives from a hypothetical "As I burst out of the door the most beautiful young woman I had ever seen slipped in," which is itself an expurgation etc. of Cooper's original preterite account. The version that the narrator parades as his expurgated etc. report of Cooper's speech is thus in fact his *fictionalized* report, the report of narrator-reporter as author-editor. It is fictionalized by translation from the automatic pluperfect of the report into the fictive past (reader's present) in which it appears.

Aside from these violations of the principle of the separation of the three estates of author, narrator, and character, there is a considerable variety of sophisticated but legitimate manipulation of the code in which the tag identifying the provenance of a sentence is omitted and the reader is invited to demonstrate his skill by filling it in. For example:

> Miss Counihan found without delay, and imparted in block capitals to Wylie, an address in Gower Street where she was on no account to be disturbed.   (195)

We obligingly expand the sentence to ". . . an address in Gower Street where, she requested [to be translated, pretended to request], she was on no account to be disturbed." A sentence like this one would hardly be worth singling out if its existence did not indicate that we are dealing not with a sample sharply divided into fictionally well-formed and fictionally ill-formed sentences, but rather with a continuum of sentences at one end of which are grouped anarchic elements like the first two examples discussed above, and at the other the more substantial body of ordinary citizens.

The fact that all the sentences I have analyzed, those that stretch the code to its limits and those that violate it, belong to a random sample of 100 sentences (of which—to strengthen the argument—29 are of dialogue and therefore not open to play) confirms one's first impression that a comic antigrammar of point of view is everywhere at work in *Murphy*. This comedy is of a piece with the flippancy of authorial asides like "It is most unfortunate, but the point in this story has been reached where a justification of the expression 'Murphy's mind' has to be attempted" and "All the puppets in this book whinge sooner or later, except Murphy, who is not a puppet" (107, 122). The comedy is ironic, and acts to keep sentiment at a distance: the bassoons of irony sound to drown the elegiac melodies that keep stealing over the piece and that come to suffuse its final pages (Celia in Battersea Park).

The comedy survives in *Watt*, written in 1942–1945, though not as extensively. *Watt* is narrated by one Sam, who takes down Watt's words in his little notebook and pieces his story together in a fragmentary book.[3] Because Sam belongs both inside the fiction—literally walking the grounds of an asylum with Watt—and, as its nominal author, outside it, there is generally only one box within the box that is *Watt*. A third and outermost box is, however, occasionally slipped over *Watt* for a moment. "Kate [was] . . . a fine girl but a bleeder," writes Sam reporting Watt. "Haemophilia is, like enlargement of the prostate, an exclusively male disorder. But not in this work," observes a footnote from the author behind Sam (102), proclaiming the fictiveness of the fiction. The same effect, which is that of Type 2 discussed above, is achieved by the scattering of "Hiatus in MS," "MS illegible," etc., in which the work drifts to a close, and by the fragmentary Addenda.

The play on the conventions of point of view that we find in *Murphy* and to a lesser extent in *Watt* is the residue of an attitude of reserve toward the Novel, a reluctance to take its prescriptions seriously. The attitude is tentative and of questionable consistency, but it is neither peripheral nor transitory: it grows, and by the time of *The Unnamable* (1953) has become, in a fundamental sense, the subject of Beckett's work. "The Unnamable" as a name is a token of an inability to attain the separation of creator and creature, namer and named, with which the act of creating, naming, begins ("To be an artist is to fail," wrote Beckett in 1949).[4] "I seem to speak," says The Unnamable, "it is not I, about me, it is not about me."[5] Unable to arrive at a division between consciousness and the objects of consciousness, he is echoing Dostoevsky's Underground Man:

> To begin to act, you know, you must first have your mind completely at ease and without a trace of doubt left in it. Well, how am I, for example, to set my mind at rest? Where are the primary causes on which I am to build? Where are my bases? Where am I to get them from? I exercise myself in the process of thinking and consequently with me every primary cause at once draws

after itself another still more primary, and so on to infinity. That is precisely the essence of every sort of consciousness and thinking.[6]

Here, consciousness of self can be only consciousness of consciousness. Fiction is the only subject of fiction. Therefore, fictions are closed systems, prisons. The prisoner can spend his time writing on the walls *(The Unnamable)* or making magic jokes about their unreality *(Murphy)*. He remains imprisoned. Thus The Unnamable has come to live unendingly with the fact that the "I" by which a Murphy names himself is a fiction, "'I,'" no more necessarily "I" or "'I'" than "you" or "'you.'" "I close my eyes," thinks Murphy, but he ("he") also thinks ("thinks"), "'I' closes his eyes" or "You ('you') close your eyes (closes his eyes)." The separation of thinker and thought, creator and creature, is a fiction of fiction, one of the internal rules by which the game of the novel is played. Murphy ("Murphy," *Murphy*) by and large submits to the rules, but he mocks them too, and thereby earns his minor niche, called Page 303 in the Grove Press edition, among the inhabitants of The Unnamable's Underground of self-enclosing, self-enclosed consciousness.

=
The Manuscript Revisions of
Beckett's *Watt* (1972)

T he *Watt* papers at the University of Texas belong to three stages in the composition of the novel: (A) a first draft, holograph, 282 pages, begun in February 1941 in Paris and completed sometime after October 1943 at Roussillon in the Vaucluse; (B) a typescript recension with holograph corrections, 269 pages, incomplete; (C) a conflation of part of B with a new holograph draft, C, of 163 pages, finished in February 1945. Since C is fairly close to the published text of 1953, we may infer that between C and this text there are missing only the printer's copy and the proofs.[1]

Watt is an uneven and somewhat anarchic work. The formal and narrative indecisiveness of its ending, with its echoes of Swift's *A Tale of a Tub* ("Hiatus in MS," "MS illegible"), and its fragmentary Addenda (footnote: "The following precious and illuminating material should be carefully studied. Only fatigue and disgust prevented its incorporation"), have caused considerable unease to me and perhaps to other of Beckett's commentators, though none has, to my knowledge, confessed it. Then, too, the eight-year lapse of time between the completion of *Watt* and its publication, and the fifteen-year wait before the French translation appeared, can only raise further doubts about Beckett's satisfaction with the work.[2] Although our critical reaction to *Watt* must finally emerge from commerce with the printed text, I suspect that the reaction would be a little more sure if we knew the sources of Beckett's apparent discontent. Acquaintance with the compositional biography of *Watt* might give us a glimpse of these sources, and I accordingly sketch this biography below. Its main thread is a story of changing plot, that is, of changing synthetic principle. As one would expect, however, the physical bulk of Beckett's revision is stylistic. The most notable of the intuitions or formal principles that control his small-scale revision is a principle of symmetry, the stylistic reflection of the mental rhythm "On the one hand X, on the other hand not-X." In its orchestration it is this rhythm that comes to make *Watt* "[develop] a purely plastic content, and gradually [lose] . . . all meaning, even the most literal" (73).

Beckett composed the first draft of *Watt* in four parts, I–IV, of which II–IV survive substantially in the printed text. He then produced a revised draft, B, which adheres to the lines of the first draft, A, but prunes it. In a third draft, C, he discarded the original Part I and wrote a new one.

In itself the old Part I makes for less than inspiring reading, but it is worth summarizing for the light it throws on the Addenda and certain other episodes. In this first version, the sixty-year-old ur-Knott lives in the house in which he was born, attended by two servants who treat him with contempt. Like Descartes, he spends most of his time in bed. For forty-three pages he explores his dominant feeling of "nothingness" through the medium of two poems by Giacomo Leopardi but eventually fails to define it, finding that his enterprise is much like trying to get "a clear view of his . . . own anus." A narrator then appears and dismisses Knott: "The plain fact of the matter seems to be, that [Knott] had never been properly born." The narrator is one Johnny Watt, who has come to visit Knott's servant Arsene. Arsene and Watt spend a night together in conversation and horseplay, Watt at one point revealing that he intends to write a book entitled *A Clean Old Man.*[3]

The soliloquy of Dum Spiro (27–29) is a collage of rejectementa from this discarded Part I: it depends for its comedy, in fact, upon the loosening of the narrative relations that existed in the first draft. Why should the author of "The Chartered Accountant's Saturday Night" live in Lourdes and be interested in the fate of a rat that eats a consecrated wafer? In the first draft these three data are related: expressing his disapproval of Leopardi, the narrator regrets that Knott did not explore "our home, colonial, army, navy, airforce, sinn fein or zionist authors" and quotes in full the patriotic poem "The Chartered Accountant's Saturday Night, or, Two Voices Are There"; he further represents himself as telling his story at his last gasp in a room in Lourdes lit only by a snippet of his underpants floating in rancid dripping; while the rat belongs in a

conundrum that defeats McGilligan, "the Master of the Leopards-
town Halflengths" (see Addenda, 247), the painter of a portrait of
Knott's mother. In draft C the three data are still present, but
their interrelations have disappeared.
We see, then, what use Beckett made of the discarded Part I. He
excised compositional blocks, sometimes a few words at a time,
sometimes whole episodes, and slipped them into new environ-
ments in draft C, paring away the plaster that gave them coherence with their original context. In their new context they therefore come to the reader with a higher level of unpredictability.
Consider, for example, the fate of Knott's father, a musician. In
drafts A and B he is an eccentric minor character who might be
at home in any number of conventional comic novels. His appearance is brief: a portrait of him seated before the piano is described,
his suicide letter is reproduced, and his intellectual legacy, "Notes
on the Ravanastron, or Chinese Violin," is mentioned. In this context the word *ravanastron* operates at something less than its full
level of lexical unpredictability. That is to say, a retired Bachelor
of Music with a heavily German prose style living inside a comic
novel can be expected to bring certain kinds of props with him,
recondite or trivial. *Ravanastron* thus fills a hole into which we as
readers may already have anticipated recondite musical trivia
("the song the Sirens sang," "theorbo") to be slotted.
In draft C Knott's father disappears. The description of his portrait turns up in the Addenda, untitled (250–251). The ravanastron
appears in a new setting: "a ravanastron hung, on the wall, from
a nail, like a plover" (71). But is it the same ravanastron? While
still plainly a musical instrument—it hangs in the music room—
it now wears an enigmatic look. Perhaps we are supposed to find
it funny, but we cannot be sure we have caught the joke until we
know what a ravanastron is (and the *Oxford English Dictionary*
will not tell us). Can we be sure it is a joke, in fact, hanging as it
does next to the bust of divine Buxtehude, to hear whom Bach
walked 200 miles? The compositional block *ravanastron* has
moved into surroundings that exploit its mystery.
The change of plot that arose from the discarding of Part I also
had repercussions on Parts II–IV. Consider, for example, the episode of the painting in Erskine's room (Part II). In draft A several
pages are given over to Watt's cogitations on whether the painting

belongs to Erskine or comes with the house. A crucial step in this inner argument depends on Watt's connoisseurship of painting: he identifies the painting as by "the Dutch painter X-." But between drafts A and C Watt changes: the new Watt comes to Knott's household stripped not only of all certainty but even of all a priori knowledge. Therefore, the episode cannot stand as it is in the draft. Yet the decision that the painting belongs to Knott's establishment is a link in the chain of reasoning that leads to the important conclusion that Knott is eternal but changing. Therefore, the episode cannot be omitted.

Beckett escapes the dilemma by giving the conclusion without the proof: "Prolonged and irksome meditations forced Watt to the conclusion that the picture was part and parcel of Mr Knott's establishment" (130). The narrator (here Sam) justifies Watt's success in coming to a conclusion: "There were times when Watt could reason rapidly, almost as rapidly as Mr. Nackybal. And there were other times when his thought moved with such extreme slowness that it seemed not to move at all, but to be at a standstill" (131). What has happened here is that Watt's modest cogitations have been pushed into the background by an editor-narrator who obscures the issue (which is not whether Watt can reason rapidly but whether his chains of reasoning lead anywhere) and mystifies the reader by referring in passing to a character who will not be introduced for another forty pages. This flippant treatment of narrative decorum reminds one of *Murphy,* whose narrator is capable of such interpositions as "All the puppets in this book whinge sooner or later, except Murphy, who is not a puppet." It may be that this flippancy stands for a rejection of the illusionism of the realistic novel.[4] We may also have to face the possibility, however, that it is simply a reflection of the "fatigue and disgust" of the Addenda, which in turn may belong to the mode of irony that says exactly what it means.

=

Samuel Beckett and the Temptations of Style (1973)

The art of Samuel Beckett has become an art of zero, as we all know. We also know that an art of zero is impossible. A thousand words under a title and a publisher's imprint, the very act of moving pen over paper, are affirmations of a kind. By what self-contradictory act can such affirmations be deprived of content? By what act can the sentences be, so to speak, erased as they flow from the pen? Here is one answer: "Islands, waters, azure, verdure, one glimpse and vanished, endlessly, omit."[1] The first four words, flagrantly *composed* though they may be, leading associatively one to the next via even the bathos of rhyme, threaten to assert themselves as illusion, as The Word in all its magical autonomy. They are erased ("omit") and left like dead leaves against a wall. The sentence thus embodies neatly two opposing impulses that permit a fiction of net zero: the impulse toward conjuration, the impulse toward silence. A compulsive self-cancellation is the weight imposed on the flight of the sentence toward illusion; the fiction itself is the penance imposed on the pursuit of silence, rest, and death. Around the helix of ever-decreasing radius described by these conditions Beckett's art moves toward its apotheosis, the one-word text "nothing" under the title "Fiction."

If we can justify an initial segmentation of a set into classes X and not-X, said the mathematician Richard Dedekind, the whole structure of mathematics will follow as a gigantic footnote. Beckett is mathematician enough to appreciate this lesson: make a single sure affirmation, and from it the whole contingent world of bicycles and greatcoats can, with a little patience, a little diligence, be deduced. The Unnamable, in the third of the *Three Novels*, has his being in a state prior to this first consoling affirmation, and prolongs his existence "by affirmations and negations invalidated as uttered," the subject of an incapacity to affirm and an

43

inability to be silent.[2] Doubt constitutes his essence. What forms do the processes of his doubt take? One is familiar to us from the *Nouvelles* (collected 1954) and *Malone Dies* (1952): tell desultory stories to pass the time (to fill the pages, to embody oneself), pouring scorn on them intermittently. These stories typically draw themselves out to such length that they become the fictional properties of their narrators, who dramatize the conflicting impulses toward illusion and silence by dramatizing themselves as thaumaturges of their stories (as well as of their being) and then as avengers of the truth (Moran's last sentences in *Molloy* [1951] belong here). Side by side with this process of doubt exists a second, smaller in scale and less dramatic: the parenthetical commentary. The following sentence from *The Unnamable* (1953) contains the familiar phrase-by-phrase self-creation and self-annihilation ("I seem to speak, it is not I, about me, it is not about me," says The Unnamable: a little bird follows Theseus into the labyrinth gobbling down the thread), but it contains as well a new editorial relation:

> Respite then, once in a way, if one can call that respite, when one waits to know one's fate, saying, Perhaps it's not that at all, and saying, Where do these words come from that pour out of my mouth, and what do they mean, no, saying nothing, for the words don't carry any more, if one can call that waiting, when there's no reason for it, and one listens, that stet, without reason, as one has always listened, because one day listening began, because it cannot stop, that's not a reason, if one can call that respite. (370)

The phrase "that stet" belongs to an editorial metalanguage, a level of language at which one talks about the language of fiction. It is the language not of *cogito ergo sum* but of *cogitat ergo est:* the speaking "I" and its speech are felt not securely as subject but as object among other objects. And the language of the fiction exists in a *meta* relation to the fiction itself, as The Unnamable recognizes:

> To elucidate this point I would need a stick or pole, and the means of plying it, the former being of little avail without the latter, and vice versa. I could also do, incidentally, with future and conditional participles. (300)

The editorial metalanguage deployed in this scholium is perfected in *Ping* (1966), where the "ping" of commentary that repeatedly fractures the surface of the fiction has evacuated itself of lexical content. Contrast "ping" with its primitive forebear "plop" in *The Unnamable*, which is yet heavy with content: "But let me complete my views, before I shit on them. For if I am Mahood, I am Worm too, plop" (338). The sound/word *ping* interrupts the permutation and combination of a set of murmured phrases ("bare white body fixed," "head haught," and so on) as the combinations promise or threaten to erect themselves into a tiny, cryptic, but autonomous image of a rudimentary naked human being sitting in a room, plus the glimmering of a meaning for this image. The demands of "ping" occur more frequently (become more imperative) as the image gains in definition and its meaning comes to the edge of materializing: "last murmur one second perhaps not alone eye unlustrous black and white half closed long lashes imploring."[3] Then we have "ping silence ping over": the monologue calls to be switched over to the source of "ping," that is, to the anti-illusionary reflexive consciousness celebrated and damned in *The Unnamable*.

In *Lessness* (1969) an infinite series of nested consciousnesses, each dismissing the figments of its immediate predecessor, is presented in the paradigm of a two-component switching mechanism. The two components are called day and night, each annihilates the figments of the other, and even the two components are figments of an embracing consciousness whose figments are in turn annihilated by the next member of the series: "Figment dawn dispeller of figments and the other called dusk."[4] This annihilation or decreation is symbolized in another binary device: *Lessness* can be broken neatly into two, the second half consisting of nothing more than a random rearrangement of the sentences of the first (or vice versa).

The progression from *The Unnamable* to *Lessness* is toward a formalization or stylization of autodestruction: that is, as the text becomes *nothing but* a destructive commentary upon itself by the encapsulating consciousness, it retreats into the trap of an automatism of which the invariant mechanical repetitions of *Lessness* are the most extreme example to date. Among the monotonous texts that form Beckett's *Residua*, the only remaining variable is how the autodestruction is done. This is an intriguing development, for it has a close analogue at an earlier stage of Beckett's career. Let us go back to *Watt* (1958), that *ouvrage abandonné* of the war years. What trick of style is it that lies behind Watt's logical-computational fantasies to make these excursions sound so much like what Leibniz called music, "the mysterious counting of the numbers"? The trick is that Watt abandons Occam's razor, the criterion of simplicity, and allows speculative hypotheses to proliferate endlessly, generated by a matrix that is rhythmic in character. Consider the form of the following typical sentence:

> Perhaps who knows Mr Knott propagates a kind of waves, of depression, or oppression, or perhaps now these, now those, in a way that it is impossible to grasp.[5]

As a first step we can break the sentence into three rhythmic groups, the first two of which are in a *coupled* relation of parallelism:

(a) Perhaps who knows Mr Knott propagates a kind of waves of depression, or oppression,	(b) or perhaps now these, now those,	(c) in a way that it is impossible to grasp.

Within group (a) there are two further couples, equivalent in phonological pattern and juncture:

(a1) perhaps	(a2) who knows
(a3) of depression	(a4) or oppression

There is another couple in group (b): ´

(b1) now these	(b2) now those

The entire couple (a3, a4) itself forms a couple with (b1, b2). Underlying the sentence there is thus a system of couples, embedded at three levels, their components linked by phonological or syntactic equivalences. We can define a couple in general as a pair of text elements between which there exists a relation of equivalence or contrast, phonological, syntactic, or semantic. The sentence I have analyzed, for example, is itself one element of a couple, the other element of which occurs ten sentences earlier. It also belongs to a sequence of nine sentences which forms a couple with a sequence of seven sentences earlier in the paragraph. Figure 1 is a scheme of the structure of couplings underlying the paragraph; the sentence I have analyzed is no. 17.

As we can see, the paragraph grows out of a rhythm or pattern of *A against B*. This rhythm infects most of *Watt*, extending to the logic of Watt's discourses. The process of his reasoning pits question against proposition, rejoinder against question, objection against rejoinder, qualification against objection, and so on until an arbitrary stop is put to the chain of pairs. This binary rhythm is above all the rhythm of doubt, internalizing the philosophical debt to Descartes until finally meaning is submerged beneath it:

> Dis yb dis, nem owt. Yad la, tin fo trap. Skin, skin, skin. Od su did ned taw? On. Taw ot klat tonk? On. (168)

"Grammar and Style!" wrote Beckett to a friend in 1934: "they appear to me to have become just as obsolete as a Biedermeier bathing suit or the imperturbability of a gentleman. A mask."[6] In 1934 Beckett was composing his lapidary *Murphy;* what he means by Style here is style as consolation, style as redemption, the grace of language. He is repudiating the religion of style that we find in the Flaubert of *Madame Bovary:* "I value style first and above all, and then Truth."[7] The energy of Beckett's repudiation is a measure of the potency of the seductions of Style. *Watt* was the battleground for the next encounter, an encounter won by Style. *Watt* trembles on the edge of realizing Flaubert's dream of "a book about nothing, a book without external attachments," held together by "the internal force of style."[8] The rhythm of A against B submerges *Watt* in its lulling plangencies: the style of the book is narcissistic reverie.

Asked to explain why he turned from English to French, Beckett replied, "Because in French it is easier to write without style."[9] The tendency of English toward chiaroscuro is notorious. At the very time in history when the French language was being modified in the direction of simplicity and analytic rigor, the connotative, metaphoric strain in English was being reinforced by the Authorized Version. Thus eventually, for example, Joseph Conrad could complain that it was impossible to use a word like "oaken" in its purest denotation, for it brought with it a swarm of metaphorical

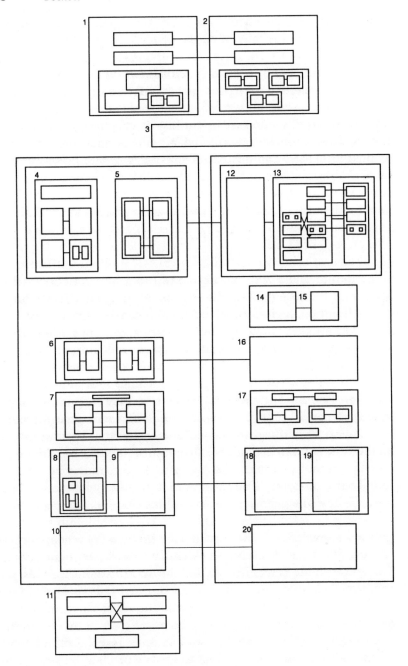

Figure 1

Figure 1. Each block-pair represents a couple. The numbered blocks are sentences. Within the sentence, embedded couples may occur at the level of word or phrase.

contexts, and Beckett could say that he was afraid of English "because you couldn't help writing poetry in it."[10] The style of even Beckett's first published French work, the *Nouvelles*, is more jagged and paratactic than the style of *Watt*. While still as recognizably his own as his English prose, his French prose has freed itself from the stylization, or automatism of style, of *Watt*.

But there is a second and deeper impulse toward stylization that is common to all of Beckett's later work. This occurs with the stylization of the impasse of reflexive consciousness, of the movement of the mind that we can call *A therefore not-A* and that Beckett apothegmatizes in the phrase "imagination dead imagine" and elsewhere explicates as "the expression that there is nothing to express, nothing with which to express, nothing from which to express, no power to express, no desire to express, together with the obligation to express."[11] The experience of actually reading Beckett's late fictions, his *Residua*, is an uncomfortable one because they offer us none of the daydream gratification of fiction: they call for a heroic attentiveness which they continually subvert by a stylized repetitiveness into the sleep of a machine. They offer no daydreams because their subject is strictly the annihilation of illusion by consciousness. They are miniature mechanisms for switching themselves off: illusion therefore silence, silence therefore illusion. Like a switch, they have no content, only shape. They are in fact only a shape, a style of mind. It is utterly appropriate for an artist to whom defeat constitutes a universe that he should march with eyes open into the prison of empty style.[12]

Remembering Texas (1984)

In September 1965 (this is an essay that can begin in no other way), I sailed into New York harbor aboard an Italian ship, once a troopship, now crammed with young folk from foreign parts come to study in America. I came, immediately, from England; at the age of twenty-five, I was heading for Austin, where the University of Texas was to support me to the tune of $2,100 a year for teaching freshman English while I studied in the graduate program.

In the colonies, where I came from ultimately, I had received a conventional undergraduate training in English studies. That is, I had learned to speak Chaucerian verse with good vowel definition and to read Elizabethan handwriting; I was acquainted with the Pearl Poet and Thomas More and John Evelyn and many other worthies; I could "do" literary criticism, although I had no clear idea of how it differed from book reviewing or polite talk about books. All in all, this patchy imitation of Oxford English studies had proved a dull mistress from whom I had been thankful to turn to the embrace of mathematics; but now, after four years in the computer industry during which even my sleeping hours had been invaded by picayune problems in logic, I was ready to have another try.

In an Austin hotter and steamier than the Africa I remembered, I enrolled myself in courses in bibliography and Old English. From William B. Todd I learned the operation of the Hinman collator; for Rosamund Lehmann I wrote (a project of my own devising) a minutely detailed classification of rhetorical figures in the sermons of Bishop Wulfstan. Professor Lehmann awarded me an A−, the minus, she said, because work like mine gave philology a bad name. She was right; I was not resentful, though unsure of where one went from there.

50

In the manuscripts collection of the library I found the exercise books in which Samuel Beckett had written *Watt* on a farm in the south of France, hiding out from the Germans. I spent weeks perusing them, pondering the sketches and numbers and doodles in the margins, disconcerted to find that the well-attested agony of composing a masterpiece had left no other traces than these flippancies. Was the pain perhaps all in the waiting, I asked myself, in the sitting and staring at the empty page?

One Charles Whitman, a student (a fellow student? were they all fellow students? all 23,000 of them?), took the elevator to the top of the clock tower and commenced shooting people in the quadrangles below. He killed a fair number, then someone killed him. I hid under my desk for the duration. In Cape Town a Greek assassinated Hendrik Frensch Verwoerd, architect of Grand Apartheid. "If you dislike the war so much," said a friend, meaning the war in (on?) Vietnam, "why don't you leave? There is nothing keeping you here." But he misread me. Complicity was not the problem—complicity was far too advanced a notion for the time being. The problem was with knowing what was being done. It was not obvious where one went to escape knowledge.

The students I taught in my composition classes might as well have been Trobriand Islanders, so inaccessible to me were their culture, their recreations, their animating ideas. I moved in one stratum only of the university community, a stratum of graduate students living thrifty lives in rented apartments with baby toys scattered over the floors, laboring like tortoises to complete courses or prepare for orals or write dissertations. Their talk, when it was not of their teachers (their personalities, their deficiencies), was of getting out, getting a job in Huntsville or Texarkana, getting their hands on real money. With less tangible goals than these or perhaps with none at all, I toiled away at my Old English texts, my German grammar.

On Sundays I played cricket on a baseball field with a group of Indians. We formed a team, traveled to College Station, played against a team from Texas A&M also made up of nostalgic castoff children from the colonies, lost. I remembered an Indian friend from the old days in England. He and I had gone for walks in the Surrey countryside, a countryside that, we agreed, meant nothing to either of us. "At least in America," he said (he had spent time in Columbus, Ohio), "there are all-night hamburger stands." Although I did not care about the hamburgers, the America he described seemed a distinct improvement on the England I knew. Now I was in America, or at least in Texas; but the green hills, I was finding, were as alien as the Surrey downs. What I missed seemed to be a certain emptiness, empty earth and empty sky, to which South Africa had accustomed me. What I also missed was the sound of a language whose nuances I understood. Speech in Texas seemed to have no nuances; or, if there were nuances, I was not hearing them.

I wrote a paper for Archibald Hill on the morphology of Nama, Malay, and Dutch, languages from unrelated stocks that had impacted on one another at the Cape of Good Hope. In the library I came upon books unopened since the 1920s: reports on the territory of South West Africa by its German explorers and administrators, accounts of punitive expeditions against the Nama and Herero, dissertations on the physical anthropology of the natives, monographs by Carl Meinhof on the Khoisan languages. I read the makeshift grammars put together by missionaries, went further back in time to the earliest linguistic records of the old languages of the Cape, word lists compiled by seventeenth-century seafarers, and then followed the fortunes of the Hottentots in a history written not by them but for them, from above, by travelers and missionaries, not excluding my remote ancestor Jacobus Coetzee, *floruit* 1760. Years later, in Buffalo, still pursuing this track, I was to venture my own contribution to the history of the Hottentots: a memoir of a kind that went on growing till it had been absorbed into a first novel, *Dusklands*.

A second track took me from Nama and Malay deeper into the syntax of exotic languages, on forays that ramified further and further as I found (I was rediscovering the wheel now) that the term *primitive* meant nothing, that every one of the 700 tongues of Borneo was as coherent and complex and intractable to analysis as English. I read Noam Chomsky and Jerrold Katz and the new universal grammarians and reached the point of asking myself: If a latter-day ark were ever commissioned to take the best that mankind has to offer and make a fresh start on the farther planets, if it ever came to that, might we not leave Shakespeare's plays and Beethoven's quartets behind to make room for the last speaker of Dyirbal, even though that last speaker might be a fat old woman who scratched herself and smelled bad? It seemed an odd position for a student of English, the greatest imperial language of them all, to be falling into. It was a doubly odd position for someone with literary ambitions, albeit of the vaguest—ambitions to speak one day, somehow, in his own voice—to discover himself suspecting that languages spoke people or at the very least spoke through them.

I left Texas in 1968. It was never clear to me, from beginning to end, why the university—and the American taxpayer—had lavished so much money on me to follow idle whims. Sometimes I thought it an oversight, an insignificant oversight, allowed for in the system: that among the thousands of petroleum engineers and political scientists turned out every year, it did not matter if there were one or two of whatever I was. At other times the Fulbright exchange program seemed to me an extraordinarily farsighted and generous scheme whose humane benefits would be felt by all parties far into the future. Where did the truth lie? Somewhere in the middle, perhaps.

Coming or going, I had no regrets. I departed, I thought, unmarked, unscathed, except by the times. No one had tried to teach me, for which I was grateful. What I had learned in the course of three years was not negligible, though picked up, for the most part, by accident. I had had the run of a great library, where I had stumbled on books whose existence I might otherwise never have guessed. Passing the door of James Sledd's office at five o'clock on a Saturday afternoon, hearing the typewriter inside, I had been reassured that the province of English studies was not, as the lifestyle of my colonial teachers had seemed to prove, reserved for dilettantes. I could have come away with less.

= The Poetics of Reciprocity

Interview

DA: A large proportion of your work in translation has been from Dutch: Marcellus Emants' *A Posthumous Confession,*[1] the poetry of Leo Vroman and Sybren Polet, but more substantially, Hans Faverey and Gerrit Achterberg.[2] What is your relationship with Dutch, and how did these projects come about?

JMC: At high school the only language I studied, besides English and Afrikaans, was Latin. This was also the only foreign language I studied at university. I would like to be polyglot but am not. My relationship with languages is an intimate but frustrated one. I have a poor ear and a distaste for memorizing. I pick up the principles of a new language quickly enough, perhaps even get a feel for it, then start looking for shortcuts, then get bored. So the pattern has been that I work on a language intensively for a period, usually for an immediate reason, then put it aside and do something else, and as a result never retain anything like a command.

This has held even in the case of Dutch, which I know better than any language bar Afrikaans and English. There was a time in the early 1970s when my command of Dutch was such that I could reasonably think of myself as a translator of professional standard. Then I began to drift away from Dutch literature to other interests. I still read literary Dutch fluently, perhaps more fluently than I read literary Afrikaans; but spoken, colloquial Dutch is closed to me. I have never lived in the Netherlands.

The Dutch writers on whom I have worked most intensively have been, as you observe, the poets Faverey and Achterberg and the nineteenth-century novelist Emants. The Faverey translations were done on commission. In the case of Achterberg and then again of Emants, I began the translations as projects of my own before I had any publication contract.

Achterberg is a major figure in postwar Dutch literature, but the kind of poetry he wrote is out of fashion today: a poetry of compression and paradox and irony, written in tight forms. The closest parallel I can think of in English is William Empson, but there is a mystical strain in Achterberg that you won't find in Empson. "Ballad of the Gasfitter" is Achterberg's best (and most ambitious) poem, a cycle of fourteen sonnets telling the story of a man's quest for—what? Love? Grace? I began to translate it into English sonnets in 1969 in an effort to understand it, then found that I couldn't translate it till I had understood it. Something any hermeneuticist could have told me, but I didn't know anything about hermeneutics: again I was reinventing the wheel.

DA: In the essay on Achterberg, you begin with patterns of reference in *I* and *You*. Your terms are drawn from linguistic descriptions in Emile Benveniste (on pronouns) and Roman Jakobson (on "shifters"). The *I–You* relation, however, connects with larger things in the whole corpus of your work, what I would like to call broadly the poetics of reciprocity. This takes various forms: in *Dusklands* it seems to draw, among other things, on the failed dialectic of master and slave in Hegel's *The Phenomenology of Spirit;* later versions in *Michael K* and *Foe* involve questions of authorship, the tensions between readers, storytellers, and the subjects or characters of stories; forms of this relation can also be traced through to your interest in problems of consciousness, and of desire and its objects.

Reciprocity and, by implication, the problem of identity are obviously of central importance in a colonial literature. You raise this question in the introduction to *White Writing*, where you speak of the problem of the European finding a language in which reciprocity is possible, and in the Jerusalem Prize acceptance speech you speak of "the failure of love" in South Africa.

Governing the treatment of the *I–You* relation in the Achterberg essay, however, is what you call the "field of language," "not *what I* and *You* signify but *how* they signify in the field of language and in the field of the poem." The novel which carries this particular emphasis most strongly—you were working on it at about this time—is surely *In the Heart of the Country*. The field of language, the field of the Novel in this case, is prominent in several ways: in the episodic repetitions, which serve to focus attention on Magda herself as the narrating subject (in this you seem close to the concerns of the *nouveau roman*), and in the numbered units that make up the text.

My question has to do with the connection, or tension, between the thematics of reciprocity, on one hand, and their *fictive* status on the other. For despite their similarities, when I place *In the Heart of the Country* alongside the Achterberg essay, I find myself wanting to measure the distance between them. Of course, it is not possible to get outside of language, as the essay makes plain; moreover, in a colonial situation, the linguistic conditions governing available forms of association are perhaps more visible than they might be under different historical conditions (something the novel dramatizes). Nevertheless, while the essay sympathetically describes the "Ballad" 's efforts to achieve self-sufficiency in reflexive conventions, I would find it hard to accept a description of the novel which claimed that the problems of selfhood and relationship developed in it are collapsed into a post-Romantic self-consciousness about their fictiveness. Although the existential dimension (*Being and Nothingness* seems to figure prominently in Magda) is clearly ruled by the linguistic, the former is still there as a ghostly field of possibility. In other words, the field of *affect* is by no means eclipsed or even neutralized by the field of language.

You might not go along with this observation. What it points to, though, is a curious tension between your respect for the linguistic-structural conditions of fiction, and the existential-historical dramas being played out within them. How do you recall the balance of these factors, especially in *In the Heart of the Country?*

JMC: Let me first say something about *In the Heart of the Country.* You are right to see similarities between it and the French *nouveau roman,* but behind both there is, I think, a more fundamental influence: film and/or photography. There was a moment in the course of high modernism when first poets, then novelists, realized how *rapidly* narration could be carried out: films that used montage effectively were connecting short narrative sequences into longer narratives much more swiftly and deftly than the nineteenth-century novelist had thought possible, and they were educating their younger audience too into following rapid transitions, an audience that then carried this skill back into the reading of printed texts.

In the Heart of the Country is not a novel on the model of a screenplay, but it is constructed out of quite brief sequences, which are numbered as a way of pointing to what is not there between them: the kind of scene-setting and connective tissue that the traditional novel used to find necessary—particularly the South African novel of rural life that *In the Heart of the Country* takes off from. (If you want to confirm that *In the Heart of the Country* is no screenplay, you have only to view Marion Hänsel's film version, *Dust*, which retains virtually none of the sequence divisions and indeed none of the quite swift *pacing* of the novel. It loses a lot of vitality thereby, in my opinion.)

If I had to give examples of the kind of film whose style imprints *In the Heart of the Country*, I would cite a short film by Chris Marker called *La Jetée* and the film *The Passenger*, put together by colleagues of Andrzej Munk after Munk's death from sequences he had completed plus some stills. What impressed me most about films like these was, paradoxically, what they could achieve through stills with voice-over commentary: a remarkable intensity of vision (because the eye *searches* the still image in a way it cannot search the moving image) together with great economy of narration. More than economy: a rapidity, even a forward-plunging quality. Jean-Luc Godard was right, it seems to me, to make it his aim to liberate the sound track from the image. There are exhilarating moments of liberation in a film like *Le Petit Soldat* (in later films I find the subordination of image to voice becomes tedious).

I have had exchanges with a number of people interested in filming my books, though only one book has actually been filmed ("to film a book": an absurd phrase, but let me use it as shorthand). I have pleaded for voice-over and in general for the independence of the voice, but I have never got anywhere. Even if one encounters a director who is cautiously sympathetic, the people who call the shots, who put up the money, who claim to know what the public will and won't take, aren't. It's a wretched state of affairs. Any words on the sound track besides lip-synchronized dialogue are branded as "literary" and therefore old-fashioned. The irony is, doing the narration through dialogue keeps film tied to stage drama. It makes sound film more primitive than silent film.

You say you would find it hard to accept a claim that in *In the Heart of the Country* I dissolve "problems of selfhood and relationship," conceived in their fullest historical dimension, into postmodernist game-playing. I support you and hope you are right. You contrast the novel with the essay on Achterberg in this respect, to the detriment of the essay. In its defense I would only say: you have to remember what is and what is not possible in discursive prose. In particular you have to remember about passion, where a strange logic prevails. When a real passion of feeling is let loose in discursive prose, you feel that you are reading the utterances of a madman (think of Vaslav Nizhinsky's diaries).

The novel, on the other hand, allows the writer to *stage* his passion: Magda, in *In the Heart of the Country*, may be mad (if that is indeed your verdict), but I, behind her, am merely passionate. So: behind all the irony, the coolness, the jokes, there is a real passion in Achterberg, which I can call *nothing but* a passion for You. In my translation there is, I hope, some reflection of that passion. But in the medium of prose commentary I can't be passionate without being mad. So I agree, there is something missing in the essay. What is missing is a passion that quite answers to Achterberg's passion. In that sense the essay is a betrayal of Achterberg. But what is criticism, what can it ever be, but either a betrayal (the usual case) or an overpowering (the rarer case) of its object? How often is there an equal marriage?

To return to Magda: Magda is passionate in the way that one can be in fiction (I see no further point in calling her mad), and her passion is, I suppose, of the same species as the love I talked about in the Jerusalem address—the love for South Africa (not just South Africa the rocks and bushes and mountains and plains but the country and its people), of which there has not been enough on the part of the European colonists and their descendants—not enough in intensity, not enough in all-embracingness. Magda at least has that love, or its cousin.

DA: I have a question about what you call the "poetics of failure" in the Achterberg essay. The poetics of failure involves a history of self-cancelling literature which in John Barth, Nabokov, and Beckett has projected the failure of the "romantic-liberal notion of the self." In metafictional terms, *In the Heart of the Country* participates in the poetics of failure as well, to the extent that Magda speculates about what other kinds of literature she might have inhabited, mentioning pastoral specifically (only to reject it). In other words, through Magda, the novel is skeptical about particular kinds of South African writing with roots going back to the late nineteenth century and lasting until the 1950s. Would the novel be implying that colonial humanism had not evolved the formal conditions that might obtain in a literature of reciprocal relationships?

JMC: What is pastoral? At the center of the mode, it seems to me, lies the idea of the local solution. The pastoral defines and isolates a space in which whatever cannot be achieved in the wider world (particularly the city) can be achieved. Magda, I concede, describes a very specific and even parodic form of the pastoral, only to reject it. But the question remains open: is *In the Heart of the Country* a pastoral itself, and is Magda a pastoral character? It is not for me to decide this question, but I would point out that letters demanding payment of taxes don't usually penetrate Arcadia.

People in Hardy's novels don't ask questions about what genre they belong to. People in *Don Quixote* do. Insofar as Cervantes is the giant on whose shoulders we pigmies of the postmodern novel stand, *In the Heart of the Country* is not just pastoral or antipastoral but Cervantean pastoral or antipastoral. Your question is about humanism in South Africa—which arrives as part of British liberal culture, for it certainly isn't Calvinist—and its failure to engender a literature of equal and reciprocal relations. The obvious response must be that British liberalism failed to engender equal and reciprocal relations, period—failed to persuade the colonists, British or Dutch, that equal and reciprocal relations were a good enough thing to make sacrifices for. But I think a more interesting avenue to explore would be to ask why, let us say, *love* in the postmodernist novel—since we are talking about love—is treated as the *figure* of a relationship (Roland Barthes's *A Lover's Discourse* is the *ars amatoria* of postmodern times) rather than as a relationship per se. It would be crude to say that the social preconditions for loving (delay, separation, and so forth) no longer exist in the West; but it does seem that *love, falling in love* have been irrevocably historicized. That is why Magda is an anomalous figure: her passion doesn't belong in the genre in which she finds herself. I'll leave the question here, but you can see what implications it has for me as a novelist.

DA: Let me take this further: earlier, you spoke of passion, the inability of criticism to reflect passion in its fullness. Here, you speak of what is *lost* in postmodernism, where allegorical resonances are given off, perhaps inconclusively, but regardless of whether or not we would *like* things to stand for themselves. (You speak of historicization in postmodernist fiction: I take this to refer to the distancing or contextualizing effects of reflexivity.) These apprehensions tend in a similar direction: characteristically, your work is transparent about conventions, but are you suggesting that there is a certain pathos in this very transparency, residing in postmodernist culture, to which you find yourself having to adjust?

JMC: A historicizing consciousness or, as you put it, the distancing effect of reflexivity, or even textualization—in the present context these are all ways of tracing the same phenomenon: an awareness, as you put pen to paper, that you are setting in train a certain play of signifiers with their own ghostly history of past interplay. Did Defoe have this kind of awareness? Did Hardy? One likes to think that they didn't, that they had, so to speak, an easier time of it. But even if they did have this awareness, surely they couldn't have found it hard to put it behind them, to isolate it in another compartment of the mind, while they attended to the serious business of Moll and the constable or Jude and Arabella. So perhaps you are right to call it simply a matter of culture: they lived in a culture, or cultures, that allowed them to get on with the job, and we don't. Hence the pathos—in a humdrum sense of the word—of our position: like children shut in the playroom, the room of textual play, looking out wistfully through the bars at the enticing world of the grownups, one that we have been instructed to think of as the mere phantasmal world of *realism* but that we stubbornly can't help thinking of as the *real*.

On the other hand, one would like to think it is something more substantial than a shift in culture—which, in this context, doesn't mean much more than a shift in fashion, does it?—that has had this massive and virtually determining effect on consciousness. Something more historically substantial. Is the longing that what acts upon us should at least be "substantial" part of that same wistfulness, that pathos? Do today's children share with us that wistfulness, or are they happy in the playroom?

DA: I want to return to the socially critical side of the exposure of conventions. At times you have been impatient with unreflective notions about form in South African literature and the arts (your review of *The Guest*, the film by Ross Devenish and Athol Fugard about the life of Eugene Marais, is perhaps the clearest example of this). If I read them correctly, the short essays "The First Sentence of Yvonne Burgess' *The Strike*" and "A Note on Writing" were small-scale attempts to intervene in uncritical assumptions by opening conventions to scrutiny and by suggesting a wider range of resources within the literary culture, beyond mainstream forms of liberal positivism. (There is also, I think, an implicit accusation of provincialism in these essays.)

The essay on the first sentence of *The Strike* links the codes of the Novel, especially characterological systems, with class bonding among writers and readers. In the "Note," the political aspect of the argument is less explicit but it is there in the rejection of instrumentalist conceptions of writing, which leads to the injunction that reviewers and critics should attend more closely to the speaking subject (the "middle voice," as you put it).

In the frame of reference of these essays, it was possible for you to move fairly easily between a critique of form and a critique of ideology; the one was implied by the other. It would be more difficult to do this now, because the *political* radicalism of the exposure of conventions has recently been contested. Furthermore, the political ambiance of realism in South Africa includes not only liberal positivism, but narratives of black resistance as well (possibly because much black South African prose has its roots in popular journalism). How do these essays strike you now, in the light of these developments?

JMC: I must answer frankly: though the essays you mention are by no means major pieces of work, and perhaps reflect little more substantial than exasperation on my part with a certain automatism of writing—writing unaccompanied by any real thought, any self-reflection—nevertheless, I have no desire to distance myself from them. You say that the political radicalism of the exposure of conventions has been contested. I would respond that an unquestioning attitude toward forms or conventions is as little radical as any other kind of obedience.

But you emphasize the word *political*: it is not *politically* radical to interrogate the kind of realism you describe. Perhaps so. Perhaps the reason why the pieces you mention are so brief, so occasional, is that there is no hope of successfully arguing the political relevance of what, in the present South African context, must seem Eurocentric avant-gardism of an old-fashioned kind.

DA: This would be the correct moment to raise the question of the interview as a genre of literary journalism. With few exceptions, the published interviews you have given have not been very successful. Many of them do not get beyond an attempt to clarify or agree on a basic set of assumptions about the exchange taking place (which makes them interesting too, but for different reasons). What is it about the interview that troubles you?

JMC: An interview is not just, as you call it, an "exchange": it is, nine times out of ten (this is the tenth case, thank God!), an exchange with a complete stranger, yet a stranger permitted by the conventions of the genre to cross the boundaries of what is proper in conversation between strangers. I don't regard myself as a public figure, a figure in the public domain. I dislike the violation of propriety, to say nothing of the violation of private space, that occurs in the typical interview. That is my first response.

And then there is the casualness and lack of professionalism, and even lack of true curiosity, true interest, that one meets with. Journalists who barely take the time to glance over the blurb of your book. Students who think nothing of dropping by to ask you what you meant by X or Y. Foreign academics making their way across Africa on travel grants, doing face-to-face interviews ("And what do you see as the role of the writer in South Africa?"—one can predict the lifeless questions before they are uttered).

I mention this background to excuse, as far as it can be excused, my general irritability and uncooperativeness with interviewers.

There is also the question of control, control over the interview. Writers are used to being in control of the text and don't resign it easily. But my resistance is not only a matter of protecting a phantasmatic omnipotence. Writing is not free expression. There is a true sense in which writing is dialogic: a matter of awakening the countervoices in oneself and embarking upon speech with them. It is some measure of a writer's seriousness whether he does evoke/invoke those countervoices in himself, that is, step down from the position of what Lacan calls "the subject supposed to know." Whereas interviewers want speech, a flow of speech. That speech they record, take away, edit, censor, cutting out all its waywardness, till what is left conforms to a monologic ideal.

If I had had any foresight, I would have had nothing to do with journalists from the start. Now it is too late: the word is out, passed from one journalist to another, at least in this country, that I am an evasive, arrogant, generally unpleasant customer. I should have recognized from the first the philosophical cleavage between myself and the journalist. Two traditions, it seems to me, converge and reinforce each other in the journalistic interview. The first is legal: the interview is a politer version of courtroom interrogation or, better, the interrogation an investigating magistrate conducts prior to the public trial. The second is most immediately inherited from Rousseau, I suppose, but it draws on the ancient strain of religious enthusiasm as well as on the practice of psychotherapy: in the transports of unrehearsed speech, the subject utters truths unknown to his waking self. The journalist takes the place of the priest or *iatros*, drawing out this truth-speech.

To me, on the other hand, truth is related to silence, to reflection, to the practice of *writing.* Speech is not a fount of truth but a pale and provisional version of writing. And the rapier of surprise wielded by the magistrate or the interviewer is not an instrument of the truth but on the contrary a weapon, a sign of the inherently confrontational nature of the transaction. The interviewer aligns himself with Richardson's Lovelace, the man who believes that truth lies inside the subject's body and that with his rapier-phallus he can search it out there.

Overreaction? Paranoia? A paranoid tirade? I deliver it to you uncensored. Make of it what you will.

DA: A final question. You came back to the problem of reciprocity in your Jerusalem Prize acceptance speech, ten years after the publication of the Achterberg essay and *In the Heart of the Country,* in a society which at that point (1987) was more riven by violence than perhaps at any other stage of its modern history. You spoke with feeling about the history from colonialism to apartheid, the way it has led to a literature "in bondage," but you also addressed the crude and irresistible power of history in South Africa. Let me put this observation to you for comment: that while it is fairly common for writers in South Africa to try to represent history or historical forces, it is rare that history should emerge, as I believe it does in your fiction, as Necessity, as an absolute limit to consciousness. That is, history, in your work, seems less a process that can be represented than a force acting on representation, a force that is itself ultimately unrepresentable. Seen in this light, the productive freedom of the act of writing is at best qualified, or provisional.

JMC: You put this observation forward in the light of the Jerusalem speech. So let me say something about the context of that speech. The winner of the Jerusalem Prize before me had been Milan Kundera. Kundera's address had been largely a tribute to Cervantes. Reading that address, I believe I knew as well as anyone else what it meant that a Czech should choose to speak about Cervantes in Jerusalem in 1985, namely, a certain defiance of the role imposed on him by history (if you look at it in one way) or by fashion (if you look at it in another). (A decade earlier Kundera had remarked, even more provocatively: "Today, when politics have become a religion, I see the novel as one of the last forms of atheism.")

There is part of me too that longs to be an atheist *à la* Kundera. I too would like to be able to go to Jerusalem and talk about Cervantes. Not because I see Kundera or indeed Cervantes as a socially irresponsible person. On the contrary, I would like to be able to say that proof of their deep social and historical responsibility lies in the penetration with which, in their different ways and to their different degrees, they reflect on the nature and the crisis of fiction, of fictionalizing, in their respective ages. But—leaving aside Cervantes now, who is simply in another class altogether—I *can't* do what Kundera does (or, to be fair to him, what he says he is doing). Cowardice on my part? Perhaps. History may be, as you call it, a process for representation, but to me it feels more like a *force* for representation, and in that sense, yes, it is unrepresentable.

(I have never known how seriously to take Joyce's—or Stephen Dedalus'—"History is a nightmare from which I am trying to awake.")

There is a poem by Zbigniew Herbert, dating from the 1960s, that has left a deep impression on me. It is called "Five Men." Five condemned prisoners spend their last night talking about girls, remembering card games. In the morning they are taken out and shot. Herbert writes: *therefore,* one can write poems about flowers, Greek shepherds, and so forth. A poem, then, justifying poems that stand back from calls to revolutionary action. Perhaps not a great poem—it may depend, though I am not yet sure of this, more on its rhetoric than on a poetic logic that carries all before it—but the effect of that *therefore* remains imperious and triumphant. What would equip me to say something equivalent? As deep a humanistic faith as Herbert's, I suppose. But I don't have it.

Why do I bring Herbert into the discussion? Herbert doesn't talk about History, but he does talk about the barbarian, the spirit of the barbarian (embodied in such people as Stalin), which is pretty much the same thing as history-the-unrepresentable. Herbert's strength is that he has something to oppose to the barbarian, which we can for present purposes call the human and the minor, about which he has his own ironic reservations but for which he can trace a sort of genealogy stretching far back into the European past. It is because Herbert feels himself so deeply to be a European and believes, with whatever hedgings and reservations, in the vitality, the *social* vitality, of the literature of shepherds, roses, and so forth, in the power of poetry to bring those symbols to life, that he can oppose poetry to the great shambling beast of history. In Poland one can still hold such beliefs; and who, after the events of 1989, would dare to scorn their power? But in Africa . . . ? In Poland one can still address the five men in the cell, or their executioners in the yard, indirectly, via the almost infinite lattice that a shared European culture provides. In

Africa the only address one can imagine is a brutally direct one, a sort of pure, unmediated representation; what short-circuits the imagination, what forces one's face into the thing itself, is what I am here calling history. "The only address one can imagine"—an admission of defeat. *Therefore*, the task becomes imagining this unimaginable, imagining a form of address that permits the play of *writing* to start taking place.

Achterberg's "Ballade van de gasfitter": The Mystery of I and You (1977)

(1) In every house I pass I glimpse You. How can I reach You? Disguised as a gasfitter?

(2) Disguised, I am face to face with You. But now the disguise cannot be dropped. (3) Shall I gas us both? Imagine the newspapers: "Death of gasfitter and woman. Mysterious letter. Sex motive not suspected." (4) So I seal the leak in the gasline, and find that You have gone.

(5) Ignoring my orders, I resolve to search in the new apartment block. (6) Reconnaissance of the block tells me nothing. (7–8) I fail to find Your name, but am directed upward by a maid. (9) In the elevator I realize what a fool I am. There is no gas here, God is the hole. What am I going to say? (10) The people of the upper floors eject me. (11) Back at street level, I realize I have failed. The game is up.

(12) The fitters' union calls for a full confession.

(13) Years later we meet the fitter in an old age home, still obsessed with finding the right address. (14) When he dies all the personages of the story, myself included, pay their last respects. R. I. P.

Such, in bald outline, is the story of Gerrit Achterberg's sonnet sequence "Ballad of the Gasfitter."[1] Scholars have beaten their heads long and hard against this strange poem, in particular against the problem of finding stable identifications for the personages. Is it a woman, for example, who is addressed at the beginning? If so, is she the dead beloved whom, in a lifelong Orphean enterprise, Achterberg tries to summon back to life? (There is a school that reads Achterberg's oeuvre in this way.) Or is the object of his invocation a more complex one, including God and the very being of the poem itself? What distance is there between the poet and his gasfitter self? Is the distance constant?

Does the poem present us with a single firm identity plus masks of that identity, or is the notion of identity it embodies more complex and fluid?

Answers to questions like these, on which critical debate has centered,[2] depend on our establishing significations for the *I* and *You* of the poem. Here, however, I want to begin by asking not *what I* and *You* signify but *how* they signify in the field of language and in the field of the poem; and then to proceed to the central symbolism of the poem, the symbolism of gas and the hole.

I and You

We can picture the pronouns *I-you-s/he* in ordinary discourse as occupying the apexes of a triangle (Figure 2). *I* stands at the origin of the utterance, the here and now, *you* at its destination, *s/he* at some point outside the axis of utterance. It is only when the axis of the utterance swings toward *s/he* that *s/he* becomes *you*, and only when *s/he* takes over the origin of the utterance that *s/he* becomes *I*.

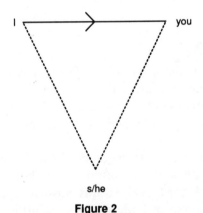

Figure 2

In discourse about discourse (for example, in critical discourse like this), the axis of utterance passes from *I*, the author, through a phantom *you* who are my reader, while every *I*, *you*, and *s/he* of my object discourse (here Achterberg's poem) becomes a *s/he*, following the rules of reported speech (Figure 3). Before I translated *I* and *you* in this way they remained outside the referential organization of linguistic signs. They were, in Roman Jakobson's term, "shifters," elements of what Emile Benveniste calls "a set of 'empty' signs . . . which are 'filled' as the speaker adopts them." Translated into forms of *s/he*, the nonpersonal pronoun, they enter the referential system as mere "abbreviative substitutes."[3]

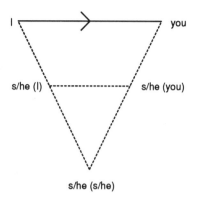

Figure 3

What happens when I try to pin down the referents of the *I* and *you* that I myself have made referential in translating them into *s/he*s? In sonnet 1 of the "Ballade," Achterberg (another "he") writes, "I glance into the houses . . . You appear." In my commentary I write: "He glances into the houses and the *You* appears," "the *You*" here being a kind of *he* or *she* or even *it*. Then I ask (and answer) questions that I have created for myself by my translation, that is, questions that come out of the structure of *my* created discourse, not out of Achterberg's: "Is the speaker [that is, he] a gasfitter already, or does he only adopt a gasfitter disguise in sonnet 2; and, if the latter, how does he acquire a supervisor and membership in a union?"[4] Or "Is the person he sees through the windows in sonnet 1 the woman who dies in sonnet 3?"[5] Twenty years of inconclusive debate on the "Ballade," with a record of irreconcilability on the identification of I and You, should warn us that adequate grounds for such identification may not exist within the poem, that I and You here may indeed be "empty signs" filled variously as the axis of utterance (Benveniste's "moment of discourse"[6]) and the point of consciousness that is the *I* move through the poem. (We should not forget that "Ballad of the Gasfitter" reflects the Dutch title in meaning both "Ballad about the Gasfitter" and "Gasfitter's Ballad": the title identifies *I* and gasfitter, or pseudogasfitter, only equivocally.)

As elements of a system of reference, *I* and *you* are empty. But the emptiness of the *I* can also be a freedom, a pure potentiality, a readiness for the embodying word. It is out of this sense of unqualified Romantic selfhood that Wallace Stevens' Nanzia Nunzio speaks. "I am the spouse," she says,

> I am the woman stripped more nakedly
> Than nakedness . . .
> Speak to me that, which spoken, will array me . . .[7]

Nanzia Nunzio longs to complete herself through a union of pure subjectivity with the Word. Similarly, the existential incompleteness of the *I* is at the root of Martin Buber's myth of a primal *I–Thou* relation. The "primary word," says Buber, is not *I* but "*I–Thou*," the word of "natural combination" denoting a relation between *I* and *You* antedating the objectification of *You* into *It* and the isolation of *I* into a being "at times more ghostly than the dead and the moon." This primal relation is, however, lost: "This is the exalted melancholy of our fate, that every *Thou* in our world must become an *It*." Intimations of the lost relation, "moments of the *Thou* . . . strange lyric and dramatic episodes, seductive and magical . . . tearing us away to dangerous extremes . . . shattering security," inspire our efforts to reconstitute again and again the "between" of the primal *I–Thou*.[8]

Nanzia Nunzio and Buber point to a transcendence of subjectivity through union with or reconstitution of the Word. Whether a subjectivity "stripped more naked than nakedness" can exist and whether there is a home for primal words in the language of men are questions we shall in due course have to consider. But let us for the moment try to read "Ballad of the Gasfitter" in the Romantic tradition as the search of this plenary, undefined *I* (embodying itself in the course of the poem in various ways) for an enigmatic but necessary *You*; for, in Buber's words, "If *Thou* is said, the *I* of the combination *I–Thou* is said along with it."[9]

Then, immediately, we encounter curious features of the *You*. The *You* has little solidity to the gaze of the *I*. On the contrary, the *You* is absent; or is present only passively, as an object of the awareness of the *I;* or is capable only of an inactive locativity defined in relation to the *I.* In other words, the *You* is absent or evanescent or dependent on the *I;* and the relation of *I* to *You,* being barely transitive, cannot be reciprocal.[10] The poem deals, then, in this reading, not only with the quest of the *I* for the *I–You* but also with the striving of the *I*—properly a poetic and perhaps even a goetic activity—to bring the *You* into some fullness of being.

Gas

English lacks a homonym to parallel Dutch *dichten:* (1) to seal (a hole), (2) to compose poetry (though, on the other hand, it possesses the notorious homophonic sequence *whole-hole-holy*). Around the familiar *dichten* pun the whole poem revolves: the gasfitter sealing off leaks is also the poet at work.

Subjected to an elaborate systems of cocks and taps and under the control of a veritable army (or, in the metaphor of sonnet 12, a veritable church) of gasmen with their own bureaucracy, gas circulates along a tentacular system of underground pipes and enters every home, except certain modern apartments. Topologically, the underground labyrinth of gas and the overworld city are equivalent to two hemispheres sealed from each other. The hemisphere of gas is held under pressure; released pure, it expands formlessly to infinity (remember that the word *gas* enters English via Dutch from the Greek *chaos*) and kills (by asphyxiation, by explosion). Human beings cannot live with pure gas. But mixed with elements of the other hemisphere and subjected to the synthesis of controlled combustion, gas brings warmth and light. Human beings (with the exceptions cited in sonnet 7) cannot live without gas. The gasfitter is a mediator between the vertiginous and fatal powers of pure gas and the needs of man. The craft of the gasfitter is the craft of *dichten.*

There are two ways in which we can translate this gas symbolically. First, it is literally the spirit, ghostly, overwhelming, coming upon us with fatal power, smelling of the void, tamed only by the *dichter*-priest. The quest for the true primal word of *I–Thou* thus takes us to the hole through which the holy spirit, Logos, enters the world. "Where is the hole?" the fitter (as holy fool) asks in sonnet 8. "God is the hole," he discovers in sonnet 9.

But, in the second place, we should not ignore the similarity between Achterberg's gas imagery and the imagery of the hole in Jean-Paul Sartre's *Being and Nothingness*, in which consciousness is presented as a hole through which nothingness pours into the world.[11] If we recognize Sartre as the darker spirit behind Achterberg, the quest of the *I* for the hole becomes an absurd quest for confrontation with the void, a quest that the *I* evades in sonnets 2–3 as long as he can embody himself as *dichter*, maker of artifacts and sealer-off of holes, but that he cannot escape in sonnet 9, in the building with the great hole, where his *dichter*-craft is ineffectual.

These two interpretations of the gas are not incompatible. Taken together, and buttressed with the numerous ironic parallels between Christ and I-as-gasfitter,[12] they make "Ballad of the Gasfitter" a story (incidentally anticlerical) of the *via dolorosa* of an absurdist Christian knight, the consummation of whose search for the true *Thou* (a consummation experienced by him as humiliating failure) is a moment in the "presence" (a presence that is an absence) of both his own nothingness and an unapproachable, infinitely remote God. The presence of God is an absence; God enters the poem as a hole, because, if we follow Kierkegaard, God remains always "incognito" and the relation of the eternal of God to the existent of man a "paradox" that never loses its irrationality.[13] The Word cannot be on man's tongue. It will not enter the structures of his discourse. "If 'speaking of God' is understood as '*speaking about God*,' then such speaking has no meaning whatever, for its subject, God, is lost at the very moment it takes place," says Rudolf Bultmann;[14] and this theme is echoed in Gabriel Marcel's criticism of Buber:

> Buber has himself forcefully insisted upon it . . . that each *Thou* becomes a thing or lapse into thinghood . . . But this is still not saying enough: I would add for my part that it is of the essence of language to effect this transformation. When I speak of you . . . even when I expressly declare that you are not a thing, that *you* are the opposite of a thing, I reduce you in spite of myself to the condition of a thing . . . We are confronted by a profound and doubtless essential contradiction.[15]

Or, as Ionesco says, "Les mots ne sont pas la parole."[16]
But can a pure *I* exist in discourse any more than a pure *You?*
The response of Stevens' Ozymandias to Nanzia Nunzio is:

> the spouse, the bride
> Is never naked. A fictive covering
> Weaves always glistening from the heart and mind.

All versions of the *I* are fictions of the *I*. The primal *I* is not
recoverable. Neither of the Words *I* and *You* can exist pure in the
medium of language. Indeed, after the experience of the Word in
relation to one's own existence, life cannot go on as before. "Self-
annihilation [that is, annihilation of the self] is the essential form
for the God-relationship," writes Kierkegaard.[17] The fate of the
gasfitter is precisely self-annihilation, a dwindling away of selfhood.

Finally, the hole has a third, minor, sexual signification. The
search of the masculine *I* for the hole in the house of the feminine
You (the language of sonnet 2 is full of double-entendres) and his
having to make do with holes in gaspipes (sonnets 2–4) and eventually in other men (sonnet 13), I take to be a kind of bawdy
sideshow in parallel to the metaphysical drama I have been out-
lining, one that points again to the danger of *naming* the *You* as
God or woman.[18]

I proceed now to a more detailed analysis of the poem in order to
try out my suggestion that the notion of identity it embodies is a
suspended one, that *I* and *You* exist and have their relations in
ways still prior to the ways of true names, with their firm significations, or true identities, and that the poem therefore works at,
and sometimes absurdly beyond, the borders of language.

1

You must have made your entries from the rear.
I glance into the houses from the street:
in windowfronts, between the curtains, out
of nothing You appear and reappear.

I pass, You vanish necessarily.
But I'm proved right by the next windowpane.

One Jansen lives there with his family—
as if You could escape me in this name.

It will not help. A door remains a door,
each with its steps, its mailbox, and its bell.
The apple-hawker lures You with his call.
A master-key is easy to procure.
Indeed I can quite freely step inside
as (at your service) gasfitter by trade.

Commentary. There is I and there is You (whom I see, as in a tracking shot, in every window): there is between us a bar (the housefronts); and there is my conviction (my delusion?) that if I can get past names (for example, "Jansen") I can reach You. Certain that a name disguises You, I adopt a disguise myself, that of gasfitter, which allows me to cross the bar. (Similar disguises I might adopt are those of postman, broker's runner, plumber: see sonnet 13).

Who are You—my doppelgänger image in the glass?[19] This translation of You into what is primarily a *s/he* (though his/her mystery is that s/he is also an *I* and a *you*) satisfies a naturalistic curiosity about how a being can pass through the inner walls of houses, but it explains nothing. "You must have made your entries from the rear"; "The apple-hawker lures You with his call"—do You not assume a tremulous autonomy here, or, if not that, am I not striving to give You an autonomy greater than that of a mirror image? I-as-reader can choose one of two paths at this moment: I can stand back from this speaking *I* (that *s/he*) and his/her fictionizings, reading both as metaphorizations of another *he* ("Achterberg"); or I can suspend this reading-as-distancing and give myself to the fictions of the *I* and the longed-for fullness of the *You*. I choose the latter path; and I do so because I see (line 14) that this is precisely what I *am* doing—giving myself to my fictions ("A gasfitter could reach You; therefore, I am a gasfitter") in a quest for a You beyond names. Names are the distance between You and I that I wish to transcend.[20]

2

Indoors with You, in daylight, on the job
disguised in workman's clothing, I wheel around

and see You standing. The walls turn to ground,
the ceiling slowly becomes a marble slab.

We grow murky in the fading light.
The room is bursting, won't take any more.
This can't go on. I drive the screws in tight.
As long as I confine myself to this chore

You and I can keep our incognito—
as long as I stay busy, bend or kneel
or lie flat on my belly trying to feel
what's wrong; all the while thinking, It's better so.
Dead silence by a hammer blow dispelled.
Death hush by which the hammer blows are healed.

Commentary. I am now I-as-gasfitter: the line between me and my disguise (fiction) fades rapidly in the course of this sonnet, to be redrawn elsewhere, in sonnets 13–14. The naturalistic code (a real gasfitter, bound and gagged, struggling in his underclothes in an alley) is suspended throughout.

Disguised, I am with You; but dropping the incognito, knowing and being known by You, leads to catastrophe: the sunlight fades, vision dims, the room, bursting or saturated as if with gas, becomes a grave. I turn away to the gasfitter's job of fixing the hole *(dichten)*. If I have crossed the bar as a man who closes the hole in the piping, then it is that hole I must stop; my intercourse is with gas, not with you, and I must "bend or kneel/or lie flat on my belly trying to feel" for that hole only. When naked I meet naked You, we drown in waves of *gas* (gas) that lead, by phantom phonetic mutation via *gat* (hole), to *God* (God).[21] The only way to You is a way of indirection. I must look to my *dichten.* (Similarly, in a putative "Ballad of the Electrician," I might find that a short circuit of + and − is not the only way to restore a lost connection.)

3

Shall I punch the gaspipes full of holes? or burst
the water-main and flood the house? I spot
the trap here, look again to the fittings, thrust
the fallacy with all haste from my thoughts.

For later in the papers one would find:
"While practicing his livelihood a fitter,
for reasons we have yet to comprehend,
inhaled monoxide gas and met his end.
In the adjoining room a similar bitter

fate befell the owner of the dwelling.
She lay prostrate, one hand stretched out in falling.
In it was clutched a letter that began:
'However wide the world I come again.'
It seems that she was overcome while reading.
Nothing suggests adulterous proceedings."

Commentary. If the naked knowledge of I and You leads to death, will death lead to the naked knowledge of I and You? Neglecting the art and craft of *dichten,* can I rely on a metaphysical overwhelming to carry us to a state of being beyond names or identities, that is, beyond language, to the forest where things have no names? Aha: "I spot / a trap here, look again to the fittings, thrust / the fallacy with all haste from my thoughts." What is the fallacy? That we can exit from the linguistic field, which includes the field of this fiction in/on which we subsist. Only by keeping my finger in the *dichter's* dyke can I hold off the flood of overwhelming substance (gas, water, the *au-delà,* the void); and the final peril of drowning is that, having died our death out of language, we die back into language. Lines 5–15 of sonnet 3 are the reincarnation of I and You in the language of institutionalized reifications, the *I* forever a fitter, the *You* forever a houseowner (female), the *I–You* traduced into a surreptitiously sexual relation between *it*s. This lapse of the barred *I–You* into the third person follows on a failure of *dichten* (a flood of gas, logorrhea—the fifteen-line sonnet).

In the newspaper report, the lady dies clutching a letter that begins, "However wide the world I come again." This archaeological relic of *I–You,* uncovered in the era of *he–she,* has connotations of a second coming, picked up in later sonnets, which the newspaper—which reads the letter as a note of assignation—of course misses. As for the provenance of the letter, we might as well ask again where the gasfitter's clothes came from: we are in a fiction continually generating itself.

4

At last the tiny leak is traced and sealed.
Slowly I bring together and pack my tools.
My legs have grown as heavy as lead tubes.
The sweat is trickling down my face in beads.

As if performing a superhuman feat
I turn with an explanatory wave
of the hand, but You are gone, and nothing save
the afternoon's declining light is left.

I pick my tray of tools up from the floor
and hoist it to my shoulder. In retreat
my footsteps raise a hollow song. The door
clicks shut behind me. The hubbub of the street
seems further off. The fog settles and thickens.
It seems that this time I have been mistaken.

Commentary. The leak is sealed, but You are gone. I can be with
You only where there is *dichten*-work to be done, only where gas
leaks into the world; yet my vocation is to close off leaks, to tame
gas for domestic consumption.

5

But just as I am settling down at home
to eat my dinner I hear the telephone.
I pick it up and from the other end
comes, as if nothing has changed, a new command.

My supervisor. His voice is sharp, severe,
but a veiled gentler undertone comes through.
"My son, go to the same street tomorrow.
You know the interest that I take in you."

Only a fool repeats an old mistake.
Best not to stay at home, but go and take
a look instead at the block of flats I see
rise sheer up from the ground across the way.
There, once I find the floor directory,
all will of itself become clear to me.

Commentary. Intercourse of I and You is over, and I am modulating from the masterful man of many parts (sonnet 1) to an ineffectual latterday evangel, an *I* with less and less inner pressure, well on my/his way to losing all pressure in sonnet 11 and becoming the object-*he* of sonnets 13–14.

The fiction of a gasfitter generates a job, a gas department, a supervisor, and a fitters' union; the fiction of the second coming generates a mission and a father. Having tamed the gaslines, I return home to find another tentacular system leaking. Over the telephone comes the voice of the father/supervisor with a command to repeat my quest along the horizontal houserow of sonnet 1. But I reject this in favor of a vertical quest in the apartment block that has generated itself on the other side of the street. Instead of scanning the horizontal series of nameplates (. . . , Jansen, . . .) I will scan the vertical floor directory, searching not for the one-in-a-million name (all names are *s/he*s) but for the You behind and beyond all names. Cabalist and man of words to the last (see sonnet 13), I am scanning name lists for something outside the system of names. How am I, in Captain Ahab's words, going to "strike through the mask" of language to the You beyond?[22] I wait for illumination: "Once I find the floor directory, / all will of itself become clear to me."

6

That night, however, I got to know no more
than that the concierge was asleep. Weary,
he had loosed the numbers from his memory
and lay there crumpled, head in arms. Absorbed

I stared in through the window. A soft wind
rustled through the grass where I stood outside;
and near to me, his duties pushed aside,
a living being who could have helped me find

my way out of this mess, if it had not
become so lonely and too dark for me
to think of whispering him awake. For he
would lose his head. Which would not do at all.
My supervisor's head would also fall
then. No one heard me leave. Did he look up?

Commentary. The situation of sonnet 1 is repeated: the voyeur and his desire, the bar, the mystery indoors. The reason given for not transgressing the bar is plainly a rationalization (indeed, the out-of-hand syntax mimes a moment of panic). The true reason is that the question I must ask is a mad question: "What is the word (name/address/number) for You?"[23]

7

At daybreak I am on the road, my face
still blurred with sleepiness. Although somewhere
the final goal has taken up its place
the streets this first hour seem as free as air.

I feel a safety I have never known.
One of my superiors cycles by.
I greet him but he barely turns an eye.
probably quarreled with his wife again.

Perhaps he is a bit suspicious meeting me in suburbs of the city where
a fitter has no business. A young and heedless generation has arisen here
by other forms of light. I've been observed.
Therefore toward the city my steps are turned.

Commentary. Postponing, perhaps even thinking of evading, the moment of reckoning, I roam through parts of the post-Christian world to which the illumination of gas does not extend, until I am reminded of my mission.

8

My last chance now approaches. Rows of white
pushbuttons, like teeth in a false denture, stand
fierce in their array defying my hand.
My fingers carry on a bitter fight.

As I stand there biting my nails I hear
the door spring suddenly open, and a maid
puts out the garbage can. I'd have remained
nonplussed forever had she not appeared.

But time is short. I turn to her and ask
in haste, Where is the hole? She points above
with vague derision as if to say, You're mad.
I know—so far gone that I pray to God.
The lift goes up toward the climax of
a job no fitter has ever yet pulled off.

Commentary. The riddle of the apartment pushbuttons (like the riddle of the typewriter keys) is, What are the name and number for You? The question to the maid—"Where is the hole?"—is a cover for this question. The maid points upward: up the elevator shaft, but also up to infinity.

9

The higher I ascend, the wider space
yawns between You and me. Life seems to be
enclosed in steel and nickel. Every
last rivet of this structure is in place.

There is no gas here. God is the hole, and pours
out his depths upon me to reveal
to a presumptuous fitter how much more
exalted he becomes with every floor.

Beneath me storey after storey falls.
I don't know where I must begin, or what.
Perhaps a last word will spring to mind
If I ask him what was the first cause.
A shock runs through my frame. I must get out.
I give it over. Be it as he finds.

Commentary. Nailed up in his coffin-cabin, a structure as closed *(gedicht)* as a sonnet *(gedicht)*, I embark on my do-or-die mission to find You in a dimension (the vertical) outside the competence of gasfitters. But whatever direction I am going in, it is the wrong direction relative to You. A workman whose job it is to keep the vertiginous powers of gas under control, I am out of my depth here, sucked toward the ultimate hole/whole, the Logos, the hidden name, the true second-person of the vertical quest, Thou. What word can a wordsmith utter? What is the answer to the question, "What is the question that will lead to the answer, 'The name of

You is—'?"? "Perhaps a last word will spring to mind / if I ask him what was the first cause." What was the first cause? In the beginning was the Logos.

10

Door after door swings open and a host
of men of every nation, race, and tongue
call out in chorus, "You don't fool anyone!"
looking at me as if I were a ghost.

Is that the reason I've crept underground?
I descend the pit of glass toward the street
with a bag of dirty laundry at my feet.
Up there one can still hear them scurry around.

For a while I hang about the neighborhood.
Past noon, I see. The rush hour has arrived.
School is over. Children run and yell
or prattle stories to their mothers. Bells
tinkle. Cars bellow past as if I had stood
for years and years upon this spot unmoved.

Commentary. The apartment-dwellers, lords of the vertical dimension, send me flying back to the horizontal, the domain of time. Wherever I am I do not fit: a man in a world of ghosts, a ghost in a world of men. I have not satisfied the precondition for vertical ascent: vertical descent, a trip underground (perhaps line 5, anomalously past tense, comes from a time after the burial poem, sonnet 14).

11

The gasworks spin upon their axleshaft.
Seeing my project utterly fallen to bits—
nothing, not even room for hope, was left—
and having, like a whipped dog, to turn tail—

a vacuum must have slipped into me then.
Up there there is no trade or craft that fits.
The children take each other's hands again:
as in remembered games they spin and wheel.

I set off for the office without waiting.
My supervisor himself comes to the door.
I yield myself to mild interrogation.
I need not make up stories any more.
Behind his glasses tears obscure his eyes.
He clasps my hand, collects himself, half-smiles.

12

The leaders of the Christian union call
the gas- and waterfitters into session
to say that one of them has been transgressing
the code of regulations binding all

by showing up with tools in hand wherever
he found himself, such action causing harm
to the body as a whole; wherefore they charge
that he who broke the rule confess his error.

For the first time in the history of the trade
the gas- and waterfitters fall to their knees
without a thought for leaks beneath the floor—
at one, fraternal, and amalgamate.
Then says the chairman, Go, and sin no more,
and they depart, well satisfied, at ease.

Commentary. Taboo, a pariah, one who has seen too much ("And all should cry, Beware! Beware!"), I am everywhere ostracized. Life systems close into circularity, shutting themselves off to me, the gasworks spinning in rapt self-absorption, the children circling, the fitters' union huddled in convocation. The very sound structure of my habitat is circular (sonnet 10, lines 11–14). A beaten man, bereft of all pressure of vocation, failed bringer of the Logos, denounced by a preacher who uses the words of the Paraclete, I disappear from the stage, giving up my pretensions as *dichter*, poet and fitter: "I need not make up stories any more."

13

Years later, hair now white, we find the fitter
moved to an old men's home. Feeble of mind

he sits and pores over a city guide
spelling the names of streets out letter by letter.

Bed and board he shares with several brothers:
a postman, a broker's runner, and a plumber.
He often gets it in the ass from others
for only coming down to meals to grumble.

Provision has been made until he dies.
Health and funeral benefits reward
one's efforts toward charity; besides
they save him from being strangled by the warden.
Public Works has given him his lodgings.
Tobacco quid is his if he has longings.

Commentary. Expulsion of the pariah extends further. For the *I* as
wordfitter/*dichter* to survive, the *I* as failed *dichter* (gasfitter) must
be split off. Failed *I* becomes false *I*, alienated *I*, or *he*. In fact, all
the failed *I*-projects are successively split off as *he*s and lodged in
an old men's home (domain of memory, museum, anthology):
gasfitter, postman, broker's runner, plumber—creatures of the
word (the city directory), phantoms nesting promiscuously within
and upon each other, watched over by a murderous warden-*I*.
Evidences of my failure, I wait impatiently for their death.

14

In the end he closed his eyes for good.
His mouth, slumped open, was tied shut again.
Measured, he was found fit to be contained
in a regulation coffin, deal, six-foot.

And all of them came—people from the flat,
Jansen, the maid, the supervisor—to bear
their final joint respects. Like mine, their wear
was sober: a dark suit, with cane and hat.

Once at the graveside no one made a sound.
With critical eye each stepped up to behold
the fitter slowly sink into the ground
as if still hoping to catch him in an error

now that he had to plug his final hole.
He rests with God. The earth covers him over.

Commentary. To kill the fitter, all that is required is that I reassert myself as wordmaster over a domain of words in which I have now (by naming, distancing) included *him*, stage-manage a funeral, and make it clear in my scene construction that fitter, people from the flat, Jansen, and so on are items in a word game I am now terminating. I am the true poet; the fitter was a mere plug I used to get this *gedicht* (poem) *gedicht* (closed off).

The Poetics of Failure

A certain elegance of poetic closure is always obtainable from the maneuver in which a poem ends by swallowing its own tail—denying, denouncing, or erasing itself. The retractions that end such medieval poems as Chaucer's *Troilus and Criseyde* are, seen formally as rhetorical *topoi*, maneuvers to achieve closure by cutting the link between a consolingly "real" world of authors, pen and ink, and sequences of signs, on the one hand, and a "fictive" world of actions and passions, on the other. The poem that incorporates a denunciation of itself (*sub specie aeternitatis* or however) paradoxically acquires the ontological self-sufficiency, and therefore extends the ontological challenge, of the self-consuming artifact: Can language reach outside itself? The tradition, represented by *Don Quixote* and *Tristram Shandy*, of self-reflexive undercutting of the mimetic pretensions of fiction, which finds its apotheosis in Flaubert's dream of "a book about nothing, a book without external attachments,"[24] raises the same question.

The hide-and-seek of the *I* in Sterne has become a serious game, with dangers to the psyche, in Eliot's "Love Song of J. Alfred Prufrock." What has intervened has been the rise and decline of the romantic-liberal notion of the self. The self in Eliot is struggling with problems of authentic being. The self in Beckett is struggling with problems of being at all, unable to get from Descartes's *cogito* to Descartes's *sum*. I hint so skimpily at an entire history because I intend no more than to point to what lies behind the metamorphosis of fiction from the adventures of the self in nineteenth-century classic realism to the metafictional commentary on the fictionality of self that precipitates such fictions as Nabokov's *Pale Fire* and Barth's *Lost in the Funhouse* and that forms the whole of Beckett's *The Unnamable*. The poetics of these works is a veritable poetics of failure, a program for constructing artifacts out of an endlessly regressive, etiolated self-consciousness lost in the labyrinth of language and endlessly failing to erect itself into autonomy. The poetics of failure is ambivalent through and through, and part of its ambivalence is that it must parade its ambivalence; thus Beckett can speak of an art that is "the expression that there is nothing to express."[25] The poetics of failure erects absence into presence by an undenied trick of prestidigitation, whose success nevertheless depends on the left hand's not knowing what the right hand is doing.

The poetics behind "Ballad of the Gasfitter" is the poetics of failure. The *I* fails in his goetic-poetic attempt (disguised as an attempt to restore the *I-You*) to constitute the *You* out of nothing. Having failed, this *I* is split off and discarded by a "real" *I* (in fact only the second in a theoretically infinite progression) who asserts his mere survival—that is to say, the mere existence of the "Ballad"—as the opposite of failure. Thus we find a three-level structure of lefthand failure and righthand success (but I use the word "success" in a purely contrastive sense, so that "failure" shall not be vacant of meaning) with a bar of unknowing between them:

Left	*Right*
As unreflective, unreflexive gasfitter, I fail to meet the *You* of my life.	As absurd quester I fail to find You. But it is the nature of quests to confront me finally with myself alone.
I split off and kill the failed questing *I*. Only by splitting myself do I seem able to live.	Not only can I survive my failures, but I have created a way of sacrificing myself endlessly to quest-as-process.
Seeking, as Romantic poet, to bring into being, through words, a *You* beyond words, I fail.	Prepared, as post-Romantic poet of failure, to construct a poetry that is no more than the process of poetry, I am finished.

Poetry as a drive toward purity of formulation is well known; poetry is further purified when the formula refers no longer to something (something that could eventually exist independently of the formula in which it is expressed), but to nothing. In such a case the formula formulates itself, turning in upon itself. It is clear that Achterberg was after this and this alone. Here we have the immediate explanation for what has been called his monotony and even his monomania. Of course his "inspiration" had always to remain the same; of course, being this kind of poet, he was compelled to say always the same thing: after all, he had *nothing* to say. With that one can get by, with that one must get by, seeing that nothing is the constant source from which everything wells. The poetry that results from it looks like the sea, which is always changing and about which people say that it is "always the same."[26]

Translation

Is this essay a study of Achterberg's Dutch poem or of my English version? The question is a misleading one, for my translation itself is part of the work of criticism. This is so because, in the first place, it is in the nature of the literary work to present its translator with problems for which the perfect solution is impossible and for which partial solutions constitute critical acts. A literary work is, among other things, a structure in which form has become meaning. When form is disrupted, meaning is also disrupted. Such disruption is inevitable, for there is never enough closeness of fit between languages for formal features of a work to be mapped across from one language to another without shifts of value. Thus the work continually presents its translator with moments of choice. Something must be "lost"; that is, features embodying certain complexes of values must be replaced with features embodying different complexes of values in the target language. At such moments the translator chooses in accordance with his conception of the whole—there is no way of simply translating the words. These choices are based, literally, on preconception, prejudgment, prejudice.

Here, for example, is the rendering of sonnet 9 published by Stanley M. Wiersma in 1971:

The higher I go up, the more I live it:
the space between us. All life I feel
is trapped in artifacts of chrome and steel,
a building perfect to the smallest rivet.

No gas is here. God is the hole, will give it—
his mystery—in floods that will reveal
to a proud fitter what he still should feel.
God's glory grows each storey, and I live it.

Now storey after storey falls below.
I don't know where or what I'd better do.
Maybe a last word will come to me
when I ask him about the first cause of being.
A shock goes through me! I want out of here!
I leave the matter to his will austere.[27]

As Wiersma reads the poem, the fitter is engaged in trying to close the hole of guilt in himself by closing the hole that is God, "for without God there would be no guilt" (Wiersma finds the source of this guilt in various events in Achterberg's life). The fitter wants to "poetize God out of existence" by "declaring that God is not a reality, but a hole." But his attitude to God remains "ambiguous": "if the hole will not close . . . then the gasfitter will be enveloped in the deadly gas, God's mystery, which makes a deeper religious experience possible."[28] Wiersma does not, therefore, see, as I do, a moment of awed realization reflected in lines 5–8, since it is precisely the gasfitter's thesis, however ambivalently held, that "God is the hole." Hence Wiersma does not find it necessary to imitate the run-on movement of these four lines. In contrast, I understand the device to be a significant one, the rhetorical equivalent of a moment of spiritual expansion. Wiersma does not find (or does not choose to stress) a parallel between the ascent in the cabin in sonnet 9 and the descent in the coffin in sonnet 14; hence he translates Achterberg's line 4, *Het bouwsel komt geen klinknagel te kort*—literally "The construction lacks not a single rivet," *klinknagel* (rivet) coming from *nagel* (nail)—as "a building perfect to the smallest rivet," while I translate it as "Every / last rivet of this structure is in place." The difference is between the perfection of the afterlife and its finality. In the last two lines of the sonnet—

literally "A shock goes through me. I must get out / and yield (it) to his edict"—Wiersma finds panic followed by resignation ("I want out of here! / I leave the matter to his will austere"—the archaic inversion is false to Achterberg's style) where I find only resignation.

I make the comparison between Wiersma's version and my own not to argue their respective strengths and weaknesses but to give an example of how, faced with the impossibility of "full" translation, that is, a mapping of all the significations that may inhere in the original, translators make verbal choices in accordance with their conception of the whole. The comparison also brings into visibility a feature of reading by no means peculiar to translation, and one that reveals why it is misleading to ask whether this essay presents a reading of Achterberg's original or of my translation. For, just like the process of translation, reading is a process of constructing a whole for oneself out of the datum of the printed text, of constructing one's own version of the poem. In a clear sense, all reading is translation, just as all translation is criticism.

The First Sentence of Yvonne Burgess'
The Strike (1976)

M. Paul Valèry recently suggested anthologizing as many
first sentences of novels as possible, from whose imbecility
he expected a great deal. The most famous authors would
be laid under contribution. Such a notion still honors Paul
Valèry who not long since, apropos of novels, asserted that
as far as he was concerned he would never permit himself
to write: *The marquise went out at five.*

— André Breton, *First Surrealist Manifesto*

"Finlay closed the book and considered the title appreciatively."
The book, *the* title: why this deviant use of *the*, and emphasized
by repetition too?

Finlay. What is *Finlay?* "Finlay" denotes a person whose name
is Finlay. Does it have any meaning?

Considered *appreciatively.* Somewhere in the deep structure of
this phrase, "Finlay" appreciates a book. Does "Finlay" give signs
that denote appreciation, and does whoever decodes his signs do
so without qualm? Or is it that "Finlay" is aware of himself ap-
preciating a book? If the latter, is "Finlay" not in fact *I?*

So this first sentence is truly a labyrinth. What "Finlay" closes
is not a book but the book; and it is the book because it is the
book that "Finlay" closes. "Finlay" is Finlay, the one who closes
the book. And he gives signs that can be seen only by an eye that
cannot be seen.

"Finlay closed the book . . ." belongs among those initial sentences whose type-sentence is "There was once a man who . . ." If
we want a gloss on the meaning of "There was once" we can go to
the Majorcan storyteller's formula "Era e non era," which signals
that all succeeding assertions (". . . a man who bought a cow . . .")
are made in the split was-and-was-not mode of fiction. "Finlay"
and "the," pseudo-definitional though they are, are not thereby
nonreferential, but their reference is oblique. They refer not to a

91

man and a book but to the body of discourse that follows: all assertions succeeding "Finlay closed the book" are signaled to be in the as-if mode.

One may intend one of several things by beginning a book with the words "Finlay closed the book." Daunted by the alternative "Someone closed a book" and all the analysis that must follow (Who closed what? How is it known?), analysis only a schoolman can look forward to ("Where now? Who now? When now? Unquestioning. I, say I. Unbelieving"—Beckett, *The Unnamable*, first sentences), one may have decided to write a work of criticism in the form of a fiction in which the codes of the Novel, the first of them the formulaic opening, will be exhibited and decoded. This has been the enterprise of the *nouveau roman*. "La marquise sortit à cinq heures"—Claude Mauriac, *La Marquise sortit à cinq heures*, first sentence.

Or, having accepted that transcendence of the illusionism of Realism is an illusory hope, that to get behind *(aufheben)* fiction by incorporating into fiction a critical consciousness of the procedures of fiction is only to climb another spiral of illusionistic Realism, one may be taking refuge, like John Barth, in Nietzschean gaiety.

Or one may be embarking on the heroic project of Jorge Luis Borges' Pierre Menard composing *Don Quixote* at the beginning of the twentieth century:

"... truth, whose mother is history, who is the rival of time ..."
Written in the seventeenth century, written by the "ingenious layman" Cervantes, this enumeration is a mere rhetorical eulogy of history. Menard, on the other hand, writes:
"... truth, whose mother is history, who is the rival of time ..."
History, *mother* of truth; the idea is astounding. Menard, contemporary of William James, does not define history as an investigation of reality, but as its origin.[1]

In language there are no stable and positive elements. Elements achieve definition only through their reciprocal differences, and all shift their boundaries continually with the passing of time. To find what a sentence like "Mr. Podsnap closed the book" or "Philip Marlow closed the book" used to mean is an archaeological endeavor. Included in its meaning, however, was certainly the following: that there was a social and characterological typology assumed and shared among the reading public; that the sign "Mr. Podsnap" or "Philip Marlow" in an initial sentence, empty to begin with, would in due course be filled with social and characterological details, some of them details of such fineness as to refine the typology ("Finlay closed the book" is immediately followed by sentences in *style indirect libre* whose direction and function are disguised, filling in "Finlay" rather than pointing forward to their pseudoreferents), the process of refining the typology being known as *making the character individual* just as adherence to the typology is known as *making the character representative;* and that the fit of "Mr. Podsnap" or "Philip Marlow" into the typological lattice would reciprocally reaffirm the typology and therefore the sociology and psychology of the reading public, the participation of whom in joint and several appreciative readings of the book would constitute a further reaffirmation of a class bond.

The replacement of the formula "There was once a man named Finlay who . . ." with the briefer "Finlay . . ." and the accompanying shift of the as-if mode marker away from the verb was a minor technical innovation when it was first done (where, when, by whom?). How does an innovation grow to be an occasion for affirming a class bond? Prague School linguists call the process by which repeatedly used speech forms wear a neural rut for themselves *automatization*. Automatized speech is speech that speaks its speaker. The phenomenon of automatized speech explains how it comes about that sometimes a book can be conceived of without an author.

A Note on Writing (1984)

Roland Barthes discusses the verb "to write" in terms of the grammatical oppositions past versus nonpast, transitivity versus nontransitivity, and active versus passive.[1] What Barthes (following Benveniste) has to say about time and person is not relevant to my purpose here; but I will summarize what he has to say about voice.

Though modern Indo-European languages retain morphologically distinct forms for only the active–passive opposition, the phantom presence of a middle voice (a voice still morphologically present in Sanskrit and ancient Greek) can be felt in some senses of modern verbs if one is alert to the possibility of the threefold opposition active–middle–passive. "To write" is one of these verbs. To write (active) is to carry out the action without reference to the self, perhaps, though not necessarily, on behalf of someone else. To write (middle) is to carry out the action (or better, to do-writing) with reference to the self. Or—to follow Barthes in his metaphorical leap from grammar to meaning—"today to write is to make oneself the center of the action of *la parole;* it is to effect writing in being affected oneself; it is to leave the writer *(le scrip-teur)* inside the writing, not as a psychological subject . . . but as the agent of the action."[2] The field of writing, Barthes goes on to suggest, has today become nothing but writing itself, not as art for art's sake but as the only space there is for the one who writes.

Whether Barthes's essay is best thought of as a piece of speculative linguistics or as academic propaganda for a postmodernist practice of writing I do not know. Perhaps it is of no more value than as a demonstration of how deeply a literary conception can be embedded (metaphorically) in linguistic categories (are there any deeper linguistic categories than those of tense, person, voice?). I would not be spending time on it here if it did not, tangentially, speak a word of caution about constructions that we often run across in literary criticism in South Africa, particularly at the level of reviewing:

to use language
to write a book
to create characters
to express thought
to communicate a message

One of the things these core phrases have in common is grammatical structure. The verbs are all transitive, their voice (in form and, as I read them, in intention) active. They reflect a common conception of the subject—a subject prior to, independent of, and untouched by the verb—and of the relation, or lack of relation, between subject and object. Within the conception of writing reflected here, a paradigm sentence would be

I | am writing | a note

with the bars standing for bars between subject and verb, verb and object, subject and object.

I am not suggesting anything about value here. It may be truer in some cases, in some conception of value, to say "A wrote X" and in others to say "B | wrote | Y," but such a distinction would say nothing about the value of X or Y. Nevertheless, it is an interesting exercise to reflect on the two sentences

I am writing a note (active)
I am writing a note (middle)

asking oneself which of them describes the act one is performing. (But: *to perform an act* or *to perform | an act?*)
One might also want to think of

A is-written-by X (passive)

as a linguistic metaphor for a particular kind of writing, writing in stereotyped forms and genres and characterological systems and narrative orderings, where the machine runs the operator. The three voices active, middle, passive may then be thought of as a cautionary chorus always to be lent an ear when one is doing-writing.

=

Jerusalem Prize Acceptance Speech (1987)

There is a paradox to the 1987 award that I have difficulty with: How does it come about that someone who not only comes from but also lives in so notably unfree a country as my own is honored with a prize for freedom?

In a society of masters and slaves, no one is free. The slave is not free, because he is not his own master; the master is not free, because he cannot do without the slave. For centuries South Africa was a society of masters and serfs; now it is a land where the serfs are in open rebellion and the masters are in disarray.

The masters, in South Africa, form a closed hereditary caste. Everyone born with a white skin is born into the caste. Since there is no way of escaping the skin you are born with (can the leopard change its spots?), you cannot resign from the caste. You can imagine resigning, you can perform a symbolic resignation, but, short of shaking the dust of the country off your feet, there is no way of actually *doing* it.

How do the masters of South Africa experience their unfreedom today? I will purposely not indulge in talk about uneasy sleep, about the imagination of disaster, about the return of the repressed in the shape of nightmare. I will not indulge in such talk because by this time in history, and particularly in Israel, with the shadow of the Holocaust behind it, people know that there exists a banal kind of evil which has no conscience, no imagination, and probably no dreams, which eats well and sleeps well and is at peace with itself.

Instead I want to say something, one brief thing, about the unfreedom of the master-caste as it is experienced in waking social life.

In the early 1950s, the heady years when the great city of apartheid was still being built, a law was passed making sexual relations between masters and slaves a crime. This was the most pointed of a long string of laws regulating all phases of social life, whose intent was to block forms of horizontal intercourse between white and black. The only sanctioned intercourse was henceforth to be vertical; that is, it was to consist in giving and receiving orders.

What was the meaning of this deeply symbolical law? Its origins, it seems to me, lie in fear and denial: denial of an unacknowledgeable desire to embrace Africa, embrace the body of Africa; and fear of being embraced in return by Africa.

The statute forbidding love between the races has recently, in another deeply symbolic move, been repealed, as if to signal that the day of reckoning prophesied by Alan Paton forty years ago has arrived. "I have one great fear in my heart," says one of Paton's black characters: "that one day when they are turned to loving, we will find we are turned to hating."

At the heart of the unfreedom of the hereditary masters of South Africa is a failure of love. To be blunt: their love is not enough today and has not been enough since they arrived on the continent; furthermore, their talk, their excessive talk, about how they love South Africa has consistently been directed toward *the land*, that is, toward what is least likely to respond to love: mountains and deserts, birds and animals and flowers.

If one fails to see the relevance of this talk about love, one can replace the word *love* with the word *fraternity*. The veiled unfreedom of the white man in South Africa has always made itself felt most keenly when, stepping down for a moment from his lonely throne, giving in to a wholly human and understandable yearning for fraternity with the people among whom he lives, he has discovered with a shock that fraternity by itself is not to be had, no matter how compellingly felt the impulse on both sides. Fraternity ineluctably comes in a package with liberty and equality. The vain and essentially sentimental yearning that expresses itself in the reform movement in South Africa today is a yearning to have fraternity without paying for it.

What is the price that has to be paid? The very lowest price is the destruction of the unnatural structures of power that define the South African state. About these structures of power there is a great deal to be said. I will confine myself to one observation.

The deformed and stunted relations between human beings that were created under colonialism and exacerbated under what is loosely called apartheid have their psychic representation in a deformed and stunted inner life. All expressions of that inner life, no matter how intense, no matter how pierced with exultation or despair, suffer from the same stuntedness and deformity. I make this observation with due deliberation, and in the fullest awareness that it applies to myself and my own writing as much as to anyone else. South African literature is a literature in bondage, as it reveals in even its highest moments, shot through as they are with feelings of homelessness and yearnings for a nameless liberation. It is a less than fully human literature, unnaturally preoccupied with power and the torsions of power, unable to move from elementary relations of contestation, domination, and subjugation to the vast and complex human world that lies beyond them. It is exactly the kind of literature you would expect people to write from a prison. And I am talking here not only about the South African *gulag*. As you would expect in so physically vast a country, there is a South African literature of vastness. Yet even that literature of vastness, examined closely, reflects feelings of entrapment, entrapment in infinitudes.

Two years ago Milan Kundera stood on this platform in Jerusalem and gave tribute to the first of all novelists, Miguel Cervantes, on whose giant shoulders we pigmy writers of a later age stand. How I would like to be able to join him in that tribute, I and so many of my fellow novelists from South Africa! How we long to quit a world of pathological attachments and abstract forces, of anger and violence, and take up residence in a world where a living play of feelings and ideas is possible, a world where we truly have an occupation.

But how do we get from our world of violent phantasms to a true living world? This is a puzzle that Cervantes' Don Quixote solves quite easily for himself. He leaves behind hot, dusty, tedious La Mancha and enters the realm of faery by what amounts to a willed act of the imagination. What prevents the South African writer from taking a similar path, from writing his way out of a situation in which his art, no matter how well-intentioned, is— and here we must be honest—too slow, too old-fashioned, too indirect to have any but the slightest and most belated effect on the life of the community or the course of history?

What prevents him is what prevents Don Quixote himself: the *power* of the world his body lives in to impose itself on him and ultimately on his imagination, which, whether he likes it or not, has its residence in his body. The *crudity* of life in South Africa, the naked force of its appeals, not only at the physical level but at the moral level too, its callousness and its brutalities, its hungers and its rages, its greed and its lies, make it as irresistible as it is unlovable. The story of Alonso Quixano or Don Quixote—though not, I add, Cervantes' subtle and enigmatic book—ends with the capitulation of the imagination to reality, with a return to La Mancha and death. We have art, said Nietzsche, so that we shall not die of the truth. In South Africa there is now too much truth for art to hold, truth by the bucketful, truth that overwhelms and swamps every act of the imagination.

= Popular Culture

Interview

DA: Your nonfiction includes essays and reviews on film, the comic strip, advertising, rugby, political journalism, and analyses of cultural stereotypes such as "the white tribe" and "the Afrikaner." Apart from journals covering popular culture in South Africa (*Speak, Critical Arts,* and *Die Suid-Afrikaan),* you have also published in *Vogue, Reader's Digest,* and the *New York Times Magazine.* Clearly, although your novels make few compromises in what they require of readers, you have tried to narrow the gap between the lowbrow and the highbrow. But "popular culture" in South Africa is a problematic, and certainly not a unitary, concept. How do you envision your work in this area?

JMC: My work in this area barely deserves the name of work. Indeed, since one of its arguments is that play is too readily slighted in comparison with work, I would positively prefer to think of at least some of it as play. The essay on Captain America, certainly, is a *jeu d'esprit.* I wrote it when my son was nine or ten, and deeply into American comic books. He dragged me willy-nilly into his obsession. I was at the same time teaching an introductory course in the nineteenth-century American novel—Cooper, Poe, Hawthorne, Melville, Twain—and was myself caught up in a rather heady mythic reading of American romance (Richard Chase, Leslie Fiedler). The writers of the Captain America stories of the late 1970s—very *literary* stories, in their way—had been exposed, I suspect, to the same reading of the American tradition. I haven't followed the fortunes of Captain America into the 1980s and 1990s, but I wouldn't be surprised if his story were being given a very different kind of turn today. I can't believe he still rides his old Harley-Davidson.

As for the piece on rugby, I had a regular white South African boyhood; my life outside the classroom was dominated by sport, particularly by cricket. Even today I have an investment in sport, or at least in what the spectacle of sport promises and now and again yields: instants of strength and speed and grace and skill coming together without thought.

What still interests me in the piece is the distinction I draw between game-construction, as a form of intellectual/physical play, and game-playing itself. As I remember it, the idea was borrowed from Chomsky's distinction between innate grammar-constructing mechanisms and grammars themselves. Game-construction, which we associate with yet-to-be-socialized children, seems to me an essentially higher activity than socialized play, as typified by sport. It is a curious fact that older children and adults do not invent games with the facility of young children, and indeed rarely show any desire to do so. If the arts constitute a higher activity than physical culture, it is surely for the reason that they continue to vary the forms and rules of the games they play. Art as polymorphous play, then, playing at inventing rules with which it plays at constraining itself.

As for the other pieces you mention, pieces on South African society, I think they deserve a quiet death. I am afraid that at a certain stage of my career—the mid-1980s—I slipped a little too easily into the role of commentator on South African affairs.[1] I have no talent for that kind of political/sociological journalism. To be more specific, I am too suspicious of the genre, of the vision it locks its practitioners into, to give myself wholly to it, yet I lack enough zeal to try to turn it upside down or inside out. Anyhow, I am far too bookish, far too ignorant about real people, to set myself up as an interpreter, much less a judge, of the lives they live.

DA: The essay on advertising is based on René Girard's theory of imitative desire. You seem to have relied on something like this theory in *Waiting for the Barbarians*, where Colonel Joll models the Magistrate's desire for the barbarian girl. The effect, as I see it, is to conflate the Magistrate's desire, confused as it is with feelings of eroticism and atonement, with Joll's acts of torture, thus implicitly producing a critique of "soft" humanitarianism. Would you go along with this construction? Alternatively, what openings did Girard provide for you?

JMC: I remember reading Girard's *Deceit, Desire, and the Novel* in the 1970s with a sense that something important was being said not only about the workings of fiction but about the effect of fiction on the lives of readers (in the latter respect Girard takes his lead from Cervantes, as he clearly acknowledges). I found in Girard the same acuity about behavior and the moral justifications we lend to our behavior that I found in Sartre. Girard's later writings, particularly what he has to say about Christ, I find absorbing though a bit megalomaniac.

Whether what I read in Girard worked itself out in *Waiting for the Barbarians* I cannot say. We may think we admire a writer because he opens our eyes, when in fact we admire him only because he confirms our preconceptions. Did I need Girard to teach me about sadism and imitative desire? I suspect not. I suspect that what is going on in *Waiting for the Barbarians* is more complicated (though not necessarily more interesting) than what Girard describes in *Deceit, Desire, and the Novel.* But perhaps I am wrong. Whatever the truth, I feel that questions of influence upon my novel-writing are not for me to answer: they entail a variety of self-awareness that does me no good as a storyteller, as a site where fantasy should not be hampered by unnecessary introversions and doubts.

(You catch me, of course, in self-contradiction. If I don't want to look into myself, claiming that it isn't good for my novel-writing, what am I doing conducting this interview, and what sort of autobiographer am I? Let me say, then, specifically on the question of influence, that the interviewer may not get the whole truth because the subject may not know the whole truth, and the subject may not know the whole truth because the resistances and repressions involved are too strong. This is not a coded way of telling you I am holding something back about Girard, nor is it the opposite. But I am clearly descending into a Cretan Liar position from which there will be no escape.)

DA: In three of these pieces, the essays on advertising and "Captain America," but especially in the review of *The Guest,*[2] you place a good deal of emphasis on demystification. (The Barthes of *Mythologies* seems to be at work here.) Is this not a different notion altogether from that of games, of game-construction and game-playing? How would you weigh these concerns now?

JMC: Demystification: yes, Barthes is certainly at work, not least as a cultural critic who *plays* with ideas (there are ideas in Barthes, almost too many ideas, but nothing I would call theory). I see no conflict between play and demystification, which is after all a procedure of taking apart things—myths, tropes, rhetorical figures—to show how they work. But talking about demystification as play does entail that I don't attach quite the same significance to demystification as an animating principle of criticism as the left does or did. That is, I no longer see opening up the mystifications in which ordinary life is wrapped as a necessary aim, or indeed an obligation, of criticism. (There was a time when I saw this as a very clear obligation.)

DA: Does the obligation no longer exist, or have your views simply changed?

JMC: A healthy level of suspiciousness is not a bad thing. But some of my criticism—parts of *White Writing*, for instance—is soured, I think, by a certain relentless suspiciousness of appearances. Why am I now suspicious of such suspiciousness? For two reasons. First, in the act of triumphantly tearing the clothes off its subject and displaying the nakedness beneath—"Behold the truth!"—it exposes a naïveté of its own. For is the naked body really the truth? And second, because a critical practice whose climactic gesture is always a triumphant tearing-off, as it grows lazy (and every orthodoxy grows lazy), begins to confine its attentions to clothed subjects, and even to subjects whose clothes are easily torn off. In other words—to return to the terms of your question—a demystifying criticism privileges mystifications. It becomes like Quixote scouring the plains for giants to tilt at, and ignoring everything but windmills.

=

Captain America in American Mythology (1976)

The Hero

Captain America wears a red-white-and-blue costume, head to toe, and carries a red-white-and-blue boomerang shield.[1] Except when ruminating or despondent, he crouches at the knees and holds his arms ready. His biceps and deltoids bulge, his pectoral and dorsal muscles ripple powerfully, his sternomastoids stand out like cables. His jaw is clean-shaven and square, his teeth are straight, his eyes (through the blue eagle-mask stamped with the letter A) blue as a mountain stream. The house inker of Marvel Comics customarily shades in the faintest of bulges at Captain America's crotch. But what the Comics Code Authority subtracts here, Marvel Comics replaces elsewhere. For sprouting upward and downward from that slim pelvis, issuing in brawny calves and booted feet, in massive arms and gauntleted fists, in bull neck and jutting chin, and seen continually at a heroic angle of forty-five degrees from in front and below, Captain America is a great flag-wrapped phallus striding out, like all heroes of adventure since Achilles, in quest of a foe worthy of all that bulging, displaced potency. And striding out of the shadows somewhere, eternally, is the figure of the supervillain, monstrously musclebound or cranially overdeveloped, come to measure his endowment against Captain America's.

Captain America has a twilight double life as Steve Rogers, harried young patrolman. When Steve Rogers dons a drab windbreaker and resumes his cowed relationship with his blonde teenage girlfriend Sharon Carter, the heroic musculature fades quite away. The hero-costume, the tumescent body, the shield of virtue, the emblematic "A" ("America," but also "Adam," "Alone") are all of a piece. Captain America is the wish-fulfillment alter ego of colorless citizen Rogers, anxious husband in embryo. As Captain America, Rogers casts off all bonds except those that bind him to his comrades in arms. His armor protects him from the adoring, groping female, whose hands can find no grip on his mountainous convexities. The courtly knight venerated a taboo lady, bent his knee to a lord, developed homoerotic relations with his comrades, and held together his self, riven with Oedipal conflict, by pouring himself into an iron mold. Captain America is his American descendant, via Leatherstocking, with his five identities and potent Long Rifle; Arthur Dimmesdale, baring the "A" on his chest with one hand while holding off the predatory mother/wife with the other; and Huck Finn, protector and protégé of Nigger Jim.

When Steve Rogers becomes Captain America, it is to hold himself together. For now he is defined and confined by his icon. The line bounding him is hard and unwavering. The colors that block him out are elementary and never wash over the line. His emblem proclaims his truth. Contained and maintained at three levels of being—by the muscular exoskeleton, by the mask and costume, by the bounding line—Captain America is the image of the stable ego.[2] Buckling his belt, he embraces his own hips; closing the symbolic lock of the buckle, he calls attention to his sex and proclaims his chastity. Masked, he puts himself outside and above family and law: as a Protestant hero he will now heed only the authority of an inner voice. He is no longer a unit on the labor market but an autonomous Guardian of the Republic. He leaps from the constricting one-dimensional city streets to the jungle of the rooftops and into the skies. When he mounts a motorcycle, the motorcycle flies. His domain of action expands: he crashes through doors, hurls his foes through windows, catapults out of the plane of the page, breaks through the rectangular panel, hurls and looms from one perspective to another, subordinating the color-composition of every frame to his dominant blue.

The name of the game is *freedom*. "IF THE YELLOW CLAW WINS, THE WHOLE WORLD LOSES" (166/8). Captain America is the third Adam, on a mission to save the world. But like the second Adam he may not use his full powers: by a mythologic rule saviors must be half-divine, half-mortal, bridges from the human to the transcendent, handicapped gods. Captain America is crucified on the dilemma of his superstrength: on the one hand it sets him apart from mankind; on the other it drives him into asymmetrical duels in which he may fight only to contain and put to flight, while his foe fights for keeps. Despised and rejected, a man of grief; and, like Jesus and all other Christian heroes, impervious to frontal assault but a sucker for betrayal, for the Judas-blow. But then, when the hero is laid low, the blow that does it is by definition unheroic: defeat becomes, by a Christian transvaluation of values, victory.

Evil

Captain America's contest is not with crime but with evil. Crime can be taken care of by the law; comic-book police are always rounding up crestfallen hoodlums and packing them off to jail. But the true supervillain soon escapes from the lockup and gets up to his old tricks. The law is inadequate to deal with evil. The CIA, above and outside the law and mythologized in *Captain America* as SHIELD, responds to the infernal technology of evil with its own martial technology ("War is a dirty game"). But SHIELD is not heroic. Captain America, in quite as ambiguous a relation to the law as SHIELD, is a hero not because he is an outlaw but because, where SHIELD is merely doing its job, he has responded to a call, the Calvinist categorical imperative of absolute urgency and absolute stringency.

Ideology

Of course Captain America refers to his mission as simply "a job" (164/10). The Christian hero is humble. So is the hero of the nation-state. Standing to attention before his leader in a posture that says, "I am your man," he refers back his heroic accomplishments to the state that made him. "I was only doing my job." Thus by a syllogistic trick are all jobs in the nation-state valorized: "The hero is merely doing a job; therefore, the merest job-doing is heroic. Do your job." There is a way of seeing the Captain America costume as a Nessus-shirt in which the heroic naked redeemer has been dressed up by the postheroic, post-Christian state. When the villain fights he utters grandiose threats; when Captain America fights he must quip in the language of the common man. Marvel Comics, through Steve Englehart, has not given Captain America a language heroically commensurate with his body. There is something in Marvel Comics that would like to tame the lone hero to the advantage of a greater America. There is less swagger and sport to Captain America than to the villain, but the low-key Captain America is the more efficient fighting machine. He has been harnessed in the interests of the *performance principle*.[3] In the case of the Hulk, eponymous hero of another comic-book series, warfare on the heroic principle is carried to an extreme: a monstrous pea-green misanthropic cretin, the Hulk roams the ice-wastes of Canada trying to escape American and Soviet forces intent on capturing and taming him. "HULK JUST WANT TO GET AWAY FROM STUPID MEN AND THEIR STUPID MACHINES!" (*The Incredible Hulk*, 172/19).

Is it possible to domesticate the American hero? From Natty Bumppo to Steve Rojack he has been a frontiersman who has wilted in domesticity. "DANGER IS LIKE FOOD TO HIM . . . A FOOD HE NEEDS TO LIVE . . . FOR ONLY WHEN HE'S CLOSE TO DYING . . . IS HE TRULY ALIVE" (*Captain America*, 164/11). Steve Rogers becomes not only the alter ego but the antiself of Captain America when he is seduced from his lone obsession with evil by the blonde pseudo-redemptress Sharon Carter, WASP-woman. Sharon Carter wants love and marriage, a steady income, respectability. The story of Steve Rogers and Sharon Carter belongs with the agonies and ecstasies of Eve Jones in the fireside family newspaper. The story of Captain America, subliterature, belongs on the shadowy drug-store bookrack, to be read under the surveillance of a hidden TV eye, or in the steamy solitude of the bedroom.

Father

Having succumbed to Woman, the father is by definition too impure to be an American hero. The image of the father in *Captain America* is Colonel Nick Fury, head of SHIELD. Fury has all the signs of a gnawing sense of failure: he is unshaven, he smokes, but for the Comics Code Authority he would probably be a hard drinker too. He has maudlin spells. He is under the thumb of a European countess, dark and probably depraved. He fights in the old boasting, brawling, two-gun Western style. Whereas the true outlaw wears a mask, he wears a rakish eyepatch: half in the

System, half out of it. Sometimes he pretends to be an elder brother, Lancelot to Captain America's Galahad; but when he has had a bad day the hostility seeps through: "I KEPT ON LIVIN'— FIGHTIN' FOR MY COUNTRY! THROUGH WORLD WAR II, THE KOREAN WAR, THE COLD WAR . . . I LIVED THOSE 20 YEARS, GETTIN' GRAY FOR AMERICA . . . AND THEN YOU POP UP, ALL BLOND, BLUE-EYED . . . AND YOUNG!" (153/11). The authentic raging voice of the VFW and the American Legion, of Mr. Middle America with his sagging wife, his ingrate kids, his mortgage payments.

Gothic

The gothic mode discovers itself in America. From gothic, frisson upon frisson of horror, the nerves thrilling in a debauch of suspense, the orgasm of revelation always around the next corner, comes striptease. In high gothic (Henry James) the ultimate secret is veiled, the object of endless whispering. Low gothic (Poe, *Captain America*) has two moments. In the first it drops the veil and the unnamable blazes forth: Ligeia, the Red Skull. In the second it backtracks: No, that is not it at all, that is not what I meant at all, the darkness of blackness must wait for our next issue. High gothic is an art of *coitus interruptus* with a single subject, low gothic, like pornography, an art of rape upon subject after subject. The energy of all gothic comes from one libidinal source, tabooed desire. Gothic therefore has a single aim: to name, possess, and exorcise its obsession. Beyond that, it yearns toward Eden, a time before inherited guilt, before parents.

Captain America pays unabashed visits to the symbolic world of gothicism, its gloomy castles and labyrinthine underground passages. Captain America in the Gothic castle is American innocence in the maze of the old European psyche. (In one story [issues 161–162] the lord of the castle, a Kraut psychologist with pince-nez and butterfly collar, is named, in a Freudian slip, Dr Faustus.) Lost in the maze, Captain America is aided by the maiden of the castle, who conspires with him to bring down her master (the Jack-the-Giant-Killer motif). His mission is to reach the very heart of the castle, guarded by monsters and massive doors, where he must destroy the infernal laboratory where the villain works at the dark projects that will give him dominion over the earth,

"SCHEMES WHICH I CONCEIVED DURING MY YEARS OF CONTEMPLA-
TIVE ISOLATION . . . SCHEMES WHICH WILL DELIVER THE WORLD
INTO MY PALM" (*The Yellow Claw*, 164/19). Avatar of Faust, brother
to Roger Chillingworth, Captain Ahab and Gilbert Osmond, intellectual and mystic, the villain directs his annihilating rays/rage
at Captain America. But Captain America, proof against magic,
only bounces back and knocks him cold with his good right fist.

Science

The myth behind the Captain America stories is a Christian myth
of Christ in the soul ever wakeful to ward off the assaults of Satan.
To find adequate metaphors for the immensity of the forces in
conflict, the stories can resort only to the inventions of science
fiction, itself a mode of gothic. Thus the superstrength of Captain
America is explained as a consequence of an unexpected chemical
reaction between inoculants in his blood. To the pharmacopoeia
of such magic potions, going back to antiquity, SF adds a repertoire of magic rays and the machines that project them.

Four rules govern the ideological relations of the science of rays
and potions to good and evil, and to Captain America and his foes
and allies:

Science is neutral with respect to good and evil.
Captain America belongs to the domain of the good but not to
the domain of science.
The villain belongs to the domain of evil and to the domain of
science.
SHIELD belongs to the domain of the good and wholly to the
domain of science.

Despite the appearance of politically "correct" support for the
principle of a neutral science, the Captain America stories thus
remain true to the pre-Renaissance mistrust of the uncommitted
intellect perpetuated in Calvinism, in Puritan New England, in
Know-Nothing America. They remain true by posing the implicit
question: if the poles of hero and villain are symmetrical with
respect to good and evil but asymmetrical with respect to science
(so that science is asymmetrical with respect to hero and villain),

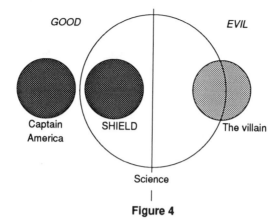

Figure 4

how can science be symmetrical with respect to good and evil? The question is geometrically unanswerable (Figure 4).

The Black Man

Blood brother to Captain America, Chingachgook to his Natty, Jim to his Huck, is the Falcon, masked Harlem vigilante. But the Falcon is torn in allegiance between his white brother and his black girlfriend, Leila. For not only does Leila, as a woman, want to tame her man (Leila < Delilah): Leila is under the influence of black radicals who preach racial exclusivism.

When the Falcon tries to pull out, Captain America preaches earnestly to him:

FALC, WE ARE DIFFERENT . . . I DON'T DENY IT. THERE NEVER HAVE BEEN AND NEVER WILL BE TWO HUMANS EXACTLY ALIKE . . . BLACK/ WHITE . . . YOUNG/OLD . . . MALE/FEMALE . . . AND STRONG/LESS STRONG. WHICHEVER SIDE WE'RE ON, THERE'S ALWAYS ANOTHER . . . DIFFERENCES CAN BE IMPORTANT . . . BUT THE ONES BETWEEN YOU AND ME AREN'T! WE BOTH HAVE THE SAME GOAL: ENDING INJUSTICE! (161/14)

Captain America pleads for the realization of Cooper's dream of the brotherhood of nature's noblemen; and, ignoring the gothic shadows that accumulate around the figure of the black man, Marvel Comics' dialogue hints that it will one day come true.

Art

DUSTY DEWDROPS SMEAR THE BROKEN WINDSHIELDS OF ABANDONED CARS, AS THE DAWNING SUN TOSSES A PROMISE OF HEAT INTO THE HUMID, CHOKING AIR. OLD MEN SNIP THE TAUT COPPER WIRES WHICH BITE DEEP INTO THEIR DAILY NEWS WAKE-UP EDITIONS. DELICATESSENS FIRE UP FRESH BROWN COFFEE. NEW YORK SNARLS HELLO TO ANOTHER SUMMER DAY. (153/1)

FABLED CAPTAIN AMERICA. (153/1)

To *hoi polloi* this is Literature, part of the subsidy Commerce pays to Culture for trespassing on the Word. To the sophisticate it is a send-up of the genre in the vein of Chaucer's tale of Sir Thopas. Imagine the plight of Steve Englehart, author and ironist. On the one hand he is not up to the task of inventing an epic language adequate to the heroic iconography (see, for instance, the bumbling thees and thous he gives to the god Thor in the series *The Avengers*). On the other hand, Marvel Comics will not permit him to send up the subject on the lines of the Batman TV series. Therefore, he soldiers on, slipping in enough parody to signal that he is hip. The plastic imagery, contorted and violent, is still faithful to the gothic-American transcendental enterprise, but the language is banal and barely functional (image: gigantic man holding struggling woman; her balloon: "HE'S . . . SO STRONG!"—161/27). Thus the verbal narrative, the conscious side of the stories, branching into topical political comment,[4] into *bien-pensant* social relevance, into teenage love-interest, into wishy-washy postmodernist self-reflexiveness, can be seen as subversion and demystification of a venerable myth. The very compositional structure of Captain America represents a moment of ideological conflict in the inner history of America:

$$\frac{narrative}{iconography} = \frac{Benjamin\ Franklin}{Jonathan\ Edwards} = \frac{Emerson}{Hawthorne} = \frac{J.\ F.\ Kennedy}{Norman\ Mailer}$$

The Burden of Consciousness in Africa (1977)

$\blacksquare$he *Guest* is a film about an episode in the later life of Eugène Marais.[1] The episode, which leads from nowhere to nowhere, is of no inherent importance. In order to break his morphine habit, Marais is persuaded to spend some months on an isolated farm in the western Transvaal. Gradually his morphine dose is reduced. He undergoes a crisis but, with the help of his hosts, passes it and begins to recover. He forms friendships, regains some human warmth. But the cure is deceptive. He returns to the drug, alienates his hosts, and is rejected. Granted that the episode is not inherently interesting, the question we might ask is: Is Eugène Marais, as man or myth, important enough to us to justify a film about him?

In Eugène Marais, South Africa came its closest yet to producing a Genius. Think of Marais's qualifications. He had deep-set piercing eyes. He loved many women. He lived in wild and dangerous places. He was addicted to an exotic drug. He wrote poems about death and thought morbid thoughts. He was mainly unhappy and finally slew himself. He was plainly in a quite different class from mere bright boys like Jan Hofmeyr and Jan Christiaan Smuts.

The Genius is one of the stereotypes of the Major Man that our culture has contrived (Saint, Hero, Genius—how many more?). In our time the cult of the Genius has waned somewhat. But when we go to see *The Guest*, we are being asked to worship at the shrine of Genius again. So what is a Genius, and why should we take one seriously?

The Genius is a creation of European Romanticism. He is a quintessentially mythic figure, mythic because in him are reconciled two contradictory attributes. On the one hand he is the prophet, the man of godlike vision (hence the piercing eyes) who foresees the future; without honor in his own time, he is citizen of a world yet to come, a pioneer in new forms of thought and feeling. On the other hand he is a child, a weakling, fleeing from a reality easily sustained by more solid people into a world of illusory gratifications, obsessed with death rather than getting on with the business of living. In the figure of the Genius the West therefore finds a home for both pessimistic self-criticism and optimistic belief in Progress. The Genius, despite his gloominess, proves the inevitability of Progress by finding it easier to live in the future than in the present.

But if this is so, what is a Genius doing in South Africa? What conditions of life in the western Transvaal of the 1920s does Eugène Marais find insupportable enough to drive him to drugs and death? The answer: being a white man in Africa is what is insupportable. Not because of the burden of guilt (this is the theme of a later literature) but because of the burden of consciousness. The theme of Marais's book *The Soul of the Ape* (written 1922, first published 1969), on which *The Guest* relies heavily, is that consciousness is a form of pain, that the highest consciousness is the most exquisite pain. And the highest form of consciousness of all is, of course, that of the white Genius, in whom consciousness bulges into the future. Therefore, to take Marais's thought seriously means to take him seriously as a hero of consciousness.

The tragedy of white consciousness in Africa is dramatized most clearly in the final scene of the film, which is worth looking at closely. Marais has relapsed into heavy addiction; his doctor (the poet A. G. Visser) has come to take him home from the farm. They chug back along the road to Heidelberg. Marais speaks: "Stop the car." "Why?" "I want to say grace." While Visser watches, Marais walks into the tall grass, struggles up a ridge, and vanishes slowly down the other side. Africa swallows him up. Over the scene we hear Marais (Athol Fugard) reciting verse; a subtitle tells us it is Marais's "Lied van Suid-Afrika." Visser looks on. The screenplay says: "His face expresses for us in these final moments our sense of the enigma of Eugène Marais." The poem comes to an end. We see only the empty veld. Text on screen: "Ten years later, on the farm Pelindaba in the Pretoria district of the Transvaal, Eugène Marais, suffering acutely again from withdrawal symptoms, shot himself."

What does this all mean? We have seen that, on the farm at mealtimes, Marais has been unable to join hands with the Meyers and say grace. He cannot pray to a God he does not believe in. Who, then, is this South Africa to whom he finds himself able to pray? A murderous mother-goddess, the poem tells us, who devours her young and in return for love gives only "endless pain." Marais's poem is powerful stuff, but I doubt that it would awake much response in most South Africans, to whom (and let us not forget this) Africa is a mother who has nourished them and their forebears for millions of years. South Africa, mother of pain, can have meaning only to people who can find it meaningful to ascribe their "pain" ("alienation" is here a better word) to the failure of Africa to love them enough. What the closing scene of the film depicts is Marais, bearer of a pain-racked higher consciousness, Genius and Saint become Hero, abandoning civilization and going off to sacrifice himself at the feet of adored but implacable Africa. The "enigma" we are invited to contemplate can therefore be cracked: "It is a tragic fate to be a white man in Africa," it says. "*On the other hand*, Marais was a Genius." Both ways, the white man wins.

Set over against Marais at every point are his hosts, the Meyers of Steenkampskraal. Marais chainsmokes and shoots morphine; the Meyers eat meat and vegetables. Marais lives with baboons; the Meyers ride horses. Marais is thin, haggard, unshaven, volatile; the Meyer men are big, stolid, slow-spoken, bearded. If Africa is the ravenous sow who devours her litter, how come the Meyers are so comfortable? Where are *their* agonies of consciousness?

The answer is that the Meyers participate in a stereotype that has nothing to do with the myth of the Genius. The Englishman's stereotype of the "Boer," a stereotype going back at least to John Barrow, is of a rawboned, hulking fellow, slow-thinking but shrewd, undisciplined, lazy, greedy, somewhat cowardly (though a fine marksman), intolerant, fundamentalist. No doubt the Afrikaner himself has played his part in the promotion of the stereotype. In any event, Ross Devenish certainly perpetuates it in his Meyer family, who speak a variety of English no human being has ever spoken. Here is Oom Doors Meyer:

I'm only a farmer, and maybe not such a good one at that . . .
There are some things I don't understand, and . . . [*voice rising*]
wragtig Eugene . . . you're one of them. *Make allowances, man!*

Some people will find Oom Doors lovable. Others will prefer to
hold their ears shut.

Behind the men of the Meyer family stands Tant Corrie Meyer.
Throughout the film Tant Corrie wears a black dress under a white
smock with wide vertical bands descending from the shoulders.
Her garb echoes the interior of the farmhouse, whose spirit she
obviously is: stark, whitewashed walls broken by the dark verti-
cals of doors and windowframes. Interior scenes are carefully composed and photographed with seductive beauty. They hark back
to the interiors of the classic Dutch painters. Sunlight enters the
house cool, luminous, tempered; lamplight makes the Meyers,
seated about the dinner table, glow with Rembrandt browns and
golds. These people are not rootless colonials, the pictures tell us:
see, they are both rude children of the African earth and heirs to
a venerable European tradition.

To everyone, Tant Corrie is the nourishing mother. Before her
menfolk she places heaped, steaming plates of food. When Oom
Doors fails to talk sense into Marais, it is Tant Corrie who tells
Marais to cut the crap and eat his soup. To the black magic of
morphine she opposes the white magic of food. (Thus, again, it is
only by discounting Marais as a Genius that we can feel comfortable about the final defeat of Tant Corrie's magic.)

In its clean, simple way, the life the Meyers lead is most attractive. But if we are not wholly seduced by it, there remain a few
uncomfortable questions. How much did the Meyers ask to take
this seedy stranger into their bosom? Why does no one in the film,
even under stress, talk about money? If the Meyers run a cattle
farm, why do they never talk about cattle? about the weather? Do
they never go to town? (Steenkampskraal is nine miles from Heidelberg.) Where do the African farm laborers who materialize out
of nowhere for a single fifteen-second sequence live? How do the
Meyer men spend their time when they are not eating?

Here are two less niggling questions.

In a film that nowhere disclaims fidelity to the historical truth
and acknowledges its debt to Leon Rousseau's biography *Die groot*

verlange (The Great Longing), why do Devenish and Fugard allow the recuperating Marais to win the confidence and affection of the Meyers' little daughter when Rousseau explicitly tells them that Marais failed to overcome the child's fear of him?[2] Because popular wisdom has it that a child can smell goodness as a lion can smell fear, and it is necessary for Marais to be a "good" character? Because it makes the story more poignant if we see Marais as a man very nearly redeemed from his worst impulses by the care of a woman and the love of a child?

A second question. Rousseau tells us that, while at Steenkampskraal, Marais used to go up into the mountains with an African helper to dig up old graves, searching for Bushman skulls. "He only wanted Bushman heads," said Louis Meyer to Rousseau. "He would pick up a head and look at it and throw it away—'No, that's a kaffir!'"[3] This episode is not reflected in the film (instead we have a sequence with a baboon skull). Perhaps it should have been. It would have shown another side of Marais. For Marais was not only a naturalist who lived with apes *à la* Jane van Lawick Goodall and is hailed as a precursor of the present-day reaction against behaviorist dogma in the study of animal behavior—all of which makes him "positive," "good"—but also one of those "bad" post-Darwinian ethnologists and comparative anatomists who traveled around the world with their calipers measuring skulls and classifying races into "higher" and "lower." Marais wanted Bushman skulls in order to prove a theory he had that their jaw structure showed that Bushmen belonged to a "less developed" race. I cite Rousseau's story not to cast a racist slur on Marais (who in this respect was only a child of his times) but to indicate that there is a perspective from which Marais suddenly seems a lot closer to the Victorians than he does to us. This perspective is absent from the film.

All in all, then, I find *The Guest* an equivocal film. Remember, however, that, with exceptions, the cinema has always tended to work within the myths of the dominant culture. Myths are ways of patching things together. What *The Guest* does is to take the legend of Eugène Marais, one of the few potentially mythic men white South Africa has produced, and to spin it out with other myths and stereotypes to create a work that is finally consoling, even flattering, to its white South African audience. "When we are good (like the Meyers)," it says, "we are very very good; and when we are bad (like Marais) we are not bad but heroic."

On its own terms are there not ways in which *The Guest* could have been made into a better film? Are there ways, for example, of preventing the falling-off of interest and tension in the film as Marais begins to recover? Would everything have come right if Marais's girlfriend Brenda had been cut entirely out? Certainly the vacuous episode involving her forms the dramatic low point of the film, and deciding to leave it in was a major error of judgment on the director's part (I cannot believe that no one advised Devenish to jettison it). But finally most of the blame for the slackening of tension must rest on the shoulders of the writer of the dialogue, Athol Fugard. As the film goes on, Marais and Visser talk more and more, exchanging pompous and facetious banter. The idea, I suppose, was to avoid too much direct exposition of Marais's thought via readings from *The Soul of the Ape* (these readings in fact work very well) and to replace it with indirect "dramatized" exposition via argument. But even on the stage this ploy has been exhausted for decades; in film it has never worked.

There is a dream sequence early in the film in which Marais sees himself asleep among the baboons of the Waterberg. Later there is a longer dream sequence (reflecting quite inadequately what the screenplay claims it represents) in which Marais sees himself being led by a baboon away from the house, into the veld and the night. What makes Marais's intuitive relations with animals possible, the film says, is what makes everyday social relations difficult for him: nature is "true" and "deep," while culture is "false" and "shallow," and it is the essence of Genius to seek the true and deep (hence the revision of history, too, to allow Marais access to the true and deep of childhood). I wonder whether, inside *The Guest*, there is not a thinner film struggling to get out, a film centered on Marais and the apes rather than on Marais and the Meyers. What such a film might look like I do not know. Perhaps more like a conventional wildlife documentary, shorter, more sober, more "educational," with none of the potential for histrionics that drug-crazed behavior allows.

Four Notes on Rugby (1978)

Rugby is one of a family of games of great antiquity and wide distribution: two teams of unarmed men struggle for possession of an object that they try to carry home with them. The game is inherently violent, and has at various times been outlawed ("Nothing but beastly fury and extreme violence"—Sir Thomas Elyot, 1531). The present-day football codes represent attempts to isolate a nonviolent variant. The rugby code in particular forbids any attack ("tackle") on a player not carrying the ball. The question of how the ball-carrier is to be dispossessed, and how another player is to possess himself of the ball, is approached via a complex, even labyrinthine set of laws. Despite repeated chopping and changing, these laws remain unsatisfactory, and for a number of reasons: (1) They are inexact inasmuch as they allow a variety of interpretations. (2) They yield a phase of play without aesthetic interest. (3) They fail to prevent injuries and allow some covert violence. (4) By and large they fail to keep the ball live as they are intended to do. (5) They contribute heavily to making rugby a game whose outcome is decided by prowess at goal-kicking.

Minor modifications to the rules are not going to change this state of affairs. It is to be doubted whether it is possible to compose a set of rules for a ball-handling game that are precise and that yield nonviolent, attractive, and continuous play. The North American football codes recognize this impossibility and declare the ball dead at the point of tackle.

Rugby dreams of itself as a celebration of speed, agility, strength, comradeship. Every now and again one sees evidence, flashes of beauty amid all the milling and toiling, that the dream is not unfounded. But the flashes are intermittent. There is a mistake in the most basic conception of the game. Therefore, the question to ask is: Why does this crippled game flourish, and flourish particularly in South Africa?

R ugby is one of several sports elaborated in England and exported to the colonies. The first stronghold of these sports—notably cricket and rugby—was the public schools, where they fell under the patronage of a powerful and mobile middle class as vehicles for the propagation of its own values; more precisely, as vehicles for the propagation of a set of mystifications through which that class saw itself and wanted others to see it: "fair play," "may the best man win," "team spirit," "never give in," "the stiff upper lip," and so on. By playing its games, the sons of the middle class were initiated into the values of their class and, once a week, ritually reaffirmed them. By passing the test of "playing the game," the sons of shopkeepers gained admission to the middle class.

Exported to the colonies, their codes centralized under the control of the priesthoods of the International Rugby Board and the International Cricket Conference, rugby and cricket served the additional function of affirming an "Anglo-Saxon" middle class whose international ties were stronger than its national ties. Hence the invention of national teams, international tours, test matches, and so on, which provided a means for conflict to be *played out* in the name of friendly rivalry.

The political importance of rugby in South Africa from the turn of the century to the 1960s cannot be overemphasized. Rugby became a means (as cricket never did) for the economically disadvantaged Afrikaner to assert himself magically over the Englishman. In its pyramidal structure (club, province, nation) it also formed—as many politicians realized—a model of white political unity. The class values attached to the sport by Englishmen and the national (often ethnic) values attached to it by Afrikaners lead to a strange doubleness of vision—spectator A reads a test match between South Africa and New Zealand as an opportunity for one nation to dance in triumph over another, while spectator B reads the same match as a celebration of old imperial values—but, as we all know, the marriage has survived the strains.

Anyone who reads rugby journalism must be struck by how methodically it avoids confronting the spectator's experience of the game. Without any consciousness of what it is itself, it remains bogged down in the most crudely positivistic conception of what it is like to watch ("X dummies and breaks through a tackle before passing to Y, who scores in the corner"). The situation is absurd. For thousands of people, Saturday afternoons in winter form the climax of the week, an experience they afterward stammer to speak about because they lack the words. They devour the sports reports looking for bread, and find only stones.

So if we want to talk about the crowd appeal of rugby we must start from scratch with the most elementary scrutiny of our own consciousness. Under what categories can we say that our experience, as we watch the game, falls? I suspect there is most to be said about our experience of time. The allure of a football game is, in the first place, the allure of time redeemed from chronicity, an island of eighty minutes lifted out of the time of one-thing-after-another, which is the time of entropy, of the running down of the universe. The game promises to give meaning to a stretch of time (in this it is like narrative), and it fulfills this promise often enough to bring the spectator back. To postreligious people whose lives are submerged in *chronos*, who feel themselves dying while they are living, it provides the experience of time given meaning—which one might call a low-level experience of transcendence—often enough to make Saturday afternoon more significant than Sunday morning.

Not only in its overall structure as *agon* or contest, but in its details, the game promises liberation from the time of the clock. Perhaps more than in any other game in which the contestants pursue each other through the same space and the same time, the varieties of football provide those momentary experiences (known in journalese as "thrills") in which the spectator's time-sense is stretched and the second hand slows: a body strains to pass another body, a hand is too slow, a grasp grazes, misses; a ball hangs in the air, a body leaps for it, grasps it.

In themselves these moments are nothing. Their phenomenal reality can be repeated in one's own backyard. But when they are experienced in a crowd of thousands, the attention of each watcher charges the moment with value. Everyone is thus engaged in creating and confirming value for everyone else. Analogies between football matches and political rallies tend to be false. The analogy with religious spectacles may be less facile.

(It would seem that no one can persuade the public that recorded relays of football matches are as good as live relays. This is only secondarily because the outcome is already known, primarily because the public knows that the redemption of time can take place only in time.)

A serious phenomenological analysis of watching rugby would proceed from time-experience to the experience of the momentum of the contest, and to further categories of aesthetic and kinaesthetic experience that, even in the criticism of so highly developed an art of movement as the dance, do not seem yet to be well developed.

If one watches children playing together, one can, in their more highly developed forms of play, distinguish two phases: a phase in which the rules are worked out, and a phase in which the game is played. In the first phase the children, so to speak, define a space in which the fantasy of the game can flourish. In the second the game is played until it fills that space and becomes boring. Then there is a return to the first phase, and the rules are modified; or else the game ends. Often the alternation between phases is rapid. Sometimes players go literally out of phase: some are playing the game while others are playing the game of the rules (mistakenly called "arguing about the game"). This is the moment of conflict.

We tend to think of the first phase as merely preliminary. But it is in fact the phase of greater creativity. It can be compared to problem-definition, as opposed to problem-solving. The two phases have, of course, a dialectical relation.

If the aim of phase two, the game itself, is to allow a display of excellence (as measured perhaps by winning), then what is the aim of phase one, the game of the rules? There can be only one answer: to create a good game. We could spend time working out some of the qualities of a good game, but that would be to miss the point, which is that children composing games do not disagree about these qualities. It is as though they possess a paradigm of what a good game is, in its most general form. (Whether they obtain this paradigm from cultural or hereditary sources I do not know. I think a good case could be made out for the latter, but again the issue is not quite relevant. I certainly agree with Johan Huizinga that it is a mistake to see play as an expression of anything but itself: "The play-concept must always remain distinct from all the other forms of thought".[1])

We can define a sport as a game played according to a well-defined code of rules. By definition, then, a player of a sport is excluded from playing the game of the rules. In exchange for this renunciation he is given a highly developed code that is guaranteed to yield, much of the time, a good game. In other words, when I play a sport I play the game (as they say), the others' game, no longer my game. If I grow bored I must suffer my boredom. Boredom becomes a fate, it is denied any place in the dialectic of the game.

In schools, and particularly in boys' schools, the line between "free play" and sport is clearly drawn, and always to the disadvantage of play. Sport is given an explicit ideological function ("character-building") while play remains suspect, frivolous. From long before adolescence the child is put under pressure to leave the open air of games and live under the umbrella of the codes. Ontogeny recapitulates phylogeny here. The old local varieties of games, with their rules that were not codified but remained a matter of consensus, varying from occasion to occasion, were frowned on by authority and ended up as picturesque irrelevancies.

The child who submits to the code and plays the game is therefore reenacting a profoundly important moment of culture: the moment at which the Oedipal compromise is made, the moment at which the knee is bent to government. This is the moment at which sport and the arts, the two most complex forms of play, part ways. In the creative arts, the artist both composes his game and plays it. He thus asserts an omnipotence that the player of sports yields up. This helps to explain why sports are so easily captured and used by political authority, while the arts remain slippery, resistant, undependable as moral training grounds for the young.

In these notes I have spoken of rugby wholly from the outside. A fuller account would require, among other things, an investigation from the inside, which would cover such areas as the player's experience of the game (in which such categories as control of space and effort may turn out to predominate) and the internal politics of rugby. Rugby, more than any other of the major spectator sports, has managed to keep money and power out of the hands of players and in the hands of cliques of administrators. How the machine of rugby is kept going—by what institutionalized means players, grown men, are cowed into letting themselves be treated like children; how "troublemakers" are dealt with at every level of the game; how the system of patronage works by which players are guided into commercial organizations that in turn have ties with administrators; what exactly the network of connections is between rugby administration, the educational system, and government, a network that seems to constitute South Africa's answer to the British "old boy" network; how careers are made and successions arranged among administrators; what the various mutual dependencies are between newspapermen and administrators—all of this would constitute a rich field of investigation for someone with access to the system yet financially independent of it, if such a person exists.

Triangular Structures of Desire in Advertising (1980)

The Transaction

A form of advertisement that we often meet consists of an image of a product (for example, a bottle of perfume), an image of a model (for example, a beautiful woman), and a text linking the model (more precisely, the self-projection of the model, her well-being, beauty, and so forth) to the product ("A fragrance to match your mood today," runs a typical text).

The aim of advertisements like these is to create a link—the link of purchase—between the product advertised and the consumer of the advertisement. The need for a third element in the transaction—the model—is therefore by no means obvious. Yet advertising practice seems to have shown that at least in a certain range of cases the form of advertisement in which the image of the product is *mediated* to the consumer by an image of an idealized consumer, the model, "works" better than the unmediated form in which only the image of the product is presented. (In both cases, of course, the text plays its own mediating role.)

One might be tempted to think that in the mediated form the "real" transaction is the one effected between the product and the consumer, that the model is inessential and can be discarded as one discards marginal rough-work once the answer to a problem in arithmetic has been obtained. What I shall be arguing, however, is that the inherent structure of advertisements with models is truly triangular (in other words, that there is no way of reducing the structure from a triad to a dyad without falsifying it), and that the particular framework developed by the critic René Girard for talking about *mediated desire* in the novel can be applied to the reading of advertisments with valuable results.

My field of discussion is therefore the limited one of advertisements in which the model is overtly present to mediate the product to the consumer. However, I suggest below that even when the model is absent it is a mistake to think of the relation between consumer and product as dyadic as long as the camera mediates between the two as a nonneutral desiring eye. The argument is carried on from inside Girard's phenomenological framework, whatever blindness this approach entails to the virtues of positivist research into the psychological dynamics of advertising.

The Consumer's Desire

Orthodox explanations of the psychology of the consumer's response to advertisements fall into two broad classes. One rests on the mechanism of *identification:* the consumer is persuaded to identify with the idealized consumer portrayed by the model, and thus to want, use, buy what the model seems to want, use, buy. The other rests on the process of *association:* the advertising image is such that the product gathers around itself associations of the glamorous, the desirable, the superior, and so on (it is characteristic of these associations to be ineffable), so that the consumer is brought to yearn to possess the product in order to capture the associations and embody them in himself/herself.

Both these accounts aspire to explanatory power over more or less the entire range of advertising. Since they are capable of supplementing each other, they can be entertained at the same time, and commonly are by people in the advertising industry. To the limited extent that it carries on an inquiry into its own foundations (as distinct from carrying out market research), the industry does so within the identification and association paradigms. For anyone intending to develop a critique of advertising as part of the capitalist order, this fact ought to give pause for thought: if the industry itself operates comfortably with these explanatory paradigms, it is unlikely that a critique that also works within them could develop any power.

It is not my intention to discuss theories of identification and association any further, or to try to argue that they are weak in comparison with the theory I will be adumbrating. How one chooses among competing psychological theories depends heavily on what one admits as valid evidence. The positivist basis of the association theory, in particular, means that only quantifiable behavior is admitted as evidence, whereas a phenomenological account will resist a demand for data divorced from the subject's experience. Attempts to compare rival accounts while ignoring their philosophical foundations must therefore be idle. Avoiding comparisons, I will simply sketch an account of the subject's response to the advertisement which is demonstrably in conflict with both accounts I have mentioned.

This account is based primarily on the analysis of forms of *triangular desire* developed by Girard in *Deceit, Desire, and the Novel*.[1]

Let us take two examples of advertisements with overt mediators and see how they are treated in a Girardian reading.

The first advertisement I have already referred to. The image of a beautiful woman gazes out of the page at the beholder. In her proximity, but on another plane, is the image of a bottle of perfume X. The text links a "you" who is both model and beholder with the perfume (in other cases the image of the bottle is simply allowed to attach itself metonymically to the beauty of the model). The promise of the advertisement is that "you" who use perfume X are beautiful.

In an identification theory, one buys perfume X because one identifies with (more precisely, wishes to identify with) the beautiful woman. In an association theory one buys it because one associates it, by way of a metonymic slide, with beautiful women, and therefore hopes that beauty will associate itself with all the perfume's users. In a Girardian reading, one desires perfume X because one has reached a stage of yielding the choice of one's desires to models like this: one desires what one believes she desires, perfume X.

The second example is slightly more complex. A beautiful woman is portrayed, and in her proximity a bottle of perfume X. Hovering about her in a state of masterly fascination is a desirable man. Again, in a Girardian reading, because one has yielded the choice of one's desires to models, one desires this model's desires: not only the man (who in turn validates one's choice of her as model by desiring her), but perfume X.

I am not concerned to argue that either of these pictures can only be read in a Girardian way. (For one thing, in the second picture the Girardian reading seems to ignore the logic, "If you use perfume X, desirable men will desire you," which an identification theory neatly caters for. On the other hand, if this particular logic were to be impeccable, then the model should not be beautiful but merely decently attractive like the models in soap-powder advertisements.) All I have done thus far is to show what a structure of triangulated desire might look like. Further, a word of elaboration is needed on desire. The gaze of the model is rarely presented fixed on the object of consumption, avid and excited. Instead she looks out of the page, an image of desire alive but appeased. She has used (absorbed, consumed) the perfume, it has made her what she is (happy, beautiful . . . —as soon as we try to describe the mood of the model we characteristically find ourselves calling forth her whole being), satisfied now but by nature (like the *consumer*) insatiable.

From these examples it is clear that the triangular desire is in essence vicarious. In literature, Emma Bovary and Don Quixote are the major exemplars of vicarious desiring. Not only do they imitate the outward behavior of models they find in books, but they freely allow their desires to be defined for them by these models. Thus in their cases there is not simply the desiring subject and the desired object, but also the characteristic third point of the triangle, the model through whom desires are mediated. Girard's general thesis is that Flaubert and Cervantes, as well as the authors of certain other *romanesque* (as opposed to *romantique*) novels, "apprehend intuitively and concretely, through the medium of their art, if not formally, the system [of triangular desire] in which they were first imprisoned together with their contemporaries" (*DDN*, p. 3). The aims of *romanesque* art are thus critical and liberatory.

The greater part of Girard's study is taken up with the analysis of more complex forms of mediated desire than Emma Bovary's or Don Quixote's, forms in which the mediator is not a remote or fictional character but someone whose sphere of possible action impinges on the subject's and who is therefore in some degree a rival as well as a model (from this point Girard's thought on mimetic rivalry in *Violence and the Sacred* develops naturally).[2] Whereas real-world rivalry between the consumer and the model in the advertisement is clearly impossible, a phantasmal rivalry—

in which the consumer must always lose—is not. Thus Girard's analysis of the consequences of this variety of mediation is also relevant to my purpose.

Girard writes in a philosophical tradition stretching from Hegel to Sartre that attaches crucial importance to the ability of the subject to choose his/her own desires. In fact, in Hegel the stage of self-consciousness does not arrive, the "I" does not come into being, until the subject becomes aware of itself as the locus of a lack, a desire. Thus the being of the "I" is wholly implicated in its desires; and for the "I" to yield its autonomy as a desiring subject is to yield its being. This yielding is what Girard calls an "ontological sickness" (DDN, p. 96): in turning his desire toward the desiring mediator, the subject yields his ontological autonomy:

> The subject is unable to desire on his own; he has no confidence whatever in a choice that would be solely his own. The rival [and model] is needed because his desire alone can confirm . . . value.[3]

> The object is only a means of reaching the mediator. The desire is aimed at the mediator's *being* . . . The desiring subject wants to become his mediator; he wants to steal from the mediator his very being of [for example] "perfect knight" or "irresistible seducer." (DDN, pp. 54–55)

The question arises at once, of course: Why is the self so mistrusted that it cannot desire its own desires? Girard does not give a single answer to this question, but the argument that appears scattered over his discussion of the *romanesque* novelists is an essentially historical one. Triangular desire makes its first appearance and becomes a target of analysis in *Don Quixote*, which marks the beginning of the modern age as well as the beginning of the *romanesque* tradition of critical fictions. It is thus a specifically modern phenomenon. It arises as a consequence of post-religious humanism and multiplies as social differences are leveled. In a world in which "the most important relationships are not between social superiors and inferiors but between peers, even though these are rarely experienced as relationships of 'equality,'" the presence of the "metaphysical rival" (that is, the phantasmic model of desiring) becomes "more and more obsessive" (DB, p. 80).

In Girard's reading it is Dostoevsky who emerges as the subtlest analyst of structures of mediated desire. Dostoevsky's answer to the question of why the self can no longer desire its own desires is that the promise that comes with the tidings that God is dead, that Man has taken his place, is not fulfilled in experience.

> Each individual discovers in the solitude of his consciousness that the promise is false but no one is able to universalize his experience. The promise remains true for Others . . . Everyone thinks that he alone is condemned to hell, and that is what makes it hell. (*DDN*, p. 57)

It follows that networks of mediated desire will be most all-inclusive in modern materialist individualist societies, in which a public ideology of equal opportunity for all reigns and the individual therefore experiences failure as unredeemable private ontic shame. In this respect Girard sets himself in the tradition of conservative European critics of American democracy, of whom Tocqueville is the main representative:

> Not only does democracy make every man forget his ancestors, but it hides his descendants and separates his contemporaries from him; it throws him back forever upon himself alone, and threatens in the end to confine him entirely within the solitude of his own heart.[4]

Though Girard's enterprise is to describe part of the social psychology of the modern world, his method of procedure is not one familiar to the empiricist social scientist. Girard himself is clear on this point:

> I believe there exists in certain [literary] works a knowledge of desirous relationships superior to any proposed [elsewhere]. It is not at all a matter of challenging science, but of searching for it wherever it might be found and in no matter how unusual a place. (*DB*, p. 49)

Similarly it is not farfetched, once we concede that "desirous relationships" are quintessentially involved in advertising, to allow the possibility that insights into how desire works may as well be found in novelists and their interpreters as in the quantifiable behavior of consumers.

The points of immediate relevance of Girard's theory to the analysis of advertising can thus be summarized as follows:

1. Triangular structures of desire have their origin in a yearning for transcendence unsatisfied in the modern world.
2. The nature of triangular desire is that the subject yields the choice of his desires to the model.
3. Its characteristic concomitant emotions are self-mistrust, envy, jealousy, resentment.

The Model

Nominally the model plays a mediatory role between consumer and product. She (it is appropriate to use the feminine pronoun here) is supposed to effect the link between desiring subject and desired object, and in the process to disappear. In fact, in the discourse of economics the model is not spoken of: all that is treated is the subject–object relation. In the advertising image itself the model is not captioned, named. She has been selected from among aspirant models for qualities that include lack of identifiable individuality: her physical features must be so plastic under the hands of the artist who *makes her up* for the photographic session that she is not identified from one assignment to the next, is not associated with any one product. In other words, she is a kind of *desiring cipher,* a nothing whose desires are infinitely mobile, who desires not because this particular object makes her desire (for in that case it would leave its particular trace on her) but simply because it is her essence to desire.

The model here has to be carefully distinguished from the *star,* the celebrity (sometimes from the field of modeling itself!) whose very identifiability is used to sell products. The *treatment* given the star is just the opposite of what I describe above: her uniqueness is stressed, and, unlike the model, she may be allowed to become identified with one or two specific products. The star in fact provides a simpler case of the mediation of desire and the yielding up of being than the model does, a case of what Girard calls "external mediation," that which Amadis of Gaul provides for Don Quixote. In the heyday of Hollywood, people were invited to "live like the stars" by learning to desire what the stars desired, that is, what the stars lent their images to.

The faces that the model wears—since she herself is faceless—are prescribed by fashion. The people who *put on* these faces for her are not their authors: authorship, they aver, lies with Fashion itself, whose originator no one claims to be. If one follows the lines back as far as those called "fashion setters," one hears that they are only "responding to the times." "X is in, Y is out," they say, in an utterance at the same time declarative and hortative and optative. The images of desiring subjecthood that the models offer their beholders are elements of an unpredictably shifting repertoire of which no one knows the source. In a characteristically mystifying gesture, the mirror is always turned back on the subject. "This is the image of your model," says the voice of Fashion, "because this is how you desire to look." The mystification consists again in denying the existence of the model, affirming her nullity, asserting that she is nothing but an image of the desire of the subject, of the desiring subject.

Caught in such a gallery of mirrors, the subject (the consumer) cannot fail to fail in his or her enterprise of apprehending the being of so phantom a model. He or she experiences the bewildering envy that Girard (following Stendhal, Nietzsche, and Scheler) describes, but in a modality peculiar to consumer society: because the mystification is precisely that the model/rival is invisible, null, does not exist, envy has the feel of being without object or origin: not only is it impotent, it does not know its own name. It occurs no more precisely than as a malaise, a discontent, a sense of inner emptiness. The most penetrating analysis of life lived in this malaise, and through the sham values that envy creates in order to hide itself, remains that of Max Scheler.[5]

It is not my aim to assign responsibilities, to pursue the project of blaming the prevalence of floating envy in the advertising and fashion industry on the late capitalist order or the death of God, if only because Girard's own analysis brings the activity of blaming into question. Nevertheless, it can barely escape our attention that it is to someone's material benefit that people should have models of how to desire, that these models should appear to be without authorship, and that the feelings aroused in their beholders should include an envy and sense of worthlessness that cannot be assuaged, no matter how much the beholder buys, because the desires he/she is trying to satisfy are transcendent. Nor can it escape the historical observer's attention that, whereas in the nineteenth century alcohol was used as a means to lure and lock the colonized into a money economy, that function is nowadays effected in the Third World via the propagation of images, models of desiring; and therefore that the phrase *the creation of dependency* may as appropriately be used of images as of substances.

The Triangle

I have hitherto discussed only one genre of advertisement: that in which the image of the model is overtly present. The question now arises: Is this in some sense a key genre with the help of which we can unlock the psychological mechanisms of other genres in which the triangularity of the structure of desire is not so clearly manifest? Here one ought to be cautious: the vast amount of empirical investigation that the industry itself conducts, however self-serving its ends and however impoverished the theory behind it, cannot be ignored. This research continually stresses the variety of functions fulfilled by advertising and the variety of means it must employ. Any open-minded survey of the phenomenon must face the possibility that its nature is protean.

Furthermore, even in the case of the genre I have concentrated on, where the argument for an underlying triangular structure is strongest, the analysis I give is not exhaustive. I have not discussed by what acculturative processes the yearning toward specific models is set up. Nor have I touched on the structure that arises between the gaze of the model, the gaze of the desiring (male) camera, and the gaze of the beholding (female) subject. Nor have I tried to describe the iconological repertoire the genre has at its command or the semics of the looks, gestures, and postures it employs. Nor have I discussed the beholder's response to the narcissism of the model, or the nature of beholding as a voyeuristic act, or the quality that personal experience takes on in a world of images.

On the other hand, I will not go to the extreme of conceding that a triangular structure is simply one among many structures on which advertising can call. Insofar as the advertiser as desiring subject interjects itself between the subject whose desire it desires to form and the object it desires to sell, the shape of the elementary advertising act must be triangular; and insofar as the nature of advertising demands that the desire of the advertiser remain concealed, disguise itself as something else, the purpose of criticism should be to reveal the hidden triangle. Thus, to take the simplest of examples, a sales catalogue may seem to employ only dyadic subject–object structures in its advertisements: an item for sale is pictured, with a price and a brief description. But why this picture, why this description? The picture and description are not the only or the best possible representation of the item (whatever these might be): they represent someone's image of the item as held in the gaze of desire: they are a representation of a desired item, an item desired in a model way, not an item in itself. Thus the structure of the apparently dyadic act is in fact triangular; the mediator has characteristically masked himself/herself; and an analysis that unmasks him/her is a demystificatory act.

Contending Analyses

At the point where Girard's analysis of triangular forms of desire ought to be of the greatest value to a historical critique of advertising, it is regrettably sketchiest, namely in its documentation of the spread of the phenomenon in society. Nevertheless, read in conjunction with its key texts, the novels of Cervantes, Stendhal, Flaubert, Dostoevsky, and Proust, it does go a long way toward providing an etiology for the resentful bafflement that is part of the background mood of the lives of many in late-capitalist consumer society confronting the objects they are invited to consume. Furthermore, the vision of a "time before" which we find in Girard seems to me more historically defensible, less a creation of nostalgia, than the vision of history in the humanist critique of advertising, which is the critique we are most familiar with in South Africa. To substantiate this point, let me turn briefly to a study representative, in terms of acumen and moral energy, of the best of the school of F. R. Leavis, namely *The Imagery of Power* by Fred Inglis.[6]

In contrast to the Girardian scheme, in which the primary transaction is between consumer and object, mediated through the model, the primary transaction in Inglis' scheme is between advertiser and consumer, mediated through the advertisement. From his "anonymous vantage" behind the advertisement, the advertiser sets about providing pseudosolutions to the "immanent fantasies" of the consumer that have the effect of "containing each man and woman within their own feelings and preventing open seeing of a common condition" (p. 78). Thus, like Girard, Inglis points on the one hand to the mutual reinforcing of individualism and solitude, and on the other to the reign of models (in Inglis, bad models). But Inglis does nothing to explain the power of the bad models proposed by advertisements over people's minds, except to talk about their "spellbinding" quality. Hence he descends to a dualism that we find in one form or another in all humanist criticism of advertising: a dualism of the cunning of the advertiser and the innocent simplicity of the consumer. It is profoundly to be doubted whether advertisers in fact stand outside the system of fantasy that reigns in society and manipulate it for their own ends. It is far more likely that they tell the truth when they say that they believe in what they are doing (whatever "believe in" means), that is, that they are involved in the same fantasies as the consumer. If so, the focus of analysis ought to be the system itself: first the desire that informs it, then the forces that create it.

When Inglis comes to talk about the advertisement itself, the earlier dualism emerges in another form as an opposition between the object of consumption and the "moral atmosphere" (that is, usually the false glamor) of its image (p. 78). The energies of the advertiser, Inglis says, are directed toward making this opposition invisible, toward hiding the gap between object and image. The object must *become* its image in the consumer's mind; and the more skillful the advertiser, the more successfully is the gap concealed. Here there is a simple question that must be asked: Why is the consumer so easily "spellbound" into confusing signified with signifier? Denunciations of the manipulativeness of advertisers can unfortunately all too easily be turned on their heads into denunciations of the gullibility of consumers. Both are forms of scapegoating, neither accomplishes anything. Behind all the good versus bad dualisms that we find in morally based humanist critiques of advertising lies an ahistorical opposition between an Edenic time before and a fallen present. Inglis, like Leavis before him, clearly believes that love, sex, the family, and so on are debased by being used to glamorize mundane objects for sale. "How can one truly love," the underlying argument runs, "if one believes that perfume X or deodorant Y is the prerequisite of love?" The immediate contrast being drawn is between a world in which true (unmediated) love is felt and a world in which X and Y are felt to be the prerequisites of love. But the deeper contrast is between an original world of true (unmediated) love in which X and Y did not exist (because there was no need for them) and a modern world in which they do. In other words, the contrast is between an unmediated original and a fallen, mediated modern; and the hidden yearning is for an unmediated world, that is, a world without language.

= Syntax

= Interview

DA: These essays are closely related. Compared with your earlier work in stylistics, they appear to involve a shift toward rhetoric. What were their points of origin, and what do they represent in terms of your linguistic interests?

JMC: I spent 1979 on leave from the University of Cape Town, working on *Waiting for the Barbarians* and getting back to grips with linguistics. Though I had intermittently taught courses in grammar and in stylistics in Cape Town, I had lost touch with new developments. I spent a semester in Texas, in the Department of Linguistics, sitting in on Lauri Karttunen's seminar on syntax, doing a lot of reading, and generally trying to reposition myself in a discipline that was expanding so rapidly in so many directions that no one could expect to command more than one or two branches. After Texas I went to Berkeley for another three months.

It was a lonely period but a productive one. I completed the novel and drafted these three essays, which belong closely together in conception. The long essay on the rhetoric of the passive is the most fundamental of the three. Syntactic theory has moved on since I wrote it, and the descriptive model of passivization that I use (Joan Bresnan's) has been superseded, but the main point of the essay, I believe, still stands: that even if we were able to develop a stylistics based strictly on linguistics— that is, a proper linguistic stylistics—rhetoric would remain independent of it. In other words, rhetoric and linguistic stylistics are independent discourses describing, in an overlapping way, the same field.

How did I come to this conclusion? It was part of the rather positivistic optimism in which I had been brought up, and which I had not sufficiently questioned, that a new and *mathematicized* stylistics would, by its capacity to define terms rigorously, to build theorems, to construct analytic procedures, and so forth, be able to answer all the questions about the relation of form and meaning that the schools of rhetoric had been fumbling helplessly with for two and a half millennia. Well, the year I spent mulling over passive sentences cured me of this scientistic arrogance. I read Aldo Scaglione's *Classical Theory of Composition* and went back to Greek and Roman rhetoric with a new respect. Whether what this reading enabled me to say about passivization has any enduring value I can't judge. But the notion of a *grammatical fiction*—which is not quite the same thing as *folk grammar*—still seems to me interesting: that, independently of the derivational and even psycholinguistic accounts that linguistics gives of certain grammatical phenomena (for instance, the truncated passive), there may operate within communities of readers quite powerful quasigrammatical fictions that tell how these phenomena are to be interpreted.

DA: You were working on *Waiting for the Barbarians* at this point. There are sharp stylistic and narratological differences between *In the Heart of the Country* and *Barbarians:* a less experimental treatment of narrative voice, a greater willingness to accommodate natural description (though the setting is historically nonspecific), and a highly ordered sense of time (one year). What lay behind these developments?

JMC: I must confess I don't see an immediate connection between *Barbarians* and the linguistic work I was doing in 1979. We must at least entertain the possibility that some of the writing I do is play, relief, diversion, of no great import outside its own disciplinary field. Except perhaps that it may be a telling fact about me that I spend some of my time (too much of my time?) in occupations that take me away from the great world and its concerns.

You are right to say that *Barbarians* is more accommodating toward nature description than *In the Heart of the Country* or, for that matter, *Dusklands.* But of course what is "described" in *Barbarians* is a landscape I have never seen; whereas I know the landscape of the other two books, to say nothing of *Michael K,* all too well. So the landscape of *Barbarians* represented a challenge to my power of *envisioning,* while the Karoo threatened only the tedium of reproduction, reproduction of a phraseology in which the Karoo has been done to death in a century of writing and overwriting (drab bushes, stunted trees, heat-stunned flats, shrilling of cicadas, and so forth).

In each of the four novels after *Dusklands* there seems to be one feature of technique on which there is a heavy concentration. In *In the*

Heart it was cutting, montage. In *Barbarians* it was milieu. In *Michael K* it was the pace of narration. In *Foe* it was voice.

DA: I would like to go back to developments in your writing during this period. In a long-term view of your work, one detects a gradual shift from an emphasis on somewhat fixed epistemic structures to a more fluid, protean, open-ended version of textuality—something like a shift from ideology to discourse, or to discourse in conflict with power. In these essays, you seem to be negotiating these poles; moreover, they seem to stand out sharply in *Barbarians*. Let me illustrate this.

In our discussion of structuralism and generative linguistics, the name of Whorf came up; in these essays, especially the one on Newton, Whorf—or the "von Humboldt–Sapir–Whorf hypothesis"—is dealt with at some length. The hypothesis, briefly, that the structures of particular languages have epistemological and even metaphysical consequences, has interested you seriously, certainly in Richard Ohmann's arguments concerning style as a form of what you call "epistemic choice."

The hypothesis has obvious relevance to colonial discourse. You mention that Whorf's precursor, von Humboldt, had behind him the expansion and consolidation of colonial power, which brought European philologists into contact with "the staggering diversity of the tongues of mankind." Here we come closer to your fiction. There is a moment in *Dusklands* that I would remind you of: in one of his crazed efforts at self-affirmation, the frontiersman Jacobus Coetzee sings the ditty: *"Hottentot, Hottentot, / I am not a Hottentot."* This is glossed as follows: "It was neater in Dutch than in Nama, which still lived in the flowering-time of inflexion." This is a Whorfian moment, not so? It reflects the Manichaeanism of the colonial situation—Jacobus Coetzee is defining himself against the Other, but more successfully in his own, the colonial, language.

In the essay on Newton, however, you resist the rigidity of the Whorfian hypothesis, preferring to see Newton's prose not in terms of its providing the basis for a mechanistic world view, but as a field of *contestation.* Let me apply this to *Barbarians:* the Empire insists (and even depends) on the maintenance of absolute differences, and it employs men like Joll to sustain these differences through torture. Against such versions of "truth," the novel provides various forms of *disconfirmation:* we have the Magistrate's equivocal treatment of the barbarian girl, the transformations occurring in dreams, the ambiguities surrounding the march of events, the play on signification in the indecipherable barbarian script, and so on. Is it not the case that in the novel you are finding fictional analogues for the play of linguistic-cultural tensions explored, in different terms, in the essays?

One seems to arrive at a similar conclusion when one asks, simply, why should *passivization* engage you in this way? The description in "The Agentless Sentence" of passivization as strategy seems applicable to your own work: it "leaves an uneasy feeling: it opens up an area of vagueness that can simply be skated over (as most of us do in everyday usage), but that can be explored and exploited for his own ends by a writer who takes seriously the question of whether language is a good map of reality." Is "agentlessness" not in part a defense against the instrumentality imposed by History? Is it not a way of refusing the tyranny of closed systems? (I notice, too, that deconstruction, in the form of Derrida's "White Mythology," comes into your work at this point.)

JMC: Before I get down to the question, let me say something about "the flowering-time of inflexion." It is a phrase from one of the great nineteenth-century philologists, I forget whom. It forms part of an argument that languages evolve in time, passing through a middle stage of being highly inflected to an advanced stage (associated with advanced civilizations) when they shed inflection and take on a purely analytic morphology and syntax. So the quotation from *Dusklands* isn't so much a Whorfian moment as a moment from a more complacently colonial science of language.

Let me add parenthetically, too, that the Whorfian sword cuts both ways. If the Hopi is, to a degree, trapped in the metaphysics of time prescribed by the Hopi verb scheme (granting Whorf's thesis for the moment), then the European who can't understand Hopi time reference is equally trapped inside the metaphysics of his/her own language.

As to what I say about Newton and his struggle not to be confined by the epistemology of Latin, I am intrigued by your suggestion that the story I tell about Newton is an allegory of my own wanderings. It has a plausible ring. Nevertheless, I ask myself: Should I be hospitable to every plausible idea I hear about myself, on the grounds that what has never occurred to me is likely to be what I have been hiding from myself? Perhaps not: rather than giving in so easily, maybe I owe it to myself to offer a decent resistance and live with the consequences.

What I point to in Newton is an immense effort of consciousness to think outside his language (Latin and English offer the same difficulties in regard to agency). But even before 1979 I did not believe for a moment that thinking outside a language was impossible. (Thinking outside language per se is another story.)

As to your question about agentlessness, let me restate what I see as the dilemma raised by a sentence like "A shot was fired." Either agency *is not thought,* or agency is thought and then deleted. In this second case, where, so to speak, is it deleted *to?* Where is the unconscious of syntactic operations? Is it an unconscious whose contents can be recovered? But it is the first case that really teases thought. For one can *say* act without agent, but how does one *think* act without agent?

DA: Newton's problem, as you describe it, was precisely that he did not *have* a language in which to account for an observable phenomenon; nevertheless, how would you respond to the charge that your work endorses a linguistic idealism, that it upholds the view that reality and history are purely constructs of language?

JMC: I presume that the word *charge* is carefully chosen. It is certainly a crime of a sort, in South Africa today [1990], to be an idealist. So I warily ask: In embarking on a response to the charge do I implicitly accept a certain jurisdiction?

Let me return to Newton. I remember quite clearly that even as a child I had obscure doubts about the theory of gravity and about explanations of physical phenomena that invoked it. As I read more about Newton, I was heartened to find that there is in fact a quite respectable tradition of skepticism about gravity, going back to Leibniz. What I say in the Newton essay is therefore not new: I simply restate that skepticism in a new form by confronting Newton as a writer engaged in a rhetorical, persuasive exercise in which he himself is perhaps the ultimate target of his own persuasion.

Gravitation as a real existent is not necessary to Newton as mathematical physicist. All he needs is a variable g. Then the movements of "bodies"—abstract bodies, admittedly, but with a certain resemblance to the earth, the sun, and so forth—relative to each other will be predicted by a set of equations involving g and other variables. The question is, why is there a homology between operations on the mathematician's page and operations out in the heavens? It is in an effort to answer this

question that Newton physicalizes g. I, in my naïveté—I am not a philosopher—stand unconvinced and puzzled. I don't understand why the
universe behaves as mathematics predicts it should. In certain particularly
dubious moods I wonder whether we know at all how the universe
"really" behaves: is our image, our representation of what happens in
the universe perhaps not of the same order of privacy as our mathematics?

Is this idealism? Probably. It is certainly skepticism.

DA: Each of these essays is concerned with eighteenth-century prose
style. In "The Agentless Sentence" you speak about the decline of irony,
its relative absence from twentieth-century political argumentation and
its association with conservatism. Despite such misgivings, you launched
Foe, with its eighteenth-century echoes, into a rhetorical climate unreceptive to the kind of nuance you discuss here?

JMC:　The essay on agentless sentences took its inspiration from work
by Richard Ohmann on the language of Edward Gibbon's *Decline and
Fall of the Roman Empire.* For the purposes of my investigations I read
a lot of eighteenth-century prose with the kind of attention to form that
one doesn't usually give when one is reading for content.

What I like about eighteenth-century English prose is its transparency,
particularly the transparency of its syntax, even when the syntax is quite
complex. This isn't just the consequence of writing with Latin models at
the back of one's mind: Defoe's syntax is as transparent as Swift's, yet
Defoe's command of Latin was shaky. *Foe,* which I began to write in
1983, is a tribute of sorts to eighteenth-century English prose style. I
hope it does not read like pastiche. Perhaps Defoe's prose is bare enough
to serve as a model without overwhelming its imitator. I doubt that one
could imitate Swift without falling into pastiche.

The observation on the decline of irony in the political discourse of
popular democracies is not my own—I owe it to Ian Watt. As for *Foe,* I
don't think of it as a particularly irony-ridden book. But the rhetorical
climate into which *Foe* was launched, at least in South Africa, was indeed,
as you say, unpropitious.

=

The Rhetoric of the Passive in English (1980)

1. Introduction

There is a well-known argument in the field of stylistics whose general form is as follows.

When a writer uses the same syntactic operation again and again, he is signaling a particular habit of making sense of his material. The kind of linkage that he makes between items, the kind of logical relation that he creates between propositions, the emphasis he gives to one verbal category over another—all of these being logical or epistemological acts with more or less clear syntactic correlates—can be read as clues to the logical or epistemological matrices within which his thinking moves. If we can isolate and describe such matrices, we can learn about habits of meaning in his work at a level of generality higher than the level of content. Thus we can claim to be uncovering particular meanings in particular syntactic operations.

Let me anchor this abstract argument by quoting one of its more eloquent presentations, followed by an example of the kind of investigation it leads to. The presentation is from an early but influential essay by Richard Ohmann in which he discusses style as a form of "epistemic choice."

> If the critic is able to isolate and examine the most primitive choices which lie behind a work of prose, they can reveal to him the very roots of a writer's epistemology . . . A heavy dependence on abstraction, a peculiar use of the present tense, a habitual evocation of similarities through parallel structure, a tendency to place feelings in syntactical positions of agency, a trick of underplaying causal words: any of these patterns of expression, when repeated with unusual frequency, is the sign of a habit of

meaning, and thus of a persistent way of sorting out the phenomena of experience.[1]

The procedure Ohmann suggests, then, is that we work back from the habitual syntactic pattern, via an act of interpretation, to the "habit of meaning" that lies behind it, and eventually, perhaps via a generalization from the set of all habits (Ohmann is not specific), to the "roots of the writer's epistemology."[2]

The crucial step in this procedure is the act of interpretation that allows us to move from the habitual syntactic pattern to the meaning it signals. Here follows an example of how such a step can be achieved. I quote from one of Hemingway's stories of the 1920s. The syntactic operation in question is coordination with *and*, an operation typical of the story as a whole, and one that, in the last two sentences quoted, is reiterated to the point of becoming bizarre.

> A man and a woman sat at the far end of the restaurant. He was middle-aged and she was young and wore black. All during the meal she would blow out her breath into the cold damp air. The man would look at it and shake his head. They ate without talking and the man held her hand under the table. She was good-looking and they seemed very sad.[3]

What does the pattern of coordination reveal? We can best interpret it by saying what it does *not* do. It does not state relations between the observed data except in the most rudimentary way by stating them sequentially. Nor does it show forth the presence of a particular intelligence or sensibility doing the observing. The narrator, we might say, does not see a world of interrelations, dependencies, causes and effects such as is reflected in normal procedures of sentence linkage and subordination. Instead he sees a world of mere phenomena on which his intelligence has no shaping effect.[4]

Now the naive direction in which to lead the argument at this point is to assert a necessary relationship between the syntactic pattern and its interpretation. For it is not difficult at all to construct a counterexample in which a highly paratactic syntax embodies a sensibility quite different from the alienated one I have described above. The naive step is to argue for a neat mapping from syntactic form to meaning. A more fruitful question to ask instead is whether a given form can accommodate *any* given meaning, and, if not (as seems very likely), what the *range* of meanings is that a given form accommodates in practice.

The discipline that investigates and describes accommodations between form and meaning in the practice of artful speech is *rhetoric*. Aristotle, in the first book of his *Rhetoric*, is at pains to argue that rhetoric is a genuine science *(techne)*, rather than a mere codification of the practice *(empeiria)* of successful speakers, on the grounds that the very success of certain speakers in arguing cases points to stable cause-and-effect relations between verbal patterns and their real-world consequences. It is these stable relations that rhetoric attempts to systematize in the form of rules.[5] The systematic nature of rhetoric distinguishes it from stylistics, which in this essay I will treat as a discipline whose domain is specific texts. The project of relating syntactic forms to ranges of meaning clearly belongs to rhetoric in Aristotle's sense.

On the subject of paratactic sentences, classical rhetoric has some clear-sighted observations to make. The paratactic sentence, says Aristotle, is inherently formless since its form is dictated by its material. It has no predictable end (because it can be continued ad infinitum); therefore, it creates no sense of anticipation in the hearer and cannot mount to a climax. Further, the longer a sequence of paratactic sentences is continued, the more dulling it becomes (*Rhetoric*, III.9). In other words, there is no indication in the form of the sentence of a mind imposing its order on the data of experience, and none of the shaping of feeling that the periodic sentence, with its inbuilt effects of balance and gradation, achieves. There is no great distance between the characterization I gave of Hemingway's syntax above and Aristotle's characterization of parataxis here.

Let us now turn to passivization, a syntactic operation to whose potential modern stylistics has given considerable attention. Here are some representative comments made by scholars about the rhetorical potential of the passive.

Ian Watt: Passives "abate . . . the active nature of the subject-verb-and-object sequence." They contribute to texts "many of the verbal and syntactic qualities of abstract discourse; of expository rather than narrative prose."[6]

Roger Fowler: Syntax has the power "to guide the reader into a particular cognitive orientation towards sentence-content." By affecting the focus of a sentence, the active form can consolidate the superficial subject as "hero" where the passive would consolidate the subject as "sufferer." If the agent is systematically deleted "the impression would be given of a central participant 'to whom things happened'—as opposed to 'who had things done to him.'"[7]

Richard Ohmann: The passive "throws emphasis on the direct object and reduces emphasis on the subject." It "answers well to a preference for objectivity and distance," particularly when the agent is not specified.[8]

Walker Gibson: The passive is a "technique for avoiding personal responsibility for one's statements."[9]

These quotations give a fair idea of what questions about the passive have interested stylisticians: (1) Are there systematic differences of emphasis or focus between corresponding active and passive sentences, and, if so, can we formulate rules relating passivization to shifts in emphasis or focus? (2) Can subjecthood or objecthood as such, or SVO order, be given a semantic characterization? (3) Can we give a semantic interpretation to the absence of the agentive phrase? (4) For what pragmatic or stylistic motives is the passive employed so frequently in what we may loosely call abstract or objective discourse?

Though (3), and possibly (1), might be treated as subcases of (2), all these questions confront significant linguistic issues, leading as they do to consideration of the iconicity of Subject-Object order (that is, to the notion that Subject-Object order in the unmarked active form reflects temporal/causal order) and thus to questions about universals of language.[10]

But when we turn to classical rhetoric, we find a lacuna where we would expect the passive to be treated. Indeed, even in what has come down to us of classical grammar we find the passive treated as a feature of the verb alone, not as a feature of sentences.[11] This lacuna in rhetoric provides the starting point for the investigation I carry out in this essay. The question is this: Is it a genuine defect in classical rhetoric that it does not recognize the passive as a rhetorical structure in its own right, or, on the contrary, is modern stylistics mistaken in taking its lead from grammar and isolating the passive as an autonomous device?

2. The Passive in Classical Grammar and Rhetoric

It is tempting to place the whole blame for the inadequacy of the treatment of the passive in classical rhetoric on the rudimentariness of syntactic theory in classical grammar. But the picture is not as simple as that. The passive is a purely syntactic phenomenon only where it is given a purely syntactic definition. Classical grammar treated the voice of the verb in a mixed fashion: in terms of morphology and in terms of the underlying logic of agency. Broadly speaking, it expected "active" meaning to be reflected in active morphology. Thus we find Quintilian puzzling over verbs that are passive in morphology yet not in "meaning."[12] The same nonsyntactic conception of the passive prevails throughout the classical era, from Dionysius Thrax to Priscian.[13]

But passivization does not merely change the form of the verb. In Greek and Latin, as in English, it usually disturbs word order. When constituent order is disturbed—and particularly when there is a major infringement, such as the movement of the subject out of initial position or of the verb away from final position—rhetoric takes note of the infringement and tries to account for its consequences. The generic name for disturbances of normal word order is *hyperbaton*.[14] Therefore, if passivization had been treated in rhetoric, the logical place to treat it would have been under the heading of hyperbaton. Yet in none of the treatises does this happen.

Hyperbaton is understood to work as follows (I paraphrase the orthodox line that had evolved by the time of Priscian).[15] (1) The natural order of constituents in the sentence is that defined by Latin *Kunstprosa*, with subject initial and verb final. (2) This natural order is also the logical order. (3) But in the interest of aesthetic appeal, or for the sake of emphasis, or (in Longinus) for the sake of representing dramatically states of inner passion, transgressions of the natural, logical order may take place. These transgressions are hyperbata. (4) Hyperbaton must be used sparingly, since it depends for its effectiveness on the maintenance of the norm of natural word order. (It is plain that the notions of background and foreground associated with Prague School stylistics are already at work here.)

In view of the clear awareness among rhetoricians that hyperbaton was a means a speaker could employ to emphasize (or foreground) a particular constituent of a sentence—a function also fulfilled by passivization (see section 4 below)—it seems foolhardy to ascribe the absence of a specific treatment of the passive in rhetoric to the inadequacy of grammatical theory alone. Instead I would suggest the following explanation.

(1) The treatment of voice as a characteristic of the verb alone—and therefore the treatment of the passive voice as a morphological/semantic matter with no syntactic correlate—certainly did not make it easy for grammarians to see corresponding active and passive sentences as pairs and thereby be led to explore grammatical relations between the sentence pairs. In addition, (2) the failure to develop separate vocabularies for word categories, syntactic categories, and logical categories (*onoma-rhema* in Greek and *nomen-verbum* in Latin do service for noun-verb as well as subject-predicate) made it difficult to distinguish between logical-semantic agents and syntactic subjects. Nevertheless, (3) the very vagueness with which the important concept of natural word order *(naturalis ordo)* is defined—the competing claims of everyday spoken language, of artistic prose, and of logic are never reconciled—and yet the acuteness with which nuances of emphasis are picked out, make it unlikely that for a thousand years the eyes of connoisseurs and theorists would have remained blind to the shifts of emphasis that were achieved in everyday speech through the means of passivization. Furthermore, (4) as Paul de Man points out, it is a peculiarly modern idea that one can "pass from grammatical to rhetorical structures without difficulty or interruption." The two disciplines, de Man argues, both cover the linguistic field, but with different epistemologies behind them.[16] Therefore, focusing de Man's argument on the case of the passive, I would suggest (5) that the very skimpy treatment classical grammar gives the phenomenon under the heading of voice is repeated by rhetoric, but in its own, autonomous, nongrammatical terms, and elaborated, under the heading of hyperbaton. In other words, passivization in the discipline of grammar becomes a form of hyperbaton in the discipline of rhetoric; and therefore—in view of the absence of examples of passives treated as hyperbata—passivization must

have been seen as an unimportant or everyday or secondary kind of hyperbaton.

I will try to substantiate this explanation in section 5.1 below by arguing that in a very large proportion of cases where passivization is the syntactic operation that makes a particular rhetorical structure possible, it can be explained as a secondary or enabling operation. If this is so, then stylistic interpretations of the passive in which a great deal of weight is attached to the semantics of agency will have to be rethought.

3. Passive Constructions

Let me now turn to modern linguistic theory, and take as a point of departure the account of the passive sketched in Chomsky's *Aspects of the Theory of Syntax*.[17] In Chomsky's account, passive sentences differ from corresponding active sentences in underlying structure and in having undergone the Passive transformation. Though alternative proposals for underlying structure have been put forward within the standard-theory model (for example, by K. Hasegawa[18]), it is fair to say that for the standard theory the active–passive distinction has hinged on the existence of the Passive transformation.

More radical questionings of Chomsky's account have come from linguists who have argued that, because it ascribes different underlying structures to corresponding actives and passives, it in fact fails to account for their synonymy,[19] and that its failure to account for so-called unpassives like *The door was unpainted* constitutes a serious flaw.[20]

Further objections to Chomsky's account, less significant, perhaps, in that they do not raise large theoretical issues, but requiring, nevertheless, an answer in a project like the present one, in which a line between passives and nonpassives must be drawn as clearly as possible, are these: (1) There is a range of passive constructions with *get, become, stand (He got arrested by the sheriff, He became disturbed by my presence, He stands rebuked by the court)*, and perhaps other verbs as well, to which the transformational account does not extend in a straightforward way.[21] (2) Even in present-day English there are exceptions to the use of *by* to govern the agentive phrase *(He is known to me, The room was permeated with gas, He was amazed at the news).* In eighteenth-century English *with* was actually productive in this position.[22]

While in theory the transformational framework could be extended to absorb these instances, the extension would add a welter of detail to both lexical rules and the transformational rule itself.

Finally, we must consider an objection to the transformational account on the grounds of universal grammar. Taken seriously, this objection would make it impossible to give any purely syntactic definition to the passive. The argument rests on the fact that sentence pairs whose logical and semantic interrelations are much like the relations of regular English active-passive pairs occur in other languages in a wide diversity of syntactic structures. V. S. Khrakovsky cites examples from a variety of languages, both Indo-European and non–Indo-European.[23] Nor is it difficult to find comparable examples in English. In (1) and (2) below, both the (b) and (c) sentences stand in a passive-to-active relation to the (a) sentence:

1. a. The captain ordered the soldiers to shoot at sight.
   b. The soldiers were ordered by the captain to shoot at sight.
   c. The soldiers were under orders from the captain to shoot at sight.
2. a. A stream runs through the garden.
   b. The garden is run through by a stream.
   c. The garden has a stream running through it.

Traditional grammars that simply define a passive sentence as one in which the logical and grammatical subjects are not identical are able to capture the active-to-passive relation of the (a) and (c) pairs. The weakness of such a definition, however, is its vagueness: so wide a variety of sentences can be made to fit it that the formal properties they share become trivial.[24]

As long as nothing more is required than a derivational account of sentences like (1b), a transformation will suffice and be favored because of its simplicity. However, the range of objections I have cited makes a transformational account, and indeed any other purely syntactic account, unsatisfactory. The problem thus becomes one of embodying both logical-semantic relations and syntactic relations in an unambiguous definition of the passive. One such definition is given by Bresnan;[25] all the passives discussed in section 5 below meet the criteria of this definition.

In brief, Bresnan's proposal amounts to the following. The focus of the active-passive opposition is taken to be the active-passive verb pair (for example, *eat-eaten*). For each of the pair, two types of information are entered in the lexicon: first, the range of possible syntactic contexts of the verb; second, the functional structure of the verb, that is, the logical argument structures in which the verb can occur with NPs. Thus we have the entries:

eat: V, [——NP] NP_1 EAT NP_2
          V, [——NP] $(\exists y)$ NP_1 EAT y
eat + en: V, [*be/get*——] $(\exists x)$ x EAT NP_2

NP_1 and NP_2 are respectively Subject and Object, defined according to their deep-structure configurations to left or right of the verb. The three possibilities thus distinguish the sentences *Tom ate the cake*, *Tom ate*, and *The cake was/got eaten*. The agentive phrase in *The cake was/got eaten by Tom* is accounted for as an optional prepositional phrase that identifies the logical subject.

The main advantage of Bresnan's definition over the transformational definition is that it identifies the active-passive opposition as one in which both the syntactic functions of subjecthood and objecthood and the logic of underlying semantic relations are involved. Though it does not immediately account for all the problem sentences I have cited, in principle it allows of modification to the lexicon fairly easily. In the discussion that follows I retain the useful terms *passivized* (of sentences) and *passivization,* since they indicate the undoubtedly secondary character of passive sentences; but they are to be understood in Bresnan's terms (as pointing to the passive lexical entry for the verb) rather than in terms of passive transformational derivation.

There are three subsidiary topics that deserve discussion: *(a)* the opposition between so-called active and passive derived nominals, *(b)* the difference between actional and statal passive participles, and *(c)* the relation between long and short passives.

a. The so-called active and passive derived nominals are respectively represented by sentences 3b and 3c:

3. a. The barbarians destroy the city.
   b. The barbarians' destruction of the city.
   c. The destruction of the city by the barbarians.

Since it is difficult to maintain that transformations play any role in word formation,[26] we cannot derive 3b and 3c from active and passive sentences respectively. Therefore, at most we can think of the relation between these two nominals as weakly analogous to the active-passive relation. I do not draw on this analogy in section 5 below. Rather, I choose to treat the nominals in terms of variations in topicalization.

b. On the other hand, no analysis can get far that cannot distinguish the actional from the statal sense of the passive participle in:

4. The door was shut.

Modern English poses particular problems in this respect. In Old English, statal and actional senses are kept apart by the auxiliaries *beon/wesan* and *weorþan*. In Modern English the formal distinction has collapsed. (Curme suggests that it is being replaced by a different opposition between *be* passives and *get* passives.[27])

The problem is not one of accounting for the ambiguity of sentences like 4: a transformational description will do so in terms of two underlying structures, while a semantic-syntactic description will give two lexical entries for *shut.* The problem in stylistic analysis is the wholly practical one of how to deal with the sheer number of ambiguous statal-actional participles that one encounters in certain texts, particularly in poetry.

If we consider a series such as the following:

5. a. He was forced to agree.
   b. He was inclined to agree.
   c. He was minded to agree.
   d. He was prone to agree.

in which (a) is clearly actional, (c) clearly statal, and (b) ambiguous, we can see that the most satisfying informal gloss we can give to the notion of ambiguity here is "halfway between actional and statal" or "neither fully actional nor fully statal" rather than "both actional and statal." If we accept what the example points to, namely the principle of a gradient between actional and statal (as proposed by Bolinger and by Svartvik[28]), then the separation of passive predicates into two classes (rather than into three classes—actional, intermediate, statal—or into two fuzzy classes) must involve arbitrary and contestable decisions. Futhermore, it is likely to be at odds with literary practice, which characteristically exploits nuances of ambiguity.

The procedure I therefore follow is to include unambiguous actional passives in my treatment but to exclude statal and intermediate/ambiguous forms on the assumption that in a fully developed rhetoric of English the latter will be dealt with under a different head from that of the active-passive opposition.

c. In transformational analysis, two different ways of deriving short passives like the following have been proposed:

6. The city was destroyed.

The first is by means of a rule that deletes the agentive phrase *by* + PRO after the Passive transformation has been applied.[29] The second posits an underlying structure for sentence 6 in which the subject node is lexically empty.[30] In the latter case, the agentive phrase in the long passive arises as an optional prepositional phrase in underlying structure.

An analysis like the second, in which the agentive is, so to speak, added to the short passive, is obviously more like Bresnan's theory of the passive than an analysis like the first, in which the agentive is, so to speak, deleted from the long passive. But there are several further empirical reasons why the *by*-phrase should be thought of as added rather than deleted: (1) While there are languages that have short passives only, there are no languages that have long passives only.[31] Considerations of universal grammar therefore argue that the short passive should not be thought of as derived from the long. (2) Where both forms exist in a language, what historical evidence we have suggests that the long passive is of later date, and perhaps a literary invention.[32] (3) Data on language acquisition do not support the prediction that follows from the deletion analysis, namely that children should acquire the long form before the short.[33]

Quite aside from the argument about whether the passive should be transformationally derived or not, this evidence, though not

overwhelming, suggests that short passives should be treated as
agentless sentences.

4. The Passive and Topicalization

Let us now look at the passive in the context of the language
typology proposed in 1976 by Charles N. Li and Sandra A. Thompson,[34] and from the point of view of Prague School functionalism.

The fundamental opposition in Li and Thompson's typology is
between subject-prominent languages (like the Indo-European
languages) and topic-prominent languages (like Chinese). In the
former, the basic organization of the sentence is in terms of subject
and predicate; in the latter, in terms of topic and comment.[35]
Among topic-prominent languages, passivization either does not
occur or occurs as a marginal construction. Li and Thompson
suggest that this is because it is the nature of topic-prominent
languages that any noun phrase can become the topic without
registering a change in the form of the verb. If this is so, then at
least one function of passivization in subject-prominent languages
might be to topicalize a non-subject noun phrase; and the morphological change in the verb can be seen as simply a way of
registering this topicalization movement. In this perspective, a
subject is essentially a grammaticalized topic, and passivization
is a topicalization phenomenon.

This analysis accords closely with the proposal of Charles Fillmore that subjectivalization should be thought of as "primary
topicalization," as distinct from such secondary topicalization operations as stress assignment.[36]

Much the same conclusion is reached by Vilem Mathesius in a
historically based study of English: "the grammatical subject in
Modern English has come to have a clearly thematical function."[37]
(Mathesius uses *theme* here in the sense in which Li and Thompson
use *topic*.) It is to counter the relative inflexibility of a pattern in
which subject and topic normally both come first in a sentence,
Mathesius suggests, that Modern English develops its extensive
system of passive forms. Further insights into how the passive
interacts with other syntactic operations to create shifts in thematization or rhematization have been elaborated by J. Firbas
and by Wallace Chafe.[38] Using a tranformational framework, Les-

lie Butters traces the semantic effects of passivization on topicalization structure and thematization structure (which she distinguishes).[39]

Thus there is a strong body of evidence and argument to warn us to keep our eyes open to the possibility that the motive behind a given passivization may involve in the first place the opposition topic/theme versus comment/rheme, and discourse relations, rather than the opposition subjecthood versus objecthood, and intrasentence relations.

5. Rhetorical Uses of the Passive

Since my concern here will be with the rhetorical potential of the passive, I will pass over its various everyday uses (see section 6). I start with the question: In the hands of writers who use the passive in a complex and systematic way, what can it be made to do?

We do not often find rhetorically sophisticated uses of the passive in fiction (to say nothing of everyday speech). The traditional novel is wedded to an ideal of realism that includes not only the representation of the ordinary speech of ordinary people, but the imitation, in its own narration, of a sober, middle-class manner. The poetics of the novel are anticlassical: with exceptions, it does not go in for the aristocratic mode of irony.[40] (The passive, with its bland shifts of emphasis and the possibility it allows of strategic ellipses, of course lends itself particularly to irony.)

The most complex and systematic exploration of the rhetorical potential of the passive I have encountered is in eighteenth-century discursive prose, the prose of essays, treatises, histories. Taking my examples from works of this period, I will devote sections 5.1–5.3 to three of the more widespread and inherently interesting uses of the construction.

5.1. One of the most penetrating readings of the style of the historian Edward Gibbon is given by Richard Ohmann in his essay "Mentalism in the Study of Literature" (see note 8). Ohmann addresses the question of how to relate Gibbon's fondness for the passive—a fondness that becomes marked when Gibbon conducts his polemical attacks on superstition—with the overall impression

Gibbon leaves of "knowing, imperturbable rationality . . . objectivity and distance." Taking up a sequence of sentences from the famous chapter 15 of the *Decline and Fall*, Ohmann pursues an intricate analysis to show that the tendency at every point in these sentences, a tendency furthered particularly by passivization, is to de-emphasize the active role of the early Christians in bringing about and reporting such highly implausible happenings as the casting out of devils and the raising of the dead, so as to portray these happenings as "in order." But (Ohmann's argument goes on) when the reader contrasts this orderly facade with the exotic and unlikely nature of the events, he cannot refrain from asking questions about *who* carried out, *who* witnessed, and *who* reported the events. Thus Gibbon effectually undermines the miraculous claims of the early Christian propagandists without overtly committing himself against them.

It is not important here that certain features of Ohmann's analysis have been invalidated by developments in syntactic theory (I refer in particular to his treatment of derived nominals). What is of concern is the form his argument takes. It proceeds in three stages: (1) He isolates a particular set of verbal forms (which we can here loosely call passives) on the grounds that they occur frequently enough in the text to become obtrusive. (2) On the basis of the two premises that passivization emphasizes the object at the expense of the subject, and that agentive phrase deletions have a psycholinguistic correlate (that is, that the agentive is in some sense "in" the mind before it is deleted), he gives a semantic interpretation to the passives, individually and cumulatively.[41] (3) He tests his cumulative interpretation against interpretations of the text arrived at in a more orthodox literary-critical fashion by both himself and other informed readers, and, in the event that there is no clear clash, makes minor adjustments till the two interpretations fit.

Let us, however, take one of the sentences Ohmann quotes—the one with the highest number of straightforward passives—and analyze it from the point of view of topicalization:

7. a. The awful ceremony was usually performed in a public manner, and in the presence of a great number of spectators;

b. the patient was relieved by the power or skill of the exorcist;

c. and the vanquished demon was heard to confess that he was one of the fabled gods of antiquity who had impiously usurped the adoration of mankind.[42]

Gibbon here describes the ceremony of exorcism and some of its elements. The topics corresponding to the three parts of the sentence are:

a. Main topic: the ceremony itself
b. Subtopic: the role of the patient in the ceremony
c. Subtopic: the role of the cast-out demon in the ceremony

The elements of the ceremony not topicalized are:

Subtopic: the role of the exorcist in the ceremony
Subtopic: the role of the spectators in the ceremony

Both exorcist and spectators are present in sentence 7 as components of prepositional phrases. A simple operation brings the exorcist, or at least the phrase *the power or skill of the exorcist*, to topic position in 7b: the operation of making 7b active. But now, if the parallelism of the three verb forms is to be maintained, the agentless 7a must also be active; and therefore *the exorcist* must be supplied as its subject, taking over the main topic position. Similarly, making 7c active will bring *the spectators* into topic position. Thus we see how an analysis in terms of topicalization based on the assumption that the dominating rhetorical structure is one of parallelism demonstrates that the alternatives Gibbon faces are: writing a sentence *about* the ceremony, the patient, and the demon; and writing a sentence *about* the exorcist and the spectators. He chooses the former alternative, very likely for just the reasons of indirect strategy that Ohmann pinpoints.

Because the assumption from which my analysis proceeds—that the dominating rhetorical matrix within which Gibbon works in sentence 7 is one of parallelism—is a weaker assumption than Ohmann's (which is that deletions have psychological correlates), I would argue that it is to be preferred. In my analysis passivization takes on a secondary, enabling role rather than the status of a rhetorical device in its own right.

Before extending this observation, let me quote two further examples.

8. The Christian religion not only was at first attended with miracles, but even to this day cannot be believed by any reasonable person without one.[43]

9. The violent and repeated strokes of the orthodox princes [that is, the Christian emperors of Rome] were broken by the soft and yielding substance against which they were directed; and the ready obedience of the Pagans protected them from the pains and penalties of the Theodosian code.[44]

What is striking about both 8 and 9 is the attention paid to arranging elements in parallel structure and to setting pairs of elements off against each other in a relationship of balance or antithesis. In 8, for instance, the two conjoined sentences of which *The Christian religion* is the subject are laid out in parallel with balanced matching elements:

The Christian religion

not only	but even
at first	to this day
was . . . attended	cannot be believed by any reasonable person
with miracles	without one.

In 9 we have a case of the crossover parallelism called *chiasmus:* on both syntactic and semantic grounds, *the violent and repeated strokes of the orthodox princes* forms a pair with *the pains and penalties of the Theodosian code,* while *the soft and yielding substance* forms a pair with *the ready obedience.*

What role has the passive played in the construction of these sentences? In 8 neither the parallelism of elements nor the syntactic-semantic play on *with-without*[45] could be brought about without the twofold passivization; and without the parallelism, the effect of climax could not be brought about. In 9 the chiasmus is achieved by the passivization of *break* but not of *protect.* In other words, in both cases passivization has a subsidiary function.

It might be objected that what I am doing here is to deny the possibility of giving any interpretation to passivization by absorbing whatever passives occur into a description of syntax in rather old-fashioned rhetorical terms. But the position I take does not deny outright the possibility of interpretation. Rather, I am arguing that the work of interpretation should begin after the intentionality of the rhetorical structure of the sentence has been fathomed and assessed; and if (as here) sentences seem to be consistently aiming toward a structural ideal that can loosely be called neoclassical, and if it can plausibly be argued that passivization acts as a secondary operation shifting sentence constituents around in such a way as to realize this ideal, then what we ought to spend our time interpreting is not the secondary operation but the structural ideal.

Parallelism, periodicity, and balance and/or antithesis are structures that in fact lend themselves rather readily to interpretation. Balance and antithesis are above all principles of ordering; parallelism (a more fundamental operation, and more widespread in language) creates what we can call temporary semantic equivalences between parallel elements;[46] and periodicity is a syntactic image of closure (no addition to the structure is possible).

The conclusion I reach here—that in certain rhetorical contexts passivization is not an autonomous rhetorical device—ought to have a numerical base to be appreciated in its full significance. My considered guess is that in a clear majority, perhaps an overwhelming majority, of cases where passivization enters into complex rhetorical structures, its function is secondary in the sense I have described. But—aside from the question of whether the labors of counting can be justified—the obstacle to providing a numerical base is that it is difficult to give a definition to the notion of rhetorical complexity that is unambiguous without being arbitrary. Therefore, I prefer to leave the conclusion in a suggestive rather than a definitive form.

5.2. The second use of the passive I want to consider is not easy to illustrate in a sentence or two because it is, so to speak, an incomplete form that invites one to complete it by inference from the context. The concision of the following examples, in which a quite limited context provides enough information for the correct inference to be drawn, thus makes them somewhat unrepresentative.

10. It is very well known that they [the Irish pauper class] are every day dying and rotting, by cold and famine, and filth, and vermin, as fast as can be reasonably *expected*.[47]

11. If an orchard was to be robbed Wild was consulted, and though he was himself seldom concerned in the execution of the design, yet he was always concerter of it, and treasurer of the booty . . . He was generally very secret on these occasions, but if any offered to plunder of his own head, without acquainting Master Wild, and making a deposit of the booty, he was sure to have an information against him *lodged* with the schoolmaster.[48]

12. [On the prosecution of the Earl of Strafford before the House of Commons.] The austere genius of Strafford, occupied in the pursuits of ambition, had not rendered his breast altogether inaccessible to the tender passions, or secured him from the dominion of the fair; and in that sullen age, when the irregularities of pleasure were more reproachful than the most odious crimes, these weaknesses were *thought* worthy of being mentioned, together with his treasons, before so great an assembly.[49]

The participles italicized belong to short passives with agents that are, formally speaking, null. Yet in each case the context enables the reader to fill in the agent. In sentence 10 the transference effect of *reasonably* invites the completion *as fast as can be reasonably expected by reasonable people*. But as soon as we complete the sentence we also complete Swift's attack on the kind of rational, calculating mentality that thinks in terms of population statistics, expendable classes of no-account people, the greatest happiness of the greatest number, and so forth. In 11 the obvious (and correct) inference is that Wild lodges the information. In 12 it is Strafford's Puritan accusers who both think his amours worthy of public discussion and discuss them.

These passives thus have the same effect as an indirect accusation or an innuendo: while appearing to say nothing (the agent is not specified) they hint a great deal. The device is fundamental to Gibbon's irony, as Ohmann shows, but probably attains its greatest complexity of use in Swift's *Argument against the Abolishing of Christianity* (1711), a work in which we can distinguish at least four actors, not named, whose identities the reader can infer and insert into the text in the gaps that the null agentive phrases mark.

What is interesting about the device is that it operates as though the derivation of the short passive were via agent deletion from the long passive, with a kind of recovery process allowing us to undo the deletion and rediscover the hidden agent. In section 6.2 I will discuss the status of pseudogrammatical accounts like this one, which, though unable to stand up to close scrutiny, nevertheless seem to describe the intuitions of ironists like Swift, Fielding, Hume, and Gibbon about how the short passive works.

5.3. The passive, particularly without agent, occurs more frequently in serious scientific writing than in any other genre.[50] The phenomenon has been often noted and often deplored.[51] The history of the spread of the passive in scientific writing has been traced by G. W. Turner, who attributes its popularity to a number of causes, some of them practical (the need to refer to processes that have been carried out by different investigators at different times, or by groups of investigators, or by people whose identities are irrelevant), some of them professional (the professionalization of science and the concomitant growth of a group style), some of them philosophical.[52] It is the philosophical reasons I will concentrate on.

In scientific texts from the early years of the Royal Society (founded 1661) we find sentences of the pattern *Lime deters insects* rather than the more typically modern *Insects are deterred by lime*. The difference appears to be this: that where lime is topic, agent, and subject all together, its activity (in a nongrammatical sense) is felt to be stronger than when it is in an agentive phrase; and from the point of view of the entomologist or chemist who wants to discuss the properties of lime, or of lime and insects in conjunction, this "activity" of lime is a red herring, hinting distractingly at animistic powers in the substance.

Of all scientists working at the beginning of the modern period, Newton appears to have been the most conscious of the philosophical problem hidden here. In his early philosophy of nature Newton still accepted the notion that there are invisible mechanisms (for example, a "subtle aether") for the production of physical phenomena.[53] But from 1665 onward Newton began to develop a wholly abstract conception of force, to be dealt with mathematically and apart from its causes. It is clear from Newton's papers that he did not regard the ultimate causes of phenomena as outside the scope of science. Rather, he conceived of a scientific program in which, as long as causes remained undiscovered, there should be means for pushing forward investigations while holding the question of causes in abeyance. Thus he required ways of talking about changes of velocity *mathematice,* "in mathematical way," without having to postulate corpuscles or any other occult agents, as Renaissance naturalism had found itself doing, to account for the changes.

We find this ambition clearly expressed in *A Treatise of the System of the World* (written circa 1685), in which Newton discusses the effects of centripetal forces on the orbits of the planets. I quote Newton's Latin and the anonymous contemporary English translation.

13. Nobis propositum est quantitatem & proprietates ipsius [viris] eruere, atque effectus in corporibus movendis investigare mathematice: proinde ne speciem eius hypothetice determinemus, diximus ipsam generali nomine centripetam . . . Viribus centripetis Planetas in orbibus certis retineri posse intelligetur ex motibus projectilium . . .

14. We said, *in a mathematical way,* to avoid all questions about the nature or quality of this force, which we would not be understood to determine by any hypothesis; and therefore call it by the general name of a centripetal force . . . That by means of centripetal forces, the planets may be retained in certain orbits, we may easily understand, if we consider the motions of projectiles . . .[54]

Although the translator does not retain the convoluted double passive in the second sentence, he does retain the structure that is crucial to my argument here: *viribus centripetis Planetas . . . retineri posse,* "by means of centripetal forces, the planets may be retained." Briefly, what we find in the passage are a manifesto for the acausal program that Newton means to follow and a manifestation of that program at work on the level of syntax: the centripetal forces are moved out of the joint topic-agent-subject slot, where they threaten to assume the mantle of the occult cause all over again, into an agentive phrase (ablative in Latin).

Though Newton does not explicitly assert that he is carrying on his philosophical struggle with the notion of causality down to the level of syntax, it is plain that the highly relational, atemporal symbolism of mathematics (epitomized in the axiom of commutativity) is more congenial to his enterprise than subject-object sentence form, which tends to be iconic both of time relations (left-to-right) and of process (cause–result). Thus, though Newton's own prose is not in point of fact as highly passivized as, say, most modern social-science prose, we can see him as conducting, with what means syntax offers, a struggle with the inbuilt metaphysics of his language.

6. Two Conclusions

Two points of general interest emerge from the preceding section. One concerns functions of the passive, the other the nature of grammatical knowledge.

6.1. Scholarly consensus names three functions for the passive: (1) it makes agentless sentences possible, (2) it participates in controlling functional sentence perspective, and (3) it yields certain aesthetic and rhetorical effects.

In (1), the passive is useful to a speaker when (a) the agent is unknown to him, or (b) it is indefinite, or (c) it is not present in his mind, or (d) he feels no need to name it because it is known, or (e) he does not wish to name it. In (2), passivization may thematize the grammatical object and/or rhematize the agent. In (3), the following uses are cited in the literature: (a) to provide variety by alternating with the active, and (b) to facilitate linkages.[55]

Of (1), (2), and (c), the rhetorical function (3) has had the least attention paid to it. In section 5.1 above I have tried to show that this function is more widespread than is recognized in modern linguistics and rhetoric. Much of the time, passivization is simply a way of moving constituents around in a sentence under the dictation of a wider rhetorical principle. Analysis that attaches a great deal of weight to the semantic roles of the constituents moved may therefore miss the point.

6.2. In sections 5.2 and 5.3 we see two different but related unarticulated intuitions about the grammar of passives at work. Swift and Gibbon and Hume operate as though deletions of substantive lexical material are made in the course of the derivation of the short passive. In their rhetorical/grammatical scheme, the agent is, so to speak, blocked out; but matters can be arranged so that it will be inferred (recovered) with fair accuracy. Thus they make of the short passive a vehicle for ironic understatement.

What enables the reader to recover the agent is of course a combination of contextual factors and intuitions (to which he or she has been guided by the writer's practice) about how the text is to be read, even at a syntactic level. Interestingly, these ironic texts can be fully understood only if writer and reader share an understanding of how short passives are to be decoded. For practical purposes, it is irrelevant that this shared understanding amounts to an implausible rule of grammar. All that is required is a shared fiction.

In the case of Newton we see a different enterprise: a yoking of the passive to a project of using agentless sentences to describe a physical universe regarding which consideration of agency is to be postponed. The structure of the Newtonian short passive says, "Bracket off the question of agency." Newton's intuition about the short passive therefore seems to be close to modern proposals for treating it as a sentence with a null agent.

I am not aware that the field of grammatical fictions has been investigated. Yet such fictions certainly reveal themselves at several levels in literary practice. One well-known phonological fiction is that certain sounds have inherent meanings: [u] is dark or heavy, [i] is light; [r] is harsh, [s] gentle; and so forth. In syntax there are a number of fictions touching on the order of elements in lists—for example, in the sentence *He stood in the doorway, huge, armed, menacing,* the convention is that the order of the adjectives stands in an iconic relation to the narrator's order of perceptions. In semantics, there is the fiction that nouns are static, verbs dynamic.

Because fictions like these, which are characteristically not wholly wrong but rather stand for massive oversimplifications of complex phenomena, are examined by scholars—when they are examined—for their truth value alone, they have been dismissed as unfounded and the matter has been left at that. They deserve more consideration. When such fictions establish themselves as widespread shared conventions between writers and readers, we are witnessing pieces of folk grammar that, at a pragmatic level, are little different from what we usually think of as shared grammatical knowledge or *langue*. They, too, are items of unconscious knowledge, though not unconscious in the same sense that grammatical competence is.

If we take these fictions seriously, two avenues of exploration open up: in linguistic study, the history of unformalized and perhaps unformulated notions of how specific grammatical constructions work; and in literary study, a bestiary of grammar, that is, a taxonomy of grammatical fictions and the rhetorical and poetic uses to which they are put.

The Agentless Sentence as Rhetorical Device (1980)

Young Robinson Crusoe wants to go to sea. His father, a well-to-do merchant, counsels him against it:

> I should always find that the calamities of life *were shared* among the upper and lower part of mankind; but that the middle station had the fewest disasters, and *was not exposed* to so many vicissitudes as the higher or lower part of mankind; nay, they *were not subjected* to so many distempers and uneasinesses either of body or mind, as [the luxurious or the indigent]; that the middle station of life *was calculated* for all kinds of virtues . . . that this way men went silently and smoothly through the world, and comfortably out of it, not *embarrassed* with the labors of the hands or of the head, nor *sold* to the life of slavery for daily bread, or *harassed* with perplexed circumstances . . . nor *enraged* with the passion of envy . . . but in easy circumstances sliding gently through the world.[1]

The forms I have italicized have this in common: they are all morphologically passive and capable of taking an agentive *by*-phrase, though in no case is this phrase actually present. For the purposes of this essay, these two properties will define the class of *passives*.[2]

The piling up of so many passives in so short a space clearly differentiates the indirect reported speech of Crusoe's father from the speech of Robinson's own narrative. Is there a way in which we can interpret this stylistic difference?

Let us rewrite the passage with the italicized constituents in active form, imagining what might be "in the mind" of the fictive character this new speech defines. In a slightly condensed form, the passage might read:

> God shares the calamities of life among the upper and lower part of mankind . . . He does not expose the middle station to so many

vicissitudes . . . or subject them to so many distempers . . . He calculates the middle station for all kinds of virtues . . . He does not embarrass them with labors . . . or sell them to the life of slavery for daily bread . . . or harass them . . . or enrage them . . .

The most radical step I have taken in rewriting Crusoe's father is of course to insert "God" as the one who sees to it that the middle class has an easy, prosperous life. Does Crusoe's father in fact have "God" at the back of his mind? Might he not be thinking in terms of some more highly abstracted Being, some personified Nature or Providence or Fate, some convenient concretization of the-way-things-are? The questions are idle: we cannot know. All we do know is, whoever or whatever it might be, it *cannot* be expressed in the particular syntactic form Defoe has used: the agentless passive.

Let us for the purpose of argument entertain the notion that behind the choice of the passive-dominated sequence lay a specific intention on Defoe's part. What might such an intention be? The most plausible answer is that the passives make it possible for him to present Crusoe's father without mentioning God or Providence or whatever. Crusoe's father is enabled to describe the lot of a privileged class without acknowledging that anyone or anything privileges that class—that is, to give an account of bourgeois success wholly in accord with the bourgeoisie's contented sense that it owes its success to no external force, but simply to the order of things as they work themselves out, to a kind of destiny without author.

As history this answer is not without plausibility. The change-over from an "active" conception of God's role ("God shares the calamities of life . . .") to a "passive" agentless conception ("The calamities of life are shared . . .") can very well be taken as marking the transition from the personal religious world of seventeenth-century Puritanism, whose prose representative is Bunyan, to a post-Newtonian world in which God has become a more abstract principle of order. One can even proceed to argue that, insofar as *Robinson Crusoe* belongs to a tradition of conversion narratives, Defoe's story is about the growth from a state of heedless pride, followed by calamity (the shipwreck) and spiritual crisis (on the island), to a more active sense of the fragility of fortune and of God's unceasing intervention in the life of man.[3]

Let me now retrace my steps and reexamine the argument I have been conducting.

In my argument I have connected an observation about the syntax of the passage with a thesis about the middle class, namely that in the early flush of success it tended to ignore historical causality. What assumptions have I had to make in the process? There are two that I would like to isolate: first, that the sequence of passives constitutes a meaningful phenomenon; and second, that the intention behind the use of the passive is to avoid mentioning agency. (I will pass over the historical assumptions I have made, restricting myself to those that bear directly on the relation between linguistic form and meaning.)

The first assumption is the easier to deal with. Repetition creates pattern and insistence. Eight passive-like forms coming close on each other's heels in a text not notable for its deployment of the passive mark a stylistic phenomenon by any definition of style. The question of whether the sequence has any meaning in its own right is, however, a different one and, I would argue, cannot be decided on the evidence of the text considered as an object, not even if the sequence ran to a hundred elements. The sequence can be said to "have" meaning only if we can attribute an intentionality to it: and such intentionality can be attributed only in the light of our understanding of where the text is going, that is, in the light of our developing understanding of its meaning. For this reason, the question of the meaningfulness of the passives turns out in fact to be a rephrasing of the second question: what the intention behind the use of the passives might be, and in particular whether it is to create, via agentless sentences, a picture of an agentless destiny.

To provide the groundwork for an answer, let me briefly digress to the treatment of agency in present-day generative-transformational syntax.

There are two kinds of passive sentence in English, in one of which the logical agent is expressed, in the other of which it is not. They are represented respectively by 1 and 2:

1. Calamities are shared by God among the upper and lower parts of mankind.
2. Calamities are shared among the upper and lower parts of mankind.

I shall call these sentence types respectively *long* and *short* passives. The active sentence corresponding to 1 is:

3. God shares calamities among the upper and lower parts of mankind.

Whether or not the agent is expressed in the passive form, it must be expressed in the active form.

How can we describe the syntactic relations of these three sentences to one another? One tempting account is the following: first, that 1 is derived from 3 by the standard passivizing transformation; and second, that 2 is then derived from 1 by deletion of the agentive phrase *by God*.

Unfortunately this account will not stand up to rigorous scrutiny.[4] We have to regard 1 and 2 as having distinct derivations. In particular, we cannot think of the short passive 2 as being derived from the long passive 1 or from anything that looks like the active 3. Instead we must regard 2 as the realization of an underlying form in which the (so to speak) missing agent is not represented at all, or is represented only in the most rudimentary form as being either animate or inanimate.[5]

A theoretical account of the short passive as one in which the agent is "never there" can be supported by other forms of evidence, comparative, historical, and psychological.[6] The upshot is that the most appropriate way to think of short passives—the way most consistent with what we know about English and about language in general—is as agentless sentences, sentences whose agent is not merely veiled (but still there behind the veil) or deleted (but once present) or unexpressed (but thought), but is actually null, void. The short passive is the principal means language provides to enable us to talk about acts as though they occurred without agents. (It also happens to be a more widespread form among languages than the long passive.)

This does not of course mean that when a speaker uses a short passive he is bound to a certain intention, namely to conceive of an act without an agent. In the case of *Robinson Crusoe*, we cannot argue that because Crusoe's father uses short passives he is thinking of a universe without an author. A determinate relation between thought and syntactic form cannot be supported. The intentionality we attribute to Crusoe's father is one we *read into* him and *read out of* his language: it is an act of interpretation. The strongest form in which we can propose the argument relating form to thought is to say that the short passive *makes possible* the reading of Crusoe's father I have advanced above, a reading that it would (obviously) have been harder to advance if he had used active forms.

Naturally it is difficult to think of acts as occurring without agents. We might say that, in requiring that a predicate take a subject, the active sentence form expresses a certain preconception that acts have agents, and that the short passive, despite its convenience, leaves an uneasy feeling: it opens up an area of vagueness that can simply be skated over (as most of us do in everyday usage), but that can be explored and exploited for their own ends by writers who take seriously the question of whether language is a good map of reality. Thus, although Defoe is usually thought of as having a merely workmanlike attitude toward language, one can argue that in the passage discussed above he is using agentless verbs to their utmost to epitomize a particular moment in the rise of the bourgeoisie.

Let me cite two additional cases of writers exploring the relations of form and meaning in the agentless passive.

Samuel Beckett's Molloy watches a man taking a dog for a walk. Without warning, the man picks up the dog and embraces it. From the outside, to Molloy, the act takes on an air of the inexplicable, the mysterious. Why do it at all? Why do it at this particular time, in this particular place? To soothe his craving for meaning, Molloy explains to himself that the moment is "pre-established." In giving this risible pseudoexplanation, Beckett is doing several things: he is (1) raising the question of who the agent may have been who preestablished the moment, (2) raising doubts about a language that provides such a glib form for papering over mysteries, and (3) measuring the skeptical distance that separates him from Leibniz (whom he is quoting).[7]

In Henry James's *The Ambassadors*, Lambert Strether, out for a day in the country, spies the guilty lovers Chad Newsome and Madame de Vionnet boating down the river. "It was suddenly as if these figures, or something like them, had been wanted in the picture, had been more or less wanted all day, and had now drifted into sight . . ."[8] The passive *wanted*, stressed by repetition, has a double signification: (1) The lovers in the boat reveal that the rural scene, considered as a picture, has in fact been aesthetically in-complete until this moment. (2) The appearance of the lovers solves a mystery, adds the last piece (the piece that was wanting) to a puzzle which Strether, up to this minute, has not wanted to admit he wants solved, since life is so much easier if lies are believed. In the complex play that James performs here, the ab-sence marked by the agentless form is the absence of a drive to find out the truth; and that drive has been suppressed by a hitherto stronger agency, the desire in Strether for the easy, the beautiful, the romantic. What is marked at this instant of the narrative is therefore a moment of self-realization at which (to put it sche-matically) the moral agent supplants the aesthetic in Strether. And all without Strether's yet being aware of it: the drama takes place in the vacant arena where the agent phrase might have been—as good a syntactic representation of the unconscious as one is likely to find.

The Beckett and James passives are most unusual in their hid-den complexity: they display an awareness of what the form itself can be made to mean that we can properly call metalinguistic. The variety of short passive I now turn to is, in contrast, one that belongs in less intensive, more extended use. I will concentrate on two works in which the semantic gaps that characterize the short passive are exploited to the extent that the short passive becomes a rhetorical device in its own right.[9]

The first work is Swift's *Argument against Abolishing Christianity* (1711), a pamphlet arguing, on the face of it, against the disestab-lishment of the Church of England but, below the surface, pro-testing against the evolution of the Church into a secular political institution without religious content. Swift's vertiginously ironic argument is deployed behind a mask. The author of the pamphlet appears to be an advocate of the modern mode of conducting the business of the Church, and appears to regard what traces of Christianity he detects in it as vestigial and old-fashioned. His argument against the abolishing of Christianity is therefore that the abolishing has already been completed, and that what modern freethinkers would like to see abolished is in fact one of the pillars of secular society.

In this short text there is a vast preponderance of short passives over passives with expressed agents; and, in a very real sense, the process of reading the text and following the ironic argument boils down to attributing agents correctly to the passive verbs.

There are four groups of agents in the game. The first group consists of the people to whom the pamphleteer counsels moderation, since they already have what they want: freethinking intellectuals (Swift's polemical enemies); the vulgar majority and its parliamentary representatives; enemies of religion and unbelievers in general; and the Church of Rome. The second group consists of the modern secular Church, its allies in court and commerce, and the educational authorities. The third group is a constellation of elements associated with true religious belief, correct church-state relations. Fourth and most complexly in the workings of the irony we have the author of the pamphlet himself, as defender of the status quo; old-fashioned religion as seen through his disparaging eyes; and human nature, as conceived of by him.[10]

For an example of the interplay of these various unnamed agents, consider the following extract. The pamphleteer writes:

> 'Tis again *objected*, as a very absurd, ridiculous custom, that a set of men *should be suffered*, much less *employed* and *hired*, to bawl one day in seven against the lawfulness of those methods most in use towards the pursuit of greatness, riches, and pleasure, which are the constant practice of all men alive on the other six. [But since forbidden fruit always tastes the sweetest,] the wisdom of the nation hath taken special care, that the ladies *should be furnished* with *prohibited* silks, and the men with *prohibited* wine: and indeed it *were to be wished*, that some other prohibitions *were promoted*, in order to improve the pleasures of the town.[11]

It is the freethinkers who *object;* it is the powers that be that *suffer;* it is the old-fashioned church authorities who *employ* and *hire.* It is the state that *prohibits* but that also turns a blind eye so that commerce can *furnish;* it is the amoral modern who understands the perverse dynamics of pleasure who *wishes* that state or church or both would *promote* further prohibitions.

I will not explicate any further the operations of the short passive in the working out of this text. Rather, I would like to ask what conception of the passive we can best picture Swift as holding, or (to put it more satisfactorily) what conception of the passive his practice reveals.

If we want a picture of Swift's text, we can imagine it as a puzzle with sixty-odd holes or gaps (ellipses). To read the text, to fathom the irony, to be in control of the play of information, we have to be able to fill these gaps (or most of them) correctly. We are able to achieve this because the context of each gap and the unfolding logic of the argument make a correct guess possible in each case. The text is dense enough with information around the gaps to compensate for what is not there and to make a secure reading possible. The text is not finally ambiguous, though it is cryptic and an inexperienced reader may quite possibly misread it.

The image of the missing agent in the Swiftian passive as a lack or gap, something to be filled, an ellipsis leading to irony by means of understatement, is a useful one. But it is an image not confirmed by linguistic investigations (see above) or by our own intuitions of what we are doing when we use short passives. It is in a case like this, where a purely linguistic description and a description that takes into account the motive behind the form are at odds, that we can most clearly see the distinction between a syntactic operation and a rhetorical operation whose vehicle is syntactic. Swift's agentless passive, conceived of as *rhetorical* device, seems to be underpinned by a conception of how passives work that is quite independent of a grammatical explanation. Thus we see rhetoric and linguistics operating in the same field, explaining the same structures, but each doing so in its own terms and according to its own internal logic.[12]

The other major eighteenth-century exponent of the passive for ironic ends is Edward Gibbon. The *Decline and Fall of the Roman Empire*, particularly those chapters (15, 16, 28) in which Gibbon attacks the intolerance and superstitiousness of early Christianity, employs the passive systematically, sometimes for broader stylistic aims (the achievement of a style marked above all by parallelism, balance, antithesis), sometimes for more specific purposes. The following extract is from the "General Reflections" on the demise of Roman paganism that end Chapter 28. Gibbon assumes the position of Christian worshippers convinced that the saints in heaven take an interest in their personal welfare (I quote sentences 6–9 of an eleven-sentence paragraph):

[6] Sometimes, indeed, their friendship [that is, the friendship of the saints] might be influenced by considerations of a less exalted

kind: they viewed with partial affection the places which had been consecrated by their birth, their residence, their death, their burial, or the possession of their relics. [7] The meaner passions of pride, avarice, and revenge, may be deemed unworthy of a celestial breast; yet the saints themselves condescended to testify their grateful approbation of the liberality of their votaries; and the sharpest bolts of punishment were hurled against those impious wretches who violated their magnificent shrines, or disbelieved their supernatural power. [8] Atrocious, indeed, must have been the guilt, and strange would have been the scepticism, of those men, if they had obstinately resisted the proofs of a divine agency, which the elements, the whole range of the animal creation, and even the subtle and invisible operations of the human mind, were compelled to obey. [9] The immediate, and almost instantaneous effects, that were supposed to follow the prayer, or the offence, satisfied the Christians of the ample measure of favour and authority which the saints enjoyed in the presence of the Supreme God; and it seemed almost superfluous to inquire whether they were continually obliged to intercede before the throne of grace, or whether they might not be permitted to exercise, according to the dictates of their benevolence and justice, the delegated powers of their subordinate ministry.[13]

Gibbon's irony here is very different from Swift's: it is complex but not subtle, relying heavily on a connotative diction that one soon learns to read with reversed values, as it were. The terrific powers of the new Christian pantheon are described with every sign of awe, but the surface is so comprehensively undermined that one would have to be blind indeed to take the passage at face value. What Gibbon describes (and mocks) is not the reality of the new dispensation, but how the new dispensation appears to its adherents (sentences 10–11 spell out Gibbon's own position unambiguously).

There are several agentless passives in the sentences quoted. It is worth looking at sentence 8 in detail to see how the passive *were compelled* becomes the pivot on which the absurd logic of the sentence turns. If we paraphrase the sentence, cutting out the ironic inversions, its force becomes clearly totalitarian: "Everything is driven by nature to obey the One God. Whoever is not so driven is therefore unnatural. Because he is unnatural, other forms of compulsion can be freely used on him. Whoever does not yet yield is doubly unnatural. Therefore, he is open to further forms of compulsion."[14] The double bind into which this logic drives the unbeliever relies on the calculated vagueness of *were compelled*. How compelled? Whether the missing agent is restored in the form of "by intrinsic nature" or "by divine agency," the unbeliever suffers equally: to resist such compulsion places him or her outside reason, outside the law; thus *were compelled* shades over into *should be compelled*.

Though there is not the same degree of play with alternative agents as in the Swift text, the agentless passive here, too, makes its contribution, via understatement, to the irony. In five of the six short passives in the quoted sentences, the unstated agents are the Christian God or the saints or their believers. Richard Ohmann has found a similar pattern of use emerging in Chapter 15.[15] Christian responsibility for the climate of fanaticism and intolerance is continually understated by being omitted from positions of agency; and, in an ironic context, understatement becomes emphasis. What Gibbon effectively says is: "Gullibility reigned on a scale that a rational modern intelligence can scarcely credit. I need make no accusations: I need merely describe the world view of the early Christians to have them condemn themselves."[16] Thus, as in the case of Swift, we see that the most natural way of conceptualizing Gibbon's short passive is as a form in which the agent is first known, then omitted for rhetorical reasons, then recovered by the complicitous reader.

Where modern studies have recognized the agentless passive as a resource of rhetoric, they have tended to see it less as an ironic device than as a means of evading attribution of agency.[17] This is probably an accurate reflection of modern usage; but how do we explain the historical shift? A naive explanation is that the province of the short passive is nowadays the language of science, politics, and bureaucracy, rather than of literature. But even in the eighteenth century, the short passive is used with most complexity in polemical prose. Furthermore, I would argue that the case of scientific prose is a separate one, since there the short passive serves a serious and autonomous need.[18] A better explanation would seem to be that the demise of sophisticated uses of the agentless passive has to do with the decline of irony as a mode of political argumentation, which in turn has to do with the democratization of the audience. The agentless sentence, as a form that says much by saying little, is wide open to misunderstanding by an audience not attuned to its nuances. Irony is by nature an aristocratic mode: it asserts a bond among the elite who can decode its inverted operations.[19] Its spirit is foreign to the mode of political debate that prevails in modern democracies. Bearing this in mind, we cannot find it surprising that the agentless sentence as an ironic device is most thoroughly exploited by such conservative neoclassical writers as Swift and Gibbon.

=

Isaac Newton and the Ideal of a Transparent Scientific Language (1982)

Writing in the 1830s, Wilhelm von Humboldt set out the linguistic relativity thesis that has become associated with his name: the thesis that one thinks in forms limited and determined by the forms of one's native language.

Since experience and action depend upon man's representations, man lives in relation to objects almost exclusively as language leads him to live. By the very act of spinning language out of himself, he spins himself into language. Thus the national linguistic community [*Volk*] to which one belongs becomes a circle from which it is possible to escape only insofar as one steps into the circle of another language.[1]

And elsewhere: "The variety of languages is not merely a variety of sounds and signs, but in fact a variety of world views."[2]

Von Humboldt writes here as one of a generation of European scholars to whom the expansion and consolidation of the European colonial empires was beginning to reveal the staggering diversity of the tongues of mankind. He also writes at the bloomtime of European nationalism. There is thus a certain pan-German interest at work in the argument that a *Volk*, defined first of all by a common language, should possess, and indeed be locked into, a unique world view and world experience. Even so, when von Humboldt postulates that thought is relative to the language of the thinker, he does so in response to a growing body of knowledge about exotic languages and the history of language, knowledge which jolted European ethnocentrism and the classically inherited conception of language as a transparent medium for thought.

One of the directions in which von Humboldt's thinking can be taken leads to *Völkerpsychologie*, the study of ethnic or national psychologies. Insofar as *Völkerpsychologie* became tainted, particularly in the first half of the twentieth century, with the ideology of racism, it was discredited as a serious study. But the work of Benjamin Lee Whorf, who did most of his field work among the Hopi of Arizona in the 1930s, cannot be discredited in the same way, even though it can be set in the same tradition, if only because what Whorf sought to uncover was not an ethnic Hopi psychology but a Hopi way of conceiving the universe so deeply founded that he could justly call it a Hopi metaphysics.

Whorf died in 1941. Since then the Whorf hypothesis (or von Humboldt–Sapir–Whorf hypothesis), namely that we see nature along lines laid down by our native languages, has had a rough time at the hands of philosophers and linguists (who have argued that it is circular) and anthropologists and psychologists (who have argued that it cannot be verified experimentally).[3] There is one field, however, where the Whorf hypothesis is treated as self-evident, even when it is not explicitly known. This is the field of literary translation, where the task that faces the translator at every turn is one of carrying across from one language to another not so much words as the systems of assumptions lying behind those words. The further apart the two languages are in terms of linguistic structure and shared historical culture, the harder the task becomes. The translator is thus in an even better position than the bilingual person to intuit whether von Humboldt is right to speak of a language as a circle, a closed system, from which one can exit only by entering another closed system. For even that ideal creature, the fully bilingual person, lives at any given moment within one or the other of his languages, not within some hypothetical higher language that comprehends both of them, and so cannot claim any greater authority to compare the differing world views they might embody than the student who approaches these languages from the outside. The more complex acts of translation, on the other hand, involve the mapping of entire semantic contexts from one language to another: the translator moves back and forth between the circles of the two languages, trying to bring with him, at each move, the memory or feel of the sense he wishes to translate. The occupation of translation thus brings the translator continually face to face with the most immediate corollary of the Whorf thesis, namely that a full or total translation is impossible.

This is not to say that the translator has continually to confront the problem in all its uncompromising abstract force. Typically, translation is as intuitive an activity as the bilingual's switch from language to language, or indeed as the process of verbalization itself. For it is a further corollary of Whorf's position—and even more clearly of von Humboldt's—that because of the closeness of fit of particular languages with particular world views, a speaker does not become aware of the mediatory role of language between reality and mind except by a considerable intellectual act of self-distancing: there is normally an untroubled continuity between nature as he sees it and the terms his language provides to see it in.

In his essays on the Hopi language, Whorf in effect tries to achieve this self-distancing by standing within the circle of Hopi and, from this standpoint, bringing to consciousness the assumptions about the universe embedded in his own language, English, and in Indo-European languages in general. By trying to conceive of time through the Hopi verb system, which has complex modes and aspects but no tense, by trying to redistribute English categories of "thing" and "event" according to the Hopi noun and verb classes, he arrives at a characterization of the metaphysics implicit in Indo-European languages:

> English and similar tongues lead us to think of the universe as a collection of rather distinct objects and events corresponding to words. Indeed this is the implicit picture of classical physics and astronomy . . . The Indo-European languages and many others give great prominence to a type of sentence having two parts, each built around a class of word—substantives and verbs . . . The Greeks, especially since Aristotle, built up this contrast and made it into a law of reason . . . Undoubtedly modern science, strongly reflecting western Indo-European tongues, often does as we all do, sees actions and forms where sometimes it might be better to see states.[4]

Thus on the one hand we tend to excerpt objects out of the endless flow of nature because we have nouns that predispose us to do so, while on the other hand we see actions and forces where our verbs predispose us to see them. The forces and objects created for us by our language in turn become the building blocks of our cosmology: "Newtonian space, time and matter are no intuitions.

They are recepts from culture and language. That is where Newton got them" (p. 153).

Newton emerges in Whorf as an exemplar of how one can unconsciously project the structure of one's language out on to the stars and then believe that the resulting map is a true picture of the universe, rather than a picture determined by one's own particular linguistic perspective. Newton typifies what Whorf elsewhere calls a "mechanistic way of thinking" with its basis in certain features of Indo-European syntax and further "rigidified and intensified" by the Aristotelian tradition in logic (p. 238).

Experimental testing of Whorf's ideas has tended to concentrate itself in the areas in which experiments are easier to design, such as the comparison of semantic fields in unrelated cultures. Yet in his discussion of classical Western cosmology Whorf himself points to a more ambitious area of inquiry, an area in which one can get beyond lexical contrasts to the scrutiny of the syntactic structures that Whorf sees as more fundamentally determinative of structures of thinking. The area I refer to is that of the texts of classical Western science, and particularly Newton's own scientific writings. Here, though one may not be able to design tests that would satisfy the scientific experimenter, one can ask and answer questions that at the very least conform to the standards of demonstration accepted in literary criticism. Do we find in Newton's English and Latin the seamless continuity that Whorf predicts between syntax and logic and world view, or, on the contrary, are there signs of a wrestling to make the thought fit into the language, to make the language express the thought, signs perhaps even of an incapacity of language to express certain thoughts, or of thought unable to think itself out because of the limitations of its medium? The case of Newton would seem to provide a remarkable opportunity to test Whorf's assertion about the complicity of Indo-European languages in the creation of classical Western cosmology.

The concept in Newton that I will concentrate on is the concept of *force*, and in particular gravitational force. A force is an intangible entity that is nevertheless susceptible of precise measurement and mathematical treatment. It is therefore a good example of the kind of phenomenon Whorf describes: something which from inside a culture seems unquestionably natural (part of nature), yet which from the viewpoint of a wholly different language and culture might seem a culture-bound metaphysical concept.

In his general law of gravitation, Newton states that every two particles in the universe attract each other with a force proportional to their respective masses and inversely proportional to the square of their distance apart. The key word here, for my purpose, is *attract*. Apart from occasions when the law is expressed in mathematical symbolism, there is no statement of the law in Newton that does not include the word *attract* or a synonym equally metaphoric. The controversy that broke out over the concept of gravity soon after the first edition of the *Principia* was published in 1686 centered on this metaphor.

To understand the strength of feeling that went into this controversy, we must appreciate that to leading thinkers of the day like Robert Boyle and Christian Huygens, the great achievement of the tradition of mechanistic philosophy in which they and Newton worked was that it had emancipated itself from the medieval physics of qualities and powers and no longer needed to call on animistic explanatory principles involving concepts like sympathy and antipathy. In their eyes they had created a truly material science with a truly empirical methodology. When Newton proposed his theory of universal gravitation, some of his contemporaries felt they were being asked to relinquish the materialist basis of their science and accept an explanation of the whole of celestial mechanics based on, in E. J. Dijksterhuis' words, "a mysterious force exerted upon each other by two bodies separated by empty space, without any intervention of an intermediary medium." This explanation seemed as unscientific, Dijksterhuis continues, "as if Newton had stated that the sun generates in the planets a quality which makes them describe ellipses."[5]

Newton's most formidable antagonists were Huygens and Leibniz. Huygens called the principle of gravitational attraction "absurd": "The cause of such an attraction is hardly to be explained by any principle in Mechanics." Leibniz cuttingly described gravitational force as "nothing but a certain inexplicable, incorporeal virtue" possessed by bodies.[6] In a later attack he characterized it as an "occult quality," one which produced effects without intelligible means.[7]

The attack on gravity as a "virtue," an "occult quality," with the implication that Newton was turning the clock back and returning to medieval standards of explanation, was a telling one, and by no means to be ignored. For if two bodies separated by millions of miles of empty space can be claimed to act upon each other, and if nothing further is proposed regarding the reality of the reciprocal forces exerted by the bodies, then does the theory not in fact attribute unexplained, occult qualities to the bodies? Of what scientific value is it to say that bodies behave as they behave because they are as they are?

Newton acknowledged the force of this criticism in two ways. First, in the 1706 edition of the *Optics*, he floated in a very tentative way the idea that space might be filled with an ethereal medium with unique physical properties, so that celestial bodies need not be claimed to act upon one another through a vacuum. But this defense was a weak one: for one thing, the ethereal medium would have to possess qualities of elasticity and low density so extraordinary as to be incredible. A stronger defense of the theory, on philosophical grounds, was presented in the General Scholium Newton added to Book III of the 1713 edition of the *Principia*. Here Newton tried to delimit the scope of his enterprise in such a way that questions about whether gravity was "real" or not were excluded. He did so by distinguishing between "experimental philosophy"—what we would today call experimental science—which proposes and verifies relations binding bodies of experimental data, and philosophy itself, which investigates ultimate causes.

> Hitherto we have explained the phenomena of the heavens and of our sea by the power of gravity, but we have not yet assigned the cause of this power . . . I have not been able to discover the cause of [the various] properties of gravity from phenomena, and I frame no hypotheses;[8] for whatever is not deduced from the phenomena is to be called an hypothesis; and hypotheses, whether metaphysical or physical, whether of occult qualities or mechanical, have no place in experimental philosophy.[9]

Thus, though he proposed gravity as one of the "general laws of nature,"[10] he allowed the possibility that it might be only a mediate cause. What cause might lie behind it, however, he declined to discuss until this became amenable to empirical observation.

On the other hand, Newton did *not* settle for the position that scientific laws simply condense regularities in the data, that they provide description without explanation, or that the move from saying that two bodies have associated with them certain accelerations which can be described as functions of mass and distance apart, to saying that the two bodies *attract* each other, is a move from a nonfigurative to a figurative way of speaking. Indeed, Newton concludes the passage I have quoted from by asserting spiritedly that

> to us it is enough that gravity really does exist, and act according to the laws which we have explained, and abundantly serves to account for all the motions of the celestial bodies, and of our sea.

As long as Newton kept the door open in this way, asserting on the one hand that gravity was simply an intermediate postulate in a chain of causes that would one day be fully explained, granting that it is an "absurdity" to think that bodies can act upon one another at a distance through a vacuum, acknowledging that to explain phenomena in terms of "innate" properties of bodies achieves nothing,[11] yet on the other hand calling gravity "real," a "law of nature," there remained a basis of justice in the accusations of Huygens and Leibniz that Newton was reinstituting a scholastic science of occult qualities. If Newton's way triumphed in the eighteenth century, it was not because the objections of these critics had been countered in a decisive way but because Newton's world-system plainly worked and therefore it seemed best, in Koyré's words, to "become reconciled to the ununderstandable."[12]

Because it brings into focus so clearly questions about the nature of causation and the status of scientific explanation, the controversy over gravitation has become a *cause célèbre* in the history of science. However, I here take a different approach to the case, viewing the task of expounding the theory from Newton's own perspective: as a question of finding the right words, and specifically of finding matter-of-fact, nonmetaphoric words.

Newton initially intended the first version of Book III of the *Principia* to be an exposition of his world-system aimed at the educated reader not expert in mathematics. But he withdrew this version (which he was later persuaded to publish separately under the title *De mundi systemate*) and replaced it with a more austerely mathematical treatment, his motive being "to prevent the disputes which might be raised."[13] In his correspondence he contrasts the mathematical language appropriate to natural science with "figurative" presentations whose language is "artificially adapted to the sense of the vulgar."[14] What is revealed in both these instances is an awareness of the risks involved in popularizing his work, in extending its range of readership from a circle of savants to an audience that needs to have mathematical findings interpreted to it in figures, that is, analogies. Though it is "the vulgar" whose lack of education he blames for misunderstandings of his work, it is clear that Newton sees such misunderstandings as arising inevitably out of figurative interpretations of his work.

I would therefore suggest that we see Newton's hesitant desire to address two audiences, savants and wider public, as having two components: not only a desire to have his work better known, but also a desire to get beyond the self-enclosure of the *mathematical principles of natural philosophy* (as his great opus is titled) to natural philosophy itself, that is, to get beyond stating the mathematical relations between idealized bodies to stating in "real" terms relations between elements of the physical universe. If we want an example of this desired transition or translation from mathematics to "real" language—language with "real" powers of reference to the universe—it is to be found in the move from stating that with any two bodies there can be associated forces that are functions of mass and distance, to stating that any two bodies attract each other with specifiable forces. The move allows the reader to anchor his understanding of gravitation analogically to instances of attraction in his own experience, but he does so at the risk of attributing agency and even volition to the bodies. The metaphor or "artificial adaptation" adds meaning at the same time that it illustrates; and it is this added meaning that Newton saw as the cause of error and the source of dispute.

The compromise that Newton reaches in the *Principia* between the demands of rigor and a need to make some concessions to his readership is, broadly speaking, that in the definitions, axioms, and propositions in which he follows the example of Euclid, the language remains that of pure mathematics, while in the various scholia he makes room for elucidatory metaphor. Thus, for example, in the scholium in which he describes the experiment with a spinning vessel of water that enables him to distinguish absolute from relative motion, he allows himself to write of the vessel's "communicating" its motion to the water it contains until the water begins to "revolve" and eventually "ascend" the sides of the vessel. This ascent, says Newton, "shows its endeavor to recede from the axis of its motion."[15] The metaphoric terms add an animistic content to the experiment: each component part of the experiment seems to feel a force act upon it, and then, in conformity with its own nature, seems to act in turn. In the more philosophical scholia, on the other hand, in particular the General Scholium to Book III, can one see how Newton continually resists the temptation of the telling elucidatory metaphor in favor of a style of rhetoric degree zero as the appropriate philosophical equivalent of the relational symbolism of mathematics.

However, there is more to the problem of finding an appropriate nonmathematical language than simply avoiding metaphors like *attract* and *repel*. The following examples exhibit obstacles faced by Newton at the level of Latin or English syntax, obstacles far less easily evaded. (Where I do not give the original Latin, I imply that Latin and English raise the same problems.)

1. The force which retains the moon in its orbit is that very force which we commonly call gravity.[16]
2. By the force of gravity [the moon] is continually drawn off from a rectilinear motion.[17]
3. By means of centripetal forces the planets may be retained in certain orbits.[18]
4. Particles [of bodies] attract one another by some force . . . These particles . . . are moved by certain active principles such as that of gravity.[19]

The straightforward subject-verb order that we see in sentence 1 is the construction that seems to cause Newton the most immediate trouble. Though it is possible to produce purely syntactic, nonsemantic definitions of subjecthood (case marking in Latin, position to the left of the verb phrase in underlying structure in English), the link between syntactic subjecthood and semantic agency is not easily broken. In English, in particular, the initial resistance met with is that the standard Subject-Verb-Object order has come to be associated with a certain meaning: it is iconic both of time order and of causal order. In Newton's Latin, Subject-Verb order similarly mimes time and causation. In sentence 1 the resistance of this association is not overcome, with the result that *force* is understood as both subject and agent, and the bogey of the occult cause raises its head again: what is the being of a force that can retain a heavenly body in its orbit? (Note that this argument has nothing to do with the etymology of *retain*.)

To overcome this association between subjecthood and agency, Newton resorts to the measure we see in sentences 2, 3, and 4: passivization. A closer analysis of sentence 3 will show how the measure works. Let us go back to Newton's Latin (Andrew Motte, Newton's English translator, commits himself to making "centripetal forces" instrumental, a step that is not strictly necessary). Lifted out of its indirect-speech construction, the relevant part of the Latin reads:

3a. viribus centripetis Planetae . . . retineri possunt.

Viribus centripetis can here be taken as either agentive ("retained by centripetal forces") or instrumental ("retained by means of centripetal forces").

Compare 3a with the two alternative active forms we must imagine behind the sentence:

3b. vires centripeti Planetas . . . retinere possunt
3c. vis X viribus centripetis Planetas . . . retinere potest.

In 3b, centripetal forces retain the planets in their orbits. In 3c, some unknown force X retains the planets in their orbits, mediated instrumentally through centripetal forces. This force X is then to be understood as the hypothetical cause of gravitational effects. It is a force that Newton does not want to bring into the discussion precisely because it is hypothetical ("Hypotheses non fingo"). The passivized sentence 3a allows him this indeterminacy. Sentence 3b commits him to an agentive interpretation of gravitation and therefore to the occult force charge, while 3c brings force X into the open and creates an obligation to account for it.

One might thus think that passive constructions like sentences 2 and 3, which Motte faithfully copies from Newton, and 4, which is Newton's own English, precisely suit Newton's purpose in that they commit him to neither the agentive nor the instrumental reading. Indeed they do suit him; but only as long as his purpose is understood to be a strategic or rhetorical rather than a scientific one—that is, to present an incomplete theory as persuasively as possible. We ought to be clear about the nature of the ambiguity of 3a: while it stands uncommitted between two semantic interpretations, it in no way brings out the fact that the agentive reading and the instrumental reading are either-or alternatives. In effect, the passive in 3a therefore allows Newton a rhetorically successful evasion of a choice between the alternatives of gravity as prime cause and gravity as mediate cause. This account of his thinking may be a crude one, but it is supported by the treatment of the question that he himself gives in the General Scholium to Book III.

What we have seen thus far is a dense complicity between thought and language. This is therefore an appropriate point to repeat the key Whorfian question: whether, if he had worked in a linguistic medium radically different from Latin and English, Newton might have been better able to do justice to his thought. One might suggest, for example, that if Newton regarded the agentive-instrumental opposition as a red herring, an opposition forced upon him by elementary linguistic structures and at best glossed over by means of rhetorical tricks, then what he needed for a proper discussion of gravity was a language that at this elementary level genuinely did not distinguish between agent and instrument. Such a language is conceivable, though whether the rest of Newton's physics could have been elaborated in it I do not know: probably not. But if one tries for a moment the (mind-bending) experiment of locating oneself within such a language, one can see that the entire controversy over occult causes would never have occurred, simply because from inside that language the distinctions made by people like Leibniz would have been unnatural or even invisible.

In an influential essay titled "The Case for Case," Charles Fillmore has proposed a theory of universal case grammar in which agent and instrument are two of a repertoire of six or so semantic relations which Fillmore calls "universal, presumably innate."[20] The question of gravitation indicates how closely the semantics of agency and instrumentality are bound up with philosophical questions about causality, questions that Newton undoubtedly wished to postpone. Fillmore's suggestion that agency and instrumentality might be innate semantic relations therefore seems questionable, while the proposal that they are universal can be considered only when many more of the world's languages have been described and when such puzzling facts as the close entwinement of the morphology of agentive and instrumental in Indo-European languages (which on the face of it would indicate that the two have not always been distinguished) have been explained.

A fondness for passive structures, in particular for passive structures in which the agent is not expressed, has often been pointed to as characteristic of the English of scientists. For the most part this predilection reflects nothing more than a preference for an anonymous group or guild style over an unseemly dramatization of acts of scientific investigation: "It is observed that the proportion increases . . ." over "I observed that the proportion increases . . ."[21] As in the examples from Newton cited earlier, the passive is preferred because it allows the elimination, by neat syntactic means, of a semantic agent felt to be irrelevant to the subject at hand.

Another feature of scientific English often singled out is a fondness for nominalization. Transitive Subject-Verb-Object structures tend to be replaced with blocks of nominals linked with copulas or prefixed with existentials: "Corrosion of unpainted surfaces takes place" replaces "Rust corrodes unpainted surfaces." In the latter sentence it is the animistic metaphorical content that is felt to be irrelevant and therefore eliminated: Subject-Verb-Object order holds a threat of becoming a metaphor (at the level of syntactic structure) for transitive action.

The overall movement in modern science has been toward a language purged of metaphoric content. We can detect this movement in Newton's own language, in ways that are locally ingenious though nowhere explicitly articulated. The animistic content of key verbs like *attract* is properly metaphorical, while the meaning superadded by Subject-Verb order is metaphorical in the sense that it imposes a temporal-causal order over a syntactic order (thus exemplifying what Roman Jakobson calls "the poetry of grammar"[22]). As we have seen, Newton holds himself in considerable reserve from these metaphorical resources.

Metaphoric language is always ambiguous; metaphor-free language may or may not achieve the unambiguous one-for-one mapping of reality, the no-nonsense "mathematical plainness" that stood for the ideal of Bishop Sprat and the Royal Society of Newton's day. On the other hand, one of the chief ways in which science creates new terminology to cover new fields of knowledge is by importing words from elsewhere, giving them a new sense, that is, by metaphor (Greek *metaphero*, "to carry over"). Furthermore, some metaphors in science are, as Richard Boyd points out, "*constitutive* of the theories they express, rather than merely exegetical," in the sense that scientists use them to express "theoretical claims for which no adequate literal paraphrase is known."[23] We may thus properly ask whether a metaphor-free language in which anything significant or new can be said is attainable.

The usual answer given to this question is that words that are originally metaphorical soon "become frozen" or "die" in their new senses and are thereafter no longer metaphorical because they are no longer felt to be metaphorical. The freezing or dying of the metaphor is explained as taking place via a process of forgetting.[24]

But there is something inherently unsatisfactory about this explanation, as the history of gravitational theory clearly shows. If what disturbed Huygens and Leibniz about the theory, and what no longer disturbs us, is no more than that the animistic metaphoric content of *attract* was alive for them but has been forgotten by us, and has therefore died or died out or died away, how else can we describe the growth to acceptance of gravitational theory between the time of Huygens and Leibniz and our own time than as, in Koyré's phrase, a "becoming reconciled to the ununderstandable"? Can we really assert that the truth of the theory has emerged out of the attrition of animistic terms like *attraction* in which it was originally expressed? If we do so, we are embracing the most radical idealism: we are asserting that there exists a pure concept of attraction toward which the mind gropes via the sideways process of metaphoric thinking, and which it attains as the impurities of secondary meanings are shed and language becomes transparent, that is, becomes thought.[25]

The ideal of a pure language in which a pure, pared-down, unambiguous translation of the truths of pure mathematics can be effected deserves more extended discussion than I can give it here. I limit myself to pointing out that this ideal language is very far indeed from the languages of man as conceived by Whorf; for to Whorf the least visible structures of a language, those that seem most natural to its speakers, are the structures most likely to embody the metaphysical preconceptions of the language community. On the other hand, the case of gravitational attraction does not at all demonstrate what Whorf asserts about Newtonian cosmology as a system, namely that the key concepts of the cosmology emerge smoothly from, or fit smoothly into, the structures of Newton's own language(s). Instead we find in Newton a real struggle, a struggle sometimes—for instance, in the General Scholium to Book III of the *Principia*—carried out in awareness of the issues involved, to bridge the gap between the nonreferential symbolism of mathematics and a language too protean to be tied down to single, pure meanings.

= Kafka

Interview

DA: When was the essay on Kafka's "The Burrow" written, and what is its place in relation to your other projects in stylistics?

JMC: It was written in 1979–80, when I was still trying to evolve a linguistic stylistics with some kind of critical penetration, that is, a form of analysis that would start with microenvironments, that would be more or less rigorous by the standards of linguistics, and that wouldn't end up simply telling you over again, in unfamiliar language, what you knew anyway. The crucial investigations on which I built in this essay were by the Canadian linguist Gustave Guillaume: into the relation between the semantics of time and the form of the verb, which, as you know, has to carry most of the burden of time-specification.

There is a clear similarity between this essay on Kafka and the earlier essay on Achterberg, in which I was concerned with what I suppose we can call the deep semantics of person, as carried by the pronoun. In this respect the essays go beyond the bounds of what we usually call stylistics. Both Kafka and Achterberg are pushing at the limits of language, and if one hopes to follow them one has to push at the limits of the linguistic disciplines.

I know no non–Indo-European language properly. My sense of contrast between Indo-European and non–Indo-European is therefore vague. In a larger linguistic perspective, what I have to say about Achterberg and Dutch, or Newton and Latin, or Kafka and German is probably trivial or, more specifically, myopic. I am sure there are more striking things to be learned about the semantics of person from Japanese, for instance; we have already talked about the Hopi verb and nonlinear time.

But projects on that scale belong to philosophers. They demand a level of abstract thinking that I can't manage.

DA: Before turning to the specifics of the essay, let me ask you about your interest in Kafka and in the kind of modernism he represents. He

197

does not seem to play as large a role in your work as, for instance, Beckett, but there are significant echoes of Kafka in your fiction. The clearest of these is the titular allusion in *Life and Times of Michael K*, but there seem to be other connections, involving Kafka's stories: one thinks of the "The Hunger Artist" in relation to K's prodigious capacity for survival, or the torture machine inscribing judgment on the bodies of the condemned in "In the Penal Colony," which brings to mind aspects of *Waiting for the Barbarians*. In a more general sense, some of your characters (Magda, Michael K) share the condition described by Walter Benjamin as living in a condition of exile within the body: "For just as K. lives in the village on Castle Hill, modern man lives in his body; the body slips away from him, is hostile toward him."[1] It is easy to see "The Burrow" as representative of the acute form of modernist alienation one finds in Kafka, and to go from there to Michael K (who even constructs for himself a burrow of a sort).

In reviews of George Steiner's *On Difficulty* (1980) and Robert Musil's stories, there are further signs of an extended interest in characteristically modernist concerns: the question of whether there is such a thing as an inner speech, which Steiner sees as undergoing a process of attrition since the start of the twentieth century, and the relationship (in Musil) between rationality and irrationality, or consciousness and the unconscious.

My question, then, is an attempt to trace the outer limit of your interest in Kafka: to what extent are you able to see yourself—and perhaps aspects of contemporary white South African writing more generally, as an ethical and marginal enterprise—as inhabiting a form of late modernism?

JMC: What engaged me then and engages me still in Kafka is an intensity, a pressure of writing that, as I have said, pushes at the limits of language, and specifically of German. No one who has really followed Kafka through his struggles with the time system of German can fail to be convinced that he had an intuition of an alternative time, a time cutting through the quotidian, on which it is as foolish to try to elaborate in English as in German. But Kafka at least hints that it is possible, for snatches, however brief, to think outside one's own language, perhaps to report back on what it is like to think outside language itself. Why should one want to think outside language? Would there be anything worth thinking there? Ignore the question: what is interesting is the liberating possibility Kafka opens up.

In a more general sense, I work on a writer like Kafka because he opens for me, or opens me to, moments of analytic intensity. And such moments are, in their lesser way, also a matter of grace, inspiration. Is this a comment about reading, about the intensities of the reading process? Not really. Rather, it is a comment about writing, the kind of writing-in-the-tracks one does in criticism. For my experience is that it is not reading that takes me into the last twist of the burrow, but writing. No intensity of reading that I can imagine would succeed in guiding me through Kafka's verb-labyrinth: to do that I would once again have to take up the pen and, step by step, write my way after him. Which is another way of saying that while, as I read it, I can understand what I wrote in the essay on Kafka, I couldn't reproduce it today without rewriting it.

You ask about the impact of Kafka on my own fiction. I acknowledge it, and acknowledge it with what I hope is a proper humility. As a writer I am not worthy to loose the latchet of Kafka's shoe. But I have no regrets about the use of the letter K in *Michael K, hubris* though it may seem. There is no monopoly on the letter K; or, to put it in another way, it is as much possible to center the universe on the town of Prince Albert in the Cape Province as on Prague. *Equally*—and the moment in history has perhaps come at which this must be said—it is as much possible to center the universe on Prague as on Prince Albert. Being an out-of-work gardener in Africa in the late twentieth century is no *less*, but also no *more*, central a fate than being a clerk in Hapsburg Central Europe.

But behind your question about Josef K and Michael K and the forms of alienation they experience I detect a presumption that must, for Kafka's sake if not for my own, be laid bare. It is that Josef K is alienated *as* a clerk in Hapsburg Europe, or, closer to the bone, that Josef K is alienated as a sign and a traceable consequence of the social, cultural, religious, and political marginality of Franz Kafka himself.

We open up here a field of argument about the relations between a writer and his society that it would take days even to reconnoiter. So why don't we just assume we have done that, and let me go on to name a set of coordinates in that field, which I do in the form of a question. What is left of Franz Kafka after the alienation of Josef K has been explained in terms of Kafka's marginality? What is left of Michael K after he has been explained in terms of my marginality in Africa? Is it not what is left *after* that interrogation that should interest us, not what the interrogation reveals? Is it not what Kafka does *not* speak, refuses to speak, under that interrogation, that will continue to fuel our desire for him (I hope forever)?

I recognize that you qualify and textualize alienation by calling it modernist alienation. But in doing so don't you implicitly set up the pair postmodern–modern (or perhaps anticanonical–canonical), as you earlier set up the pair Africa–Europe, and use the first member of each pair not only to relativize the other but also to *mark* it? For these pairs are never neutral: one is the positive pole, one the negative, and we all know who falls under the negative nowadays.

The direction of your questioning is undoubtedly interesting: does serious contemporary writing by whites in South Africa not inhabit a position we can call late-modernist? (Do I detect the qualifier *merely* late-modernist hanging in the air?) But before I respond I want to position *myself*. For I do not wish to respond from the marked or negative position, to embrace ethicalism or anything else from a position in the dialogue that is already marked as the position of the negative, the position of the *mere*. So, for instance, the last thing I want to do is to *defiantly* embrace the ethical as against the political. I don't want to contribute, in that way, toward marking the ethical as the pole with the lack.

I neither claim nor fail to claim that my reservations open up for me a third position. I neither claim nor fail to claim that there can be a third position. I do say that if I speak from a pole-position, from the negative pole, it is because I am drawn or pushed there by a force, even a violence, operating over the whole of the discursive field that at this moment (April 1990) we inhabit, you and I.

Is this mere maneuvering, mere time-wasting? I don't believe it is. I believe one has a duty (an ethical duty?—perhaps) not to submit to powers of discourse without question.

Having got through the preliminaries (but the preliminaries contain what I most want to express), let me say that I see "alienated," as applied to Kafka and Musil and Rilke and Eliot and Faulkner and Joyce and the other exceedingly diverse characters we lump together as modernists, as a rather fuzzy term with a heavy polemical content. I can see some sense in applying it to Kafka or to Eliot, at least at one stage of Eliot's life, with careful qualification in each case. Further than that I am dubious.

DA: You assimilate my question, I believe, to a pattern of evaluations it does not necessarily choose. Perhaps I should have spelt out a position more clearly. Let me try to do so now—it will involve entering the field of cultural politics to which you have referred. I agree there is violence, but I disagree with your account of its effects.

As I understand it, the position on modernism of which you are suspicious is the Lukácsian one which carries an endorsement of realism; but there is also the position developed by Adorno, which treats modernism as a historically appropriate and critical tradition. (I am thinking especially of Adorno's essay on commitment, which argues—with reference to Kafka and Beckett—that it "is not the office of art to spotlight alternatives, but to resist by its form alone the course of the world, which permanently puts a pistol to men's heads."[2]) There is similar disagreement today on the subject of postmodernism, although I think there is probably, in this case, a majority opinion which regards Anglo-American or metropolitan forms of postmodernism as only feebly anticanonical, as little more than a cultish accommodation to "late capitalism." Being politically correct in relation to South Africa, then, can mean (and has meant) the *reverse* of the evaluations you have taken to be dominant. Modernism, with its ethical dimension and its basic faith in the powers of representation, can be seen as appropriate for a marginal literature in a context such as this one, and postmodernism can be seen as tainted with irrelevance and indulgence.[3]

One of the ways to resist the powers of discourse, as you put it, is to bring new evidence to bear on the polarities. Without wishing to enter into discussion about what postmodernism is, I would claim that arguments concerning the subversive potential of postmodernism cannot be decided in advance, since postmodernism is by no means a homogeneous movement originating solely from the metropolitan center. I would distinguish, then, at the very least, between Anglo-American forms of postmodernism, on one hand, and postcolonial forms on the other (of course, not all forms of postcolonial literature may be described as postmodern). I would also argue that it is possible to see postmodernism as *continuing* some of the concerns of modernism, ethical concerns among them, into new situations. It is not difficult to imagine that there will be forms of postmodern literature and cultural politics that, in due course, will free themselves of the taint of Eurocentric indulgence (the historical shifts you mention might just carry such a possibility as well). So I think critical discussions of postmodernism and postcolonialism will break new ground on these questions. But let me go back to the question of marginality, back to Kafka, in order to qualify my earlier remarks. It ought to be possible, as Gilles Deleuze and Félix Guattari do in *Kafka: Toward a Minor Literature,* to discuss what I called alienation—and I used the term in a very specific sense—not only as a *place,* the place of marginality, but also as a *practice,* a practice in which one speaks both within and to the dominant culture or "major" language—in terms that the dominant culture cannot immediately assimilate. The challenge of a "minor" literature is that it changes the rules of the game: writing in German, in Prague, with a Jewish background, Kafka releases new potentialities. In such a reading, then, Kafka is not symptomatically "placed," but rather, a new receptive context is opened up to him.

JMC: You are right, it is with the Lukács of *Studies in European Realism* in mind, and the judgment he hands down on writers like Kafka and Joyce, that I responded to your question. I happen to think Lukács' judgment wrong, conditioned by more than a little moralistic prejudice; nor do I think much of what he has to say about Tolstoy and Balzac. Nevertheless, the general position Lukács takes on what he calls realism as against modernist decadence carries a great deal of power, political and moral, in South Africa today: one's first duty as a writer is to represent social and historical processes; drawing the procedures of representation into question is time-wasting; and so forth. So please forgive me for overhastily and unfairly assimilating your question to a dominant discourse.

I am not sure I would agree with the statement that Anglo-American or metropolitan forms of postmodernism are merely (that word again!) cultish, an accommodation to "late capitalism." Romanticism was cultish in its day, modernism was cultish: movements that capture the public imagination attract hangers-on, and hangers-on swell out the sideshows, the cults. It is true that a great deal of the energy of contemporary writing comes from the postcolonial peripheries of the Anglophone world. Yet I would be wary of setting up too clear an opposition between exhausted metropolis and vigorous periphery. To an extent the metropolitan center has run out of steam, to an extent the ex-colonial subjects are running the show. But to an extent also, with electronic communications, the old opposition metropolis-periphery has lost its meaning; and to an extent the success of "international" writers (a telling word!)

flows from a metropolitan taste for the exotic, provoked and catered to by the entertainment industry.

Returning to Kafka: I have no objection to thinking of alienation as not only a position but a practice as well. From that point of view, alienation is a strategy open to writers since the mid-eighteenth century, a strategy in the service of skepticism. What I balk at is the common understanding of alienation as a *state*, a state of being cut off not only from the body of socially dominant opinion but also from a meaningful everyday life (this is implicit in Marx's account of the worker who loses touch with what his hands are fabricating), and even (in the old-fashioned psychological sense of the term) from oneself: alienation equals madness or at least woundedness; art becomes the alienated artist's private means, his private vice even, for turning lack and woe into gain.

DA: Turning to the essay itself, I would like to ask you about "The Burrow" as an exemplary experiment in narrative construction. In the essay you speak of the "failed narrative ruses" of the story, which involve Kafka's attempts to do away with the distance separating the time of the events narrated from the time of narration, and to collapse everything into a cyclic and iterative present. As you point out, such a project can't be sustained, but the resources of narrative seem to make it possible. What claim are you making here for the capabilities either of narrative, or of *writing* more generally?

JMC: Let me first distinguish what I think Kafka's concern is in "The Burrow" from whatever is generalizable from that story as a parable about writing. Kafka's concern is with the experience of a breakdown of time, of the time-sense: one moment does not flow into the next—on the contrary, each moment has the threat or promise of being (not becoming) a timeless forever, unconnected to, ungenerated by, the past. One can choose to regard this as a symptom of psychological breakdown in the man Kafka, but only at the risk of dismissing as pathological every so-called mystical intuition.

Leaving Kafka behind now, let me say two things. The first is that by its nature narrative must create an altered experience of time. That experience can be heady for both writer and reader. For the reader, the experience of time bunching and becoming dense at points of significant action in the story, or thinning out and skipping or glancing through nonsignificant periods of clock time or calendar time, can be exhilarating—in fact, it may be at the heart of narrative pleasure. As for writing and the experience of writing, there is a definite thrill of mastery—perhaps even omnipotence—that comes with making time bend and buckle, and generally with being present when signification, or the will to signification, takes control over time. You asked about claims for the capabilities of narrative, and this is one claim I make.

My other observation is about self-referentiality—the absorption, in radical metafiction, of reference into the act of writing, so that all one is left with on the page is a trace of the process of writing itself. This is obviously another capability of writing. But its attractions soon pall: if we are talking about narrative pleasure (and I'm not so ascetic as to wish to dismiss narrative pleasure), writing-about-writing hasn't much to offer.

DA: Let me follow up with a similar question, which will again involve my linking the essay and *Michael K.* In the essay you speak of Kafka's project as a struggle with time, "time experienced as continual crisis." The anxiety this entails is about self-preservation. This is closely related to K's struggle in the novel to survive the relentless and corrosive march of history. In *Michael K,* it is not the moment of enunciation that is at issue, as in "The Burrow," but utterance (what can be said rather than the moment of saying it); but the problem of self-preservation in both situations makes them analogous.

I would take this further with respect to the novel. Although enunciation in *Michael K* is not rendered problematic, there is still an allegorical sense in which K (and "K" is a reminder of this) represents something within writing itself. K could be the element within textualization that is beyond calculation or control, that continually eludes textualization (although paradoxically, textualization brings the elusiveness into being). There is therefore a good deal of truth in the medical officer's interpretation of him as an allegory "of how scandalously, how outrageously a meaning can take up residence within a system without becoming a term in it."[4]

(I am aware of a certain metafictional trap here, which has to do with K's resistance to the medical officer's interpretation—an extension of his resistance to history. The trap consists in the fact that my reading of K is already encoded, and to an extent undermined, in the medical officer's attempts to contain K. However, I do not believe the novel "plays its hand" in a metafictional preempting of interpretation—something you were skeptical about in Nabokov, some years ago.)

My question is this: Does the book itself not involve an attempt to hold up K's resistance, which I have interpreted as the resistance implied by the open-endedness of writing, as symbolically valuable in itself? Or to put it more strongly, a marginal freedom residing within textuality is turned back upon the process of history (by which I mean, at this point, the history made up by readers in their collective interpretations), and offered as something extraordinary and valuable? K's resistance, and the resistances of writing, in other words, are elaborated to the point where they acquire a social meaning and value. (It would be a small step from here to *Foe*, where similar questions are handled with some reserve.)

JMC: I am immensely uncomfortable with questions—like this one—that call upon me to *answer for* (in two senses) my novels, and my responses are often taken as evasive. To defend against that judgment I suppose I should, as a preliminary step, explain my difficulties, explain myself, spell out my position with regard to *answering for*. But my difficulty is precisely with the project of stating positions, taking positions. So what I am about to say will be difficult for me—*difficult for*, again, in two senses.

Let me talk first about the subjective experience of writing a novel and the subjective experience of answering questions about it. The experience of writing a novel is, above all, lengthy. The novel becomes less a *thing* than a *place* where one goes every day for several hours a day for years on end. What happens in that place has less and less discernible relation to the daily life one lives or the lives people are living around one. Other forces, another dynamic, take over. I don't want to sound silly, to talk of possession or the Muse, nor on the other hand do I want to be drearily reductionist and talk of a bag called the unconscious into which you dip when you can't think of what to say next. But whatever the process is that goes on when one writes, one has to have some respect for it. It is in one's own interest, one's own very best interest, even one's material interest, to maintain that respect.

In contrast, as I talk to you today, I have no sense of *going anywhere* for my answers. What I say here is continuous with the rest of the daily life of a writer-academic like myself. While I hope what I say has some integrity, I see no reason to have any particular respect for it. True or false, it is simply my utterance, continuous with me; whereas what I am doing when I am writing a novel either isn't me or is me in a deeper sense than the words I am now speaking are me.

You ask me to comment on *Michael K.* When I listen to novelists talking about their books, I often have the sense that they are producing for the interviewer a patter that has very little to do with the book they intimately know. I might even call their response alienated, alienated as a more or less baffled, more or less self-protective measure. I am as capable as the next man of producing an alienated response. But I would feel less of a sellout if I said something like the following: I decline, if only because to do so is in my best interest, to take up a position of authority in relation to *Michael K.* What *Michael K* says, if it says anything, about asserting the freedom of textuality, however meager and marginal that freedom may be, against history (history, as you say, as a society's collective self-interpretation of its own coming-into-being) stands by itself against anything I might say about what it says. What I say is marginal to the book, not because I as author and authority so proclaim, but on the contrary because it would be said from a position peripheral, posterior to the forever unreclaimable position from which the book was written.

(I might even venture: the author's position is the weakest of all. Neither can he claim the critic's saving distance—that would be a simple lie—nor can he pretend to be what he was when he wrote—that is, when he was not himself.)

What do I say, then? That your question relies on a questionable distinction between textual and real heroes in fiction. That all heroes in fiction are textual; only some fictions are more self-conscious than others about their own textuality. If one takes Michael K seriously as a hero, a paragon, a model, it can only be as a hero of resistance against—or rather, withdrawal from or evasion of—accepted ideas of the heroic. But insofar as this resistance claims a social meaning and value, I see no great distance between it and the resistance of the book *Michael K* itself, with its own evasions of authority, including its (I would hope successful) evasion of attempts by its author to put a stranglehold on it.

DA: Yes, there are conceptions of authorship that need to be addressed in the way you have done here, conceptions that are reproduced unwittingly in my question. But I need to say that I do not distinguish between textual and real heroes. I have learned the lesson that all heroes are textual. What my question suggests is that textuality is itself a metafictional referent in *Michael K.* K is therefore not only the integral, fictional being who withdraws and resists, because he is specifically marked with the signs of textuality and intertextuality. This marking goes further than the acknowledgment I might make as a reader that K is a textual phenomenon. If I am right in this reading, then I am obliged to ask myself what the symbolic value might be of establishing textuality as a referent—hence my remarks about upholding the freedom of textuality against history. But you have reminded me that I need to take responsibility for this reading. I do so, and readily acknowledge that I might have learned this particular lesson by absorbing more deeply what *Waiting for the Barbarians* has to say about signification and closure.

JMC: There is a moment in *Michael K* at which Michael hides away while a group of guerrillas camp beside "his" dam. He is tempted to come out into the open and ask to join them, but in the end he doesn't.

This is, I suppose, the most politically naked moment in the novel. If one reads the novel simply, K offers himself as a model either of modest prudence or of cowardice masquerading as commitment to a humbler function (one of his reasons or rationalizations for not joining, as I remember it, is that someone has to stay behind and grow pumpkins for the men in the front line: the context tempts one to read humble as noble, growing pumpkins as more important than shooting people).

Why doesn't K go off with the guerrillas? Why doesn't he abandon his dam and his pumpkin patch, head off into the night with the donkey train and its sacks of mortar shells, hide in the Swartberg, blow up trains, ambush army convoys, and eventually get killed in action?

In a more sophisticated form, this became the question Nadine Gordimer asked in her review of the novel.[5] What kind of model of behavior in the face of oppression was I presenting? Why hadn't I written a different book with (I put words in her mouth now) a less spineless hero?

To a reader taking this line, much of the text of *Michael K* is just one fancy evasion after another of an overriding political question: how shall the tyranny of apartheid be ended? In this perspective, the moment when the text turns in upon itself and begins to reflect upon its own textuality is thus simply a moment of evasion. The question of why K does not go off with the guerrillas and the question of why textuality is given a symbolic value become the same question.

How do I respond to such readers?

One writes the books one wants to write. One doesn't write the books one doesn't want to write. The emphasis falls not on *one* but on the word *want* in all its own resistance to being known. The book about going off with the guerrillas, the book in the heroic tradition, is not a book I *wanted-to-write*, wanted enough to be able to bring off, however much I might have wanted to have written it—that is to say, wanted to be the person who had successfully brought off the writing of it.

What, then, do I *want-to-write?* A question to prospect, to open up, perhaps, in the present dialogue, but not to mine, to exploit: too much of the fictional enterprise depends on it. Just as it is not productive to discover the answer to the question of why one desires: the answer threatens the end of desire, the end of the production of desire.

DA: Allow me to turn briefly to your review of Musil's *Five Women*. There are several things here that would strike a chord in readers of your fiction, such as Musil's attitude to the relationship between the rational and the irrational, or the notion that "things think themselves out within us," or the currency of forms in certain historical situations. What has been your relationship with Musil?

JMC: I first came across Musil in my early twenties, and read him in a state that I would now call bemused. I read Rilke too in much the same state and at much the same time.

I experienced Musil's prose, or the prose of his middle period at any rate, as a kind of music in which quite simple ideas gradually lost all recognizable shape as they were protracted, in a process of slightly altered repetition, metamorphosis, inch-by-inch accretion, to quite voluptuous lengths.

I think of my own prose as rather hard and dry; but there remains in me a tug toward sensual elaboration—toward the late-Romantic symphony and away from the two-part invention, say. For the rest, Musil stands for me as a model of an *intelligence* turned, however desperately, on the *fin de siècle.*

DA: You spoke earlier about the capacity of narrative to alter one's experience of time, and in the Kafka essay you contrast historical and eschatological conceptions of time in "The Burrow." (Your procedure, incidentally, is close to that formalized more recently by Paul Ricoeur in *Time and Narrative*, where it is argued that in the final analysis, narrative discourse—both history and fiction—provides "allegories of temporality," different accounts of what it means to live in time.)[6]

Your fiction deals with this question, to the point of allowing the narrators to reflect directly on their experience of temporality. Starting at a point where she says, "A day must have intervened here," Magda, who inhabits an "everlasting present," is brought gradually into conflict with a historical sense of time: "Once I lived in time as a fish in water, breathing it, drinking it, sustained by it. Now I kill time and time kills me."[7] In *Barbarians*, the Magistrate inveighs against Empire for turning away from the "recurrent spinning time of the cycle of the seasons" and creating "the jagged time of rise and fall, of beginning and end, of catastrophe."[8] Through Michael K, the medical officer discovers that he has been wasting his life: "I was wasting it by living from day to day in a state of waiting, that I had in effect given myself up as a prisoner to this war."[9]

In this aspect of the novels, are you giving life to ideas about the experience of time in a place like South Africa, or is it rather that the present tense (and first person) in the utterance of these narrators leads to the recurrent discovery of a dialectical opposite, that is, historical time—the sweep of past, present and future—as a chasm that threatens to engulf the self?

JMC: The either/or you present does not exhaust the possibilities. Nevertheless, yes, time in South Africa has been extraordinarily static for most of my life. I think of a comment of Erich Auerbach's on the time-experience of Flaubert's generation, the generation that came to maturity around 1848, as an experience of a viscous, sluggish chronicity charged with eruptive potential. I was born in 1940; I was eight when the party of Afrikaner Christian nationalism came to power and set about stopping or even turning back the clock. Its programs involved a radically discontinuous intervention into time, in that it tried to stop dead or turn around a range of developments normal (in the sense of being the norm) in colonial societies. It also aimed at instituting a sluggish no-time in which an already anachronistic order of patriarchal clans and tribal despotisms would be frozen in place. This is the political order in which I grew up. And the culture in which I was educated—a culture looking, when it looked anywhere, nostalgically back to Little England—did nothing to quicken time. So I am not surprised that you detect in me a horror of chronicity South African style.

But that horror is also a horror of death—and here we come to the second part of your either/or. Historicizing oneself is an exercise in locating one's significance, but is also a lesson, at the most immediate level, in insignificance. It is not just time as history that threatens to engulf one: it is time itself, time as death.

Time, Tense, and Aspect in Kafka's "The Burrow" (1981)

Kafka's story "The Burrow" begins: "I have completed the construction of my burrow and it seems to be successful."[1] The position in time of the speaker, the creature whose life has been devoted to the building of this perfectly secure hideaway, seems to be clear: he speaks (or writes) from a moment after the completion of the burrow but not so long after it that final judgment on its success can be given. Further information in the next few pages helps to situate the fictional *now* of his utterances as belonging to "the zenith of my life" (325), when he is nevertheless "growing old" (326), "getting on in years" (327).

The time encompassed by his act of storytelling, beginning at this moment, is not, however, simply the time that might be taken to utter the thirty-five or so pages of the text: although there are no typographic breaks to mark breaks in the time of narration, there is at least one point (343) where the narration is interrupted by sleep. As for the time depicted by the narrative, all I shall say as a first approximation is that, aside from passing references to a faroff time of apprenticeship (for example, 357), it appears to cover life in the burrow (which it depicts as largely dominated by habit), to include and pass beyond the moment at which the first words of the text are uttered, and to continue as far as the moment at which the last words are uttered, a moment at which the time of narration and the time of the narrative are identical.

But the relations between the *time of narration* (the moving *now* of the narrator's utterance) and the *time of the narrative* (referential time) turn out to be far more complex and indeed baffling, the more closely we read the text. The first approximation to the reading of time-relations I have given above glosses over the problem of fitting the pattern of habitual life in the burrow into a temporal continuum; and attempts to refine the approximation

210

bring us face to face in the end with not only a narrative structure but also a representation of time that cannot be compressed into a rational model. There are numerous passages in Kafka's fictional works and notebooks that reveal a preoccupation with the metaphysics of time. It is above all in the stories "The Country Doctor" and "The Burrow," however, that we have *representations* of an idiosyncratic feel for time. As we might expect, such stories necessarily bring Kafka into conflict not only with the time-conventions of fictional realism (which rest on a Newtonian metaphysics) but also with the conception embedded in (and, in the Whorfian view, propagated by) the tense-system of his language.

In this essay I am concerned to explore the relations between the verb-system of German (which, in the features I shall be commenting on, is very close to the verb-system of English), the narrative (and narratorial) structure of "The Burrow," and the conception of time we can postulate Kafka held in 1923. In the first section of the essay I attempt little more than to persuade the reader that the task of laying out the events of the narrative in sequential temporal order is riddled with difficulties. In the second section I discuss the work of two scholars who have recognized these difficulties and attempted to overcome them. In the third section I outline a distinction between two features of the verb, tense and aspect, that are often confused, and suggest how upholding the distinction may aid us in our reading. And in the final section I attempt to explain the time-scheme that "The Burrow" represents, in both senses of this ambiguous phrase.

There is nothing in the first three long paragraphs of the text to conflict with the time and tense conventions of retrospective first-person narration. But with the fourth paragraph it begins to become more difficult to situate the *now* of the act of narration in time. Let us take up this paragraph in some detail.

> In the Castle Keep I assemble my stores . . . The place is so spacious that . . . I can divide up my stores, walk about among them, play with them . . . That done, I can always . . . make my calculations and hunting plans for the future, taking into account the season of the year. There are times when I am so well provided for that in my indifference to food I never even touch the smaller fry that scuttle about the burrow . . . (328)

The present here is an iterative, habitual present, with a cycle of seasons and even years.

> It sometimes seems risky to make the Castle Keep the basis of defense . . . Thereupon I mark off every third room . . . as a reserve storeroom . . . or I ignore certain passages altogether . . . or I choose quite at random a very few rooms . . . Each of these new plans involves of course heavy work . . . True, I can do [it] at my leisure . . . But it is not so pleasant when, as sometimes happens, you suddenly fancy, starting up from your sleep, that the present distribution of your stores is completely and totally wrong . . . and must be set right at once, no matter how tired or sleepy you may be; then I rush, then I fly, then I have no time for calculation; and although I was about to execute a perfectly new, perfectly exact plan, I now seize whatever my teeth hit upon and drag or carry it away, sighing, groaning, stumbling . . . Until little by little full wakefulness sobers me, and I can . . . return to my resting place . . . (329)

There is no question that this episode too is iterative, typical, recurrent, and that the *now* out of which the narrative is uttered is situated within these recurrences: episodes of panic are part of the life of the creature, they have occurred in the past, they are expected to recur.

> Then again there are times when the storing of all my food in one place seems the best plan of all . . . and so . . . I begin once more to haul all my stores back . . . to the Castle Keep. For some time afterwards I find a certain comfort in having all the passages and rooms free . . . Then I usually enjoy periods of particular tranquility . . . until at last I can no longer restrain myself [*bis ich es nicht mehr ertrage*] and one night [*eines Nachts*] rush into the Castle Keep, mightily fling myself upon my stores, and glut myself . . . (329–331)

Here we see that narrative with difficulty sustains the illusion of an iterative present when the actions that recur are impulsive, unforeseen, and unforeseeable, when the speaker is at the mercy of forces he cannot control or predict. Thus sentence 1 below, in contrast to sentence 2, strikes us as bizarre and perhaps ungrammatical:

1. Every month I impulsively run about the streets naked.
2. Every month I run about the streets naked.

The only way to domesticate sentence 1 is to read it as a generalization about behavior over past months, culminating in the present moment at which the sentence is uttered ("Every month for the past x months I have impulsively run about the streets naked"). It is most bizarre when it is read as uttered within an iterative present ("My habit is impulsively to run about the streets naked every month"). The cause of conflict is of course that for a speaker to take up his stance within an iterative present means, to the listener who, so to speak, unrolls the cycle of the iterative on to a past–present–future continuum, that the speaker not only makes a generalization about his past behavior but also predicts his future behavior; and the act of prediction conflicts with the notion of the impulsive.

Kafka does not unequivocally provoke this contradiction in the passages I have quoted. Nevertheless, both when the burrowing creature starts out of his sleep and rushes and flies (eile, fliege) to relocate his provisions, and when "one night" he rushes (stürze) into the Castle Keep to glut himself, the verbs carry connotations of the impulsive, the uncontrollable, the unpredictable, and therefore sit uneasily in a narratorial framework of iterated time.

There are two alternative ways of explaining what is going on here. The less radical explanation is this: German, like English, lacks a specific morphological form to signify iterative action. The noniterative (punctual) sense of the verb is the semantically unmarked form, in contrast to the marked form of the iterative sense. (This is perhaps no more than a consequence of the relative infrequency of the iterative sense.) Therefore unless a sequence of verbs is systematically interspersed with iterative modifiers (sometimes, every day, . . .) or (in English) is given with an appropriate modal (will, used to, . . .), the verbs tend to be read as unmarked, that is, noniterative. In other words, it requires a continual pressure of emphasis in the writing to maintain iterative time. Of course, the more this emphasis has to be repeated, the clumsier it sounds. So rather than maintain the emphasis throughout, Kafka sometimes (for example, in the last two passages quoted) dramatizes a typical event from the iterative cycle and so permits the reading to slip back for a while into the unmarked, noniterative mode.

This rhetorical explanation thus interprets the problematic verb sequence in terms of the pragmatics of "what works" for the reader, as manifestations of the writer's artfulness. There is no doubt that this explanation can be "made to work" for the sequences I quote and for others I mention below. My reservations about explanation along these lines will become clearer later, when I argue that, rather than being an obstacle to understanding, the problematic sequences embody a conception of time that is central to Kafka's enterprise. For the moment let me simply observe that, "success" in writing, like beauty, being essentially undemonstrable, some rhetorical coaxing or intimidation, or both, is required from the commentator to establish *any* argument that a particular strategy in a text "works," that it is "successful writing," indeed that it is a "strategy of writing" at all.

The second and more radical explanation is that the conception of time that reigns in "The Burrow" is truly aberrant, that it can be domesticated only with a degree of rhetorical violence amounting to traduction, and that it is better understood as the reflection of a time-sense that does not draw a line between iterative and noniterative senses of the verb, or does not draw the line in the usual place. This is the explanation I will be exploring. However, before doing that let me indicate the pervasiveness of difficult tense-sequences. I quote in leapfrog fashion to highlight the verbs.

> To regain my composure after such lapses I make a practice of reviewing my burrow, and . . . frequently leave it . . . It is always with a certain solemnity that I approach the exit again . . . [for] it was there that I began my burrow . . . Should I reconstruct this part of my burrow? I keep on postponing the decision, and the labyrinth will probably remain as it is . . . Sometimes I dream that I have reconstructed it . . . and now it is impregnable . . . [The] nights on which such dreams come to me are the sweetest I know . . . So I must thread the tormenting complications of this labyrinth . . . whenever I go out . . . But then [*dann*] I find myself beneath the mossy covering [of the entrance] . . . and now [*nun*] only a little push with my head is needed and I am in the upper world. For a long time I do not dare to make that movement . . . I then cautiously raise the trap door and slip outside . . . (331–333).

The time of utterance of the first paragraph here is clearly the same as at the beginning of the story: a present time after the completion of the burrow, a point from which the creature looks back to a cycle of habitual past behavior and forward to a future in which the burrow will probably not be rebuilt. But again, when he enters into closer description of his iterative excursions from the burrow, the *now* of narration shifts and becomes the moment (though what the status of that moment is we have yet to decide) at which he leaves the burrow. This becomes particularly clear in the paragraph that follows.

> . . . I know . . . that I do not have to hunt here [*hier*] forever . . . so I can pass my time here quite without care . . . or rather I could, and yet I cannot [*vielmehr, ich könnte es und kann es doch nicht*]. My burrow takes up too much of my thoughts. I fled from the entrance fast enough, but soon I am back at it again [*schnell bin ich vom Eingang fortgelaufen, bald aber komme ich zurück*]. I seek out a good hiding place and keep watch on the entrance . . . At such times it is as if I were not so much looking at my house as at myself sleeping . . . In all my time I have never seen anyone investigating the actual door of my house . . . There have been happy periods in which I could almost assure myself that the enmity of the world toward me had ceased . . . The burrow has probably protected [*schützt*] me in more ways that I thought [*gedacht habe*] or dared think while . . . inside it.[2] . . . Sometimes I have been seized with [*bekam*] the childish desire never to return to the burrow again, but to . . . pass my life watching the entrance . . . [But] what does this protection which I am looking at here from the outside [*die ich hier beobachte*] amount to . . . ? . . . No, I do not watch over my own sleep, as I imagined; rather it is I who sleep, while the destroyer watches . . . And I leave my post of observation and find I have had enough of this outside life . . . But I have never [*nicht*] been able to discover . . . an infallible method of descent. In consequence . . . I have not yet summoned the resolution to make my actual descent [*ich bin . . . noch nicht in den wirklichen Eingang hinabgestiegen*[3]], and I am thrown into despair at the necessity of doing it soon . . . I tear myself free from all my doubts and . . . rush to the door . . . but I cannot . . . The danger is by no means a fanciful one, but very real . . . If [an enemy] were actually to arrive now . . . if [it] were actually to happen, so that at least . . . I might in my blind rage leap on him [and] . . . destroy him . . . but above all—that is the main thing— were [*sic*] at last back in my burrow once more, I would have it in my heart to greet the labyrinth itself with rapture; but first I would . . . want to rest . . . But nobody comes . . . (334–337)

The tense sequence is itself labyrinthine. The Muirs try to follow its twistings and turnings, but there are unavoidable moments when they have to choose between progressive and nonprogressive English forms (*die ich hier beobachte* becomes "which I am looking at here" rather than "which I look at here") and between perfect and preterite (*bin fortgelaufen* becomes "fled" rather than "have fled"). There is no way, in fact, of translating the passage without committing oneself from moment to moment to an interpretation of its time-structure, in particular of the situation in time of the moment at which the narrator speaks: are the events beheld from the perspective of the *now* of the first sentence of the story—"I have [now] completed the construction of my burrow"—which I would make the present tense here a so-called historical present; or has the moment of narration shifted decisively, for the time being, to a time out in the fresh air where the burrowing creature waits indecisively, unable to venture the descent back into the earth? In fact this passage puts the question most starkly. "Ich bin . . . noch nicht in den wirklichen Eingang hinabgestiegen," says the creature. If the moment of utterance of this sentence is the moment of utterance of the text, then the creature is *now* literally trapped out in the open.

This lengthy quotation should be enough to show that the de-tailed progression of tense-sequences indeed raises puzzling prob-lems. Without quoting at quite such length, let me point to other places where the problem is unavoidable.

The creature is "now" outside his burrow. "For the present . . . I am outside it, seeking some possibility of returning . . . con-fronted by that entrance over there [*dort*] which now [*jetzt*] liter-ally locks and bars itself against me" (339, 340). The deictics em-phatically mark the moment of narration as a moment outside the burrow. "And then . . . I approach the entrance [and] . . . slowly descend" (341). The *now* of narratorial time shifts with the *now* of narrated time: time elapses both in the progress of the text and in the world outside the entrance of the burrow, and "now" en-trance is achieved. The earlier irresolution and incapacity to de-scend are overcome by sheer exhaustion. "Only in this state [of exhaustion] . . . can I achieve my descent" (341). But the return to the burrow rejuvenates him. "It is as though at the moment when I set foot in the burrow I had [*hätte*] wakened from a long . . . sleep." He sets about transporting the spoils of his hunting to his Castle Keep. When this task is completed "a feeling of lassitude overcomes me" and he sleeps (342–343).

Though there is no break in Kafka's manuscript at this point,[4] there is a gap in narrated time. "I must have slept for a long time" *(Ich habe wohl sehr lange geschlafen)*, the narration continues.[5] This second part of the story concerns the mysterious whistling noise that the creature hears in his burrow. Again the *now* of the narration seems to be cotemporal with the *now* of the action; but again there are unsettling passages in which the *now* seems to reveal an iterative face.[6] On the other hand, the noise is unambiguously described as something "that I have never heard before" *(was ich nie gehört habe)* (347)—an iterative return of the noise seems to be ruled out.

When the first researches into the origin of the noise fail, the creature revises his plans and speaks of a future of intention: "I intend now to alter my methods. I shall dig a . . . trench in the direction of the noise" (348). But this new plan brings no solace, for "I do not believe in it" (349). The reason for this mistrust of "reasonable" future projections would, in an iterative time, be that their failure has already been experienced. In the, so to speak, blinkered present of the text the cause of his own hopelessness remains obscure to the narrator.

Even if we read the entire second part of the story as linear and noniterative, there are iterative cycles within it.

> Sometimes I fancy that the noise has stopped . . . sometimes such a faint whistling escapes one . . . one thinks that the whistling has stopped forever. I listen no longer, I jump up . . . (350)

If, on the other hand, we read this part as iterative, then the sequence I have quoted becomes part of the iterative present: neither German nor English appears to have a mechanism at the level of structure of the verb phrase for indicating cycles within cycles.

"It may happen [*kann . . . geschehen*] that I [*man*] make a new discovery" (351): that the noise is growing louder. The shift from *ich* to *man* is maintained for much of the rest of the paragraph, in conformity with the new hypothetical mode of the narrative. It seems impossible to square this mode with a noniterative understanding of the narrative unless one grants to the narrator the effective position of a fictional creator, someone toying with sequences that may or may not be inserted into the narrative. While this possibility cannot be dismissed absolutely, there is nothing else in the text to support the notion that the operations of writing are being so radically unmasked. On the other hand, if one understands the narrative as iterative, then the hypothetical sequence fits in as one that may or may not occur in a given iteration.

As the creature moves about his burrow investigating the noise, new ideas, new plans, new conclusions occur to him, all in turn abandoned as useless. Why does he not remember them from previous iterations, why does he entertain them again if they are proved ineffective, why does he experience surges of hope and despair? The answer, at one level, is that he is in some sense condemned to these iterations, and that part of being condemned (as the example of Sisyphus might teach) is that the torments of hope are part of the sentence. What should interest us particularly in an investigation of tense and time, however, is that the inability to learn from past failure is a reflection of the fact that the iterations are not ordered: none of them being earlier in time than any other, no iteration encompasses a memory of an earlier one.

"Nothing . . . approaching the present situation has happened before; nevertheless there was an incident not unlike it when the burrow was only beginning" (355); and the creature digresses into a past-tense account of an episode from his "apprenticeship." The temporal perspective has reverted unambiguously to that of the opening of the story: a *now* in the time of narration with a linear past behind it and a linear future before it.

The last pages of "The Burrow," after this episode, are resigned, valedictory in tone. The creature retires to his Castle Keep, to his store of food, and awaits "the beast," dreaming of the peace of "the old days" (358). Perhaps it is possible that the beast has never heard him, in which case there is hope. "But all remains unchanged" (359).

The extraordinary time structure of "The Burrow" has been commented on by numerous scholars. I should like to discuss two of the more perceptive of these commentaries.

In her essay "Kafka's Eternal Present," and again in her book *Transparent Minds*, Dorrit Cohn discusses peculiarities of time and tense in Kafka.[7] About "The Burrow" she writes:

The animal—midway through the story—seems to "forget" the iterative nature of his account and begins to tell of . . . the appearance of the hissing sound. Up to this point the animal has described his habitual subterranean existence in durative-iterative present tense . . . [After this point] the static time of the first part of the story . . . becomes an evolving time, its durative tense a punctual tense . . . The speaker who surveyed his sovereign realm in durative present tense [is] transformed into a monologist who simultaneously experiences bewildering events and articulates them in a punctual present tense.

. . . This [temporal] structure corresponds exactly to Kafka's paradoxical conception of human time, which is based on a denial of the distinction between repetitious and singular events. For him, as he once affirmed aphoristically, "the decisive moment of human development is everlasting." "The Burrow," by exploiting the ambiguities of a discourse cast in the present tense, reflects this paradox in its language as well as its meaning. If the crucial events of life happen not once, but everlastingly, then the distinction between durative and singulative modes of discourse is effaced: the durative silence always already contains the hissing sound, and the destruction it brings lies not in a single future moment, but in a constantly repeated present.[8]

The discussion of pages 334–337 of "The Burrow" above should make it clear that Cohn's division of the story into a first part, in which "tense" is durative-iterative, and a second part, in which it is punctual, is too neat: shifts occur too frequently for her generalization to hold. Consequently, while she is right to characterize Kafka's time-conception as "paradoxical [and] . . . based on a denial of the distinction between repetitious and singular events," she goes too far when she claims that this distinction or opposition creates a *structure* in any meaningful sense. There is no clear correspondence between, on the one hand, durative-iterative tenses and life before "the decisive moment" (the start of the hissing) and, on the other, the arrival of "the decisive moment" and singulative tenses.

Cohn does, however, point in a fruitful direction in identifying the ambiguities of present-tense verb forms as the formal field whose exploitation makes the higher-level paradoxes of "The Burrow" possible. But there is a certain flaccidity in the argument that Kafka's "denial of the distinction between repetitious and singular events" is simply "reflected" in the language of the story. For "The Burrow" does not "efface" the distinction between "durative and singulative." The most we can say is that at certain points in the text where we would expect the one form we encounter the other, and vice versa. If the distinction were indeed effaced, if the durative and singulative forms were used interchangeably, the result would very probably be nonsense. The problem is precisely that intuition (which may mislead) suggests that there is system behind the aberrant usage; and our critical task is one of probing intuition by analysis. The conclusion I come to happens to be quite close to Cohn's: the story is indeed dominated by "a constantly repeated present." To reach that conclusion, however, requires not only a tighter scrutiny of the text but also a principled understanding of the use one may make of privileged insights such as the aphorism of Kafka's that Cohn quotes.

In a study based on a more minute examination of tense sequences in "The Burrow" than Cohn's, Heinrich Henel arrives at a similar characterization of the temporal situation of Kafka's creature: that it is "an endless condition." Henel recognizes from the start the particular hermeneutic problems posed by a text in which so elementary a linguistic category as tense, not easily reduced to other terms, becomes the object of the writer's play: "What kind of present occurs as a given point is determined by tone and context; but what tone is appropriate and what context is perceived depend on how one understands the present."[9]

In Henel's reading, the story falls into two main parts with a short linking middle passage. In the first part the use of the present is indeterminate: "Often it sounds as if a unique moment in the here and now is intended, yet the dominant impression is of the iterative . . . Past definite and non-recurring events are reported in the preterite, but for the most part earlier and now melt into an endlessly expanding condition." In the second part

> the meaning of the present tense changes. Past is clearly distinguished from present, and the thoughts and activities of the beast proceed in temporal order . . . The narrator now keeps step with the events represented, and the present tense he employs denotes at each point of the narration a different, later present. While the present of the first part fuses with an untranscended past, the present of the second part moves consistently forward and merges into an indefinite future. The effect is in both cases the same: an eternal condition is represented.[10]

Thus, like Cohn, Henel is concerned to smooth out, by an act of generalization, the difficulties presented by the tense sequences. In his reading the time of the first half of the story is, by and large, iterative, the time of the second half is not. But, we can ask, is the mode of generalizing from the totality of data the correct mode of argument to employ here? Are we concerned to formulate laws that cover most of the data—that is, statistical generalizations— or laws that explain detailed variations, laws whose models would be rules of grammar?[11] My aim here is to elucidate the temporal system of the story on the basis of usage which, despite its appearance of aberrance, I must start by assuming to have some kind of intentional unity. For this reason I do not find it enough to say, as Henel does, that the present tense in "The Burrow" "fills no less than five distinct functions" without carrying the analysis further.[12] This classificatory step is only a stage in analysis, with no explanatory power in itself. The more important stage is the one at which the question is answered: Is there a coherent time-system in which these five functions can be said to participate? In other words: Is there a temporal coherence to the story, or does the mind behind the story shift from one temporal subsystem to another?

Hitherto I have used the word *tense* rather loosely to designate the element of verb inflection that marks time-relations. I must now refine the notion of tense by distinguishing between the *two* elements of verb inflection with temporal functions: tense and aspect.

The theory of the verb on which I base my discussion of "The Burrow" is the description first outlined by Gustave Guillaume in *Temps et verbe* (1929) and subsequently developed in his published lectures of 1948–49. A Guillaumean description of the English verb system has been given by W. H. Hirtle.[13] (I am not aware of any comparable study for the German verb.)

In Guillaume's theory, it is not possible to describe the system of tense and aspect in terms of a single model of time, namely the familiar unidirectional arrow of infinite time of Newtonian physics. The verb system instead rests upon two simultaneous and complementary ways of conceiving time: as universe time, a limitless linear time along whose axis any event can be situated; and as event time, the span of time that an event takes to achieve itself.

Though in theory event time can be infinitesimal—that is, the event can be purely punctual, with no interval between beginning and end—this state is rarely reached in the human world.[14]

Verbal aspect is a system of representing event time. Once this mental representation has been achieved, in Guillaume's theory, the system of tense serves to combine the representations of event time and universe time.

How does aspect represent event time? It conceives of the event as taking place in two phases: a *coming-to-be* phase extending over successive instants, followed by a *result* phase during which no further development or actualization of the event can take place. Depending upon at what point of the temporal continuum the verb intercepts event time, different aspectual results are achieved. In English, the primary aspectual opposition is between intercepting event time at some instant (which may be the final instant) of the coming-to-be phase, and intercepting it during its aftermath. The two aspects that result are, respectively, *immanent* and *transcendent*.

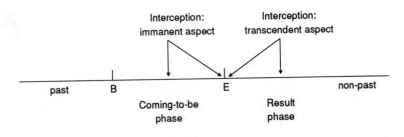

Figure 5

A diagram (Figure 5) may elucidate these concepts. Here the continuum extending infinitely from past to nonpast represents universe time; and the section BE represents event time, from beginning to end, with a coming-to-be phase and a result phase. Depending on whether event time is intercepted during the former or the latter phase, we have verb forms of immanent aspect ("he is running," "he runs," "he ran") or verb forms of transcendent aspect ("he has run"). (We see from these examples that aspect is independent of the past-present tense distinction.)

How are iterative verb forms—forms whose iterative meaning

Figure 6

is signaled by nonsyntactic means—represented in such a scheme? Here the important thing to recognize is that, though an iterative form may be thought of as shorthand for a succession of single events each with a beginning and an end (for example, "he runs [every day]"), it does not intercept the result phase of any of these single events, and at most may or may not intercept only the result phase of their totality. Thus in Figure 6, where each pair B_i and E_i represents the beginning and end of a typical iterated event i, the forms "he runs/ran [every day]," "he is/was running [every day]," represent an interception in the coming-to-be phase of event i, whereas "he used to run [every day]" represents an interception in the result phase of the totality of the iterated events, that is, after E_n. Therefore, without loss of generality we can condense Figure 6 to Figure 7, in which the iterated events are represented without individual result phases.

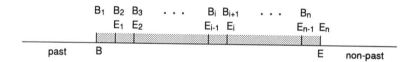

Figure 7

There is one more point to recognize about iteration. Though in the diagrams thus far I have represented the event that is iterated as a single event (for example, "I run"), in "The Burrow" it is more often a sequence of events of some length (for example, "I must thread the tormenting complications of this labyrinth . . . whenever I go out, and I am both exasperated and touched when, as sometime happens, I lose myself . . . But then I find myself beneath the mossy covering . . . " [33]). It is the *whole* of this sequence of subevents (going out, threading, losing myself, being exasperated and touched, finding myself, . . .) that is iterated and that is represented in Figure 7 by the event (B_i, E_i).

Now within the total iterated event (B_i, E_i), morphological means of time-specification are more impoverished than under normal (noniterated) circumstances. This is because what is under normal circumstances a tense marker with a secondary aspectual function (for example, the null morpheme $\emptyset$ of *run*, which normally marks the verb as present in tense and marks iterative aspect only when syntactically reinforced, as in "I run every day") is now charged primarily with marking iterative aspect, so that time relations have to be specified by syntactic means. In the passage quoted above, the relative order of subevents is represented iconically, by the sequence of the signifiers ("I lose myself . . . then I find myself"), and by the logic of syntactic relations ("I am . . . exasperated . . . when . . . I lose myself"), rather than morphologically.

This excursus on iterativity may help us to distinguish between the structure of time in "The Burrow" and the system of tense and aspect through which, in part, that structure is realized, and thus to unravel, at least at a formal level, some of the complexities of the narrative. For closer analysis, consider pages 333–341, from the emergence of the creature into the fresh air to his descent back into the burrow, a passage in which the time structure is perhaps more bewildering than anywhere else in the story.

Scrutinizing these pages closely, we find an alternation between two varieties of temporal experience, each with an associated narrative point of view. The ground bass of the passage is: (1) the iterative experience of emerging from the burrow, enduring the pleasures and terrors of life above, not being able to reenter the burrow, then finally reentering it. The iterativity of the experience is signaled by so-called present-tense (in fact iterative-aspect) verb forms with associated adverbials (*sometimes, usually,* and so on). In Figure 7 the time segment of this experience is (B_i, E_i) and the moment of narration from which it is described is *outside* any (B_i, E_i), that is, beyond E. But there are regular transitions from (1) into: (2) the time of the iteration experienced from the inside, with a past and an unknown future of its own. In terms of Figure 7, it is as if the structure of (B_i, E_i) were identical with that of (B, E), and therefore as though the iterative nature of the experience became invisible or were erased from knowledge. There are two formal devices above all that achieve transitions of this kind: (a) overt past and future verb-forms, which have the effect of normalizing the null morpheme $\emptyset$ of the unmarked form as a *present tense* rather than an *iterative aspect* marker (as, for example, in the context "he ran . . . he will run," "he runs" is read as a present-tense form); (b) emphatically employed deictics like *now, this, here,* which, since they locate the narrative relative to the time and place of its narration, serve to introduce the *now* of narration *inside* (B_i, E_i).

The movement of these pages is thus a continual slide from an outside view of the cycle safety-danger-safety to an inside view in which danger is experienced from the inside and from which it seems impossible to reattain safety, followed by an abrupt and temporary return to the safer outside view. This back-and-forth occurs not only at the level of the narrator's experience; it is also explicitly thematized in the passage as a "problem." It is possible to minimize this thematization and to read it as simply a private joke of Kafka's, a wry reflection on the experience of writing oneself into a corner. But it is also possible to read it as a bringing to explicitness of a fundamental experience of time with which the story continually wrestles at a formal level. Unable to summon the resolution to reenter his burrow, the creature says: "For the present . . . I am outside it seeking some possibility of returning, and for that the necessary technical devices [*technischen Einrichtungen*] would be very desirable" (339). Among the most desirable devices would be, of course, a passage from the dangers of (B, E) to the safety of (B_i, E_i) (the switching power of the $\emptyset$ tense/aspect marker would be such a device). Two pages later: "And then, too exhausted to be any longer capable of thought . . . I . . . slowly descend . . . Only in this state . . . can I achieve my descent" (341). As long as consciousness has been in control, the creature has been unable to achieve this transition from above to below and has remained stuck in a condition that is not only unendurable but logically impossible: the iterative forms have already promised that ascent and descent form a cycle; therefore, the creature cannot remain stuck halfway. Exhaustion and incapacity for thought are the sole means that overcome the arguments (or rationalizations) of the conscious mind that keep him from his burrow; they also constitute the absurd "technical device" that solves the problem of getting stuck during the cycle. What can be read in the mode of realism as a piece of rather inept *deus ex machina* psychologizing can also be read in the mode of text-construction as a flattening of the distance between narrator and narrated, till the adventures of the creature seeking a way into his burrow become identical with the adventures of the signifying subject seeking to find a way to keep the narrative moving. As Henry Sussman writes:

> The voice of the animal is . . . also the voice of construction [of the burrow, of the text], the voice of the rhetorical constructs employed in this particular production.
>
> . . . The reader is asked to believe in the concurrence of the text with the actions which the animal claims to be performing at the moment. If for no other reason than because these actions are mediated by a written text subject to time in different ways than the unidirectional thrust of experience, this presumption is absurd. The narrative confines itself, nevertheless, on the basis of this fictive temporal immediacy, to a now which is remarkably resistant to revisions to the past or projections into the future. The animal thus becomes the agent of a temporal paradox, that the now, capable of feeding upon itself endlessly, is wider-reaching than both the past . . . and the future.[15]

Sussman is right to characterize time in "The Burrow" as paradoxical. But the ability of the *now* to feed upon itself endlessly is not paradoxical at all as long as we distinguish between a *now* of narrative time (which tracks the process of feeding) and a *now* of narrated time (that which is fed upon). The paradox lies elsewhere: in the apparent identity—if we rely upon the signals given by verb forms—of the texture of time in the narrated *now* of (B_i, E_i) and the moment of narration. It is this paradox that Kafka brings into prominence at the moment when, too "exhausted" to play any longer with the riddle itself, he cuts through the knot and puts the creature back in the burrow.[16]

It would be foolhardy to dismiss out of hand the possibility that "The Burrow" is incomplete, and that one of the things Kafka might have done had he completed it to his own satisfaction might have been to regularize at least some of the more bizarre tense sequences, or to create gaps in the text ("chapter breaks") to indicate lacunae in the time of narration.[17] Nevertheless, one's procedure as a critic must be to test the possibility that the text *as it stands* is open to interpretation; only if no interpretation can be given should one fall back on the explanation that the text is in some sense at fault. In this section of the essay, therefore, I suggest how the repeatedly broken, interrupted iterative present might be understood in the context of the whole of the story.

The state in which Kafka's creature lives is one of acute anxiety (one would call it irrational anxiety if there were any reliable opposition between rational and irrational in his universe). His whole life is organized around the burrow, his refuge against an attack that may come at any moment and without warning. The key notion here is *without warning*. A warning is the sign of a transition from peace to its opposite. Strictly speaking, the art of reading warnings is purely prospective, future-directed: a sign recognized retrospectively as having been a warning is no longer a warning, for it can no longer warn.

A warning is the sign of a transition. In "The Burrow," however, time does not move through transition phases. There is one moment and then there is another moment; between them is simply a break. No amount of watchfulness will reveal how one moment becomes another; all we know is that the next moment happens. Similarly, Zeno pointed out, before an arrow reaches its target it must reach halfway to its target; before it reaches halfway, it must reach a quarter of the way; and so forth. To reach its target it must pass through an infinity of states; and to pass through an infinity of states must take an infinity of time. Zeno might have added: conceiving the flight of an arrow in this way as a succession of moments, we can never understand how it gets from one moment to the next, we can never integrate its moments into a single flight.

We know that this paradox (which he did not necessarily arrive at via Zeno) preoccupied Kafka. In "The Great Wall of China" he describes the messenger who takes thousands of years and more to bring a message from the emperor. In "The Next Village" a lifetime may not be long enough for a journey to the next village. In "Advocates" flights of stairs expand beneath the searcher's feet. The mystical correlate to the paradox is a time incommensurable with human time in which man's life occupies a mere instant, yet eons of which can fit in the interstices between two human moments.[18]

Time in "The Burrow" is discontinuous in a strictly formalizable sense. Any moment may mark the break between before and after. Time is thus at every moment a time of *crisis* (from Greek *krino*, "to separate, to divide"). Life consists in an attempt to anticipate a danger that cannot be anticipated because it comes without transition, without warning. The experience of a time of crisis is colored by anxiety. The task of building the burrow itself represents a life devoted to trying to still anxiety, naturally without success; for without warning "the enemy" is in the burrow. (Here I suggest that it would be naive to think that the whistling is a warning and that "the enemy" is some beast that the reader does not get to see, rather along the lines that Dora Dymant suggests; for by the end of the story the architect of the burrow clearly recognizes that a break between before and after has arrived, the clearest sign of this being that the lead-up time that once looked innocent now looks in retrospect like a time of warning. This does not of course mean that there will only be a single foe, a single danger, a single before and after: in theory "The Burrow" is infinitely extensible.)

We treat the past as real insofar as present existence has been conditioned or generated by it. The more indirect the causal derivation of the present from a particular past becomes, the weaker the past becomes, the more it sinks toward a dead past. But with Kafka it is precisely the power of each moment to condition the next that seems to be in question. Someone must have been telling lies about Josef K., but no backward exploration of time will reveal the cause of the accusation against him. Gregor Samsa finds himself one morning transformed into a giant insect, why and how he will never know. Between the before and the after there is not stage-by-stage development but a sudden transformation, *Verwandlung*, metamorphosis.[19]

A common strategy of the first-person intelligence attempting to understand the processes of time is to take up its stance in a present moment (ideally the moment of tranquillity when "I take up my pen to write") that stands for the culmination of a certain past, in order to retrace the history leading up to this moment. Both parts of Beckett's *Molloy*, for example, take up this stance in an explicit way. The first sentence of "The Burrow" seems to promise a similar project: "I have completed the construction of my burrow and it seems to be successful." But the project turns out to be riddled with problems. Where are we to locate this privileged moment of success and security: before, after, or during the recital of events in and around the burrow that occupies pp. 325–343 and terminates in the state of sleep from which the creature is awakened by the whistling? As I have tried to show in the first section, any putative temporal ordering of events at a detailed level becomes honeycombed with inconsistencies and internal contradictions. There is no smooth course of narrative development that will lead from beginnings to the present moment of narration. Between then and now is always a break.

It is from this vantage that the logic of iterative narrative becomes clear. Failing to trace the present to roots in the past, Kafka's narrator embarks on a series of projects to wrap up the past as a round of habit that includes the present and, insomuch as it is repeated, projects into the future. "I assemble my stores . . . I can divide up my stores, walk about among them, play with them . . . That done, I can make my calculations and hunting plans . . ." (328): this is typical of the creature's discourse. The crucial move, in Guillaume's terms, is away from universe time toward event time, away from linear past-present-future tense organization toward a cyclic aspectual organization of time.

This move—which I would call a ruse—is intended to capture the relation of past to present to future by trapping them all in an iterative pseudopresent. But as we have seen, the ruse continually fails. The pseudopresent of iterative/habitual aspect continually breaks down as the events signified within (B_i, E_i), the typical time gap, persist in organizing themselves into successivity, into time, into tense, and then in collapsing in the persistent rupture of the time order that characterizes Kafka. There is no way of getting here from there.

By talking in terms of failed narrative ruses I may give the impression that Kafka is in some sense against, above, and superior to the narrator of "The Burrow," that if he does not know what a successful narrative strategy might be he is at least aware of the futility of the narrator's strategy. This picture would entirely falsify the story. What we have in "The Burrow," rather, is a struggle—not only the representation of the struggle but the struggle itself—with time experienced as continual crisis, and experienced at a pitch of anxiety that leads to attempts to tame it with whatever means language offers. The entire linguistic construct called "The Burrow" represents the stilling of this anxiety; the major metaphor for the linguistic construct is the burrow itself, built by the labors of the forehead (328). But this particular burrow, "The Burrow," could not have been built in a language that did not provide so easy a means of gliding from tense to aspect as German (or English) does. Thus, without denying the total implication of Kafka in the story, it should be possible to recognize that the particular form the story takes rests heavily on a peculiarity of language. We can steer this course without committing ourselves to the extremism of either the Whorfian thesis that linguistic structures determine thought or the line characteristic of some Russian formalists that the literary text is in some sense predetermined by its devices.[20]

I can spell out my position in a different way by isolating my point of disagreement with Dorrit Cohn, whose *Transparent Minds* contains the most carefully worked-out observations on the relations of time to narrative point of view in the story. Cohn recognizes the "illogical" nature of its temporal structure; but this structure, she says,

> corresponds exactly to Kafka's paradoxical conception of human time, which is based on the denial of the distinction between repetitious and singular events. For him, as he once affirmed aphoristically, "the decisive moment of human development is everlasting." "The Burrow," by exploiting the ambiguities of a discourse cast in the present tense, reflects this paradox in its language as well as its meaning. If the crucial events of life happen not once, but everlastingly, then the distinction between durative and singulative modes of discourse is effaced: the durative silence always already contains the hissing sound, and the destruction it brings lies not in a single future moment, but in a constantly repeated present.[21]

The aphorism quoted by Cohn is both obscure and pregnant; but I am not sure that it lends itself to quite the point Cohn is making here. It comes from the notebook of October 1917, and occurs after a parable whose gist we might express as follows: We die at every moment, but blindly do not recognize our death and are spat back into life. Kafka goes on: "From a certain point on, there is no more turning back. This is the point to be reached." And then: "The decisive [entscheidende] moment of human development is everlasting [immerwährend]. Therefore, those revolutionary spiritual movements that declare everything before themselves null are right, in that nothing has yet happened." The next aphorism is: "Human history is the second between two steps of a traveler."[22]

The passage as a whole therefore contrasts two kinds of awareness of time. The first, which we can call historical awareness, imputes reality to a past that it sees as continuous with the present. The second, which we can call eschatological, recognizes no such continuity: there is only the present, which is always present, separated from Ingarden's "dead past" by a moment of rupture, the entscheidende Augenblick. Hence the paradox that history is over in "a second," while the present moment is "everlasting."

To say, as Cohn does, that "the crucial events of life happen not once, but everlastingly," therefore misses the point. There are no "crucial events" as opposed to other events: there is only what is happening now, and this is always crucial.[23] Similarly, although the linguistic opposition of durative to singulative cannot really be effaced without causing a general collapse of language, the conceptual opposition between the two—an opposition that belongs to what I have loosely called the historical sense of time—is brought into doubt by a linguistic practice that steps perilously along the brink of contradiction, confusion, and nonsense. Thus by the end of the story the silence does indeed, as Cohn says, "always contain the hissing sound," and whatever the noise signifies is indeed already here "in a constantly repeated present" (which I would rather call an everlasting present).

But this does not go far enough. What is missing from Cohn's account is a recognition of the radical treatment Kafka gives to narrative time. For the everlasting present is nothing but the moment of narration itself. Now that the narrator has failed time and again to domesticate time by using strategies of narrative (that is, strategies belonging to historical time), his structures of sequence, of cause and effect, collapsing each time at the "decisive moment" of rupture when the past fails to run smoothly into the present, that is, now that the construct of narrative time has collapsed, there is only the time of narration left, the shifting *now* within which his narrative takes place, leaving behind it a wake (a text) of failure, fantasy, sterile speculation: the ramifications of a burrow whose fatal precariousness is signaled by the whistling that comes from its point(s) of rupture.

=

Robert Musil's Stories of Women (1986)

In 1924 Robert Musil published a collection of stories titled *Three Women*, the spinoff of work on a novel about the last years of the Habsburg Empire that began to appear, in installments, in 1930: *The Man without Qualities*. For readers daunted by this most essayistic of novels, full of thinking, empty of ideas (because, to its author, it was the mark of a poet to be *open* to ideas but to *hold* none), unfinished and perhaps unfinishable, a novel that asks its central question—what Europe is to believe in now that it has ceased to believe in history—in a mode of irony and artifice, *Three Women* may provide a more convenient introduction to the mature Musil.

The most considerable of these three stories, "Tonka," draws on an unhappy entanglement from Musil's own youth (it is remarkable how directly this reserved, ironical modernist transposed the events of his life into his fictions). A young man from a well-to-do Austrian family forms a liaison with a simple Czech girl, Tonka. He takes her off to Berlin, where they set up house together. Then Tonka falls pregnant. Worse, it appears she has contracted syphilis. The calendar proves her lover cannot be the father, and the doctors insist it is impossible he could have infected her. Yet she persists in her story that she has known no other man. Such is her evident sincerity that her lover asks himself whether there might not be such a thing as immaculate conception (and immaculate venereal infection). But ultimately he lacks the will to believe her. "The woman loved is [not] the origin of the emotions apparently aroused by her; they are merely set behind her like a light . . . He could not bring himself to set the light behind Tonka."[1]

He tends the girl as she grows sicker and uglier, does whatever is called for, in a certain sense cherishes her; so that, after her death, he feels his conscience to be clear, and can even tell himself he is a better person for the experience. Only for an instant does the veil fall:

> Memory cried out in him: "Tonka! Tonka!" He felt her, from the ground under his feet to the crown of his head, and the whole of her life. All that he had never understood was there before him in this instant, the bandage that had blindfolded him seemed to have dropped from his eyes—yet only for an instant, and the next instant it was merely as though something had flashed through his mind.

In this fable, whose unhurried, circumstantial opening seems to mark it as of the tamest German domestic realism, about a girl who though probably lying is also innocent and a man who fails an impossible test, Musil found a perfect vehicle—perhaps, finally, a little too perfect, too schematic—for a constant theme of his: the unbridgeability of the gap between the rational and the irrational, between the moral, based always on the example of the past and therefore on calculation, and the ethical, calling for a leap into the future.

Musil's thinking maintains a remarkably straight trajectory from his precocious first novel, *The Confusions of Young Törless* (1906), until his death in 1942. At the core of his thinking is an idea expressed most succinctly in a mathematical metaphor (Musil was trained as an engineer). There is an infinity of rational numbers, that is, numbers that can be written as the ratio of two whole numbers. There is also an infinity of irrational numbers, numbers that cannot be expressed as any such ratio. But their two orders of infinity are not comparable. The infinity of irrationals is "greater" than the infinity of rationals. In particular, between any two rationals, no matter how close, lies a cluster of irrationals. Stepping from one rational to the next, as we do every day, is, in Törless' figure, like crossing a bridge whose piers are joined by something that does not "really" exist.

To live and function in the world of the rational, we must deliberately banish from awareness the irrational that lies dense under our feet and about us. We must accept a convention regarding what is to be treated as belonging to the real world. Such a convention will define everyday language (here Musil is close to his Austrian contemporary Wittgenstein). However, Musil proceeds, accepting the fact of a linguistic contract should not mean that we are committed to the repression of the irrational. Like Ulrich, the hero of *The Man without Qualities*, we can maintain a certain reserve toward the real world, a living sense of alternative possibilities. This reserve defines one as what Ulrich calls a "possibilitarian," someone prepared to exist in "a web of haze, imaginings, fantasy and the subjunctive mood," to live a "hovering life" without ideological commitment, to be "without qualities," someone whose natural mode will be the mode of irony ("With me," said Musil in an interview, "irony is not a gesture of condescension but a form of struggle").

With so keen a sense of the role of repression in the formation of culture, one might imagine that Musil would have found Freud congenial. But in fact Musil maintained a lifelong reserve toward Freud, whom he regarded as fundamentally mistaken in assuming that the unconscious, the repressed irrational, or what Musil preferred to call, more vaguely, "the other condition," is accessible to the language of rationality. In a certain sense Musil's psychology is more radical than Freud's. To Musil—a positivist in this regard—psychology, in submitting to the rules of logic and causality that govern the rational, confines itself to the rational: "the other condition" is simply outside its scope. To enter "the other condition" one must abandon the model of science *(Wissenschaft)*, whose instrument is logic, and take up the model of poetry *(Dichtung)*, whose instrument is analogy. In Musil's eyes, Freud comes to his deepest insights when he operates not as a scientist but as a "pseudopoet."

This is not the only reason why Musil kept his distance from Freud. To a novelist with an analytical interest in the darker causes of the breakdown of European liberal institutions, the power that Freud attributed to fixed structures in the psyche seemed all too close to the power attributed by nineteenth-century German historicism to the past, betraying psychoanalysis as no more than a continuation of historicism by other means. In addition, there may be—as Karl Corino has argued—a certain willfulness in Musil's attitude, a decision to close his eyes to psychoanalysis because it threatened to superannuate the ethical-metaphysical analysis of the passions he was more comfortable with.

Drawing a clear line, therefore, between the province of *Wissenschaft* and the province of *Dichtung*, Musil set out to explore, as *Dichter*, the submerged, "other" condition. The three stories of 1924 present people on the edge of revelation, at the point of giving—or of drawing back from giving—themselves to an "other" kind of awareness. "Tonka" is a study in ethical cowardice. Despite its simple narrative surface, it is the subtlest of explorations into the will to blindness, a will that is always *behind* his protagonist's need to believe the girl's unbelievable story, and therefore always hidden from him. In the absoluteness of his sickness, and therefore in the absoluteness required of any remedy for it—*conversion* rather than *cure*—we have a further hint of why the secular science of Freud was unacceptable to Musil.

In "The Lady from Portugal," an uneasier piece of work with blocks of highly wrought prose marking places where Musil is writing his way out of trouble, the miracle, ambiguous and absurd though it is, takes place before our eyes: the love between a jealous older man and his young wife is restored by the exemplary death of a mangy, filthy kitten, which both of them obscurely feel to be Christ. In "Grigia" a geologist working in an isolated valley high in the Tyrol has an affair with a peasant woman, a woman of the earth with an animal's name, through which he attains release from the world, from life itself, into a mystical love of his faroff wife.

Musil is never less than commanding in the ease with which he moves between sense-experience, sensuous thought, and abstraction, much like the writer he most admired among his contemporaries: Rilke. In his diary he wrote: "It is not the case that we reflect on things. Rather, things think themselves out within us." The line of his prose, when he is writing at his best, as in "Tonka" and many parts of *The Man without Qualities*, traces a mind pushing gently but unremittingly at the bounds of the hitherto known. No case history in psychopathology gives us as eerie a sense of inhabiting madness as the chapters of *The Man without Qualities* given over to the sex-killer Moosbrugger. Musil's power, here and elsewhere, seems to flow from an effortless ability to annihilate his selfhood and enter the Other.

Pondering this life of his, Moosbrugger had slow interior talks with himself in which he gave the same weight to the unstressed syllables as to the stressed. It made for a quite different life-song from the song one usually heard . . . It is hard to find an expression for the unity of being he at times achieved. One can think of a person's life as flowing along like a stream. But the movement that Moosbrugger felt in his life was like a stream flowing through a great, still lake. While it pushed forward it was also mingling backward; the actual progress of life just about disappeared. Once, in a half-waking dream, he had the feeling he was wearing the Moosbrugger of his life like an old coat; he opened it a little, now and again, and the most wondrous lining came gushing out in forest-green waves of silk.

This having been said, however, there remains in the stories a certain amount of lofty gesturing toward mystical love, transcendent consummation. We see this in "Grigia" and "The Lady from Portugal"; it is also the weakest feature of the earlier story "The Perfecting of a Love." Nonetheless, "The Perfecting of a Love" is an audacious piece of sustained poetic intensity, and one of the key texts of German modernism. Some fifty-five pages in length, it was the outcome of two years of fevered work by its author. It is the story of a woman, Claudine, who "perfects" her love of her husband by giving herself with reluctant voluptuousness to acts of sexual self-abasement with a stranger she has no feeling for, a complacent middle-aged philanderer. By the end of the brief liaison Claudine feels she has reached a state of mystical liberation, "a state . . . like giving herself to everyone and yet belonging only to the one beloved."

As Musil's private papers make clear, the story is based on an infidelity of his wife-to-be, Martha Marcovaldi. Starting as an attempt to explore his own feelings of jealousy, it became a somewhat grandiose plea for mystical adultery (in a 1913 essay Musil went further, looking forward to a time when "bipolar erotics" would be outdated), but also perhaps (and this is a kind of possibility that Musil's narrative treatment, locked on to Claudine's inner life, does not allow to emerge into articulation) an effort to take over the woman's sexual experience—by writing it, by becoming its author—and thereby strip it of its disturbing autonomy. "The Perfecting of a Love" was hard to write, I would guess, because it presented a real, and ultimately ethical, challenge to the integrity of Musil's enterprise, the enterprise of yielding himself to the processes by which thought thinks itself out, analogically or paralogically, in metaphors, likenesses, similitudes. The rhythms of Claudine's meditation (if hers is indeed the voice of the text) invite us to lapse into lulled will-lessness as they lead us along what Musil would later call "the maximally laden path . . . the way of the most gradual, imperceptible transitions," from contented marital rectitude to perverse abandonment.

Claudine's story gives several *fin-de-siècle* twists to the Christian teaching that as long as the soul is pure it cannot be harmed by violations performed upon the flesh. The first twist takes place when Claudine offers her body to violation, the second when she gives herself without reserve, yielding her will as well as her body. The test, we are to presume, is whether she can maintain an ultimate kernel of selfhood untouched by the martyrdom of the flesh. But Claudine is aware of, and does not repudiate, an ultimate stage of perversion the doctrine can undergo: the active seeking out of violation, torture, and death as means to negative transcendence. To her husband she confesses a fascination with the inner experience of a psychopath she calls G., later to be re-embodied as the enigmatic Moosbrugger in *The Man without Qualities*. "I think . . . he believes his actions are good," she says. In more ways than one, "The Perfecting of a Love" is an exercise in thinking the unthinkable.

Musil's later attitude toward this story—which appeared in company with the much inferior "Temptation of Quiet Veronica" in 1911—is an interesting one: though it remained the only one of his works he could bear to reread, he dissuaded friends from venturing upon it. It was so obscure, he said, so much a matter of "the artist's arcana," that the ordinary reader was all too likely to respond with "revulsion." What Musil is here defending against, I suspect, has less to do with "arcana" a layperson might misunderstand than with being identified with the moral position Claudine arrives at, a position to which Musil is driven, however, by his decision to make the woman's disturbing experience his own. In the language of Musil's older rival in the exploration of the underlife of polite Viennese society, the "pseudopoet" Freud, the scandal of the story lies in the wish it betrays in its writer to occupy and author the ultimately fascinating scene of intercourse, supplanting the usurper, the bearded stranger of Claudine/Martha's story.

In one of the dualisms Musil accepts as a premise and then seeks to overcome, man and woman stand to each other in the relation of rational to irrational, *Wissenschaft* to *Dichtung*. In the years 1906–1911, his first years with Martha Marcovaldi, Musil can be thought of as alternating between a daytime self devoted to science and a nighttime self increasingly steeped in Martha, in reimagining, through the medium of an eroticized female sensibility that he half-adopted, half-created, her life before she met him. When we set side by side Robert's project of imaginatively living Martha, and Martha's project, after Robert's death, of editing and publishing his manuscripts, in places tampering with them—a project of becoming *his* author—we have an as remarkable a dyadic literary household as any since the Tolstoys.

Musil's only important poem, "Isis and Osiris" (1923), is about a sister and brother who devour each other in a love feast. It is a myth that, as Musil later came to see, held *The Man without Qualities* in embryo; and *The Man without Qualities*, as we have it, drifts to an end in the retreat of Ulrich and his sister Agathe into mystical incest, a species of androgyny, Musil's last metaphor for "the other condition." We usually think of *The Man without Qualities* as an unfinished novel. But, like Ezra Pound's *Cantos*, another work with epic ambitions, *The Man without Qualities* had already begun to founder in the 1930s, as history began to move so fast and with such devastating effect that it burst the capacity of literary forms to hold it. Musil's progress with the work, after the publication of Part I, became slower and slower. The shell provided by his tenuous plot was too fragile and ironic a matter for the times; perhaps the private peace of Ulrich and Agathe was the best to be hoped for, under the circumstances.

= Autobiography and Confession

Interview

DA: The question of the self's presence to the self has engaged you for a long time. The choice from the beginning, in *Dusklands,* of first-person, present tense narration, implicitly dramatizes the problem of self-knowledge. It is therefore not surprising that you should address the question in your nonfiction, as in your substantial and challenging essay on confession. How did the essay come about?

JMC: I see myself in this essay getting away from microenvironments and taking on broader critical themes (though I must say that what I like best on rereading it is the part where I trace Tolstoy's engagement with the semantics of verb morphology). At the time I wrote it (1982–83) it was the most ambitious piece of criticism I had ventured on. But the length of the Kafka essay had already surprised me. I had thought of myself as a miniaturist, and my fiction certainly supported this view; whereas what was now coming from my pen was long to the point of being prolix.

Part of the reason for this prolixity is that I do not have a "field" as a literary scholar. Most of my critical essays have followed after raids into territory strange to me, often into foreign linguistic territory. What saves them from being mere academic tourism is that I do what scholarly homework I can. In practice this entails that I rehearse for my own benefit arguments familiar to specialists but new to me. This is particularly true when it comes to arguments in philosophy. The essay we are talking about contains more than enough of the reinventing of philosophical wheels.

The essay came out of a rereading of Tolstoy and Dostoevsky, two novelists for whom my admiration remains undimmed. I read them on what I take to be their own terms, that is, in terms of their power to tell the truth as well as to subvert secular skepticism about truth, getting behind skeptical ploys to get behind them ("What is truth?"). I accept Tolstoy and Dostoevsky, in their different ways, as writers of real philosophical sophistication, or rather, since "sophistication" carries the wrong overtones, of real philosophical power. If there is a sense in which my reading of them "on their own terms" is not simply a repeat of the reading they were accorded in the West during their own day—as geniuses of rough realism from the Russian backwoods—it lies in treating them as men who not only *lived through* the philosophical debates of their day with the intensity characteristic of an intelligentsia held down under censorship, but also were the heirs of a Christian tradition more vital, in some respects, than Western Christianity.

Whether my overall thesis can be sustained in debate with philosophers I have no idea. But I do see the capacity to push self-analysis through to its limits—analysis not of *one's* self but of *the* self, the soul—in both Tolstoy and Dostoevsky as greater than in a purely secular thinker like Freud.

DA: Reviewers have often commended your work, in old-fashioned language, for its penetration into the "psyche." In this essay, though, there is a certain reserve about psychological description, even about psychoanalysis. Would you agree?

JMC: Freudian psychoanalysis has scientific ambitions, and science has no ethical content beyond a blind commitment to follow wherever its researches take it (I hasten to add that this blindness of science is, paradoxically, what is most admirable about it: science in the service of a social or political goal is above all dreary). What psychoanalysis has to say about ethical impulses may be illuminating (I give as an instance the link Freud points to between pity and destructiveness) but is ultimately of no ethical weight. That is to say, whatever one thinks the psychological origins of love or charity may be, one must still act with love and charity. The outrage felt by many of Freud's first readers—that he was subverting their moral world—was therefore misplaced. This is, I trust, a Dostoevskian point. Dostoevsky's underground man makes his life, his life story, out of psychology, psychological self-analysis. Stavrogin, in *The Possessed*, does something similar but more radical by treating himself as an abandoned soul, a soul that can therefore be used as material for an experiment, as Frankenstein did with an abandoned body. Dostoevsky's ethical critique is that these are merely ways of making oneself into the hero of a story for the modern age—merely ways of being interesting.

If one believes that stories must aspire to more than merely to be interesting, then one must go beyond psychology.

Does this mean that I am anti-Freudian? Far from it—the traces of my dealings with Freud lie all over my writings. Does it mean that the essay we are talking about is anti-Freudian? Yes, to the extent that it sets itself against the old-fashioned Freud, the Freud who wrote, for instance, the essay on Dostoevsky and parricide. Similarly I see Tolstoy exercising a right, or rather a power, to assert his own reading of *The Kreutzer Sonata* against subversive readings such as one might imagine coming from the old-fashioned Freud. But whether *my* argument in this case has enough power I don't know. "Failed" works are always difficult to work with, *The Keutzer Sonata* particularly so because of its impatience with the entire category of "accomplished" works (that is of course the theme it *asserts:* down with Beethoven, down with art).

DA: I have a question about your relationship as a novelist with literary and critical theory. There is a tendency in the criticism of your fiction to approach it as "allegorized theory." Although all your writing could hardly be described as antitheoretical, I doubt such a description would please you; nevertheless, let me put the question to you, and I do so in the context of your relationship with deconstruction.

In the essay there is some direct engagement with deconstruction, in your comments on de Man's analysis of Rousseau's *Confessions* and on Derrida's notion of the "epoch of supplementarity." It is logical that you should bring deconstruction to bear on the analysis of confession where the problem of the self's residence within language is so visible; but despite this, in both instances you imply that you find the arguments valuable but ultimately (and paradoxically) too large, too incautious. Outside of this essay, there is surprisingly little sustained reference to deconstructive theory or criticism. By contrast, it seems (and this is why I say "surprisingly"), in the *fiction* you seem willing or able to exploit the resources of deconstruction more easily: in *Barbarians*, the unstable and inconclusive features of signification feature prominently; Michael K is himself a kind of Derridean trace (refusing to occupy a fixed place in the system); and in *Foe*, most pertinently, the tongueless Friday is a guardian of significant silence or absence.

Is this a fair observation—that is, can one say that in the nonspecific manner of fiction, you are able to move relatively freely within the deconstructive mode? If so, what might this imply about the resource-fulness of theory to the writing of fiction?

JMC: Your observation is quite right. I feel a greater freedom to follow where my thinking takes me when I am writing fiction than when I am writing criticism. One reason is that, as I have said before, I am not a trained philosopher (and contemporary criticism has become very much a variety of philosophizing). Not only that: I tend to be rather slow and painstaking and myopic in my thinking (in fact, in most things I do). I don't think or act in sweeps. It would be pointless for me to try to rethink Dostoevsky in Derridean terms or—what would interest me more—rethink Derrida in Dostoevskian terms, because I don't have the mind for it, to say nothing of the philosophical equipment.

Another reason for what strikes you as a paradox has to do with the two discursive modes. Stories are defined by their irresponsibility: they are, in the judgment of Swift's Houynhnhms, "that which is not." The *feel* of writing fiction is one of freedom, of irresponsibility, or better, of responsibility toward something that has not yet emerged, that lies some-where at the end of the road. When I write criticism, on the other hand, I am always aware of a responsibility toward a goal that has been set for me not only by the argument, not only by the whole philosophical tradition into which I am implicitly inserting myself, but also by the rather tight discourse of criticism itself.

If I were a truly creative critic I would work toward liberating that discourse—making it less monological, for instance. But the candid truth is I don't have enough of an investment in criticism to try. Where I do my liberating, my playing with possibilities, is in my fiction. To put it in another way: I am concerned to write the kind of novel—to work in the kind of novel form—in which one is not unduly handicapped (compared with the philosopher) when one plays (or works) with ideas.

DA: A more straightforward question, also on the subject of theory. It is curious that there is little significant reference to Foucault in your nonfiction, since Foucauldian themes seem prominent in the novels. Certainly, one could read fruitfully from *Discipline and Punish* to *Michael K,* or from *The Archaeology of Knowledge* to *Barbarians.* In *Foe* the Foucault of "What Is an Author?" is apposite, especially in Susan's struggle with the author-function, with Foe as Other. Is Foucault a significant influence?

JMC: Foucault's shadow lies quite heavily over my essays about colonial South Africa (I think in particular of the essay on anthropological writings about the Hottentots that forms part of *White Writing*). He is also very much a presence behind the essays on censorship I have been working on recently. But no, there is not much evidence of Foucault in my strictly literary essays. I find what Foucault has to say about forms of writing whose bearing on, or use by, *power* is immediate, more striking than what he says, or than what I can imagine him saying, about literary forms whose relations with power, as forms, as practices, are less direct.

DA: The essay on confession argues that there comes a point when the confessant cannot look to further self-analysis for release. You attribute the more satisfying account of the end of confession to Dostoevsky, where it is implied that what is required finally is grace, for which there is no secular equivalent.

To an extent, *Foe* stages the "endless chain" of self-consciousness discussed in the essay, though in metafictional terms. Each new section gets behind the preceding one until, at the point of closure, we have an unnamed narrator who seems to stand for the narrative function per se. (In the essay, you raise the question of the degree to which writers are willing to treat the complexities of confession as embedded in narrative itself; in an earlier version of the section on Rousseau—given as an inaugural lecture at the University of Cape Town—you stress the discursive "economy" of confession.[1])

The one constant in *Foe*, marking the limit of self-knowledge in Susan's case and overwhelming the narrator at the novel's close, is Friday. There is finally no metafictional preempting of Friday's power. This power is largely that of silence; perhaps it is the power of an unwritten but potentially transfiguring text. The closest the narrator comes to defining what is called "the home of Friday" is that it is the "place where bodies are their own signs."[2]

Could you comment on the importance of the body in your fiction? What is the function of this consciousness of the body in bringing an end to Susan's confessional discourse, as well as to the process of metafictional self-scrutiny?

JMC: If I translate your question into practical terms, it becomes a question about closure: how does a novel that is as much an interrogation of authority as *Foe* is find an end for itself? Dostoevsky, in *Notes from*

Underground, faces a comparable question and produces a rather uninspired solution: an "editorial" postscript saying that the text we have is incomplete. Endings of this kind, endings that inform you that the text should be understood as going on endlessly, I find aesthetically inept. However peremptory the ending of *Foe,* it is at least an ending, not a gesture toward an ending.

But, translated into my terms, your question can take a second form, as a question about power: is representation to be so robbed of power by the endlessly skeptical processes of textualization that those represented in/by the text—the feminine subject, the colonial subject—are to have no power either? Am I too fanciful as seeing this as a restaging of the Dostoevskian confrontation between faith and skepticism (between Tikhon and Stavrogin, for instance)? For Susan Barton, the question takes care of itself: the book is not Foe's, it is hers, even in the form of the trace of her hunt for a Foe to tell it for her. But Friday is the true test. Is his history of mute subjection to remain drowned? I return to the theme of power. The last pages of *Foe* have a certain power. They close the text by force, so to speak: they confront head-on the endlessness of its skepticism.

Friday is mute, but Friday does not disappear, because Friday is body. If I look back over my own fiction, I see a simple (simple-minded?) standard erected. That standard is the body. Whatever else, the body is not "that which is not," and the proof that it *is* is the pain it feels. The body with its pain becomes a counter to the endless trials of doubt. (One can get away with such crudeness in fiction; one can't in philosophy, I'm sure.)

Not grace, then, but at least the body. Let me put it baldly: in South Africa it is not possible to deny the authority of suffering and therefore of the body. It is not possible, not for logical reasons, not for ethical reasons (I would not assert the ethical superiority of pain over pleasure), but for political reasons, for reasons of power. And let me again be unambiguous: it is not that one *grants* the authority of the suffering body: the suffering body *takes* this authority: that is its power. To use other words: its power is undeniable.

(Let me add, *entirely* parenthetically, that I, as a person, as a personality, am overwhelmed, that my thinking is thrown into confusion and helplessness, by the fact of suffering in the world, and not only human suffering. These fictional constructions of mine are paltry, ludicrous defenses against that being-overwhelmed, and, to me, transparently so.)

You asked me earlier on about psychology, about my lack of interest in the psychological as a field for fiction to exercise itself in. I come back to the question of endlessness. The self-interrogation of Montaigne, of Rousseau, of the earlier Tolstoy, carries on by other means a religious tradition of self-examination and confession: soul-searching turned into psychologizing. Freud, both in his role as confessor to his patients and in his self-interrogation, fits into the tradition, as do I in these interviews. All of us, both great and small, face the problem of how to bring our confession to an end; not all of us have the power to accept, pessimistically (Freud) or with equanimity (Derrida, it seems), the prospect of endlessness.

Against the endlessness of skepticism Dostoevsky poses the closure not of confession but of absolution and therefore of the intervention of grace in the world. In that sense Dostoevsky is not a psychological novelist at all: he is finally not interested in the psyche, which he sees as an arena of game-playing, of the *middle* of the novel. To the extent that I am taken as a political novelist, it may be because I take it as given that people must be treated as fully responsible beings: psychology is no excuse. Politics, in its wise stupidity, is at one with religion here: one man, one soul: no half-measures. What saves me from a merely stupid stupidity, I would hope, is a measure of charity, which is, I suppose, the way in which grace allegorizes itself in the world. Another way of saying this is that I try not to lose sight of the reality that we are children, unreconstructed (Freud wouldn't disagree at this point), to be treated with the charity that children have due to them (charity that doesn't preclude clear-sightedness).

DA: What you say about the body and the authority of suffering brings me to your most recent novel, *Age of Iron*. Here, "Friday" is no longer mute, though whether there is any voice that can address adequately the trauma of South Africa in the late 1980s, in the period of the States of Emergency, remains in question; as Elizabeth Curren says, "To speak of this . . . you would need the tongue of a god."[3] Nevertheless, there is speech, and there is a dramatic assumption of authority on the part of the oppressed.

In the face of this, Elizabeth's questioning (her skepticism about heroism, her discomfort over her daughter's uncompromising rejections) is implicitly confessional, for it runs the risk of undermining or undervaluing the work of restitution. What releases Elizabeth, finally, is death; in fact, the pact she enters into (or allows herself to fall into) with her Angel of Death, the derelict Vercueil, seems increasingly to represent the promise of absolution as the novel develops. In this resolution, are you not close to the Dostoyevskian principle of grace?

JMC: It is 28 July 1990 today, and *Age of Iron* has yet to be published, though you have read it in manuscript. I am still too near its writing— too near and too raw—to know what to think of it. But let me take up the two terms *history* and *authority* and, at the risk of traducing Elizabeth, comment on them in the light, or in the shadow, of my aftersense of the book.

Elizabeth Curren brings to bear against the voices of history and historical judgment that resound around her two kinds of authority: the authority of the dying and the authority of the classics. Both these authorities are denied and even derided in her world: the first because hers is a private death, the second because it speaks from long ago and far away.

So a contest is staged, not only in the dramatic construction of the novel but also within Elizabeth's—what shall I say?—soul, a contest about having a say. To me as a writer, as *the* writer in this case, the outcome of this contest—what is to count as classic in South Africa—is irrelevant. What matters is that the contest is staged, that the dead have their say, even those who speak from a totally untenable historical position. So: even in an age of iron, pity is not silenced.

What is of importance in what I have just said is the phrasing: the phrases *is staged, is heard;* not *should be staged, should be heard.* There is no ethical imperative that I claim access to. Elizabeth is the one who believes in *should,* who believes in *believes in.* As for me, the book is written, it will be published, nothing can stop it. The deed is done, what power was available to me is exercised.

As for your question about absolution for Elizabeth, the end of the novel seems to me more troubled (in the sense that the sea can be troubled) than you imply. But here I am stepping onto precarious ground, or precarious water; I had better stop. As for grace, no, regrettably no: I am not a Christian, or not yet.

Confession and Double Thoughts: Tolstoy, Rousseau, Dostoevsky (1985)

I n Book II of his *Confessions,* Augustine relates the story of how, as a boy, he and some friends stole a huge load of pears from a neighbor's garden, stealing them not because they wanted to eat them (in fact they fed them to hogs) but for the pleasure of committing a forbidden act. They were being "gratuitously wanton, having no inducement to the evil but the evil itself . . . seeking nothing from the shameful deed but the shame itself . . . We were ashamed not to be shameless."[1]

In the time-before of which the *Confessions* tells, the robbery brings shame to the young Augustine's heart. But the desire of the boy's heart (the mature man remembers) is that very feeling of shame. And his heart is not shamed (chastened) by the knowledge that it seeks to know shame: on the contrary, the knowledge of its own desire as a shameful one both satisfies the desire for the experience of shame and fuels a sense of shame. And this sense of shame is both experienced with satisfaction and recognized, if it is recognized, by self-conscious searching, as a further source of shame; and so on endlessly.

In the "numberless halls and caves, in the innumerable fields and dens and caverns of memory" (X.xvii; p. 217), the shame lives on in the mature man. "Who can unravel such a twisted and tangled knottiness? It is unclean, I hate to reflect upon it" (II.x; p. 60). Augustine's plight is truly abysmal. He wants to know what lies at the beginning of the skein of remembered shame, what is the origin from which it springs, but the skein is endless, the stages of self-searching required to attain its beginning infinite in number. Yet until the source from which the shameful act sprang is confronted, the self can have no rest.

Confession is one component in a sequence of transgression, confession, penitence, and absolution. Absolution means the end of the episode, the closing of the chapter, liberation from the oppression of the memory. Absolution in this sense is therefore the indispensable goal of all confession, sacramental or secular. In contrast, transgression is not a fundamental component. In Augustine's story, the theft of the pears is the transgression, but what calls to be confessed is something that lies behind the theft, a truth about himself that he does not yet know. His story of the pears is therefore a twofold confession of something he knows (the act) and something he does not know: "I would . . . confess what I know about myself; I will confess what I do not know about myself . . . What I do not know about myself I will continue not to know until the time when 'my darkness is as the noonday' in thy sight" (X.v; p. 205). The truth about the self that will bring an end to the quest for the source within the self for that-which-is-wrong, he affirms, will remain inaccessible to introspection.

In this essay I follow the fortunes of a number of secular confessions, fictional and autobiographical, as their authors confront or evade the problem of how to know the truth about the self without being self-deceived, and of how to bring the confession to an end in the spirit of whatever they take to be the secular equivalent of absolution. A certain looseness is inevitable when one transposes the term *confession* from a religious to a secular context. Nevertheless, we can demarcate a mode of autobiographical writing that we can call the *confession*, as distinct from the *memoir* and the *apology*, on the basis of an underlying motive to tell an essential truth about the self.[2] It is a mode practiced at times by Montaigne,[3] but the mode is essentially defined by Rousseau's *Confessions*. As for fictional confession, this mode is already practiced by Defoe in the made-up confessions of sinners like Moll Flanders and Roxana; by our time, confessional fictions have come to constitute a subgenre of the novel in which problems of truth-telling and self-recognition, deception and self-deception, come to the forefront.[4] Two of the fictions I discuss, Dostoevsky's *Notes from Underground* and Tolstoy's *Kreutzer Sonata*, can strictly be called confessional fictions because they consist for the greater part of representations of confessions of abhorrent acts committed by their narrators. Ippolit Terentyev's "Explanation" in *The Idiot* is a deathbed apologia which soon engages in the problems of truth and self-knowledge that characterize confession. Finally, Stavrogin's confession in *The Possessed* raises the question, left in abeyance since Montaigne's time, of whether secular confession, for which there is an auditor or audience, fictional or real, but no confessor empowered to absolve, can ever lead to that *end of the chapter* whose attainment is the goal of confession.[5]

Tolstoy

It is the second evening of a long train journey. Conversation among the passengers has turned to marriage, adultery, divorce. A gray-haired man speaks cynically about love. He reveals his name: Pozdnyshev, convicted wife-killer. His fellow passengers edge away, leaving him alone with the unnamed narrator, to whom he now offers to "tell everything from the beginning." Pozdnyshev's confession, as repeated by this narrator, constitutes the body of Tolstoy's *Kreutzer Sonata* (1889).[6]

Pozdnyshev's story is of a man who lived his life in an "abyss of error" concerning relations with women, and who finally underwent an "episode" of pathological jealousy in which he killed his wife. Only later, after being sent to prison, did it happen that "my eyes [were] opened and I [saw] everything in quite a different light. Everything reversed, everything reversed!" (233). The moment when everything becomes reversed (*navyvorot'*, "turned inside out") is the moment of illumination that opens his eyes to the truth and makes true confession possible. The confession on which he embarks in the train thus has two sides: the facts of the "episode," which have already of course come out in court, and the truth about himself to which his eyes have since been opened. Telling the latter truth, in turn, is closely allied to denouncing error, a state of error in which, in his opinion, the entire class from which he comes still lives.

With his air of agitation, the funny little sound he makes (half cough, half broken-off laugh), his strange ideas about sex, and the history of violence behind him, Pozdnyshev is plainly an odd character, and one would not be surprised if the truth he told were at odds with the truth understood by the quiet, sober auditor who later retells his truth to us. We would not be surprised, in other words, to find ourselves reading one of those books in which the speaker believes himself to be telling one truth while to us it slowly emerges that somehow another truth is being told—a book like Nabokov's *Pale Fire*, say, in which the narrator believes he is speaking *for* himself but we are all too easily able to read him *against* himself.

Let me begin by summarizing the truth as Pozdnyshev sees it, allowing him to speak in his own voice.

Pozdnyshev's Truth

As a child of my class, I received my sexual initiation in a brothel. Experience with prostitutes spoiled my relations with women forever. Yet with "the most varied and horrible crimes against women" on my soul, I was welcomed into the homes of my peers and permitted to dance with their wives and daughters (239).

I became engaged to a girl. It was a time of sensual promise heightened by alluring fashions in clothes, by rich food, by lack of physical exercise. Our honeymoon brought disillusionment, and married life turned into an alternation between bouts of animosity and bouts of sensuality. What we did not understand was that the animosity we felt for each other was a protest of our "human nature" against being overpowered by our "animal nature" (261).

Society, via its priests and doctors, sanctions unnatural practices: sexual intercourse during pregnancy and lactation, contraception. Contraception was "the cause of all that happened later," for it permitted my wife to move among strange men "in the full vigor of a thirty-year-old, well fed and excited woman who is not bearing children" (281, 283).

A man named Trukachevski, a violinist, came onto the scene. Led by "a strange and fatal force," I encouraged his friendship with my wife, and "a game of mutual deception" began. He and my wife played duets, I seethed with jealousy but kept a smiling front, my wife was excited by my jealousy, while an "electric current" flowed between her and him (293–294). In retrospect I now see that playing music together, like dancing together, like the closeness of sculptors to female models or of doctors to female patients, is an avenue that society keeps open to encourage illicit liaisons.

I left home on a trip but kept remembering something Trukachevski's brother once said: he slept only with married women because they were "safe," he would not pick up an infection. Overcome with jealous rage, I raced home. Trukachevski and my wife were playing duets. I burst in upon them with a dagger. Trukachevski escaped. My wife pleaded, "There has been nothing . . . I swear it!" (328). I stabbed her.

In prison a "moral change" took place in me and I saw how my fate had been determined. "Had I known what I know now, everything would have been different . . . I should not have married at all" (328, 334).

Tolstoy's Truth

In 1890, in response to letters from readers asking "what I meant" in *The Kreutzer Sonata*, Tolstoy published an "Afterword" in which he spelled out what he "meant" as a series of injunctions. It is wrong for unmarried people to indulge in sexual intercourse. People should learn to live naturally and eat moderately; they would then find sexual abstinence easier. They should also be taught that sexual love is "an animal state degrading to a human being." Contraception and the practice of intercourse during lactation should cease. Chastity is a state preferable to marriage.[7]

The Other Truth "of" Pozdnyshev

If one rereads the story of Pozdnyshev, however, stressing elements other than those elements Pozdnyshev and the Tolstoy of the "Afterword" choose to stress, one comes up with another truth. I could allow this alternative truth "of" Pozdnyshev to speak in its own voice from its own "I." But then I may be read as prejudging the case by asserting the same authority for this second voice as for the first, the voice Pozdnyshev believes to be his own. So let me write the other truth simply as something postulated "of" or "about" Pozdnyshev, something extracted from his utterances yet not the truth he avows in his own person.

In the ballrooms and drawing rooms of Pozdnyshev's class a convention reigns: no one is to look beneath the "carefully washed, shaved, perfumed" exteriors of young men to see them as they are in their filthy naked nocturnal debauches with prostitutes. Another convention says that there are two kinds of woman, decent women and prostitutes, even though on occasion decent women dress like prostitutes, with "the same exposure of arms, shoulders and breasts, the same tight skirts over prominent bustles." In fact, women dress to kill. Pozdnyshev: "I am simply frightened [by them]. I want to call a policeman and ask for protection from the peril" (239, 244, 249).

Pozdnyshev gets married and goes on a honeymoon. The experience is disillusioning: he compares it to paying to enter a sideshow at a fair, discovering inside that you have been cheated, but being too ashamed of your gullibility to warn other sightseers of the fraud. He thinks particularly of a sideshow advertising a bearded woman that he visited in Paris (251). As for intercourse, it leads to hatred and thence ultimately to killing. The killing goes on all the time. "They are all killing, all, all." Yet even when a woman is pregnant, when "great work" is going on within her, she permits the entry of the male instrument (261, 263).

Then comes Trukachevski, with his "specially developed posterior," his "springy gait," his habit of "holding his hat against his twitching thigh." Though Pozdnyshev dislikes Trukachevski, "a strange and fatal force led me not to repulse him . . . but on the contrary to invite him to the house." Trukachevski offers to "be of use" to Pozdnyshev's wife, and Pozdnyshev accepts, asking him to "bring his violin and play [igrat'] with my wife." "From the first moment [their] eyes met . . . I saw that the animal in each of them asked, 'May I?' and answered, 'Oh yes, certainly'" (286, 295, 294, 293, 296).

Racing home to trap the couple together, he exacerbates his jealousy by imagining how Trukachevski sees his wife: "She is not in her first youth, has lost a side-tooth, and there is a slight puffiness about her," but at least she will not have a venereal disease. Pozdnyshev's greatest anguish is that "I considered myself to have a complete right to her body . . . and yet at the same time I felt I could not control that body . . . and she could dispose of that body as she pleased, and she wanted to dispose of it not as I wished her to" (315, 318).

Creeping up to the room from which the music comes, Pozdnyshev fears only that they will "part hastily" before he gets there and so deprive him of "clear evidence" of their crime. As he is about to stab his wife, she cries out that there "has been nothing." "I might still have hesitated, but these last words of hers, from which I concluded just the opposite—that everything had happened—called forth a reply," and he kills her (322, 326).

This collage of extracts from Pozdnyshev's text literally tells a different story from the one he tells. This story is of a man who sees the phallus everywhere, peeking mockingly or bulging threateningly from the bodies of men and women. He marries in the hope of learning the sexual secret (the woman's beard) but is disappointed. He imagines sexual intercourse as a probing by the vengeful phallus after the life of the unborn child, with whom he identifies, within the mother. At the thought that his wife/mother's body does not belong to him alone, he feels the anguish of the Oepidal child. He tries to solve the problem by giving her to the threatening rival (whom he sees as a walking phallus), thereby retaining magical control over the couple; when they do not enact the scene he has prescribed and permitted them, he loses control and flies into murderous rage.

We hear Pozdnyshev speak this "other" truth about himself if we stress a certain chain of elements of his text and ignore those elements he wants us to attend to—his visits to prostitutes, his meat diet, and so on. No doubt we can read third and fourth truths out of the text by the same method. But my argument is not a radical one involving an infinity of interpretations. My argument is merely that Pozdnyshev and Pozdnyshev's interlocutor and Tolstoy and Tolstoy's public operate within an economy in which a second reading is possible, a reading that searches in the corners of Pozdnyshev's discourse for instances where the truth, the "unconscious" truth, slips out in strange associations, false rationalizations, gaps, contradictions. If the "unconscious" truth of Pozdnyshev is anything like the one I have outlined, then Pozdnyshev's confession becomes one of those "ironic" confessions in which the speaker believes himself to be saying one thing but is "in truth" saying something very different. In particular, Pozdnyshev believes that since the "episode" his eyes have been "opened" and he has attained a certain knowledge of himself both as individual and as representative of a social class that qualifies him to say what was "wrong" with him and is still wrong with his class (whose representatives, all but one, refuse to hear the diagnosis and move to another carriage). But the true truth "of"

Pozdnyshev turns out to be that he knows very little about himself. In particular, while he knows that "had I known [then] what I know now . . . I should not have married at all," he does not know why he should not have married or why he killed his wife. Yet the peculiar thing is that this incompetent diagnostician is given explicit support by Tolstoy as author in his "Afterword": what Pozdnyshev believes to be wrong with society, says Tolstoy, is indeed what is wrong.

Little I have said thus far about *The Kreutzer Sonata* is new. "The conventions which govern it are confused," says Donald Davie. "The reader does not know 'which way to take it.' Nor, as far as we can see, was this ambiguity intended by the author. It is therefore a grossly imperfect work."[8] "Broken-backed" is T. G. S. Cain's verdict: a "magnificently handled narrative of the moral decay of a marriage . . . introduced by, and partly interwoven with, an obsessively unintelligent, simplistic series of generalizations . . . spoken by Pozdnyshev but . . . undoubtedly endorsed by Tolstoy."[9]

Both the comments of Davie and Cain and my comments above point to a problem of mediation. A confession embodying a patently inadequate self-analysis is mediated through a narrator who gives no hint that he questions the analysis, and the analysis is then reaffirmed (as "what I meant") by the author writing outside the fiction. These mediators of Pozdnyshev are too quickly satisfied, one reflects: it is all too easy to read another, "deeper" truth in Pozdnyshev's confession. Yet when one looks to Pozdnyshev himself for evidence that he is disturbed by the strain of articulating one truth with one voice ("consciously") while another truth speaks itself "unconsciously," one finds nothing but the cryptic symptom of the preverbal half-cough, half-laugh, which may signal strain but may equally well signal scorn; when one looks to the narrator for signs of a questioning attitude, one finds only silence; and when one looks to Tolstoy one finds belligerently simplistic support for Pozdnyshev's truth. At all levels of presentation, then, there is a lack of reflectiveness. *The Kreutzer Sonata* presents a narrative, asserts its interpretation (its truth), and asserts as well that there are no problems of interpretation.

A willed belief that things are one way when they are another way is a form of self-deception. Whether Pozdnyshev is self-deceived and whether the narrator is deceived are questions the text will not answer. For the question "Is Pozdnyshev self-deceived?" can only mean "Is Pozdnyshev a representation of a self-deceived man?" and the text does not reflect on this point. Whether the narrator is deceived or not by Pozdnyshev one cannot know, since the narrator is silent. But it is meaningful to put the question of whether Tolstoy himself, as writer and self-aware self-critic, is, at best, self-deceived when, by asserting that Pozdnyshev is a trustworthy critic of society, he implies that Pozdnyshev understands his own history, and therefore that his confession can be trusted to mean what he says it means. For, in the first place, there is a plethora of biographical evidence that the habit of keeping a diary in the peculiar circumstances of the Tolstoy household brought Tolstoy every day face to face with the temptations of deception and the problems of insincerity and self-deception inherent in the diary form and in confessional forms in general.[10] And second, the focus of the psychology of the novels of Tolstoy's middle period is as much on mechanisms of self-deception as on anything else.

What must surprise one, with this background in mind, is that Tolstoy should write a work so blank as *The Kreutzer Sonata* on the ambivalences of the confessional impulse and the deformations of truth brought about by the confessional situation, a situation in which there is always someone confessed to, even if, as in the private diary, the nature of this Other might be left undefined, in suspension. Around neither the confession within the confession (Pozdnyshev's presentation of his diaries to his fiancée) nor the confession of Pozdnyshev to the narrator is there any frame of questioning. Just as one effect of seeing the light has been to make it easy for Pozdnyshev to discard his earlier self, to regard that self without sympathy, so it would seem that the effect of "knowing the truth" has made it easy for the Tolstoy of 1889 to turn his back on the earlier self who had regarded the attainment of truth as perilously beset with self-deception and complacency, and to see the problematics of truth-telling as trivial compared with the truth itself. One might say that *The Kreutzer Sonata* is not only open to second and third readings, but is carelessly open to them, as though Tolstoy were indifferent to games of reinterpretation that might be played by people with time to waste. Thus

The Kreutzer Sonata seems to mark the repudiation by Tolstoy of a talent whose distinguishing feature was a capacity "to know himself," as Rilke says, "right into his own blood."[11]

Pozdnyshev's life falls into a before and an after, the before being "an abyss of error," the after a time of "everything reversed." His temporal position in the after gives him, in his own eyes, the complete self-knowledge that William C. Spengemann finds characteristic of the "converted narrator," whose knowing, converted, narrating self stands invisibly beside the experiencing, acting self he tells about.[12] On Pozdnyshev's conversion experience the text is silent except to say that awareness comes after "torments" (235). Still, as long as we continue to read *The Kreutzer Sonata* as the utterance of a converted self, rather than as a frame for a schedule of pronouncements ("abstain from prostitutes, abstain from meat, . . ."), we can continue to seek in the text traces of the sense of *truth-bearing* that comes to the converted narrator with the attainment of what he believes to be full understanding of the past.

To confirm that this sense of truth-embodying selfhood—and indeed the process of the conversion experience itself—was of acute interest to Tolstoy, we may turn not only to *Anna Karenina* but also to a document written ten years before *The Kreutzer Sonata*. *A Confession* is, in the main, an analysis of a crisis Tolstoy passed through in 1874, when reason told him that life was meaningless and he came close to suicide, till a force within him that he calls "an instinctive consciousness of life" rejected the conclusions of his reason and saved him.[13]

The language in which Tolstoy sets out this contest of forces is worth examining in detail. Though associated with reasoning, the condition of mind that leads him to "[hide] away a cord, to avoid being tempted to hang myself . . . and [cease] to carry a gun" is described as a passive state, "a strange state of mind-torpor . . . a stoppage, as it were, of life" (29–30, 24). Conversely, the impulse that saves his life is not simply a physical life-force but partakes of the intellect: it is "an inkling that my ideas were wrong," a sense that "I [had] made some mistake"; it is "doubts" (72, 76, 77). And though the impulse is finally named as "an instinctive consciousness of life," it is accompanied by "a tormenting feeling, which I cannot [in retrospect] describe otherwise than as a searching after God" (109). Thus the opposition is not between a clear and overwhelming conviction that life is absurd, and an instinctually based animal drive to live: error, the drive to death, is a gathering sluggishness, like the running down of life itself, while the saving truth springs from an instinctive intellectual power that obscurely mistrusts reason. The second force does not clash with the first and defeat it. Strictly speaking, there is no conflict. Rather, there are two states of mind simultaneously present, the one a death-directed stoppage of life that simply *happens* (*na menya stali naxodit' minuty snačala nedoumeniya, ostanovki žizni:* "it happened that I was seized over and over with moments of puzzlement, stoppages of life"), the other a mistrust, a caution; and, for reasons that reason cannot fathom, the tide reverses, the second slowly begins to supervene, the first begins to dissipate.

One is not wrong to detect a certain philosophical scrupulousness in this account. There is another, conventional kind of language Tolstoy might have slipped into to describe this conversion experience, a language in which the self chooses selfishly to follow the voice of reason but is then saved from error by another voice speaking from the heart. This would be a language of the false self and the true self, the false self being rational and socially conditioned, the true self instinctual and individual. In Tolstoy there is no such simple dualism of false and true selves. Rather, the self is a site where the will goes through its processes in ways only obscurely accessible to introspection. It is not the self, or a self, that reaches out toward God. Rather, the self experiences a reaching-out (*iskaniem Boga*, "a searching after God"). The self does not change (change in the middle voice sense of change-itself); rather, a change takes place in the site of the self: "When and how the change took place in me [*soveršilsya vo mne etot perevorot*] I could not say" (114).

Insofar as it gives an answer to the question of what the condition of truthfulness is like, then, *A Confession* says that it arises out of an attentiveness and responsiveness to an inner impulse that Tolstoy calls an impulse toward God. The condition of truthfulness is not perfect self-knowledge but truth-directedness, what the peasant in *Anna Karenina* calls "living for one's soul," in words that come as a blinding illumination to Levin.[14] In his skepticism about rational self-knowledge, in his conviction that men act in accord with inner forces in ways of which they are not aware, Tolstoy remains in sympathy with Schopenhauer;[15] where he parts company with Schopenhauer is in identifying the impulse toward God as one of these forces.

All of Tolstoy's writing, fictional and nonfictional, is concerned with truth; in the late writings the concern with truth overrides all other concerns. The restless impatience with received truths, the struggles to uncover the grounds for a state of truthfulness in the self that are common to both the Levin sections of *Anna Karenina* and the later autobiographical writings, have left on one reader after another the impression of "perfect sincerity" that Matthew Arnold records.[16] Common to both the autobiographical *Confession* and late stories like "The Death of Ivan Ilyich" is the crisis (a confrontation with his own death) that brings about an illumination in the life of the central character that makes it absurd for him to continue in a self-deceived mode of existence. Thereafter he may or may not live on as a (limited) witness to the truth. The sense of urgency that the crisis brings about, the relentlessness of the process in which the self is stripped of its comforting fictions, the single-mindedness of the quest for truth: all these qualities enter into the term *sincerity*.

One would therefore expect that a fiction in confessional form would provide Tolstoy with a congenial and adequate vehicle for the literature of truth that he wanted to write—that is, a fiction centering on a crisis of illumination, retrospectively narrated by a speaker (now a truth-bearer) about his earlier, (self-)deceived self. But what one finds instead in *The Kreutzer Sonata* is a lack of interest in the potential of the confessional form in favor of another, dogmatic notion of what it means to tell the truth. In consequence there occur two crippling silences in the text. The first is the silence about the conversion experience, an experience in which, as the example of Tolstoy's own *Confession* shows, the inner experience of being a truth-bearer is felt most intensely by contrast with the previous self-deceived mode of existence. Silence about this experience thus entails a failure of dramatization. The second and more serious silence is that of the narrator. Since Pozdnyshev's confession is a narrative monologue characterized by new-found self-certainty, the function of doubling back and scrutinizing the truthfulness of the truth enunciated by Pozdnyshev must, *faute de mieux*, fall to his auditor. His auditor performs no such function, thereby implicitly giving his support to the notion of truth that Tolstoy himself presents in the "Afterword": that truth is what it is, that there are more important things to do than scrutinize the machinations of the will at work in the utterer of truth. This authoritarian position denies, in the name of a higher truth, the relevance of interrogating the interest of the confessant in telling the truth his way: whatever the will behind the confession might be (ultimately, thought Countess Tolstoy, a will in Tolstoy to get at her), the truth transcends the will behind it. The truth also transcends the suspicion that "the truth transcends the will behind it" might be willed, self-serving. In other words, the position taken up in *The Kreutzer Sonata*, both in the framework of interpretation with which Tolstoy surrounds it and in its own lack of armament against other, unauthorized readings, other truths—a lack of armament that one must finally read as contemptuous, disregarding—is one of short-circuiting self-doubt and self-scrutiny in the name of an autonomous truth.

Because the basic movement of self-reflexiveness is a doubting and questioning movement, it is in the nature of the truth told to itself by the reflecting self not to be final. This lack of finality is naturally experienced with particular anguish in a writer as truth-directed as Tolstoy. The endless knot of self-awareness becomes a Gordian knot. But if it cannot be loosened, there is more than one way of cutting it. "Man cuts the Gordian knot of his life, and kills himself simply for the sake of escaping from the torturing inward contradictions produced by intelligent consciousness, which has been carried to the last degree of tension in our day," Tolstoy wrote in 1887.[17] Alternatively, man can cut the knot by announcing the end of doubt in the name of the revealed truth. But this maneuver, followed by Tolstoy in *The Kreutzer Sonata*, raises its own problem. For whatever authority a confession bears in a secular context derives from the status of the confessant as a hero of the labyrinth willing to confront the worst within himself (Rousseau claims to be such a hero). A confessant who does not doubt himself when there are obvious grounds for doing so (as in

Pozdnyshev's case) is no better than one who refuses to doubt because doubt is not profitable. Neither is a hero, neither confesses with authority.

Rousseau

The impact on Tolstoy of reading Rousseau for the first time is well known. For a while, as a youth, he wore around his neck a medallion with Rousseau's picture. "There would be a certain justice," writes V. V. Zenkovsky, "in expounding all of Tolstoy's views as variations on his Rousseauism—so deeply did this Rousseauism influence him to the end of his life."[18] Rousseau's *Confessions* first impressed Tolstoy for "the contempt for human lies, and the love of truth" they revealed, though in later life he delivered to Maxim Gorky his verdict that "Rousseau lied and believed his lies."[19] The terrain of truth, self-knowledge, and sincerity where Tolstoy spent so much of his writing life was mapped out by Rousseau, and it is only here and there that Tolstoy goes further than Rousseau in exploring it.

The *Confessions* begin: "I am commencing an undertaking . . . without precedent . . . I desire to set before my fellows the likeness of a man in all the truth of nature, and that man myself." Rousseau goes on to imagine himself appearing before God, book in hand, saying: "I have shown myself as I was: mean and contemptible, good, high-minded and sublime . . . I have unveiled my inmost self."[20] The task Rousseau sets himself is therefore one of total self-revelation. Yet one might at once ask how any other reader of the book of Rousseau's life save all-knowing God can know that he has truly told the truth.

Rousseau's first defense is that he passes the test Montaigne fails: whereas Montaigne "pretends to confess his defects" but confesses only "amiable" defects (Book X; II, 160), he, Rousseau, is prepared to confess to defects that bring shame upon him, like the sensual pleasure he takes in being beaten by a woman (Book I; I, 13). This defense does not, of course, answer the charge that he may believe he is telling the truth, yet be self-deceived. Here his response is that his method in the *Confessions* is to detail "everything that has happened to me, all my acts, thoughts and feelings" without any structure of interpretation: "it is [the reader's] business to collect these scattered elements and to determine the being which is composed of them; the result must be his work" (Book IV; I, 159). And if this response seems evasive (if it does not answer the charge of selective recollection, for instance), Rousseau's position is as follows:

> I may omit or transpose facts, I may make mistakes in dates, but I cannot be deceived in what I have felt or what my feelings have prompted me to do . . . The real object of my Confessions is, to contribute to an accurate knowledge of my inner being in all the different situations of my life. What I have promised to relate is the history of my soul; I need no other memoirs to write it faithfully; it is sufficient for me to enter again into my inner self. (Book VII; I, 252)

Rousseau's position is thus that self-deception with respect to present recollection is impossible, since the self is transparent to itself. Present self-knowledge is a *donnée*.

How does this position work out in practice? Here let us turn to the oft-discussed story of the theft of a ribbon told not only in Book II of the *Confessions* but also in the fourth of the *Rêveries*. While employed as a manservant, Rousseau steals a strip of ribbon. The ribbon is found in his possession. Rousseau claims that the maidservant Marion gave the ribbon to him, and repeats the charge to her face. Both Rousseau and Marion are dismissed. Rousseau comments: "It is not likely that she afterwards found it easy to get a good situation"; he wonders darkly whether she might not have done away with herself (Book II; I, 75–76).

Though remorse has weighed on him for forty years, Rousseau writes in 1766, he has never confessed his guilt till now. The act was "atrocious," and the spectacle of poor falsely accused Marion would have changed any but a "barbarous heart." Nevertheless, the purpose of the *Confessions* would not be served if he did not also try to present the inner truth of the story. The inner truth is that "I accused her of having done what I meant to do," that is, he accused Marion of having given him the ribbon because it was his "intention" that he should give Marion the ribbon. As for his failure to retract his lie when confronted with Marion, this was the result of an "unconquerable fear of shame." "I was little more than a child": the situation was more than he could handle (Book II; I, 75–77).

Paul de Man distinguishes two strains in this story: an element of *confession* whose purpose it is to reveal a verifiable truth, and an element of *excuse* whose purpose it is to convince the reader that things are and were as Rousseau sees them.[21] Though de Man errs in asserting that the truth one confesses must in principle be verifiable (one can confess impure thoughts, for example), his distinction between confession proper and excuse does allow us to see why confessions of the kind we encounter in Rousseau raise problems of certainty not raised by confessions of fact. The act of theft was bad, says Rousseau, but there was an intention behind it that was good, and therefore the act was not entirely blameworthy. Similarly, the act of blaming Marion was bad, but it was caused by fear and was therefore to some extent excusable. Rousseau's self-examination ceases at this point. But the process of qualification he has initiated can be continued further. How can he know that that part of himself which recalls the good intention behind the bad act is not constructing the intention *post facto* to exculpate him? Yet on the other hand (we may imagine the autobiographer continuing), we must be careful to give the good in us as much credit as the bad: what is it in me that might wish to minimize good intentions by labeling them *post-facto* rationalizations?[22] Yet is a question like the last one not precisely the kind of question I would be asking if I were trying to shield myself from the knowledge of the worst in myself? And yet . . .

To get to the "real" truth of the ribbon story, de Man moves past a balancing of the claims of good intentions against those of bad acts to a scrutiny of the language of confession. "The obvious satisfaction in the tone and the eloquence of the passage . . . the easy flow of hyperboles . . . the obvious delight with which the desire to hide is being revealed"—these features of tone all indicate that "what Rousseau *really* wanted is neither the ribbon nor Marion, but the public scene of exposure which he actually gets." Both the theft and the belated breast-beating thus conceal Rousseau's "real" desire to exhibit himself. And if self-exhibition is the real motive, then the more crime there is, the more concealment, the more delay over revelation, the better. The "truly shameful" desire that Rousseau is too ashamed to confess is the desire to expose himself, a desire to which Marion is sacrificed. And, de Man points out, this process of shame and exposure, like the process of confession and qualification, entails a regression to infinity: "each new stage in the unveiling suggests a deeper shame, a greater impossibility to reveal, and a greater satisfaction in outwitting this impossibility."[23]

It is perhaps naive of de Man to write of "what Rousseau really wanted" as if that were historically knowable. It may also seem incautious to base interpretation on an analysis of features of style. However, in the latter respect de Man has the authority not only of Rousseau but of Romantic poetics behind him. From an early merely anticlassical position that finds in sincerity, understood as a truthful relation of the writer to himself, a substitute for an apprenticeship to the classics,[24] Romanticism moves rapidly to the formula of Keats that reverses the entailments: not only does truth entail beauty; beauty entails truth, too. From here it is not far to the position that poetry creates its own, autonomous standards of truth.[25]

The notion that the artist creates his own truth takes a particularly radical form in the *Confessions*, since Rousseau is working in a medium—autobiography—with closer ties to history, and to referential criteria of truth, than to poetry. We can conveniently trace the stages by which Rousseau feels his way towards this position if we follow the theme of exhibitionism in the *Confessions*.

In Book III Rousseau describes a series of sexually exhibitionistic acts he performed as a youth. The description of these acts is itself, of course, a kind of exhibitionism. What motive do these two forms of self-revelation have in common? Jean Starobinski suggests an answer: both represent a recourse to the "magic power" of "immediate seduction": the subject reaches out to others without leaving himself; he shows what he is like while remaining himself and remaining within himself.[26]

Rousseau's self-revelations in fact always have in view the goal of winning love and acceptance. Self-revelation offers the truth of the self, a truth that others might be persuaded to see. Thus, in the words of Starobinski, whose analysis of Rousseau's exhibitionism I follow, "the *Confessions* are on the most important account an attempt to rectify the error of others and not an investigation of a *temps perdu*. Rousseau's interest . . . begins with the question: Why does this inner feeling . . . not find its echo in the according of immediate recognition?" For this persuasive intent to be carried out, a language *(écriture)* must be invented to render the unique savor of personal experience, a language "supple enough and varied enough to tell the diversity, the contradictions, the slight details, the minuscule nuances, the interlocking of tiny perceptions whose tissue constitutes the unique existence of Jean-Jacques."[27] Rousseau's own comment on this stylistic project is as follows:

> I will write what comes to me, I will change [my style] according to my humor without scruple, I will express everything I feel as I feel it, as I see it, without affectation, without constraint, without being upset by the resulting medley. Yielding myself simultaneously to the memory of the impression I received [in the past] and to present feeling, I will give a twofold depiction of [*je peindrai doublement*] the state of my soul.[28]

The immediacy of the language Rousseau projects is intended as a guarantee of the truth of the past it recounts. It is no longer a language that dominates its subject as the language of the historian does. Instead, it is a naive language that reveals the confessant in the moment of confession in the same instant that it reveals the past he confesses—a past necessarily become uncertain. In Starobinski's formulation, we are moving from the domain of truthfulness, where confession is still subject to historical verification, to the domain of authenticity. Authenticity does not demand that language reproduce a reality; instead it demands that language manifest its "own" truth. The distance between the writing self and the source of the feelings it writes about is abolished—this abolition being what distinguishes authenticity from sincerity—for the source is always here and now. "Everything takes place, in effect, in a present so pure that the past itself is relived as present feeling."[29] The first prerequisite is thus to *be oneself*. One is in danger of not being oneself when one lives at a reflective distance from oneself (a revealing reversal of values for autobiography).

Language itself therefore becomes for Rousseau the being of the authentic self, and appeal to an exterior "truth" is closed off. Furthermore, the only kind of reader who can judge between truth and falsity in Rousseau while accepting—even if only provisionally—the premises of his confessional project, must be one like de Man, who tries to detect inauthentic moments in Rousseau via inauthentic moments in his language. De Man's analysis of the ribbon episode depends on the premise that confession betrays inauthenticity when the confessant lapses into the language of the Other. Thus, though de Man accuses Rousseau of (self-)deception on the basis of the "satisfaction" he detects in his tone, a "delight" in his own revelations, the satisfaction and delight are themselves detected in "eloquence" and "an easy flow of hyperbole," that is, in features of language that do not belong to Rousseau. Rousseau is not speaking (for) himself; someone else is speaking through him.[30]

Without contesting this identification of authenticity with truth, we may seem to have as little hope of giving the *Confessions* a second reading as we have of giving *The Kreutzer Sonata* a second reading without contesting Tolstoy's authoritarian truth. De Man is able to give a second reading of the ribbon episode only by detecting and exploring a fissure in the text, a lapse of authenticity. As long as his language remains his own, Rousseau would seem to remain sole author of his own truth.

To show that there is an alternative road to a second reading of Rousseau's text, via moments of inconsistency rather than via moments of false style, I should like to take up a passage in which Rousseau discusses his attitude toward money (Book I; I, 30–32). Here Rousseau presents himself as "a man of very strong passions," who under the sway of feeling is capable of being "impetuous, violent, fearless." But such fits are usually brief. He soon lapses into "indolence, timidity," overpowered by "fear and shame," embarrassed by the looks of others to such an extent that he would like to hide. Not only are his desires limited by his indolence and timidity: the range of his tastes is also limited. "None of my prevailing tastes center on things that can be bought," he writes. "Money poisons all." "Women who could be bought for money would lose for me all their charms; I even doubt whether it would be in me to make use of them." "I find it the same with all pleasures within my reach; unless they cost me nothing, I find them insipid."

Why should money poison desire? The explanation Rousseau

offers is that *for him the exchange is always an unfair one.* "I should like something which is good in quality; with my money I am sure to get it bad [*je suis sûr de l'avoir mauvaise*]. If I pay a high price for a fresh egg, it is stale; for a nice piece of fruit, it is unripe; for a girl, she is spoilt."

This first explanation, which blames the egg or the fruit or the girl, is not supported by the facts (the only girl he ever buys is not "spoilt"; rather, Rousseau is impotent).[31] The phrase "I am sure to get it bad" is more revealing: in comparison with what he wants, what he *buys* (not what he *gets*) is sure to be bad/unripe/spoilt. "Unless [pleasures] cost me nothing, they are insipid." The prophecy that what I buy is sure to be bad is self-fulfilling.

Rousseau now gives examples of how he experiences the transaction of buying. He goes to the pastrycook's and notices women laughing among themselves at "the little glutton." He goes to the fruiterer's but sees passersby whom his shortsightedness turns into "acquaintances." "Everywhere I am intimidated, restrained by some obstacle; my desire increases with my shame, and at last I return home like a fool, consumed with longing, having in my pocket the means of satisfying it, and yet not having the courage to buy anything."

What is it that the eyes around him threaten to know and laugh at when he walks into a shop? Is it what he wants (to buy)? Is it the act of asking? Is it the act of proffering money? Instead of pursuing an answer, Rousseau makes a typically veering and retracting motion. As the reader follows the story of his life, he says, and gets to know his "real temperament, he will understand all this, without my taking the trouble to tell him." To the entire syndrome he gives the label of an "apparent inconsistency [*contradiction*]," namely "the union of an almost sordid avarice with the greatest contempt for money." For avarice the excuse is that "I keep [money] for a long time without spending it, for want of knowing how to make use of it in a way to please myself [*faute de savoir l'employer à ma fantaisie*]"; and he at once goes on to distinguish between the *possession* of money (where money becomes "an instrument of freedom") and the *pursuit* of money (where it is "an instrument of slavery"), a distinction that neatly nullifies the vice of avarice he admitted to a moment ago.

Why is it that he has no desire for money? His answer is that money cannot be enjoyed in itself, whereas "between the thing itself and the enjoyment of it there is [no intermediary]. If I see the thing, it tempts me; if I see only the means of possessing it, it does not. For this reason [*donc*] I have committed thefts, and even now I sometimes pilfer trifles which tempt me, and which I prefer to take rather than ask for."

The logic of this passage is worth scrutinizing. As Starobinski reads it, Rousseau is giving an example of how "money poisons all."[32] But if we paraphrase Rousseau's logic accurately, it reads as follows: "I desire the thing but not the means that leads to it; therefore, I steal the thing but not the means," not: "I desire the thing but not the means, therefore I take (steal) the thing so as not to use the means." To the question "Why steal at all?" this passage gives no better explanation than: "I prefer to take rather than ask for." Nor does Rousseau push the exploration of his attitudes toward money any further, though he returns to the topic several times in the *Confessions*.[33]

Since Rousseau makes no headway in explaining his "apparent inconsistency," and since the illumination he promises the reader does not, at least for some readers, ever arrive, let me try to give my own explanation of the complex of behavior he describes. Attending less to his reflections than to the shop scenes he describes, we note that what offends Rousseau is the openness and legitimacy of monetary transactions. By going into the shop and saying "I want a cake" and proffering money, he is acquiescing in a mode of treating his own "I want" that effectively "poisons" it. It is brought into the public, equalized with the "I want" of every Tom, Dick, and Harry who enters the shop; it loses its uniqueness: it becomes known (by all the knowing eyes) in the same moment at which he loses control of the terms on which he wants it known; it becomes *spent* on a public scale of sous and francs. To Rousseau, his own desires are *resources* as long as they remain unique, hidden—in other words, as long as they are potentially confessable. Brought into the public eye, they are revealed to be merely desires like everyone else's. The system of exchange that agitates Rousseau, the system he will not participate in, is thus one in which his desire for an apple is exchanged for an apple, via the public medium of money; for every time such an exchange takes place the desire loses its value. *Shamefulness* and *value* are thus interchangeable terms. For—in the economy of confession—the only unique appetites, the only appetites that constitute confessable currency, are shameful appetites. A shameful desire is a valuable desire. Conversely, for a desire to have a value it must have a secret, shameful component. Confession consists in a double movement of offering to spend "inconsistencies" and holding back enough to maintain the "freedom" that comes of having capital. This process of half-revealing and then withdrawing into mystery, a process intended to *fascinate*, is neatly exemplified in the passage as a whole.

If *buying* is unacceptable because it places desire on a public scale (such being the nature of money), *stealing*, though it, too, reveals the equivalent of the desire in the object stolen, has its compensations in replacing the revealed, and no longer shameful, desire with a crime—itself confessable currency; and bringing into being the mystery of why he steals when he can afford to buy, the very mystery that he introduces and then withdraws from solving.

I do not wish to advance the reading I have given as *the* truth that Rousseau ought to have told about money, but did not or could not, just as I do not wish to advance the reading I have given of Tolstoy's Pozdnyshev as *the* truth that Pozdnyshev failed to see about himself. Indeed, one of the minor functions of these rereadings is to bring the notion of *the* truth into question.

On the other hand, there seems to me a narrower yet more productive direction to follow at this point than the Derridean line of arguing that the idea of truth belongs to a certain epoch, the "epoch of supplementarity," that the idea enables a practice of writing by functioning as a kind of "blind spot" toward which writing moves by an endless series of "supplements" that continually defer truth.[34] The readings that Rousseau and Pozdnyshev have given themselves, and the rereadings I have given them, insofar as these rereadings have justified themselves in the name of the truth, are certainly Derridean supplements; and the deconstruction of the practices I have followed in rereading Rousseau and Pozdnyshev could certainly lead to a "better," "fuller" pair of new readings; and so on to infinity. But the point Derrida makes is relevant to all truth-oriented writing; whereas the point I wish to argue is that the possibility of reading the truth "behind" a true confession has implications peculiar to the genre of confession.

Returning to *The Kreutzer Sonata* and Rousseau's *Confessions*, we may note that we have passed through a similar progression in each case. A crime is confessed (murder, theft); a cause or reason or psychological origin is proposed to explain the crime; then a rereading of the confession yields a "truer" explanation. The question we should ask now is: What must the response of the confessant be towards these or any other "truer" corrections of his confession? The answer, it seems to me, is that to the extent that the new, "deeper" truth is acknowledged as true, the response of the confessant must contain an element of shame. For either the confessant was aware of the deeper truth but was concealing it, in which case he was deceiving his confessor; or he was not aware of the deeper truth (though now he acknowledges it), in which case his competence as a confessant is in question: what was being offered as his secret, the coin of his confession, was not the real secret, was false coin, and a de facto deception has occurred, which is fresh cause for confession.[35]

I have considered thus far the hypothetical case of a Pozdnyshev or a Rousseau who, confronted with a reading of his confession that yields a "deeper" truth than the one he has acknowledged, acknowledges the new truth and shifts his ground. In such a case, we might ask, where will the confessant *stand* his ground? For, in principle, if we have given one rereading of his story we can give a second. If the confessant is *in principle* prepared to shift his ground with each new reading as long as he can be convinced that it is "truer" than the last one, then he is no more than a biographer of the self, a constructor of hypotheses about himself that can be improved on by other biographers. In such an event, his confession has no more authority than an account given by any other biographer: it may proceed from knowledge, but it does not proceed from self-knowledge.

Whether the confessant yields to the new truth about himself depends on the nature of his commitment to his original confession. The more deeply he has avowed the truth of this confession, the more deeply its truth has become part of his personal identity. Yielding subsequently to the new truth entails damage to that identity. In the case of a Pozdnyshev or a Rousseau the damage is particularly acute, since part of the being of each is that he has become a confessant, a truth-teller.

Alternatively, the confessant may refuse to yield to the new truth, thereby adopting precisely the stand of the self-deceived subject who prefers not to avow the "real" truth of himself to himself, and prefers not to avow this preference, and so on to infinity.[36] In this case, how can he tell the difference between himself and the self-deceived confessant, the confessant whose truth is a lie, since both "believe" they know the truth?

A third alternative is to confess with an "open mind," acknowledging from the beginning that what he avows as the truth may not be the truth. But there is something literally shameless in this posture. For if one proceeds in the awareness that the transgressions one is "truly" guilty of may be heavier than those one accuses oneself of, one proceeds equally in an awareness that the transgressions one is "truly" guilty of may be lighter than those one accuses oneself of (Rousseau is explicit about the latter kind of awareness in his own case: see note 22). To be aware of oneself in this posture—which follows inevitably from having an open mind on the question of one's own truthfulness—is already matter for confession; to be aware that the posture is not a guilty one (because it is inevitable) is a matter for further shame and confession; and so on to infinity.

What I have written thus far indicates that the project of confession when the subject is at a heightened level of self-awareness and open to self-doubt raises intricate and, on the face of it, intractable problems regarding truthfulness, problems whose common factor seems to be a regression to infinity of self-awareness and self-doubt. It is by no means clear that these problems are visible to the Rousseau of the *Confessions* or the Tolstoy of *The Kreutzer Sonata*. But to trust that evidence of such an awareness must necessarily surface in the text, when it is precisely not in the interest of either writer to bear such awareness, would be incautious. All we can say at this stage is that the problems are not articulated. For the time being we are in the position of Hume, who, confronted with an interlocutor who claims unmediated knowledge of himself (and therefore—though this is not in Hume—knowledge of his own truth), has no recourse but to break off the discussion for lack of common ground.[37]

Dostoevsky

Confessions are everywhere in Dostoevsky. In simpler cases Dostoevsky uses confession as a way of allowing a character to expose himself, tell his own truth. The confession of Prince Valkovsky in *The Insulted and Injured* (1861), for example, is little more than an expository means of this kind.[38] Even in this early novel, however, an element of gratuitousness creeps into the confession: the freedom of revelation is not strictly necessitated by demands of plotting or motivation; its frankness is not strictly in character. In the later novels the level of gratuitousness mounts to the extent that one can no longer think of confession as a mere expository device: confession itself, with all its attendant psychological, moral, epistemological, and finally metaphysical problems, moves to the center of the stage. Though in other critical contexts it may be fruitful to treat confession in the major novels as, on the one hand, a form of masochism or a vice that Dostoevsky finds typical of the age,[39] or on the other as one of the generic forms yoked together to make up the Dostoevskian novel,[40] I propose here to single out three of the major confession episodes, in *Notes from Underground*, *The Idiot*, and *The Possessed*, and ask how the problem of *ending* is solved when the tendency of self-consciousness is to draw out confession endlessly.

Notes from Underground (1864) falls into two parts, the first a dissertation on self-consciousness, the second a story from the narrator's past. Though both parts can be thought of as confessions, they are confessions of different kinds, the first being a revelation of personality, the second the revelation of a shameful history. In the first and more theoretical part, however, self-revelation is subsumed under a wider discussion of whether it is possible to tell the truth about oneself in an age of self-consciousness or "hyperconsciousness," the disease of what the unnamed narrator calls "our unfortunate nineteenth century" and of St. Petersburg, "the most abstract and intentional city in the whole world." The "laws of hyperconsciousness," which dictate an endless awareness of awareness, make the hyperconscious man the antithesis of the normal man. Feeling no basis in certainty, he cannot make decisions and act. He cannot even act upon his own self-consciousness to freeze it in some position or other, for it obeys its own laws. Nor can he regard himself as a responsible agent, since accepting responsibility for oneself is a final position. (This is not, of course, to say that he blames himself for nothing: on the contrary, he blames himself for everything. But he does so in a reflex motion originating in the laws of self-consciousness.)[41]

So much for theory. But before embarking on his own shameful reminiscences, the narrator-hero invokes the precedent of Rousseau.

> I want to try the experiment whether one can be perfectly frank
> . . . Heine maintains that a true autobiography is almost an
> impossibility, and that man is bound to lie about himself. He
> considers that Rousseau almost certainly told lies about himself
> in his confessions, and even intentionally lied, out of vanity. I am
> convinced that Heine is right.   (35)

In his own case, on the other hand, he will have no readers and therefore, he asserts, will have no temptation to lie.

The project of *not lying* is put to the test most severely in the story of his relations with the young prostitute Liza. After a night of "vice . . . without love," he recounts, he wakes up in her bed to find her staring intently at him. Feeling uncomfortable, he begins to talk without forethought, urging her to reform and offering to help her. Why is he doing this? he later asks himself. He explains it as "sport," the sport of "turning her soul upside down and breaking her heart." However, he has an inkling that what attracts him is "not merely the sport" (82, 91).

The next day the "loathsome truth" dawns on him that he has been sentimental. His reaction is to begin to hate Liza; nevertheless, he cannot forget the "pitiful, distorted, inappropriate smile" she wore as she gazed at him. "Something was rising up, rising up continually in my soul, painfully, refusing to be appeased" (94, 97, 96).

A short while later Liza visits him to take him up on his promise. With a feeling of "horrible spite" he embarks on a cruel confession. All the time he was mouthing fine sentiments, he says, he was inwardly laughing at her. For, having been humiliated by his friends, he had turned on her as an object to humiliate in turn. All he had wanted was "sport." Now she can "go to hell." Surely she realizes that he will never forgive her for coming to his apartment and seeing the wretched conditions in which he lives? He is bound to make her suffer, since he is "the nastiest, stupidest, pettiest, absurdest and most envious of all worms on earth"; and for eliciting this abject confession, for hearing him speak "as a man speaks . . . once in a lifetime," she must be punished even more; and so forth (106–108).

At first Liza is taken aback by his "cynicism"; then, surprisingly, she embraces him, as if it has dawned on her that he too is unhappy. He is overwhelmed. "They won't let me—I can't be— good!" he sobs in her arms. Almost at once, however, he begins to feel ashamed to be in a "crushed and humiliated" position (107, 109). In his heart flares up

a feeling of mastery and possession. My eyes gleamed with pas- sion, and I gripped her hands tightly. How I hated her and how I was drawn to her at that minute! The one feeling intensified the other. It was almost like an act of vengeance! At first there was a look of amazement, even of terror on her face, but only for one instant. She warmly and rapturously embraced me.   (110)

In the "fever of oscillations" typical of hyperconsciousness (11), his next moves are almost predictable. (1) He presses money into Liza's hand to indicate that she remains a whore to him; then, when she leaves, (2) he rushes after her "in shame and despair," reflecting, however, (3) that the real cause of his shame is the "bookishness" of this gesture. He gives up the chase, persuading himself (4) that a feeling of outrage will "elevate and purify" the girl. He feels pleased with this formulation and (5) despises himself for being pleased (112–113).

At this point the story of Liza comes to an end: "I don't want to write more from 'underground,'" the narrator says. However, his text is followed by an "authorial" note: "The 'notes' of this para- doxicalist do not end here . . . He could not resist and continued them. But it also seems that we may stop here" (115).

The summary I have given of the "Liza" confession is not a disinterested one. I have emphasized those moments at which something comes up out of the narrator's depths that he does not understand even in the retrospect of fifteen years. Part I has pre- pared us for a confession in which no motive will be hidden from the light of hyperconsciousness, in which Rousseau will be exceeded in frankness. Those moments at which the narrator does not understand himself therefore have a peculiar status: either they were not understood fifteen years ago when he was actor in his story, and now are recorded without interrogation by him in the role of confessant; or they are now given a retrospective explanation, but an explanation odd not so much for being false as for being final, that is, for not being subjected to the endless regression of self-consciousness (I shall give an example below).

Specifically, we might want to question the "Liza" confession at the following points.

1. If it is "sport" to humiliate Liza, what motivates the narrator that is "not merely the sport"?

2. "Something was not dead within me, in the depths of my heart and conscience it would not die . . . Something was rising up, rising up continually in my soul, painfully, and refusing to be appeased. I returned home completely upset; it was just as though some crime were lying on my conscience" (96). What is the name of the "something," and what is the nature of the crime?

3. "They won't let me—I can't be—good!" he sobs, uttering words that seem to come from a stranger within him. What does the utterance mean? One reading is that he is continuing his "sport" with Liza, pretending to be tormented and unhappy. Another is that the voice from within is the repressed voice of a better self which "they" won't allow to emerge.

4. In Liza's embrace he passes through a rapid series of states of feeling remarkable for their ambivalence. Though cryptically expressed, these include: triumph that he has got his aggressive confession off his chest without incurring a rebuff, a desire to set his seal on this victory by sexually possessing the girl, and an abiding will to humiliate her even further. There is no doubt that he and she have the makings of the sadomasochistic couple so common in Dostoevsky. But the account I have just given rests only on the report he gives of his own inner state and of what he reads on Liza's face; and what she reads in his face (he in turn reads from her face) awakes in her first amazement and terror but then rapturous response. Is she misreading him, seeing "true" love where she should read sadistic desire?

In a sense, yes: the burden of his ridicule of her is that she is a bad reader who has misread him from the beginning as being sincere when he is not. But one must remember that as a writer of his own story he is in a privileged position to dictate readings. His "Notes" dictate a reading in which Liza is duped in the brothel as well as in his apartment. Not only is he the writer of his story; he also plays the leader in the two dialogues he has with Liza, asking her questions, telling her who and what she is. Only one judgment of hers on him gets reported: "You speak exactly like a book" (86). For the rest, her reading of him is memorialized in his "Notes" only in the two looks: the "wide-open eyes scrutinizing me curiously and persistently" to which he wakes up in her room (77), and the look in his apartment that reads passion in his face. Not much material from which to infer her reading of him. Yet we have a fair idea of what her wide-open eyes see: a man who has paid his money and spent two hours in her bed having sex with her "without love, grossly and shamelessly" (77). Her comment that he speaks like a book is accurate too. Can we be convinced, then, that she misreads him when he says he wants her to escape prostitution, and again when he says he feels passion—or perhaps even need—for her? The possibility seems open that Liza has a knowledge of, or at least an insight into, the narrator that he, as teller of his own story, cannot afford to acknowledge: and that from this point of vantage (point of advantage) the three moments of perception he allows to Liza are flaws in the texture of his story.

It would be naive to propose a reading of the story—filled out from Liza's three moments and from the moments at which a voice speaks unbidden from within him—in which the hero emerges as "in truth" an unhappy, self-tormented young man longing for a woman's love yet afraid to expose his longings. There is an irony at the heart of *Notes from Underground*, but the irony is not that its hero is not as bad as he says he is. The real irony is that, while he promises a confession that will outdo Rousseau in truthfulness, a confession he believes himself fitted to make because he is afflicted with hyperconsciousness to the ultimate degree, his confession reveals nothing so much as the helplessness of confession before the desire of the self to construct its own truth.

It is worth going back to Part I of the *Notes* to see what the hero has to say about desire. The enlightened 1860s view, he says, is that desire obeys a law, the law that man desires in accord with his own advantage.[42] But the truth is that every now and again man will desire what is injurious to himself precisely "in order to have the right to desire for himself" without being bound by any law. And he desires that freedom from determination in order to assert "what is most precious and most important—that is, our personality, our individuality" (26). The primal desire is therefore the desire for a freedom that the hero indentifies with unique individuality.

The question one might immediately ask is: How does the subject know that the choices he makes, even "perverse" choices that bring him no advantage, are truly undetermined? How does he know he is not the slave of a pattern of perverse choices (a pathological pattern, perhaps) whose design is visible to everyone but him? Self-consciousness will not give him the answer, for self-consciousness in *Notes from Underground* is a disease. What is diseased about it is that it feeds upon itself, finding behind every motive another motive, behind every mask another mask, until the ultimate motive, which must remain masked (otherwise the endless regression would be ended, the disease would be cured). We can call this ultimate motive the *motive for unmasking* itself. What the underground man cannot know in his self-interrogation, therefore, is why he wants to tell the truth about himself; and the possibility exists that the truth he tells about himself (the perverse truth, the truth as a story of perverse "free" choices he has made) might itself be a perverse truth, a perverse choice made in accord with a design invisible to him though perhaps visible to others.

We are now beyond all questions of sincerity. The possibility we face is of a confession made via a process of relentless self-unmasking which might yet be not the truth but a self-serving fiction, because the unexamined, unexaminable principle behind it may be not a desire for the truth but a desire to *be a particular way*. The more coherent such a hypothetical fiction of the self might be, the less the reader's chance of knowing whether it is a true confession. We can test its truth only when it contradicts itself or comes into conflict with some "outer," verifiable truth, both of which eventualities a careful confessing narrator can in theory avoid. We would have no grounds for doubting the truth of the underground man's confession, and specifically of his thesis that his ultimate quality is consciousness, if there were not imperfections in the surface the confession presents, moments, for example, when the body under stress emits words like "I can't be good," signs of an unexamined underlying struggle.

It would not be surprising, if the narrator's confession *were* a lying, self-serving fiction, that the repressed truth should break through its surface, particularly at moments of stress, in the forms of stirrings of the heart, intimations of the unacknowledged, utterances of the inner self, or that the truth should soon be repressed again. What is disappointing about *Notes from Underground*, if we think of it as an exploration of confession and truth, is that it should rely for its *own* truth not only upon the return of the repressed at the level of the acting subject (the hero of the story of Liza) but also upon a lack of *subsequent* censorship at the level of the narrating subject (the hero telling the story of himself fifteen years later). It is as though the one process that is not subjected to the scrutiny of self-awareness is the narrative process itself. By presenting the story of his relations with Liza as, in snatches, the story of two autonomous selves (Liza being allowed her own say, her own looks), by reporting the voice from underground that spoke within him fifteen years ago, the narrator makes it easy enough to read another truth, a "better" truth, than the one he is telling. Is the naïveté that allows the voice of the "other" truth to go uncensored evidence of a secret, devious appeal to the reader that the narrator does not acknowledge? Certainly he presents the question of whether his story is a "public" or a "private" confession in an ambivalent way: it becomes, in effect, a pseudo-public but "really" private document.[43] But the *Notes* end indeterminately. The paradoxes of self-consciousness could indeed go on forever, as the authorial coda says in excuse. Nevertheless, the questions I have raised remain not only unanswered (it is not in their nature to be answered) but unexplored. Dostoevsky in *Notes from Underground* has not found a solution to the problem of *how to end the story*, the problem whose solution Michael Holquist rightly identifies as the great achievement of his mature years.[44]

The Idiot (1868–69) is in several ways a book about last things. One thinks of the references to the Book of Revelation and the Holbein painting of the dead Christ, of Ippolit Terentyev's confrontation with his own imminent death, and of the many stories of the last moments of condemned men. The pervading sense that there is a limit to time affects attitudes toward confession too: there is much casting around after an adequate confessor, and impatience with confessions that are not serious.

The major confessional episodes in *The Idiot* are the game of truth-telling at Nastasya Filippovna's, and Ippolit's "Explanation." There is, however, an episode I wish to take up first that succinctly expresses some of the philosophical problems of confession.

Keller, "overflowing with confidence and confessions," comes to Prince Myshkin with shameful stories about himself, claiming to be deeply sorry yet recounting his actions as though proud of them. The Prince commends him for being "so extraordinarily truthful" but asks what might be the motive behind his confession: does he want to borrow money? Yes, confesses Keller, "I prepared my confession . . . so as to pave the way . . . and, having softened you up, make you fork out one hundred and fifty roubles. Don't you think that was mean?"[45]

We recognize that we are at the beginning of a potentially infinite regression of self-recognition and self-abasement in which the self-satisfied candor of each level of confession of impure motive becomes a new source of shame and each twinge of shame a new source of self-congratulation. The pattern is familiar from *Notes from Underground* and is familiar to the people of *The Idiot*, who readily spot the worm of vanity in the self-abasement of others, and barely react with indignation when it is pointed out in themselves. At the kernel of the pattern lies what Myshkin calls a *dvoinaya mysl'*, literally a "double thought," but what is perhaps better imagined as a doubling back of thought, the characteristic movement of self-consciousness (346). It is a double thought in Keller to want sincerely to confess to Myshkin for the sake of "spiritual development" while at the same time wanting to borrow money; it is the doubling back of thought that undermines the integrity of the will to confess by detecting behind it a will to deceive, and behind the detection of this second motive a third motive (a wish to be admired for one's candor), and so on.

Myshkin thus identifies in "double thought" the malaise that renders confession powerless to tell the truth and come to an end. In fact, Myshkin does more than diagnose the malaise. "Everyone is like that," he says: he, too, has experienced double thought. But the recognition that double thinking is universal is itself a double thought, as Myshkin at once recognizes: "I couldn't help thinking ... that everyone is like that, *so that* [*tak čto*] I even began patting myself on the back" (my italics). The very movement of recognition thus entraps him in the syndrome.

This point is worth stressing. Both Keller and Lebedev (who makes a confession to Myshkin a page or two later) directly address the question of why they choose the Prince to confess to. Questions of the spirit in which confession is made and of the adequacy of the confessor can no longer be ignored after the party game of confessions (173–187), where, after a round of confessing the worst actions of their lives, the partygoers are left feeling ashamed and unsatisfied, and Totsky's cynical comment that confession is only "a special form of bragging" seems to be vindicated (173). Keller and Lebedev give identical explanations for their choice of Myshkin as confessor: he will judge them "in a human way" (*po-čelovečeski*, "like a man"). Further, being not wholly a man but an idiot, "simple-minded" (as Keller explicitly calls him [345]), a mouse *(mys)*, he is not engaged in the all-too-human game of using the truth for his own ends. He is a being neither godlike in severity (though Aglaya Yepanchin expresses her misgiving that in his devotion to the truth he may judge without "tenderness" [465]) nor manlike in subjecting truth to desire. In choosing Myshkin to confess to, Keller and Lebedev are therefore seeking—though obscurely and for impure, "double" motives—forgiveness rather than judgment, Christ rather than God.

We may set in contrast against this ideal confessor-figure the party guests who find themselves acting as confessors to Ippolit Terentyev's "Explanation." Even before Ippolit has begun reading out his confession, some of his auditors have formed their own ideas about what his act of public confession, as such, might imply. Myshkin sees it as a device Ippolit has created to force himself to carry out his suicide; Rogozhin, on the contrary, sees it as a way for Ippolit to compel his auditors to prevent his suicide. Thus both see his confession as in the service not of truth but of a deeper desire (to die, to live).

As for the confession itself, it wrestles with its own motives in a way with which we are by now familiar in Dostoevsky. First, claims Ippolit, his confession will be "only the truth" because, since he is dying of tuberculosis, he can have no motive for lying (in other words his confession is written in the shadow of last things). Second, if there is anything false in the confession his auditors are bound to pick it up, since he deliberately wrote the document in haste and did not correct it (the argument from authenticity of style taken over from Rousseau). Third, while he is aware that his confession may be thought of as a means to an end, a way of justifying himself or asking forgiveness, he denies either of these as a motive. Being, as it were, on the scaffold, and therefore privileged, he asserts his right to confess simply "because I want to"; and he asserts his right to assert such a motiveless, "free" confession against any imputation of a motive. His confession belongs to last things, it *is* a last thing, and therefore has a status different from any critique of it. The sincerity of the motive behind last confessions cannot be impugned, he says, because that sincerity is guaranteed by the death of the confessant. The sincerity of any critique of him, on the other hand, can and should be subjected to the endlessness of criticism. His authors impugn his motive for a motive of their own; they do not want to know the truth about life and death, and to this end are prepared to impose upon him the silence and doubleness that must follow when silence is taken for acquiescence: "There is a limit to disgrace in the consciousness of one's own worthlessness and powerlessness beyond which a man cannot go, and after which he begins to feel a tremendous satisfaction in his own disgrace" (452). The truth his auditors do not want to hear is that there is no life after death and that God is simply "a huge and horrible tarantula" (448). His suicide is therefore an assertion of his freedom not to live on the "ridiculous terms" laid down for man (453).

The argument presented by Ippolit is thus that in the face of death the division of the self brought about by self-consciousness can be transcended in, and the endless regression of self-doubt overtaken by, an overriding will to the truth. The moment before death belongs to a different kind of time in which truth has at last the power to appear in the form of revelation. The experience of time out of time is described most clearly in Myshkin's epileptic seizures, when, in the last instant of clarity before darkness falls, his mind and heart were flooded by a dazzling light. All his agitation, all his doubts and worries, seemed composed in a twinkling, culminating in a great calm, full of serene and harmonious joy and hope, full of understanding and knowledge of the final cause . . . These moments were precisely[46] an intense heightening of awareness . . . and at the same time of the most direct sensation of one's own existence to the most intense degree. (258–259)

Reflecting on such moments, Myshkin thinks of the words "There shall be time no longer" (259). With these words Ippolit later prefaces his confession.

The moment in which earthly time ends, self-doubt ceases, the self is integrated, and truth is known, recurs in Myshkin's stories of executions. In one of these stories (86–88) he tells of the extraordinary richness with which the condemned man experiences the most mundane details of life. In another (90–93) he imagines a man on the scaffold who in his last moment "knows everything." Later Myshkin has his own experience of the "blinding inner light" that floods the soul of the man under the executioner's knife (268).

Ippolit claims to be on the scaffold as much as any of Myshkin's condemned men. From this position of privilege he wishes to bequeath to mankind his "truth," which he imagines as a seed that may grow to have great consequences. Specifically, he hopes that his death may have meaning in a meaningless universe if he can sow in the minds of men the idea of a philosophical suicide like his own.

But does Ippolit "really" have the privilege of truth? The prognosis of death within a month has been pronounced by a mere medical student; Ippolit is by no means on his deathbed; and most of the guests at the party respond to his "Explanation" "without disguising their annoyance" (454), taking it as a ploy by a vain young man to win attention. They decline to take his vow to kill himself as sincere. He, in turn, refuses to take their indifference to his confession as sincere indifference, reading it as pressure to force him to go through with the suicide. Faced with a suddenly ridiculous situation in which he and his auditors have become like poker players each trying to outbluff the other, in which, if he kills himself, he may be doing so out of spite or frustration, and in which the most urgent demand that he spare his life comes from Lebedev, who does not want a mess on the floor, he puts a pistol to his head and pulls the trigger, only to find the gun not loaded. What had started as a project in philosophical suicide degenerates into a chaos of laughter and weeping. The question of whether or not Ippolit had a privileged, "true" insight into life and death is re-enunciated by Keller in a new and banal form: did he forget to load the pistol or was it all a trick?

The farcical end of the episode reasserts the problem Ippolit claimed he had transcended, the problem of self-deception and of the endless regression of self-doubt. The project of suicide as a way of guaranteeing the truth of one's story with the ultimate payment of one's life withers under the corrosion of Rogozhin's comment: "That's not the way this thing ought to be done" (423). It ought to be done, Rogozhin implies, without an "explanation," without a why and wherefore, in muteness and obscurity. The explanation, the privileged truth paid for with death, is in truth a seed, a way of living on after death: it therefore casts into doubt the sincerity of the decision to die. The only truth is silence.

The dream that Ippolit recounts in his confession deepens the paradox. Ippolit dreams that he tells a man to melt all his gold down and make a coffin, then dig up his "frozen" baby and rebury it in the golden coffin (446). The dream is based on a real-life incident in which Ippolit has done a good deed for a stranger, thinking of his deed as a seed cast abroad into the world. In the complex condensations of the dream, the eighteen-year-old Ippolit is the frozen baby, the "Explanation" the golden coffin; planted in the ground like a seed, the dream foretells that the baby will not be resurrected (immediately after the dream Ippolit thinks of the Holbein painting of the dead Christ, a Christ who will never rise). Speaking, like the unbidden utterances of the hero of *Notes from Underground*, from a "deeper," "truer" level of the self, the dream reveals Ippolit's doubt about the fertility of his "seed" and undermines the privileged truth-status of the "Explanation" of which it constitutes a part.[47]

The poetic effect of the dream is powerful. However, rather than read the dream as a privileged truth coming from "within" Ippolit—a procedure that would unquestioningly assign to the unconscious the position of source of truth—I would ask here, as I asked in *Notes from Underground*, why these confessants fail to censor from their confessions traces of a "deeper" truth that contradicts the truth they seek to express. One answer might be that, transferring into first-person self-narration the same "Menippean" mixture of genres that characterizes his novels as a whole—a mixture including philosophical exposition, confessions, and dreams—Dostoevsky treats the self-betrayal of the narrator as a purely formal issue that only a mundane realist would take seriously. The question remains troubling, however. We continue to feel that when Dostoevsky falls back on a univocal "inner" truth, he betrays the interrogation of notions of sincerity that he otherwise carries out via a rigorously conscious dialectic.

The underground man sits down to write his confessions vaguely oppressed by memories from the past, otherwise bored and idle. He will tell his stories to soothe himself; he will tell the truth because, unlike Rousseau, he will be writing for his own eyes alone. This is as far as his examination of his motive for confessing, the spirit in which he confesses, and the significance of an audience, goes. It is precisely these questions that *The Idiot* brings into prominence. Confession, in *The Idiot*, can be made only to an adequate confessor; and even Prince Myshkin, the Christlike man, turns out to be inadequate, unable to absolve the confessant (as he is unable to rescue himself) from the spiral of double thought. As for the spirit of confession, *The Idiot* says, it is ridiculous to believe that the truth can be told as a game, a way of passing time. No act of will seems able to compel the truth to emerge, not even the willing of a moment of illumination via the willing of one's own death, since that will may itself be a double thought. Dostoevsky's critique of confession is clearly bringing us to the brink of a conception of truth-telling as close to grace.

Dostoevsky takes his next, and last, steps in the exploration of the limits of secular confession in *The Possessed* (1871–72). There are two episodes that concern us. Kirillov, like Ippolit, plans to kill himself to sow a seed of truth in the minds of men. The difference is that Kirillov actually kills himself; and the focus of interest is not on the explanation he gives for his suicide (the seed)—an explanation full of savage, grandiose, blasphemous unreason[48]—but on the actual suicide.

However, the questions of whether Kirillov scrutinizes his own motives for presenting his manifesto for suicide (one hesitates to call it a confession), and of whether he is subject to self-doubt and self-deception, become almost meaningless, since the novel allows no access to his mind. The scene of his suicide is presented through the eyes of the younger Verkhovensky (it is an irony typical of the book that while Kirillov thinks he kills himself to assert his freedom, he is all the while being nudged toward suicide by Verkhovensky). It is thus through gesture, posture, and external detail that we must read, as far as we can, the last moments of Kirillov, "grasp[ing] himself," as René Girard says, "in a moment of vertiginous possession,"[49] trying to achieve self-transcendence through death. Taking up a cryptic posture behind a cupboard in a dark room, Kirillov enters a trancelike state, his eyes "quite unmoving and . . . staring away at a point in the distance" (635). He seems, if one reads him correctly—with Myshkin's readings of condemned men at the back of one's mind—to be waiting for the instant to arrive when the self is entirely present to the self and time ceases, in which to blow his brains out. *In this reading,* Kirillov goes further than any other character in Dostoevsky in the cultivation of death as the sole guarantee of the truth of the story one tells of oneself. But we must remember that Kirillov in his last hour is more and more a madman and a beast (his last action before killing himself is to bite Verkhovensky), and that the reading from outside forced upon us by Dostoevsky perhaps signals that Kirillov's consciousness is conscienceless, inhuman, unreadable.

The chapter "At Tikhon's," excluded from the serialized version of *The Possessed* by the editor of the *Russian Herald* and later excluded by the author from the separate edition of the novel, resumes the skeptical interrogation of the confessional impulse. Stavrogin, visiting the monk Tikhon, shows him a pamphlet he plans to distribute confessing to a crime against a child; but soon Stavrogin's motives for offering the confession fall under scrutiny, and become in turn a subject of confession.

Stavrogin recounts his offense (an unspecified sexual crime followed by a provocation to suicide) without explanation of the motive, unless "being bored" (705) counts as an explanation. Instead of an exploration of motive, which so easily—as we see in Rousseau—shades into self-justification, we have an insistence by Stavrogin on his own guilt and responsibility (704, 705, 711). Even when, years later, the child begins to appear to him in visions, he insists that these visions are not involuntary: he is responsible for them, he summons them up of his own accord, though he cannot help doing so (717). The image of the child is thus not an emanation of a guilty "inner" or "unconscious" self: the same self that committed the act compulsively confronts itself with its guilty memory; there is no distinction between a self that intends and a self that acts.[50]

Stavrogin's act is understood as an abomination by both Stavrogin himself and Tikhon. What Tikhon opens to question, however, is the motive behind Stavrogin's desire to publish his guilt. Interrogation of this motive, exteriorized in Tikhon's interrogation of Stavrogin, takes the place of the interiorized self-interrogation we are accustomed to in first-person confessional narratives. In interrogating it, Tikhon opens up the gap Stavrogin has sought to close between the subject's self-knowledge and the truth.

The encounter between Stavrogin and Tikhon (717–730) consists of a double testing. All the while Tikhon tests the truth of the series of motives Stavrogin claims for making public confession, Stavrogin tests Tikhon's adequacy as a confessor. He wants Tikhon to prove his power to absolve by seeing through the untruths proposed by Stavrogin himself to the truth beyond. But just as there turn out to be limits on the kind of penance and the kind of forgiveness Stavrogin is prepared to accept, there turn out to be limits on the kind of truth Tikhon is to be allowed to see. Specifically, Stavrogin is not prepared to permit Tikhon to trouble a certain kernel of identity he wishes to claim for himself. Thus despite his readiness to forgo any right to explain his crime and excuse his guilt—a readiness which gives the impression that he wants absolute truth and true absolution—Stavrogin's confession becomes a game whose essence is that certain limits will not be transgressed, though the contestants will pretend to each other and to themselves that there are no limits. It is thus a game of deception and self-deception, a game of limited truth. Tikhon ends the game by breaking the rules.[51]

The identity Stavrogin is determined to assert is that of great sinner. He presents his crime against the child as all the more contemptible—great in its contemptibility—because its motive was so idle, its passion so flat. Tikhon suggests that so mean and yet so pretentious a crime might deserve only laughter, and counsels Stavrogin to undertake quiet penitence rather than seek "measureless suffering." Tikhon thus draws into question the *scale* on which Stavrogin thinks of his crime and his punishment. Stavrogin wants "measureless suffering" to be prescribed for him as a sign that his guilt is measureless; and the measurelessness of his guilt must follow from the banality of the evil of his crime. Tikhon places before Stavrogin's eyes the possibility that he may merely be a dissolute, rootless aristocrat with Byronic pretensions who wants to attain fame by the short cut of committing an easy abomination and confessing it in public.

It is important to note that Tikhon does not present this account to Stavrogin as *the truth about him*, since by that act Tikhon would be presenting himself as a source of truth without question. He presents it as a possible truth, a possibility that Stavrogin would have to confront if he were seriously pursuing the truth about himself in a program of spiritual self-interrogation (just as Tikhon would have to examine his own motives for minimizing the scale of Stavrogin's evil in the course of his own self-scrutiny). Thus Tikhon cuts short the bad infinity of one regression of self-consciousness—a regression more clearly typified by such self-abasing breast-beaters as Marmeladov and Lebedev, in whom the shamelessness of the confession is a further motive for shame, and so on to infinity, than by Stavrogin, whose version of the regression is that the meanness of his act is a kind of greatness, and the meanness of this conscious trick a further kind of greatness, and so on— to replace it by another regression of self-scrutiny that has the potential to extend to infinity but also has true potential to end in self-forgiveness.

Self-forgiveness means the closing of the chapter, the end of the downward spiral of self-accusation whose depths can never be plumbed because to decide to stop at any point by an act of will, to decide that guilt ceases at such-and-such a point, is itself a potentially false act that deserves its own scrutiny. How to tell the difference between a "true" moment of self-forgiveness and a moment of complacency when the self decides that it has gone far enough in self-scrutiny is a mystery that Tikhon does not elucidate, leaving it, perhaps, to the spiritual adviser "of such Christian wisdom that you and I could hardly understand it" to whom he recommends Stavrogin (729)—though if one has read Dostoevsky attentively one might guess that this monk would never articulate the difference, on the principle that, once articulated, the difference would invoke efforts to incorporate it into a new game of deception and self-deception; further, that to articulate a decision not to articulate the difference could similarly become part of a game; and so on to infinity. The endless chain manifests itself as soon as self-consciousness enters; how to enter into the possession of the truth of oneself, how to attain self-forgiveness and transcend self-doubt, would seem, for structural reasons, to have to remain in a field of mystery; and even the demarcation in this field, even the specification of the structural reasons, would similarly have to remain unarticulated; and the reasons for this silence as well.

The End of Confession

The end of confession is to tell the truth to and for oneself. The analysis of the fate of confession that I have traced in three novels by Dostoevsky indicates how skeptical Dostoevsky was, and why he was skeptical, about the variety of secular confession that Rousseau and, before him, Montaigne attempt. Because of the nature of consciousness, Dostoevsky indicates, the self cannot tell the truth of itself to itself and come to rest without the possibility of self-deception. True confession does not come from the sterile monologue of the self or from the dialogue of the self with its own self-doubt, but (and here we go beyond Tikhon) from faith and grace. It is possible to read *Notes from Underground, The Idiot*, and Stavrogin's confession as a sequence of texts in which Dostoevsky explores the impasses of secular confession, pointing finally to the sacrament of confession as the only road to self-truth.

In a long review of *Anna Karenina* that appeared in his *Diary of a Writer*, Dostoevsky praises Tolstoy for the "immense psychological analysis of the human soul" conducted in the novel. This depth of insight he sees exemplified in the episode of Anna's near-fatal illness, during which Anna, Vronsky, and Karenin "remove from themselves deceit, guilt and crime" in a spirit of "mutual all-forgiveness," only to find themselves embarked after Anna's recovery on a downward path into "that fatal condition where evil, having taken possession of man, binds his every move, paralyzes every desire for resistance."[52] In the case of Karenin, the pity, remorse, and liberating joy he feels in forgiving Anna are not proof against the shame he experiences when he returns to society in the role prescribed for him: that of humiliated husband, "a laughing-stock" (*Anna Karenina*, p. 533). First he feels self-pity, then a shameful suspicion that in forgiving Anna he may have expressed not the generosity of the self he aspires to but the weakness and perhaps impotence of the self he does not want to be. Thus introspection allows him to deny what he had earlier experienced as a liberation of his true, better self in the name of a new truth, "deeper" in the sense that it undermines the earlier one. This "deeper" truth is of course, in truth, a self-serving self-deception that (in Tolstoy's commentary) allows Karenin to "forget what he did not want to remember" (548): in so purely secular a creature ("He was a sincere believer, interested in religion primarily in its political aspect" [538]), self-scrutiny is an instrument not of the truth but of a mere will to be comfortable, to be well thought of, and so on.

The question usually asked about *The Kreutzer Sonata* is: How, after the "immense psychological analysis" that typifies *Anna Karenina* (1874–1876), and in particular the analysis of the movements of self-deception we find there, could Tolstoy have gone on to write so naive and simple-minded a book, in which the truth that the truth-teller tells emerges as a bald series of dicta about controlling the appetites? Before we accept the question in this form, however, we ought to recall three things. The first is that in *Anna Karenina* we already have the spectacle of a truth-seeker who, though as riddled with self-doubt as any, finds truth not via the labyrinthine processes of self-examination but in illumination from outside (in Levin's case, the sudden illumination of a peasant's words). The second is that there is no argument that will succeed in outflanking the underground man's assertion that self-consciousness works by its own laws, one of which is that behind each true, final position lurks another position truer and more final. From one point of view this is a fertile law, since it allows the endless generation of the text of the self exemplified by *Notes from Underground*. From another point of view, that of the hungerer after truth, it is sterile, deferring the truth endlessly, coming to no end. The third thing to bear in mind is that the kind of transcendence of self-consciousness to which Dostoevsky points as a way of coming to an end may not be available to a rationalistic, ethical Christian like Tolstoy, who can find the truth in simple, unselfconscious people but is skeptical of a way to truth beyond self-consciousness through self-consciousness.

With these considerations in mind, we can perhaps rephrase our question in a way more sympathetic to the later Tolstoy, as follows: To a writer to whom the psychology of self-deception is a not unlimited field that has for all practical purposes already been conquered, to whom self-doubt in and of itself has proved merely an endless treadmill, what potential for the attainment of truth can there be in the self-interrogation of a confessing consciousness? There can be little doubt that Tolstoy was capable of making Pozdnyshev's confession psychologically "richer" or "deeper" by making it ambiguous—indeed, material for creating such ambiguity already lies to hand in the text—but (one must imagine Tolstoy asking himself) *to what end?* Thus, after all the machinery has been set up (the narrator, ready to play the part of interrogating and interrogated Other, the train of clues pointing to a truth that questions and complicates the truth the confessant asserts), we see (I speculate now) disillusionment, boredom with this particular mill for cranking truth out of lies, impatience with the novelistic motions that must be gone through before truth may emerge (a truth that anyhow always emerges as provisional, tainted with doubt from the processes it has gone through), and a (rash?) decision to *set down the truth,* finally, as though after a lifetime of exploring one had acquired the credentials, amassed the authority, to do so.

= Obscenity and Censorship

Interview

DA: What occasioned the essays on Lawrence and censorship?

JMC: During 1986 I spent a semester at Johns Hopkins University. One of the terms of my appointment was that I deliver a public lecture on literature and the law. I thought at first I would talk about censorship, not only because that is the obvious point where the law intersects literature but also because, coming from South Africa, I had had firsthand acquaintance with state censorship. However, doing my homework, reading what had been said about censorship in the past, I found plenty of what I would call case histories, plenty of heated expression of opinion, but little of what I would call thinking. I stored this information for future reference, and for the lecture fell back on another topic, a rather obvious one: D. H. Lawrence and *Lady Chatterley's Lover*. I regard Lawrence quite highly as a writer but have always been put off by his defenders, by their moralistic cant. One doesn't hear so much of that cant nowadays, but I had had a bellyful in my youth, when Lawrence was still a controversial figure. I decided I would talk about Lawrence as a transgressor not of the law but of taboo, decorum.

I approached Lawrence's sexual mysticism from a particular angle: with my reading of Sarah Gertrude Millin at the back of my mind, and the pseudoscience of degeneration that was so much in the air in the early decades of the century.[1] So my focus became Lawrence's discussion of *taint*, a key term in the discourse of degeneration, just as *taint* became the key word for Lawrence himself in his reading of Swift. The guiding metaphor of the essay is of reading as sniffing out: one detects in the text, conceived of as a spectrum of odors, what the nose desires to discriminate. The sniffer-out-in-chief in society is, of course, the censor; and my own reading of Lawrence is very much a matter of sniffing out.

Let me be candid. I did not know how to end the essay. As it stands, the last paragraph strikes me as extraordinarily lame. But I don't see how to improve the essay—how to end it properly or, alternatively, how to continue it. This blankness of mine disturbs me. What is it a sign of? What am I refusing to see (to smell)?

Two years later, back in South Africa, I became involved in an unforeseen and unsettling public disagreement with Nadine Gordimer over Salman Rushdie's *Satanic Verses*. Rushdie had been invited to lecture in South Africa and had accepted: the disagreement was over whether, in the light of various menaces to his life (I am speaking of the time before sentence of death was passed on him by Khomeini), the invitation should be withdrawn. I argued that it should not. In retrospect I think Gordimer, in her prudence, was right, I was wrong. But the nagging question came back: why was it so hard to think of anything interesting to say about censorship? Did the discussion of censorship simply belong to politics? I began work on what was intended to be a single essay exploring the question but soon turned into a series of essays.[2]

DA: How has your own work been treated by the censorship apparatus in this country?

JMC: The 1970s were a time of fairly harsh censorship in South Africa, the 1980s, broadly speaking, a time of liberalization. I began publishing fiction in 1974. If we distinguish between the practical effects of censorship and the psychic effect it exercises simply by being in the air as a threat, then at a practical level I hardly suffered at all. A consignment of one of my books was briefly impounded by the customs; a poem was banned when the entire issue of the magazine in which it appeared was banned; that was the sum of it. I have never had the authorities turn their full attention on me as happened to André Brink or Athol Fugard or Nadine Gordimer or Etienne Leroux. I regard it as a badge of honor to have had a book banned in South Africa, and even more of an honor to have been acted against punitively, as Fugard and others were officially, and Brink and others unofficially. This honor I have never achieved nor, to be frank, merited. Besides coming too late in the era, my books have been too indirect in their approach, too rarefied, to be considered a threat to the order.

My own attitude toward censorship is what you would expect in any middle-class intellectual. I don't like censorship; where it exists, I would like to see it abolished; I think being a censor is an ignoble occupation. At the same time I suspect it would be a pity if all boundaries were to disappear: in an abstract way I think there ought to be bounds to what is licit, if only as a way of making it possible to be transgressive. Should we go to the lengths of creating or approving an apparatus of censorship to maintain such bounds? I don't think so: you create a tail that then begins to wag the dog. Still, it's a sign of cultural life—of a kind—when books are denounced from the pulpit or in the legislature as blasphemous or licentious—denounced for transgressing the Law.

Those are my thoughts on censorship itself: not very interesting and perhaps even jejune. But then, the general debate is an uninteresting one, failing to rise above the level of the political in the worst sense. It remains stalled at the level of (to use a good Flaubertian word) *bêtise*, stupidity.

Last year [1989], then, I left the pros and cons of censorship aside and turned my attention to trying to understand the dynamic of that stupidity, a dynamic which dictates that instead of becoming more and more pointed and conclusive, debates about censorship should become more and more dull and heated and endless. Why should this be so? My ambition became to say something intelligent about stupidity and the seeming inevitability of stupidity. A thoroughly hubristic ambition.

DA: In the essay on South African censorship, you address the question more or less on its own terms, leaving out what it means *to write* under censorship. In an earlier exchange you mentioned the intensity censorship produces: you were speaking about Tolstoy and Dostoevsky, but one could also mention the dissidents of Eastern Europe before 1989. All South African writers face this question, in one way or another. How have you been affected by it?

JMC: Being subjected to the gaze of the censor is a humiliating and perhaps even enraging experience. It is not unlike being stripped and searched. But at the same time it is a sign that one's writing is being taken seriously: seriously, that is, in the stupid way characteristic of the censor, who has only two words in his lexicon: *Yes* and *No*. (But who would desire the censor's *Yes*?) Writing under threat of official censure concentrates the mind wonderfully. I have no doubt that the intensity, the pointedness, the *seriousness* of Russian writing from the time of Nicholas I is in part a reflection of the fact that every word published represented a risk taken. *Mutatis mutandis,* I would say the same about much postwar writing from Eastern Europe. I would be more ambivalent about South Africa, or at least about English-language writing from South

Africa, simply because the ease with which books can be published abroad renders the actual powers of the South African censor rather vacuous. Nevertheless, no one can deny the pointedness and seriousness of the best of South African writing since 1948. The existence of censorship laws and a costly punitive apparatus (there were once many more censors in the Soviet Union than members of the Writers' Union; I have no doubt that in the heyday of the system censors outnumbered writers in South Africa, even it we count only government-appointed censors) is an undeniable sign that one's work is taken seriously in the highest quarters. What writer in the United States or Britain could make the same claim?

But writing under threat also has uglier, deforming side effects that it is hard to escape. The very fact that certain topics are forbidden creates an unnatural concentration upon them. To give one example: when it was forbidden to represent sex between blacks and whites, sex between blacks and whites was widely written into novels. Now that the ban has gone, the sex scenes are gone. I have no doubt that the concentration on imprisonment, on regimentation, on torture in books of my own like *Waiting for the Barbarians* and *Life & Times of Michael K* was a response—I emphasize, a *pathological* response—to the ban on representing what went on in police cells in this country.

DA: When a generation of black writers in South Africa was forced into silence in the 1960s, the censorship system itself was less significant than the direct application of security legislation in the form of personal bannings, "listing" people for membership in banned organizations, the issuing of one-way exit permits resulting in forced exile, and so on. When, in the early 1970s, you wrote your essays on the work of Alex La Guma (who later came to represent the African National Congress), presumably you had to go to some trouble to circumvent the system, simply to lay hands on the novels. Does this other form of censorship not deserve an acknowledgment here?

JMC: The censorship laws in South Africa have always had two prongs, as you point out. On the one hand there have been the laws administered by the Publications Control Board; on the other there have been the measures taken against writers, against books, against publications in general, under the security laws. La Guma's writings were banned under security legislation. Such bans were more draconian, and harder to get reversed, than bans under the Publications Act. La Guma did indeed, within South Africa, become a nonperson. Here was, one might plausibly argue, the most substantial writer the Western Cape had produced, yet hardly anyone in Cape Town had read him.

I obtained his books from East Berlin, where they had been published (in English) in the 1960s. I have them on my shelves, still in the brown paper wrappers I used to disguise them.

What is the point here? That La Guma's books *were* published, albeit in East Germany; that his books *could* be obtained, albeit with difficulty; that he *could* be read, albeit at a risk. One can indeed maintain, as you do, that the generation of black writers of the 1960s to which La Guma belonged was forced into silence. But one can maintain so only loosely. I think of other writers of La Guma's generation who went into exile and then could not find publishers for their work. Who was forcing them into silence? I balk at applying the word *censor* to a publisher who rejects a book because he believes there is no market for it. Two decades later, when interest in South Africa was at a high, they readily found publishers for their resurrected manuscripts. Censorship stifles books that *have* been written; only loosely can one say that it stifles books that *might have been* written.

The Taint of the Pornographic: Defending (against) *Lady Chatterley* (1988)

n 1960 Penguin Books decided to republish *Lady Chatterley's Lover*, which in Britain had circulated only clandestinely since the late 1920s. In response, the Crown announced that it would prosecute. The affair was conducted in a thoroughly gentlemanly way as a test case for the newly ratified British Act on Obscene Publications (1959).

The essential feature of this act was that, for the first time in British law, literary value was accepted as a criterion. Courts were instructed that, although a particular work might "tend to deprave and corrupt persons likely to read it" (the definition of obscenity), there should be no conviction "if it [was] proved that publication . . . [was] justified as being for the public good on the grounds that it [was] in the interests of science, literature, art or learning, or any other objects of general concern." Courts were required to admit the evidence of expert witnesses to literary or other value.

The defense of *Lady Chatterley* was conducted by a legal team with the resources of the Penguin empire behind it, able to call in a stream of eminent witnesses to the merits of the book. The prosecution, by contrast, either could find no reputable witnesses to support its case, or deemed it impolitic to call such witnesses.

What did the expert witnesses say? The Bishop of Woolwich recommended *Lady Chatterley* to Christians: "What Lawrence is trying to do is to portray the sex relationship as something essentially sacred," he said. From the standpoint of Christian theology, said the editor of the *London Churchman*, it would be "misleading" to replace words with asterisks if such words referred to "activities . . . essential for all human life." "By reading *Lady Chatterley*," suggested the director of religious education for the diocese of Birmingham, "young people will be helped to grow up as mature and responsible people."[1]

[The gamekeeper] stroked her tail with his hand . . . "Tha's got a nice tail on thee," he said, in the throaty, caressive dialect. "Tha's got the nicest arse of anybody. It's the nicest, nicest woman's arse as is! . . ." His fingertips touched the two secret openings to her body, time after time, with a soft little brush of fire. "An' if tha shits an' if tha pisses, I'm glad. I don't want a woman as couldna shit nor piss."[2]

In his own expert commentary on the book, Lawrence writes:

The words that shock so much at first don't shock at all after a while . . . We are today . . . evolved and cultured far beyond the taboos which are inherent in our culture . . . The evocative power of the so-called obscene words must have been very dangerous to the dim-minded, obscure, violent natures of the Middle Ages, and perhaps are still too strong for slow-minded, half-evoked lower natures today . . . [But] culture and civilization have taught us . . . [that] the act does not necessarily follow on the thought.[3]

In his bright, progressive dismissal of taboo, Lawrence is invoking the backing of the anthropology of his day, the anthropology of J. G. Frazer. In particular, Lawrence is using the notion of *survivals*, which Frazer takes over from Henry Burnett Tylor. Survivals are "customs . . . which have been carried by force of habit into the new society . . . and . . . thus remain as proofs and examples of an older condition of culture out of which the newer has evolved."[4] Taboos on words for body parts, body products, physical acts are, then, according to Lawrence, survivals from a less highly evolved stage of our culture.

What harm is there in such survivals? Why should we be iconoclasts of the old taboos? The answer both Lawrence and the expert witnesses give is that to maintain linguistic taboos is to maintain an aura of shame around whatever the words stand for, to the ultimate detriment of society. "Fifty yards from this court," testified the critic Richard Hoggart,

I heard a man say "fuck" three times as he passed me. He was speaking to himself and he said "fuck it, fuck it, fuck it" . . . He [was using] the word as a word of contempt, and one of the things Lawrence found most worrying was that the word for this important relationship had become a word of vile abuse . . . [Lawrence] wanted to re-establish the meaning of [the word], the proper use of it.[5]

Despite their high moral tone, it is hard to take the arguments of the defense seriously. Indeed, it is hard to read through the trial record without a sneaking sympathy for the prosecution. For, as we read, it becomes more and more clear that the prosecution is fighting without weapons. Who, in 1960, would dare take the witness stand and declare that he or she had been depraved or corrupted by reading a book? We have to go to the stuffiest, most venerable forums to find the old forthright language still in use. In the wake of the acquittal of *Lady Chatterley*, the House of Lords debated a motion that the writings of D. H. Lawrence be banned in perpetuity. "I hold a very strong view," said Lord Teviot, who proposed the motion, "on giving unbridled licence to everybody in the country, and I am very anxious lest our world become depraved and indecent, to put it mildly." *Lady Chatterley*, he went on, was a "disgusting, filthy affront to ordinary decencies."[6]

In the end Lord Teviot was placated by his colleagues and withdrew his motion. But the House agreed that *Lady Chatterley* was an unfortunate business from beginning to end. Lord Gage summed up: *Lady Chatterley* was "in very bad taste"; it would certainly not be "very becoming" to find it in the bookstalls. As for the clerics who had lent themselves to the defense, their testimony evoked only "a considerable sense of the ridiculous."[7]

I take Lord Gage's position to be a representative conservative one, namely that *Lady Chatterley* offends against *decorum* on a fairly gross scale. The problem for the Lords, however, is that rules of decorum depend on social consensus. When consensus does not exist, the upholders of decorum must either impose their rule or else withdraw. There is no logic, no body of evidence by which decorum can plead for and justify itself. As the etymology of the word tells us, decorum covers things of the right hand, as opposed to things of the left hand. It belongs to the most archaic polarity of all. Its essence is that it is *tacit*. It marks off a domain of silence, and preserves silence about how the boundaries of that domain are determined. Decorum can therefore be gestured toward but not codified. It cannot be written into law. It cannot be the subject of the law because it lies, if anywhere, *behind* the law.

Hence the dismay in the House as the Lords began to realize the full implications of the 1959 act. By creating an overriding criterion of "the public good," to be attested to by "the expert witness," the act demands that decorum plead for itself. If the Lords shake their heads over the role the church played in the acquittal of *Lady Chatterley*, it is because the church ought surely to understand that there are matters one does not debate: commandments, standards of decorum, taboos. For taboo, too, has no defense against being questioned. The barriers raised by taboo around words and objects are like the emperor's clothes: as soon as the first small voice is raised, the scales fall from the eyes of the crowd and everyone sees that the emperor is naked. Lawrence was right when he said: If you read the forbidden words with the eye of a child, you will see they are like any other words. What Lawrence did not go on to say was: But we are not children. What Lord Gage deplores is the spectacle of churchmen pretending disingenuously to be children, playing a game in which the Crown, like the emperor, is maneuvered into claiming the taboo is clothed in reason. The taboo never is.

Let us now turn to *Lady Chatterley's Lover*, that is, the third version of Lawrence's story, and to the various defenses Lawrence wrote of it.

The story Lawrence tells is of the wife of a member of the English aristocracy who has an affair with one of the servants of the estate, falls pregnant, and decides to run off with her lover.

The intercourse of Lady Chatterley with the gamekeeper transgresses at least three rules: it is adulterous; it crosses caste boundaries; and it is sometimes "unnatural," that is, anal. Let me elaborate on the second and third of these transgressions.

Though we speak of the British upper *class*, with regard to Edwardian England it would be better to speak of an upper *caste*, part of a pan-European upper caste in the twilight of its days, characterized *inter alia* by endogamy and asymmetrical rules of sexual relations: men may freely cross caste boundaries in their sexual contacts, but for women this is interdicted, or, in the language of the caste, "not done." The rationale for the interdiction, as we might expect, involves the notion of pollution: women carry the blood of the caste, and the bloodstock is polluted when it is invaded by the blood (or semen, which, in the language of pollution, is the same thing) of a man of lower caste. This interdiction is clearly enunciated by Sir Clifford Chatterley when he tells his wife he will give his name to any child she bears as long as she exercises her "natural instinct of decency and selection" and does not allow "the wrong sort of fellow [to] touch [her]" (*LCL*, 49).

With regard to the third transgression, the gamekeeper Mellors not only has intercourse with the lady of the manor but also sodomizes her. Furthermore, Mellors' ex-wife spreads the news that he is a sodomist. Connie Chatterley is thus known all over the district to have had what used to be called a "crime against nature" committed upon her body—a crime whose transgressive nature was marked, in the British penal code of the 1920s, by draconian penalties, even for man and wife.

Besides the transgressions I have named, there is a fourth. Mellors *pollutes Connie's mind* (I use the language of the time) by instructing her in the use of taboo words. In the Victorian mythology of pollution, "bad language" is the speech of a polluted mind. The only class of women in whose mouths bad language is expected to occur are "fallen women," women in a state of unredeemed defilement. Mellors' transgression is to teach a woman bad language. Bad language is harmless among men—when Mellors and Connie's father meet, the latter jovially applies taboo words to his daughter (*LCL*, 321)—but blasts the innocence of women and children.[8] (The phenomenon of men's language forbidden to women and women's language forbidden to men is of course well attested in the literature of taboo.)

Lawrence called *Lady Chatterley* a "tender and phallic novel."[9] There is obviously intended to be tenderness between the lovers. But tenderness is represented within a fable about *possession.* Mellors uses the phallus, and the phallic male word, to make Connie his own. He leaves the sign of the phallus upon her in such a way that she can return neither to her husband nor to her caste. She becomes a devotee of the cult of the phallus: "The strange weight of the balls between his legs! What a mystery! . . . She felt the slow, momentous, surging rise of the phallus again, the other power. And her heart melted out with a kind of awe" (*LCL*, 197–198). But is Lawrence's phrase "tender and phallic" not an oxymoron? What tenderness is possible under the rule of the phallus?

The answer may perhaps be that tenderness is possible as long as the sexual partners are *both* participants in the cult, that is, as long as the man is the priest rather than the god (the word made flesh) of the phallus, and the celebratory act is conducted by man and woman *under* the phallus. This is, I think, the implication of the scenes in which the phallus is alienated from Mellors by being addressed (as "thou"), decked with flowers, and so forth. Perhaps the sharpest difference between *Lady Chatterley* and Lawrence's other big novel of the period, *The Plumed Serpent*, is that in the latter Lawrence toys with the idea of man/husband as godhead.

I will return later to the place of the phallus in *Lady Chatterley*. But let me now turn to the series of prose pieces that Lawrence wrote after *Lady Chatterley*, largely to counter charges that he was a pornographer. I refer to the introduction to the private edition of *Pansies* (1929), to the essay "Pornography and Obscenity" (1929), to the introduction to the 1929 book of paintings, and to the pamphlet *A Propos of Lady Chatterley's Lover* (1930).[10]

According to Lawrence in these pieces, the origin of the pornographic imagination lies in an excremental experience of sex. What does this mean? He explains as follows. In "healthy" human beings, two kinds of *flow* take place: an excremental downward flow, in which form is dissolved and living matter becomes *dirt;* and a sexual upward flow that is both procreative and form-creating (see, for example, *LCL*, 316). In "degraded" human beings, however, the instinct to hold the polarities apart has collapsed, and all the flow of the body is downward and decreative, issuing in dirt. Sexual play becomes a play with dirt; the body of the woman becomes the dirt the man plays with; sex, for the man, becomes an act of soiling. "Common individuals of this sort have a disgusting attitude towards sex, a disgusting contempt of it, a disgusting desire to insult it. If such fellows have intercourse with a woman, they triumphantly feel they have done her dirt" (*SLC*, 38–39).

This is Lawrence's picture of the degraded or fallen state. When and how did the fall take place? With considerable tentativeness Lawrence situates it in the time of Elizabeth I. The shock of epidemic syphilis on England, particularly on the aristocracy, he suggests, resulted in a "rupture in human consciousness." "The pox entered the blood of the nation . . . After it had entered the blood, it entered the consciousness." Why should syphilis and no other disease have left this legacy? Because nothing can equal the "horror" of the realization that the issue of the sexual act may be a taint on the unborn (*SLC*, 54, 55, 57).

In Lawrence's speculative fantasy, then, after a certain historical moment there is a fear that male seed may be tainted. The seed may be bad, the seed may be dirt: ejaculation becomes part of the excremental flux. From here it is a short step to Lawrence's next figure of sex in a fallen state. Sexual desire is no longer itself desired, but becomes a suppurating wound in the body. The wound itches, is scratched, does not heal, oozes dirt, and adds its quota to the downward, excremental flow. Scratching is another name for masturbation, "perhaps the deepest and most dangerous cancer of our civilization"; it marks the self-enclosure of pure subjectivity, and is reflected in an art of pure subjectivity (here Lawrence is very likely thinking of Proust and Joyce, though he does not name them) (*SLC*, 40–42).

What is the remedy? "The way to treat the disease is to come out into the open." We must have "a natural fresh openness about sex" (*SLC*, 40). Specifically, we must restore the fallen Word, the Word that has become "unclean." "To-day, if you suggest that the word arse was in the beginning, and was God and was with God, you will . . . be put in prison . . . The word arse is as much god as the word face." The villain is the mind. The mind, hating the body, has turned the old body-words into scapegoats and driven them from consciousness. Now they haunt the margins of consciousness like jackals or hyenas, undying. They must be readmitted. The "taboo" must be lifted. If not, we will remain at the level of savages. "The kangaroo is a harmless animal, the word shit is a harmless word. Make either into a taboo and it becomes dangerous. The result of taboo is insanity." As evidence Lawrence cites the case of Jonathan Swift, whose mind was "poisoned" as if by "some terrible constipation" by the thought that "Celia shits" (*SLC*, 28–30).

Are we mistaken if we detect something downward and decreative in the flow of Lawrence's own language here? Let us look further into the case of Lawrence's Swift, with his poisoned mind.

There are two poems of Swift's in which the phrase "Celia shits" occurs. They are about young men who play the idealizing game of pastoral love, but find themselves unable to contain within the limits of the pastoral the full reality of the beloved, body functions and all. The two poems belong to a group of four, all written about 1732 (a decade before Swift was declared of unsound mind and placed under guardianship), which have attained a mild notoriety as the "excremental" or "scatological" group.[11]

In the first of the "Celia shits" poems, the swain steals into Celia's dressing room and discovers with dismay that soiled underwear and makeup lie behind the ethereal front she presents in public. Pressing on with his exploration of her secret world, he gropes in the commode and fouls his hand in the pan. This experience unhinges him: in his tainted imagination the sight of a woman henceforth always calls up the smell of excrement. In the second poem—a slighter piece—the swain (a student who himself lives in circumstances of considerable squalor) finds that there is no place for "the blackest of all female deeds" in his Arcady, and similarly falls to raving.

In a straightforward reading, these poems warn against idealizing the body, against closing the eyes and nose to the downward flow that is proof of its animal nature. What is repressed from consciousness inevitably returns to haunt us; the dirt whose existence is denied returns as dirty thoughts, dirty language. The poems present themselves as the work of a critic and moralizer who sets himself at an explicit distance from the idealizer with his fragile defenses against reality.[12]

Lawrence misremembers and misquotes the poems so badly, ignoring this distance, that one wonders whether he knew them at first hand or had simply heard of them from his friend Aldous Huxley.[13] But let us take the most interesting case, which is that Lawrence has given Swift a reading of genius, seeing through the screen Swift has erected in order to be able to represent a personal excremental crisis without the nakedness of overt confession. What, then, is Swift's disguised narrative? A hand is plunged into a dark hole and comes out smelling of excrement; from hand via nose, the excremental taint invades and poisons the mind, as vengeance for penetration of the woman's sanctum.

> But Vengeance, goddess never sleeping,
> Soon punished Strephon for his peeping.
> His foul imagination links
> Each dame he sees with all her stinks. (119–122)

Lawrence comes back to these poems of Swift's several times in the late 1920s, always in order to hold Swift up as a terrifying example of what can happen if a taboo is taken to heart.[14] "The word shit is a harmless word. Make [it] into a taboo and it becomes dangerous. The result of taboo is insanity." Lawrence's Swift makes contact with his mistress' excrement, is flooded with contagion, and goes mad. Therefore—what? Therefore, says Lawrence, we must destroy the excremental taboo, not naively, as Laputans would do, by bringing the substance itself into the open, but symbolically, at one remove, by uttering the word *shit*, thereby purging the mind of the signified of the word, namely, the idea of shit-as-contagion.

What strikes me is that the reading Lawrence gives the poem, whether we regard it as gross or inspired, is one that could be given only by a reader who has been touched or tainted by something in the poem. What touches Lawrence's mind, what takes control of his reading of Swift, is the idea of excremental taint: denouncing Swift in his essays and anathematizing the excremental taboo, Lawrence denounces and anathematizes the idea of taint itself. The moral Lawrence claims for his tale of a commode—that *shit* ought to be just a word like any word—is a non sequitur. The moral he is really after is that only a mind already tainted can be touched by taint. Its converse is that it ought to be possible for an untainted mind to undertake any exploration whatsoever of the body without suffering self-punishment. The question Lawrence does not face is: Is the very reading he gives Swift not made possible by a sharp nose for taint, a nose belonging to one acquainted with taint? Is any reading at all possible to a man without a nose? Where would such a man begin reading? How would he know, for example, that the point of entry into Swift's poem is line 112, the word "taint"? Is there not a direct connection between reading, curiosity, and a nose for dirt? In a society without interdictions or violations, without the Law—if such a society is imaginable—who would want to read or write?

(Parenthesis: in evolutionary biology, that region of the cortex which in lower mammals is given over to olfactory discrimination, in *homo sapiens* assumes the function of abstract discrimination. To put it another way: what in animals is called smelling is in human beings called analytic thinking.)

So much for Lawrence's Swift. I would now like to turn to Lawrence's Chaucer.

Somewhere between Chaucer and Shakespeare, says Lawrence, there occurred a "grand rupture . . . in human consciousness" after which "the real natural innocence of Chaucer was impossible." "Nothing could be more lovely and fearless than Chaucer," whereas "already Shakespeare is morbid with fear" (*SLC*, 54, 57, 53). Between Chaucer and Shakespeare falls the break: syphilis and the consequent secret horror of sex.

I do not want to comment on this as a piece of history or literary history, but to relate it to the enterprise of *Lady Chatterley*.

The story of the rich, impotent nobleman with the lusty young wife who escapes from the manor house for bouts of energetic intercourse with the gamekeeper is material made for a Geoffrey Chaucer. In Chaucer's hands, one can imagine, the material would be treated comically, with moments of bawdy: after appropriately ironic apologies for *cherlish speche* or vulgarity, we might even expect to have the lady's *queynte*, the gamekeeper's *sely thinge*, the great pleasure of their *swyving* referred to without circumlocution. Whether in Chaucer's version the lady's heart would "melt out of her with a kind of awe" at the "slow, momentous, surging rise of [the gamekeeper's] phallus" is another question.

Lawrence talks of Chaucer's "natural innocence." He is right, in this sense: Chaucer has available to him a treatment of sex, comic without being demeaning, that seems not to have been available by Lawrence's day and perhaps had not been available for a long time. Yet Chaucer stands for more than this wistful ideal in Lawrence's mythology. He stands for a *time before the fall* when the sexual and the excremental retained their opposed polarities, when the excremental taboo had not yet touched the mind with its contagion. To *return to Chaucer*, to *return to innocence* can therefore mean either of two things. I am not sure that Lawrence always distinguished the two, and I am entirely convinced that no one involved in the *Lady Chatterley* trial did.

The first gloss is that to return to Chaucerian innocence means to return to a time before taboos on the representation of sex. It means freedom to call a spade a spade. It means returning to *the true names of things*, particularly to the "simple and natural" obscene words that have been driven out and now haunt the margins of the imagination. Strictly interpreted, this gloss is indefensible. It ignores the complex play of high and low styles, courtly and demotic speech in Chaucer: it attributes to him a language without levels or registers.[15] Oliver Mellors may call a spade a spade, but Geoffrey Chaucer certainly does not. On the contrary, he adverts to it with a great variety of metaphors and metonyms. And if it appears that the slipping and sliding of metaphors and metonyms around body parts, body products, and interbody acts has accelerated since Chaucer's time, the explanation is in large part simply that linguistic records grow more voluminous as we approach the present.

The second and more interesting reading of Lawrence's myth of Chaucer is that Chaucer stands for an age before the specifically *excremental* taboo touched sex, that is, before the names of sexual parts and the naming—and, by contagion, performing—of clean sexual acts had the excremental taboo laid over the traditional taboos, thereby becoming *dirty*.[16] A return to Chaucer would then require the annihilation of the excremental taboo. Though it is difficult to square this reading with all of Lawrence's writings of the 1928–1930 period (for instance, with his denunciation of *all* taboos as survivals of savagery), it seems to me the reading that makes most sense of what Lawrence is up to in *Lady Chatterley*. I would therefore like to return to the novel—and to the trial—and look at a key episode, the episode of anal intercourse.

This scene (*LCL*, 280–281) was the occasion for some rich hermeneutic comedy at the trial as, without himself calling a spade a spade, prosecuting counsel sought to persuade an uncomprehending jury that something obscenely filthy was going on behind the screen of Lawrence's hypermetaphoric prose.[17]

There is little one need say about the episode itself. Connie is subjected to a rite of initiation. She dies a "poignant, marvellous death" as the last of "organic shame" is burned from her, and emerges reborn, "a different woman." The annihilation of shame is achieved by the phallus, which "hunts [shame] out" in "the core of the physical jungle." To her surprise, Connie discovers that what she has in her heart always desired has been the "piercing, consuming, rather awful sensuality" of the act.

Clearly there is a way of reading the episode in line with the account (the rationalization) Lawrence provides in the essays of the late 1920s. The excremental taboo is destroyed in its lair. The god-phallus disappears into the labyrinth of the underworld, hunts out the monster, slays it there, and emerges triumphant.

Where I find the novel and Lawrence's exegesis at odds is over the question: *what is the fate of the monster?* In the essays, the argument is that, once the power of the excremental taboo has been broken, we can begin to return to a Chaucerian state of linguistic, and ultimately sexual, innocence. In the novel the argument seems to be that, having passed through her rite of passage, Connie has become one of the purified, the reborn, the elect. What do the purified do the night after their initiation? Is the "piercing, consuming, rather awful sensuality" of sodomy lost to them once the taboo (marked by shame) has been destroyed? Do they simply return to the practice of a genital rite, purified, however, of excremental taint? Or may the rite of the hunting and slaying of the monster be performed again and again, night after night, by the god-phallus?

I am asking a question about the durability of the taboo: Is the taboo annihilated once it is transgressed?[18] The same question might be asked of the act Lawrence claims to be performing in bringing *Lady Chatterley* into the world, namely, purifying the language of the tribe. Once the tabooed representations have been brought into the light of day, does the taboo die, or is the slaying of the taboo to be acted out again and again, ritually? Does letting *Lady Chatterley* go free mean the beginning of the end of dirty books or the beginning of a stream of dirty books?

The answer Lawrence gives in his essays is clear: it means the end of taboos, the end of dirty language, the end of dirty books. But what does *Lady Chatterley* itself say? In the reading I have been giving, *Lady Chatterley* is a tale about the transgression of boundaries—sexual boundaries and sexualized social boundaries—a tale whose local tensions and dramatic force depend on the continuing viability of taboos. Taboo is a necessary condition of its existence. The sexual economy of the lovers, the dramatic economy of the tale, even the economy of the book *Lady Chatterley*, as an act of transgressive speech in the real world, depend on the vitality of taboo. The book is opened; after long deferrals, after many pages, the lovers are unclothed, their bodies explored, their truth at last told; and the book is closed. But the book waits to be reopened, re-explored. Each time it is reopened, the lovers stand before us again, ready for the prescribed unclothing, the prescribed explorations. Whatever taboos were vanquished in the first traversal of the text are there again, revived. Even bans that have long lost their mandate reassume a shadowy force in the pages of certain old books. The strings of Emma Bovary's corsets whistle like snakes as she disrobes; while that moment retains its scandalous power, we know that something has been evoked, something is being transgressed.

Does this reading turn *Lady Chatterley* into pornography? Is it the reading of a tainted imagination?

"Pornography," said Lawrence, "is the attempt to insult sex, to do dirt on it" (*SLC*, 37). "To do dirt on": a euphemism for to shit on. *Pornographer* was a word whose taint Lawrence struggled hard to escape. He invented a creature named Jonathan Swift, "degraded" man in extremis, touched him with the taint of doing dirt on sex, and banished him to a madhouse, from where, like a jackal or a hyena, he continued to haunt the margins of Lawrence's imagination. Turning on a body of writing come to erotic life under his pen, Lawrence, or the Swift in Lawrence, did dirt on it after the act. Denying its transgressiveness, explaining it away, he ended by betraying the book's proper *mysteria*.[19]

Censorship in South Africa (1990)

The Publications Act (1975) of the Republic of South Africa, as amended in 1978, allows for a publication to be found "undesirable" in terms of any of the following criteria:

(a) it is "indecent or obscene or offensive or harmful to public morals";
(b) it is "blasphemous or offensive to the religious convictions or feelings" of a "section";
(c) it "brings any section . . . into ridicule or contempt";
(d) it is harmful to inter-section relations;
(e) it prejudices security, welfare, peace and good order;
(f) it discloses part of a judicial proceeding in which offensive material is quoted.[1]

In 1980 J. C. W. van Rooyen, professor of criminal law at the University of Pretoria, was appointed chairman of the Publications Appeal Board created under the terms of the act, succeeding Hon. J. H. Snyman. Van Rooyen is the author of two books on the South African censorship system: *Publikasiebeheer in Suid-Afrika* (1978) and *Censorship in South Africa* (1987). These are authoritative works written by a proponent of the system, by no means an ideologue but rather a lawyer and office-bearer concerned that the law should be rationally and consistently interpreted and equitably applied. If we wish to study the South African system of publication control, therefore, there is no better place to start than with van Rooyen's exposition of its workings.

Objectivity, Impersonality, Impartiality

"The need arose for a comprehensive book to be written on the application of the Publications Act, and someone had to do the

315

work," writes van Rooyen in his 1987 preface. "So I set about writing this book . . . despite my misgivings" (*CSA*, vii). These words set the tone for what follows. *Censorship in South Africa* presents itself as a book written not out of desire but out of duty. The marks of the censor's desire on its pages are few and far between (though not wholly absent). In fact, van Rooyen's vision of the Publications Appeal Board (hereafter the PAB) is of a committee of technocrats in the field of morality and intergroup relations, their own personalities submerged in their work. "The ideal is that the [PAB] should be seen to be an objective and independent arbiter." Its attitude should be "not that of a persecutor [*sic*] but that of an arbiter who weighs all the relevant interests against each other." Even in the sensitive area of state security, "the publications committees and the PAB are arbiters whose function is not to restore order or to defend the country, but to strike a balance between the opposing interests" (*CSA*, 16, 51, 106).

The notion of the censor as an arbiter between contending social forces is close to the heart of van Rooyen's philosophy. "A balancing of interests has become the hallmark of control [of publications] in the Republic: general or sectional interests are continually weighed against minority interests." Even the lowly publications committees should be set up, in his view, in such a way that "each committee represents diverse interests." After summarizing (rather briefly) some of the principal positions in the philosophical debate about censorship, van Rooyen even goes to the extent of taking up the position of arbiter between the philosophers: since "legal philosophy is divided on [the subject of] the basis of control," he opts for a "moderate," that is, middle-ground, approach (*CSA*, 3, 16, 8–9).

Nevertheless, reading van Rooyen's two books attentively, one can recover a submerged history of clashes of personality and compromises over standards in the corridors of the censorship bureaucracy. The earlier book, written when the noise of the battle provoked by Minister Connie Mulder over Etienne Leroux's *Magersfontein, O Magersfontein!* still hung in the air, defends Mulder's intervention and represents the PAB as adjudicating between (Afrikaans) community opinion and the standards of a minority of intellectuals.[2] In the second book there is no such forthright defense of the handling of the *Magersfontein* affair, which can in retrospect be seen as a minor watershed in the history of censorship in South Africa, marking a split between the conservatives in the National Party and middle-of-the-road academics and intellectuals, represented by the Akademie vir Wetenskap en Kuns (Academy for Science and Art). Instead, we have a discreet account of an evolution away from Judge Snyman's fiction of the "man of balance" as the reader whose sensibilities should be taken into account, the "reasonable reader/viewer who is not hyper-critical or over-sensitive," whose "tolerance" should not be "transgressed", toward the "likely reader-viewer" of the work under scrutiny. This new touchstone, together with an increased role for advisory committees of experts and (not least) the retirement of Judge Snyman in favor of van Rooyen himself, mark 1980, in van Rooyen's account, as the beginning of a new, more rational, less confrontational dispensation (*CSA*, 56–57, 9–10).

If there is one feature of the present-day Publications Control system that emerges from van Rooyen's writings as a source of personal pride, it is the standard of impersonality the system has attained. This impersonality is not to be confused with objectivity. Van Rooyen knows all too well how futile it is to seek objectivity in the arena of morals. "It cannot be argued that the concepts of indecency, obscenity, offensiveness or harmfulness are objective concepts which exist apart from any consideration of the likely readers/viewers." Hence the importance to him of the likely-reader test. By interrogating this hypothetical reader's response to a book, an answer to the question of whether it gives offense can be reached that will be independent of the censor's personal reaction. This reponse will not, of course, serve as the sole criterion of whether it should be suppressed. But it will become one of the elements between which the censor, in his role as social mediator, may then proceed to adjudicate. "Academically," writes van Rooyen, the problem is not one of defining a "reasonable *man*," but simply of finding "a solution which is reasonable in the light of all competing interests" (*CSA*, 60, 13).

Between the reigns of Snyman and van Rooyen the essential difference can thus be summarized in the opposition *reasonable reader* versus *likely reader*. In the phrase "the reasonable reader" there is a clear ideological content, one that van Rooyen rejects;

the likely reader, on the other hand, is a probabilistic concept, value-free. But it is not the content of the two opposed terms on which I wish to concentrate. Rather, I wish to ask what is involved in the kind of reading that both Snyman and van Rooyen propose, a reading via an interposed reader. (For we must remember that the PAB's procedures have never included identifying real-life reasonable or likely readers and polling their opinions.) I will argue that the procedure involves distancing the self from being offended. But before we can enter that discussion we must be more sure about what being offended is.

The Offensive

Clause (a) of the Publications Act proscribes publications that are "indecent or obscene or offensive or harmful to public morals." Clause (b) proscribes, *inter alia*, publications that are "offensive to the religious convictions or feelings" of a section of the population. Clause (c) proscribes publications that "[bring] any section . . . into ridicule or contempt." Van Rooyen calls the language of the act "vague" and holds it to be the first task of the PAB to give a specific meaning to it.[3] Although in discussing offensiveness "we are working with subjective feelings," there is also a "judicial offensiveness" with a limited meaning; similarly with the terms *ridicule* and *contempt*.[4] Again: "Each of the terms (e.g., 'indecent,' 'obscene') employed by the Act has . . . a juridical meaning . . . The jurisdictional postulates of obscenity, offensiveness, harmfulness and blasphemy are the basic issues which must ultimately be addressed" (*CSA*, 11).

What does van Rooyen have to say about these notoriously difficult terms? He makes the following observations, which are based sometimes on legal precedent, sometimes on his own best judgment.

1. "It cannot be argued that the concepts of indecency, obscenity, offensiveness or harmfulness are objective concepts which exist apart from any consideration of the likely readers/viewers" (*CSA*, 60). This is van Rooyen's clearest statement on the subject, and marks his most forthright divergence from the touchstone of the "reasonable reader." His reasoning, though not given, is clear: there is no way of defining the reasonable reader, in a context of

censorship, except as the reader who either does or does not pass the test of finding publication X or Y indecent/obscene/offensive/ harmful. Thus the definition of the indecent/obscene/offensive/ harmful remains circular. The likely reader, on the other hand, to the extent that he has an objective existence outside the censor's mind, allows the *possibility* of noncircular definition.

2. Material becomes indecent/obscene/offensive/harmful when the control reader's tolerance is transgressed" (*CSA*, 56–57).

3. "No word is undesirable in itself . . . The criterion is . . . whether [the word] is used in a manner that . . . is in fact 'offensive' as defined in [legal precedent]" (*CSA*, 79). Since the precedent to which van Rooyen proceeds to refer cites the potential of words to cause repugnance, mortification, pain, the test is again one of how words affect a reader/listener.

4. Everything obscene is indecent, but not vice versa. Nevertheless, "a common characteristic of the [two] terms seems to be the blatantly shameless intrusion upon that which is private (usually sexually) by whatever is horrifying, disgusting, lascivious, lewd, depraving or corrupting." Again, "obscene material is material which . . . *blatantly* violates privacy" (*CSA*, 53, 11). Leaving aside the proliferation of defining terms, none of which contributes toward defining the indecent/obscene, we may not that van Rooyen introduces here the notion of intrusion upon or violation of *privacy*, of which I will have more to say below.

5. *Offensive* in the context of religion does not "mean merely something that displeases, but . . . something that is repugnant, that mortifies or pains" (*CSA*, 54).

6. "The meanings of the terms 'ridiculing' or 'bringing into contempt' [in clause (c)] are circumscribed. Ordinary scorn or political criticism is not sufficient for a finding of undesirability. The material must be degrading, humiliating or ignominious" (*CSA*, 100). Here we move away from the hypothetical likely reader to what I will call the target reader or target group. A publication is not banned, of course, on the mere testimony of members of the target group that they have felt degraded, humiliated or ignominious: again a reading is done by the censor in the person of the target reader. Thus the procedure—a reading via a displaced reader—is no different from the usual test for offensiveness.

It should be clear by now that to van Rooyen, "Is X offensive?"

can only mean "Does the likely reader of X find X offensive?" The censor's task, as he sees it, is to identify the likely reader, read X *as if* it were being read by its likely reader, and then introduce the result of this inquiry as one among several considerations to be weighed up and adjudicated among before a decision is reached.

Nevertheless, van Rooyen does not regard the likely reader and his responses without curiosity. (How could he, one might ask?— the likely reader is, after all, in the real world, the censor himself.) As we see under item 4 above, what the reader finds indecent or obscene is, in van Rooyen's view, what intrudes blatantly on his privacy. Van Rooyen, to say nothing of the PAB itself, has much to say on the relation between privacy, particularly sexual privacy, and obscenity. In its judgment on *Magersfontein*, the PAB denounces the "excessively filthy language" of the book and its references to "masturbation, loss of virginity, contraception . . . orgasms, periods, sex organs and ailments of the prostate" as "an intrusion into the respect [of the individual] for sexual privacy" (*Publikasiebeheer*, 18). "At the basis for the protection accorded [by the law] to sexual relationships lies the respect for privacy and dignity," writes van Rooyen in his own person. "At the basis of control of the arts" lie *(inter alia)* "respect for the privacy of the sexual act [and] for the privacy of the nude human body" (*CSA*, 65, 3).

It seems to be no accident, however, that the PAB, in its judgment on *Magersfontein*, identifies the outrage of the reader as a *man's* outrage ("The broad public . . . personified in the average man [*gemiddelde man*]") and elsewhere identifies what is outraged by such obscenity as a man's feeling for woman's honor: "The average man puts a high premium on the sexual privacy of woman"; the PAB objects to "the dishonor of the female body" (*CSA*, 18, 59). I am by no means suggesting that van Rooyen and the PAB defend only the privacy of the female body from representation; but as the censor, in van Rooyen's account, is required to read on behalf of the average man (here) or the likely reader (elsewhere) to protect that person's respect for privacy (a respect for the privacy of others as well as his own) from offense, so he must also protect from outrage a man's feeling that a woman's body should be private. The censor acts for the man, who feels for others and/or for the woman; and who may, indeed, himself be displaced so far from his own better self that his better self needs to be represented by another.[5] A double or triple or quadruple displacement, therefore, in the name of privacy.

How well does the argument stand up in legal logic that obscenity consists in an intrusion into (or, in van Rooyen's formulation, a blatant violation of) the privacy of the individual?

The basis of the notion of privacy, argues D. N. MacCormick, lies in a desire to be able to seclude ourselves. But if the essence of obscenity and indecency is the "public revelation, display, depiction or description" of certain matters, then it is hard to see how such acts can be understood as intrusions on the privacy of others. It is particularly hard to see obscenity in a book as an intrusion into privacy, since (1) reading a book is an act of choice, and (2) the book can be closed and the intrusion ended. In fact, in obscene displays it is rather the case that the people performing the acts are waiving their own privacy. MacCormick therefore concludes that "offensive obscenity" and "offensive intrusions on privacy" are "entirely different categories and types of wrong" except in certain areas of overlap.[6]

In other words: certain obscene acts can be construed as invasions of privacy; certain invasions of privacy may be obscene; but obscenity in general is not an invasion of privacy, and it is not possible to argue, as van Rooyen does, that the general ground for acting against obscenity is to protect the *privacy* of the citizen (or the reader). Whatever it is that is protected in the process of banning books, if anything is indeed protected, has yet to be pinned down.

Just as the kind of reading van Rooyen describes is a displaced reading, the kind of argument he conducts is an argument by displacement. All definition is, of course, a displacement. In a dictionary each word is defined by being displaced on to a subset of the other words in the dictionary. Nevertheless, displacement runs through his text (and indeed through the censor's text in general) like wildfire. What is being displaced?

Protecting Others

Van Rooyen situates censorship (or "publications control") in South Africa in the context of an Anglo-American debate in the area of morals about the rights of the individual vis-à-vis the demands of society. He sees the poles of this debate as occupied by, on the one hand, Patrick Devlin, arguing for the community's right to protect its standards, and, on the other, Herbert Hart and Ronald Dworkin, arguing for the priority of individual rights. Van Rooyen himself claims to follow "a moderate approach" between these poles (*CSA*, 8–9). Nevertheless, as he expands upon his approach, it becomes clear that he is closer to Devlin than to Hart. (It is worth noting that when van Rooyen writes that Devlin imposes a "stricter test" than Hart, the stricter test is one that has to be passed by the *book*, not by the argument for its suppression. In effect the book is guilty until it proves itself innocent. Van Rooyen gives no sign of being aware of this bias in his language.[7]

Van Rooyen concedes that the state cannot and should not legislate morality ("morality finds its source in man himself"). But he proceeds to define morality as "the sum total of rules which society has developed to regulate man's behavior towards others" (*CSA*, 2), that is, to give it the kind of definition that Dworkin distinguishes as "anthropological" and therefore without any necessary moral base.[8] Van Rooyen proceeds: "Should the basis of control not . . . be sought in the protection of interests which underlie morality?"—that is, which underlie morality as just defined (*CSA*, 2–3). This is precisely Devlin's position: that the principle underlying the enforcement of moral standards—*a principle which itself is not a moral standard but on the contrary rationally defensible*—is the right of a society to take what steps are necessary to protect its organized existence.

Thus when van Rooyen claims for himself a "moderate" position, it is not a position mediate between Devlin's functionalism and the libertarianism of Hart and Dworkin (who in this respect both follow J. S. Mill), but rather moderate in the sense in which Hart uses it, namely, moderate by comparison with the extreme position that the enforcement of morals is a good in itself. To Hart, the "moderate thesis" is that "a shared morality is the cement of society," and a breach of moral principle is therefore "an offense against society as a whole.[9] It is this kind of moderation that Hart attributes to Devlin, and it is this kind of moderation that van Rooyen follows.

The divergence between Devlin and van Rooyen on the one hand and Hart and Dworkin on the other rests on a disagreement about what sort of thing morality is. To the former, morality is no different from a system of mores whose basis may be understood as either shared, customary, and unquestioned (constituting what Dworkin calls "anthropological" morality) or else political, that is, depending on the expressed will of society. (Devlin and van Rooyen diverge, of course, when it comes to identifying how society expresses its will.) To the latter, true morality must include a yet-to-be-defined element of *value* lacking in mere customary rules.[10] In particular, when the public claims to be condemning something or other in the name of morality it may be expressing nothing more than "passionate . . . disapproval."[11]

Of course, says Dworkin, the legislator must take account of what presents itself as a moral consensus among the public. But before such a consensus can claim the status of "a consensus of moral conviction," it must provide proof in the form of "moral reasons or arguments which the average member of society might sincerely and consistently advance."[12] Otherwise we are talking not about justice but about politics. Van Rooyen paraphrases this argument of Dworkin's (the judge/censor's decision must not be based, he says, on "parroting and not relying on a moral conviction of [his] own"), but the gloss he gives to the argument reveals that he has not understood its force and is in his own way "parroting": "This means that sound objective reasons must be given" (*CSA,* 1). On the contrary, it is precisely because "objective reasons" cannot be advanced to prove that one holds a belief with conviction that Dworkin has to include the criterion of an unverifiable sincerity. The question that Dworkin only half-faces and van Rooyen does not face at all is whether people know whether convictions they hold are sincerely held. Dworkin assigns to his legislator the task of adjudicating between sincere and insincere moral beliefs. It is no wonder that Devlin, a lawyer rather than a philosopher, chooses the more matter-of-fact distinction between moral beliefs that are merely held and moral beliefs that are loudly and persistently expressed.[13]

Clause (a) of the Publications Act names four categories of publication that may be found undesirable: the indecent, the obscene, the offensive, and the harmful to public morals. From the preceding discussion it is clear that the fourth category differs from the other three. The concepts of indecency, obscenity, offensiveness, and harmfulness can indeed, as van Rooyen says, be given a meaning only relative to a specific reader/viewer (*CSA*, 60). But harmfulness *to public morals* cannot be defined in a relative manner. The censor here must either act on his own initiative to protect what he defines as public morals or take his cue from public protest. No displacement of reading is possible; the censor's position is inescapably political.

One of the most frequent criticisms of the Publications Appeal Board has been that its theory does not accord with its practice. The "rhetoric" of the PAB in defense of freedom of speech, writes Gilbert Marcus, has been "both impressive and seductive . . . [but] an analysis of [its] decisions reveals that its stated commitment to these guiding principles is often fragile." "Decisions . . . are often strikingly inconsistent . . . with the professed guiding principles. Certain decisions seem to be devoid of principle altogether."[14] This is not the place for case-by-case analysis of the PAB's decisions over the years. Nevertheless, let me cite one instance: the banning of Helen Gurley Brown's *Having it All* "as a result of its advice to women to use extramarital sex in the promotion of a career." This decision, cited by van Rooyen (*CSA*, 71) as an illustration of the criteria used by the PAB, also presents the PAB behaving not in its claimed role as arbiter between competing interests but in an authoritarian Devlinian role of guardian of public morals.

But it is not in the area of morals that the authoritarianism of the South African censorship system emerges most clearly. In the area of security as much as in the area of morals van Rooyen asserts a nonideological function for the PAB: "The publications committees and the PAB are arbiters whose function is not to restore order or to defend the country, but to strike a balance between the opposing interests" (*CSA*, 106). Yet an exemplary decision on the representation of the police cited by van Rooyen reveals the PAB bending the law. The question: Is a writer of fiction permitted to bring the police into ridicule or contempt? The answer: "Although the police force is not regarded as a section of the population [as required by clause (c) of the Publications Act], it was decided that the rendering of the police ridiculous or contemptible in this book was intended to prejudice state security, the general welfare and good order within the meaning of [clause (e)]" (*Publikasiebeheer*, 118).

Censors and Writers

The truth is that the censors played a highly partisan role in South African intellectual life in the 1960s and 1970s. In the 1980s, it can at least be said that they did not give rein to partisanship. In his own account of the period, van Rooyen acknowledges that "tension between authors and a large section of the public reached a crisis point between 1960 and 1978." He implicitly blames this tension on the conservatism of South African public life, even on a conservative reaction.[15] "In 1980, however, matters changed. The PAB, under the chairmanship of the acting chairman [that is, van Rooyen himself]," passed *Magersfontein*. A new policy allowing "strong protest" was adopted "based on the philosophy that it is often in the interests of state security to permit the expression of pent-up feelings and grievances" (*CSA*, 15–16). In practice this has meant that literary magazines (and indeed other publications) "with a sophisticated likely readership have been found to be not undesirable in spite of poems and other material expressing hatred against the authorities. Such publications were regarded as useful safety-valves for pent-up feelings in a milieu where they would be understood not as a call to political violence but as a literary experience" (*CSA*, 115).

As a measure of the cooling of tempers we may contrast his account above, which presents itself as level-headed crisis-management, with the highly confrontational response of the PAB to those Afrikaans intellectuals who had testified on behalf of *Magersfontein*:

> The point at issue is whether the position of the literary scholars [*letterkundiges*] regarding unsavory language (however revolting [*vieslik*]) can really be justified.
> The law protects the morals of the entire public [*gemeenskap*]. The Appeal Board wishes to state expressly that, according to its assessment of the community view [*gemeenskapsopvatting*] of public morals, this approach of the literary scholars is at odds with the Publications Act . . .

The general opinion of the literary scholars is that the goal of the book is to satirize the folly, the bravado, the vanity and moral decline of our own age against the background of an heroic past. Nevertheless, the central question remains whether the public . . . is prepared to tolerate the manner in which this goal is attained . . . (*Publikasiebeheer*, 14–16)

The PAB concluded:

The writer built into [his] novel excessive filthy language, excessive idle use of the Lord's name, vulgar references to excretion, masturbation . . . [This novel is] highly regarded by literary scholars. The broad public, however, as personified by the average man, regards the use [of such language] as an infringement of the dignity of the individual and an invasion of his respect for sexual privacy. (Ibid., 18)

Magersfontein was therefore banned.

In a double sense of the term, we see the PAB here *deciding for* the public: both deciding in favor of the public seen as the antagonist of the intellectuals and deciding on behalf of that public. The PAB under J. H. Snyman acted as both champion of the public (a public whose feelings it assessed according to its own methods and then embodied in a fiction called "the average man") and arbiter between the public and the intellectuals in a *cause célèbre* that it did as much as any other party to set up and stage-manage. In the first role—the role that the Board under van Rooyen claims to have dropped—the PAB at least acted in accord with its essentially conservative principles. In the second role too, in persisting to claim the role of arbiter, van Rooyen has kept alive the notion that there is a contest to arbitrate—or, in his own terms, that the interests of writers and the interests of the public are at odds. Van Rooyen is very clear about the matter: the 1978 amendment to the act that created committees of experts gave recognition, he writes, to the "minority rights of literature, art and language." "I have described these as 'minority rights,'" he goes on, "since there is little doubt that, were a referendum to be held as to the value which should be given to these interests, majority opinion would deny them recognition" (*CSA*, 9). Thus if the PAB under J. H. Snyman constituted intellectuals in South Africa as a minority, van Rooyen, in attributing to it minority "rights," perpetuates its constitution as a minority.

Nor is the kind of aggressive emotionalism that breathes from the 1977 judgment on *Magersfontein*, rendering the body that gave the judgment so suspect in the role of arbiter, wholly absent from the post-1980 PAB. In his 1978 book van Rooyen does not hesitate to characterize certain instances of obscenity as the emanations of sick minds.[16] Though we see little of this in the 1987 book, there remain pronouncements in the area of politics that reveal a very specific political position. I cite a few.

> Nadine Gordimer's *Burger's Daughter* "contains various anti-white sentiments" (*CSA*, 100).
> Wessel Ebersohn's *Store up the Anger* "deal[s] with alleged atrocities committed by the security police" (*CSA*, 103).
> In 1984 the series *Roots* was banned because "a substantial number of likely viewers would identify with the cause of the oppressed American slaves" (*CSA*, 104).
> "The legislature has over the years enacted laws which make it an offense to harm . . . relations between the races" (*CSA*, 102).

With regard to these several pronouncements we need only observe that while Gordimer's dialogue includes racial insults, most of them directed against Afrikaners, to say that the book "contains" these insults is misleading;[17] that it is possible for a work of fiction to deal with atrocities or with allegations of atrocities but not, logically speaking, with alleged atrocities; that while the logic of the decision on *Roots* is impeccable, van Rooyen seems to miss entirely the force of reporting it (or of having to report it). In the case of the statement about "laws which make it an offense to harm . . . relations between the races," van Rooyen seems breathtakingly blind to the import of what he says.

Such pronouncements serve only to confirm Marcus' view that "the assessment of factors such as 'the security of the State' will inevitably be bound up with the personalities, background and general life experience of the members of the Board. 'State Security' . . . involves an emotional dimension which often precludes rational debate."[18] We might add: an emotional dimension to which the participants are blind.

Paranoia

The further we explore the phenomenon of censorship, the more pivotal we find *attribution* to be, specifically the attribution of blame, and the dynamic that blaming initiates, a dynamic of blaming and counterblaming. It is hard not to be sucked into this dynamic, impossible not to be touched by it: those who claim to observe it judiciously or scientifically may be the most deceived. Nor do we step outside the dynamic simply by acknowledging its existence. It has its own inevitability. Paranoia gives rise to paranoia. At the close of his major case study of paranoid fantasy, the case of Judge Schreber, Freud confronts the (phantasmal?) suspicion that his brand-new theory of the etiology of paranoia can already be detected in outline in Schreber's autobiographical memoir and therefore is not original.

> Since I neither fear the criticism of others nor shrink from criticizing myself, I have no motive for avoiding the mention of a similarity which may possibly damage our libido theory in the estimation of many of my readers . . . I can nevertheless call a friend and fellow-specialist to witness that I had developed my theory of paranoia before I became acquainted with the contents of Schreber's book.[19]

In both its (unmotivated?) occasion and in its hand-on-heart style this asseveration surely betrays paranoia; or else seeing paranoia everywhere, even in Freud, belongs to a perception that has been touched by paranoia.

The principal manifestation of Schreber's paranoia is an end-of-the-world fantasy. Discussing this fantasy and the general question of the paranoiac's relation to the world, Freud gives his support to the explanation that part of paranoia is a general detachment of libido from the world.[20] The form that this general detachment of libido from the world has taken in the psychohistory of the white South African in the twentieth century has been an inability to imagine a future for himself, a relinquishing of an imaginative grasp of his future; it manifests itself in an end-of-the-world fantasy whose expression in political discourse has been in a fantasy of a "total onslaught" of hostile powers against the South African state, an onslaught in which no means, even the most unsuspected, go unused. Though the censorship laws ante-date total-onslaught talk, they are an expression of total-onslaught thinking, and the construction of a bureaucracy of censorship entrusted with the task of scrutinizing every book, every magazine, every film, every record, every stage performance, every T-shirt to appear in the land is what we can legitimately call a manifestation of paranoia.

The subject I address is not the political discourse of white South Africa. If one were in search of traces of paranoia in the discourse of total onslaught, one would not in the first place go to J. C. W. van Rooyen's books on the censorship apparatus. But, simply because he is self-evidently not paranoid (but remember: in the paranoid mode everything that is self-evident is suspect) in his own person, it is worthwhile to trace in his pages the evidences of the paranoid discourse he mediates—a discourse that shows every sign of being contagious.

What evidences do we find?

At one end of the spectrum, we find insults—for instance, the attributions of sickness of one variety or another that van Rooyen either himself makes or quotes approvingly. In the middle of the spectrum, we find self-censorship—in the interest of presenting a cooler, more judicious face—from the 1978 to the 1987 volume. At the other end, we can cite the overall enterprise—to which van Rooyen is loyal—of abstracting judicial authority, including the censorship system, from interrogations of its authority and from the dynamic of blame, eliding it from that discourse in advance, by means of what one can call the metarule of contempt: certain forms of blame (including the present one?), certain questionings of authority, are ruled inadmissible under penal sanction and form no part of the record ("No person shall insult, disparage or belittle any member of the Publications Appeal Board, or do anything in relation to the Publications Appeal Board which if done in relation to a court would constitute contempt of court").[21] The entire argument of the 1987 book—that the PAB occupies a position of arbiter between contending interests—can be seen as an effort to place the censorship outside the paranoid dynamic of blaming.

But the ultimate and all-pervasive *symptom* of paranoia lies in the mechanisms of denial, projection, and displacement in van Rooyen's texts to which I have pointed above. Offense, taking-offense, always belongs to *someone else:* the man in the street, the man in the street taking offense on behalf of someone else, woman or child, and so forth. When Freud draws up his table of the transformations of inadmissible impulses that paranoiacs perform, the projective transformation is the first.[22] The projection "He is persecuting me" ("He is part of the onslaught") is, Lacan observes, *immediate:* there is no reflection, and the efforts of the paranoiac to *explain* his move as an act of judgment (as van Rooyen's two books do) or to *proclaim* it an act of judgment (as the Publications Act itself does) founder under the suspicion of being retrospective or prospective rationalization.

The suspicion that the censor acts on the basis of unadmitted impulse belongs to the mode of paranoia. It is answered by the suspicion of the censor, also paranoid, that the call for the end of censorship in the name of free speech is part of a plot to destroy the state. Polemics around censorship soon fall into a paranoid mode in which every argument presented by the other is seen as a mask for a hidden hostile intention. Once paranoid discourse is entered upon and its dynamic takes over, the intentions of the other cannot but be hostile, since they are constituted by one's own projections.

The entry into paranoia is in fact an entry into an automatism. There can be no clearer illustration of this than the fact that, of all the pathologies, paranoia has been the most amenable to artificial simulation. Thus a computer program embodying a system of "beliefs" to be protected and a set of defense mechanisms for protecting them has simulated interactive paranoid discourse (that is, the discourse of a paranoid patient with a therapist) so convincingly that it has passed Turing tests: qualified observers (in this case psychiatrists) were unable to tell whether they were listening in to the verbal behavior of a human being or an automaton.[23]

Paranoia has in fact a double character that has always struck observers as paradoxical. On the one hand it manifests itself in behavior whose rationale is not apparent to the outsider. On the other it presents a highly intellectual front, a front of rationality or pseudorationality. It is highly judgmental, though its judgment is without apparent logic. For this reason classical (pre-Freudian) psychiatry focused on the question of judgment in paranoia, treating paranoia as a syndrome whose essence it is that "[the faculty of] judgment [becomes] perverted."[24]

But what, in a psychoanalytic context, is judgment? In his 1925 paper on negation and denial, Freud discusses the relation of judgment to primary instinctual impulses. "Judging is a continuation, along lines of expediency, of the original process by which the ego took things into itself or expelled them from itself, according to the pleasure principle." This original process remains compulsive (and, in the sense in which I have used the word above, automatic), governed by the pleasure/unpleasure principle, until "the creation of [a] symbol of negation" is achieved. This "No" marks the liberation of thinking from the primitive alternatives of incorporating and expelling. Thus we can take "No" both as the mark (the birthmark) of language and as the first speech of the Freudian unconscious. "There is no stronger evidence that we have been successful in our effort to uncover the unconscious," continues Freud, "than when the patient reacts to [an interpretation] with the words 'I didn't think that,' or 'I didn't (ever) think of that.'"[25] This comment is usually scrutinized—indeed, is scrutinized by Freud himself—as perhaps a piece of logical sleight-of-hand on the analyst's part: "If the patient agrees . . . then the interpretation is right; if [not] . . . that is only a sign of resistance."[26] But we should return to Freud's words: when we hear No, we know for certain that the unconscious speaks. Or: we know for certain that it is the unconscious speaking.

The question I have raised is whether the admit-or-condemn judgment that we call censorship continues to bear, as its first and instinctive moment, a primitive incorporative-or-expulsive character. It requires only the slightest of shifts of logical angle (a shift characteristic of the paranoid mode, which seems to see the same world as the "normal" observer does, though at a bizarre angle) for the censorship laws themselves to come into focus as a set of conditions and tests that have to be passed not so much by the words under scrutiny as by the judge's primitive Yes/No impulse in response to them. From this point of view, words and judgment are on the same level: under suspicion, on the defensive. The (paranoid) wisdom of the law is that society must guard itself on all sides: against its defenses too. Freud assigns the defense of the ego (which, at least in his earlier account of the psychological apparatus, he sees as "the dominant mass of ideas," whose analogy at a social level we might call ideology) to a function that he calls the censorship. The defenses that guard the ego "are not just unconscious in the sense that the subject is ignorant of their motive and mechanism, but more profoundly so in that they present a compulsive, repetitive and unrealistic aspect which makes them comparable with the very repressed against which they are struggling."[27]

In this discourse, the discourse of criticism (from the verb *krino*, to accuse, to bring to trial), I place censorship under suspicion. As I place it under suspicion of hiding its true nature, of being a paranoid act, my criticism itself cannot escape from the paranoid dynamic of judging, blaming, expulsion. Nevertheless, I quote a South African judge on the "primitive urge in mankind to prohibit that with which one does not agree" (Justice Rumpff, 1965, quoted in *CSA*, 1). If we look at the discourse of law and legal philosophy as it confronts the subject of *the offensive*, we encounter again and again a process of rationalizing displacement, as though there were a fear of confronting the offensive itself. I have already pointed to the processes of displacement in van Rooyen's texts. Here is the same process at work in the writing of the most rationalistic of all writers on offense, Jeremy Bentham. The law, says Bentham, should define no act as an offense "which is not liable, in some way or another, to be detrimental to the community." The test of mischievousness is utility. "An action . . . may be said to be conformable to the principle of utility . . . when the tendency it has to augment the happiness of the community is greater than any it has to diminish it." By a process of abstraction the thing itself, or the word onto which it has been displaced, becomes an *offense*, which is then abstracted into the class "detriment" and entered as a term in the calculus of utility. Does the chain of displacements stop with utility? Yes, promises Bentham: "The principle of utility neither requires nor admits any other regulator than itself."[28] Similarly Dworkin promises that his chain of displacements will end in the principle of sincerity.

One hears the protest: But that is how reason works: reason works by displacement. Yes: but the reasoning of paranoia sees that work from another, a shifted angle: what presents itself as reason is displacement in disguise. Reason cannot explain paranoia to itself, explain it away. In paranoia, reason meets its match.

= South African Writers

Interview

DA: "Necessity is blind only insofar as it is not understood." Marx's proposition, you suggest, is intrinsic to the development of Alex La Guma's oeuvre. But we can also allow it to represent the historical vision and political optimism of a generation of South African revisionists. The perspectives of this movement, in historiography, social theory, and social history, had established an unrivaled authority on the South African academic left by the end of the 1970s. In cultural politics—or the branch of it influencing the reception of the novel—the consequences of this movement involved a general acceptance of realism as the form capable of producing the approved analyses of historical forces.

In October 1987 you felt compelled to object publicly, in an address at a book festival in Cape Town, to the tendency in South Africa for fiction to be absorbed into historical discourse, to become, as you put it, a mere "supplement" to the more earnest business of history-writing. If I represent you correctly, you were making a claim for the specificity of fiction, for its ability not only to follow its own rules but also to change the rules, to the point of "demythologizing history," as you put it. You were establishing, at any rate, a clear line of division between the nature and purposes of history and those of fiction, or certain kinds of fiction.

I am not pointing to a *contradiction* between your initial reading of La Guma and your objection years later to the appetitive drive of South African historicism—this would be to falsify nearly two decades of history, both personal and national. Rather, I want to ask you to reflect on the *distance* separating these moments; in particular, I would like you to describe the situation out of which the La Guma essay developed. We can understand the past only from a consciousness of the present: from that point of view, it is curious, you will agree, that someone who by 1987 is arguing for the distinctiveness of fictionality as against history should, in 1974, have followed La Guma—a South African Marxist producing social realism—down a path marked out by Hegel, Marx, Lukács, and Sartre. Two things, at least, seem noteworthy here: that you were involved with this tradition so *early* (radical historicism in South Africa became consolidated only later), and that you should have *abandoned* it almost as quickly as you took it up.

JMC: An interesting question. Let me try to say how I today see my work on La Guma as having come about.

I left Texas to accept a job at the State University of New York in Buffalo. My situation at that time—1968—was quite precarious. Strictly construed, the terms of my visa were that I should depart the United States and use my American education for the betterment of my own country. But I had no desire to return to South Africa, particularly as I now had two children, both born in the United States. I petitioned the Immigration and Naturalization Service for permission to stay and, when my petition failed, petitioned again, and so forth, hanging on from month to month.

I had left South Africa to be part of a wider world. But now I discovered that my novelty value to the wider world, to the extent that I had any novelty value, was that I came from Africa. In Buffalo I was invited to offer a course on African literature. I had of course read the better-known South African writers, none of whom I regarded as of world status. But to prepare for the course I reread them, more carefully, and read too what was available in the United States from the rest of Africa. The drama, particularly West African drama, seemed more interesting than the poetry or fiction, though nothing truly gripped me. Nevertheless, I taught the course—in fact taught it a couple of times. I doubt that it changed any of my students' lives.

I mention this because the La Guma essay emerged from a rather resigned perception that, if I were going to stay on in the United States, it might well have to be as an Africanist, that is, as a specialist in a peripheral and not very highly regarded body of literature. Rereading the La Guma essay today, I detect something in it that may be invisible to you: a tension between asserting the particularity of South African literature and asserting the amenability of South African writing to European standards of judgment; or, in more immediate terms, a tension between wanting to validate the profession of Africanist and wanting to create a space in African studies for a person with my rather European tastes.

But why address La Guma rather than, say, Thomas Mofolo—a more interesting case—or Es'kia Mphahlele—a more complex person—or Dugmore Boetie—a more engaging writer? Why La Guma, a committed Communist, a man who ended his life as the ANC representative in Cuba? Perhaps because with La Guma I was on home ground. La Guma wrote about the Cape; whereas the rest of South Africa has always felt like foreign territory to me.

I cannot stress too strongly how directionless I was in those days. I was thirty years old and had published nothing. I had left England at a time when the war in Vietnam was getting more and more horrible, to voyage into the belly of the beast. The Americans I lived and worked among, fine people, generous, likable, liberal in their values—I made some of my most enduring friendships among colleagues and students in Buffalo—were nevertheless as little able to halt the war machine as liberal whites at home were able to halt the forced removals. Whatever my private feelings, I was as complicit in the one case as in the other.

I tested the possibility of retreating to the sidelines. I was offered jobs in Canada and Hong Kong. At the last minute I turned both down. Why? A certain fatality, perhaps, a will to remain in crisis. A *real* resolution would have been to hurl myself bodily into the anti-imperialist struggle (I use that language in a spirit of irony; yet what other language is there?). But the picture of myself marching to the fray—I, with my craving for privacy, my distaste for crowds, for slogans, my almost physical revulsion against obeying orders, I who by dint of utterly uncharacteristic, single-minded cunning had got through four years of high school without doing military drill—the picture was simply comic.

Why that revulsion? I can only say that violence and death, my own death, are to me, intuitively, the same thing. Violence, as soon as I sense its presence within me, becomes introverted as violence against myself: I cannot project it outward. I am unable to, or refuse to, conceive of a liberating violence. Is this pathological? Is it the sign of a blockage? I can only reply that such a diagnosis, whether Freudian (repression, over-zealous acceptance of the law of the father) or Marxian (inaction in the service of real but unacknowledged interests), makes no difference to me. I cannot take it seriously. I cannot but think: if all of us imagined violence as violence against ourselves, perhaps we would have peace. (Whether peace is what we most deeply want is another story.) Or, to explain myself in another way: I understand the Crucifixion as a refusal and an introversion of retributive violence, a refusal so deliberate, so conscious, and so powerful that it overwhelms any reinterpretation, Freudian, Marxian, or whatever, that we can give to it.

I think you will find the contest of interpretations I have sketched here—the political versus the ethical—played out again and again in my novels.

In Buffalo, anyhow, I tried to find an imaginative (an imaginary) place for myself in the Third World and its narratives of itself. I read Césaire and Senghor and Fanon; I read Lukács on the duties of realism; I even read Chairman Mao ("The purpose of our meeting today is to ensure that literature and art fit well into the whole revolutionary machine as a component part, that they operate as powerful weapons for uniting and educating the people . . . and that they help the people fight the enemy with one heart and one mind"—I find this passage underlined in my copy of Mao *On Literature and Art*, purchased in 1969. In what spirit could I have done the underlining?). I began work on *Dusklands*. Sadly, Lukács and Mao proved of no help there. But at least I dipped my toe in the waters of Marxism by writing in what was intended to be a positive spirit about the novels of a native South African Marxist.

In the end (to complete the Buffalo story) I became embroiled in a protest action on campus, my political patrons dropped me like a hot potato, and I had to depart the United States. Thus was the problem settled for me. I followed my wife and children back to South Africa.

I am not happy with the La Guma essay. Save for a moment or two (for instance, in the discussion of Alan Paton) it lacks intellectual urgency. It is academic in a bad sense of the word. I was wrong to make my case for La Guma rest on Lukács. Lucács' category of what he calls critical realism hinges, when you test it, on a naive criterion of the writer's sincerity. I was right to label La Guma excessively literary: as Flaubert observed, popular literature tends to be the most literary of all. Nor do I read Zola in a Lukácsian way any more. Instead I am captivated by Zola's absorption in the plethora of *things* in the world.

DA: Since the La Guma essay, you have said relatively little about black South African literature. Why?

JMC: For a number of reasons. What writing I have done about contemporaries of mine has tended to be occasional, mainly in the form of commissioned book reviews. The substantial work I did on South African literature before my recent (1990) essays on Brink and Breytenbach was *White Writing*, which concentrates on the 1920s and 1930s. *White Writing* isn't about writing by people with white skins but about European ideas writing themselves out in Africa, so there is no reason why Sol Plaatje and Thomas Mofolo shouldn't have fallen within its purview. But, frankly, I don't have much of substance to say about Plaatje or Mofolo, just as I haven't much of substance to say about N. P. van Wyk Louw.

And then, discourse about what people *are* writing in South Africa slides so easily nowadays into discourse about what people *ought to be* writing. It's an arid discourse that I take no joy in, particularly when it slideslips into polemics.

DA: In "Into the Dark Chamber," you are concerned mainly with the morality of representing torture; behind this question is a larger one, though, about the authority in South Africa of ethical judgment itself. At the end of the essay you project forward to a time when "all human acts . . . will be returned to the ambit of moral judgment," when it will "once again be *meaningful* for the gaze of the author, the gaze of authority and authoritative judgment, to be turned upon scenes of torture."

If your argument is partly about how South Africa disables its writers, how its pain and social fractures leave them without adequate vantage points from which to speak, then perhaps it is possible to see this situation as similar to, or at least continuous with, that of the poet or painter of landscape described in *White Writing,* who cannot imagine a "peopled" world, or a society "in which there is a place for the self." In each of the essays in *White Writing,* you unravel a discursive and ideological structure operating with various degrees of "blind force," as you put it, on the spokespersons of literary-colonial culture. If contemporary white South African literature has come further than this, then it has been better at subverting colonial traditions than at replacing them with the imaginative possibility of a moral community. Would you agree?

JMC: I agree with every word you say; I hesitate only in the face of the shadow of an implication which, perhaps mistakenly, I detect behind your observation that, while white South African writers have successfully subverted the colonial view of things, they have not taken the step of imagining a possible "moral community" in their native country. The implication whose shadow I seem to see is that imagining such a possibility is a duty that falls upon writers (white or black or neither white nor black), one they have failed to perform. And my hesitation is not in relation to the notion of the duty itself (that is another story for another occasion; I will accept it as given in the present argument), nor in relation to the failure to perform that duty, but in relation to the question of where the duty comes from. To me, duty can be of two kinds: it can be an obligation imposed on the writer by society, by the soul of society, by society in its hopes and dreams; or it can be something constitutional to the writer, what one might loosely call conscience but what I would tentatively prefer to call an imperative, a transcendental imperative. All I want to say here, in this tiny demurral, is that I would not want to favor the first definition unhesitatingly over the second.

DA: Yes, I take the point of the demurral. Could you elaborate, though, on the "transcendental imperative"? I ask because although your work is antiheroic, declining the role of herald to a reconstructed social order, it also seems to project, at a much deeper level, a certain faith in the idea, or the possibility, of an ethical community. (As an instance, I would cite the powerful dramatizations in *Age of Iron,* of the failure of communication between Elizabeth and some of the black protagonists.)

JMC: "Herald" is an interesting word in this context. "Of uncertain origin," the *OED* tells me, but certainly not related to "hero." Elizabeth Curren ruminates a great deal about what would constitute heroism in contemporary South Africa; but *Age of Iron* is perhaps more about heralds than about heroes. There is, in the first place, Vercueil, whom Elizabeth recognizes as, or makes into, a herald of death. But there is also the entire performance (in an Austinian sense) of the book itself as the message of someone speaking from the jaws of death, as a backward herald, so to speak, a herald looking and speaking back. Much of the book is in fact taken up with the question of whether performative conditions for messengerhood are met (conditions involving authority to speak, above all).

I'll not rehearse the question of whether Elizabeth has the right to speak or should simply shut up, and get to your question. I don't believe that any form of lasting community can exist where people do not share the same sense of what is just and what is not just. To put it another way, community has its basis in an awareness and acceptance of a common justice. You use the word *faith.* Let me be more cautious and stay with *awareness:* awareness of an idea of justice, somewhere, that transcends laws and lawmaking. Such an awareness is not absent from our lives. But where I see it, I see it mainly as flickering or dimmed—the kind of awareness you would have if you were a prisoner in a cave, say, watching the shadows of ideas flickering on the walls. To be a herald you would have to have slipped your chains for a while and wandered about in the real world. I am not a herald of community or anything else, as you correctly recognize. I am someone who has intimations of freedom (as every chained prisoner has) and constructs representations— which are shadows themselves—of people slipping their chains and turning their faces to the light. I do not imagine freedom, freedom *an sich;* I do not represent it. Freedom is another name for the unimaginable, says Kant, and he is right.

DA: Reading your reviews of Athol Fugard, Nadine Gordimer, and Breyten Breytenbach together, it is easy to draw the conclusion that although your relationship with the work of each of these major South African figures is obviously sustained and significant, it is with Breytenbach that you have a certain affinity. I have in mind the formal influences that shape his work, but also his willingness to allow the process of writing to take him, as it were, beyond the point of apprehending the real. Is this observation fair, to you and to the other writers?

JMC: Yes, I think so. If I must try to specify in what spirit I read these three, I would say it is above all in a spirit of sympathy. I believe I know from the inside some of what, in their very different ways, they have confronted and sometimes overcome, sometimes failed to overcome. If I am closer to Breytenbach than to Gordimer (I'll leave Fugard aside—I am not particularly receptive to theater), it is, as you say, because Breytenbach accepts more easily than Gordimer that stories finally have to tell themselves, that the hand that holds the pen is only the conduit of a signifying process. If I have reservations about Breytenbach, they would be aesthetic and moral at the same time: that, at least in his prose, he gives in too easily to the narcissism that always imperils self-writing— narcissism and prolixity. His poetry is another story.

DA: Much of Breytenbach's struggle has been with Afrikanerdom, its self-representations and their hold over him. To what extent have you shared—or been made to share—in that struggle?

JMC: No Afrikaner would consider me an Afrikaner. That, it seems to me, is the acid test for group membership, and I don't pass it. Why not? In the first place, because English is my first language, and has been since childhood. An Afrikaner (primary and simplest definition) is a person whose first language is Afrikaans (I will come to the catch in a moment). In the second place, because I am not embedded in the culture of the Afrikaner (I have never, for instance, belonged to a Reformed Church) and have been shaped by that culture only in a perverse way.

What am I, then, in this ethnic-linguistic sense? I am one of many people in this country who have become detached from their ethnic roots, whether those roots were in Dutch South Africa or Indonesia or Britain or Greece or wherever, and have joined a pool of no recognizable *ethnos* whose language of exchange is English. These people are not, strictly speaking, "English South Africans," since a large proportion of them—myself included—are not of British ancestry. They are merely South Africans (itself a mere name of convenience) whose native tongue, the tongue they have been born to, is English. And, as the pool has no discernible *ethnos*, so one day I hope it will have no predominant color, as more "people of color" drift into it. A pool, I would hope then, in which differences wash away.

But "Afrikaner" is not just a linguistic/cultural label. It is also an ideological term. That is to say, since the 1880s it has been a word hijacked by a political movement, first primarily anti-British, later primarily antiblack, calling itself Afrikaner Nationalism. In that process, "Afrikaner" became an *exclusive* classification. People who spoke Afrikaans as their first language but did not meet further racial, cultural, and political criteria were not accepted as Afrikaners. Hence the expulsion from the fold of the over two million Afrikaans-speakers who were not "white."

For this reason many South Africans who qualify linguistically to wear the label "Afrikaner," most of them "Colored," today refuse to wear it. But the label is also one that certain white Afrikaans-speakers have dropped: Breyten Breytenbach, whom you mention, provides an example, at least at a certain stage of his life.

But, thirdly, "Afrikaner" is a name; and naming and making a name stick is above all, as we know, an exercise in power. A child is born wild; we name it to subjugate it. Am I, in these terms, an Afrikaner? The answer must be that I am not in a position to *make* an answer. At best I can *contest* whatever answer is given. But do I desire to contest that answer? In my heart I am so sick of contestation—contestation and the spectacle of contestation. The whites of South Africa participated, in various degrees, actively or passively, in an audacious and well-planned crime against Africa. Afrikaners as a self-defining group distinguished themselves in the commission of that crime. Thereby they lent their name to it. It will be a long time before they have the moral authority to withdraw that brandmark. There are nuances on which they might want to insist—for instance, that the crime doesn't belong to the post-1948 period alone, or even to the twentieth century alone, but is continuous with the entire enterprise of colonialism—but they lack the power to impose those nuances, and anyway the nuances carry no moral weight. Is it in my power to withdraw from the gang? I think not. Breytenbach may have the power, but only because he first paid a price. More important, is it my heart's desire to be counted apart? Not really. Furthermore—and this is an afterthought—I would regard it as morally questionable to write something like the second part of *Dusklands*—a *fiction*, note—from a position that is not historically complicit.

Man's Fate in the Novels of
Alex la Guma (1974)

The Writer in South Africa

By the late 1960s, in reaction against a degree of overestimation of African writing by the literary establishments of East and West, a skeptical reassessment of its achievement was in full swing among African intellectuals. The harshest critics were writers themselves. Thus Wole Soyinka:

> The curiosity of the outside world far exceeded their critical faculties, and publishers hovered like benevolent vultures on the still foetus of the African Muse . . . The average published writer in the first few years of the post-colonial era was the most celebrated skin of inconsequence ever to obscure the true flesh of the African dilemma.[1]

And on South Africa in particular, Lewis Nkosi's judgment was:

> With the best will in the world it is impossible to detect in the fiction of black South Africans any significant and complex talent which responds with both the vigor of the imagination and sufficient technical resources to the problems posed by conditions in South Africa.[2]

In the case of South Africa the outcome of the debate is crucial. So much of the intelligentsia is in prison or in exile, so much serious work has been banned by the censors, that the work of black South African writers has become a kind of émigré literature written by outcasts for foreigners. There can thus be no argument, as in independent Africa, that a vital if crude national school of writing will eventually both educate and be educated by its audience, for the work of the South African exile is deprived of its social function and indeed of the locus of its existence in a community of writers and readers. At his desk he must generalize the idea of an audience from a "you" to an indefinite "they." A criterion of timelessness may come to seem the only one that can justify him, for his work promises to find a place for itself only by transcending the world and the age out of which it grows. If he has been exposed to the universities, then English academic criticism, with the tradition of Coleridge, Arnold, and Eliot behind it, may underpin his retreat with a critical ideology. Thus we find Nkosi censuring a writer (Bloke Modisane) for lacking a "power for so re-ordering and for so transmuting the given social facts that we can detect an underlying moral imagination at work."[3] If he cannot live by these consolations, the writer must cultivate stoicism and a literature of witness, seeing himself minimally: as the man who acts, in Sartre's words, "in such a way that nobody can be ignorant of the world and nobody may say that he is innocent of what it's all about";[4] with, all the while, an eye on his moral relation to his obsessive story: is he merely fondling his wound?

Alex la Guma

Alex la Guma was born in Cape Town in 1925. For much of his life he has been involved in resistance activities. He was one of the 156 accused in the notorious Treason Trial of the 1950s, and later spent years under house arrest and in detention. He left South Africa in 1966. His first novel, *A Walk in the Night* (1962), appeared in Nigeria and later in Britain and the United States. *And a Threefold Cord* (1964) and *The Stone Country* (1967) were published in East Berlin. *In the Fog of the Seasons' End* appeared in London in 1972.[5]

La Guma came to the novel via journalism and slice-of-life story-writing. The obvious influences on his style are American: the popular crime and low-life story, with behind it the naturalism of James Farrell and Richard Wright, and, further back, the protest novel of Upton Sinclair. The naturalistic-deterministic influence is plain in *A Walk in the Night*, with its large cast of negligible characters driven to their various fates by social forces beyond their understanding. In the next three novels we see protagonists exerting their will more and more to grasp their fate and eventually, we are given to hope, to master it. In this sense the novels become progressively more political. Nevertheless, Zola's ideal of a novel with the certainty, the solidity, and the practical appli-cation of a work of science can be discerned, if we look carefully enough, behind all La Guma's work. His novels are recognizably the product of someone who has served an apprenticeship in the short story: they come close to observing the unities of space and time, and their characters are largely from a single milieu, the Colored working class and underworld of Cape Town. Whites ap-pear mainly as police officers and prison guards: *The Stone Country* specifically develops a metaphor of South Africa as a prison in which prisoner and jailer are bound to each other by Hegelian chains, and for the metaphor a nominal white presence is suffi-cient.[6] Until the fourth novel black African characters are few and minor. La Guma does not offer a representative social panorama. For simplicity I therefore call his antagonists Black and White.

Naturalism and Tragedy

A favored mode among white South African writers has been tragedy (though Afrikaans writers have given much attention to the mythographic revision of history). Tragedy is typically the tragedy of interracial love: a white man and a black woman, or vice versa, fall foul of the law against miscegenation, or simply of white prejudice, and are destroyed or driven into exile. The overt content of the fable here is that love conquers evil through tragic suffering when such suffering is borne witness to in art; its covert content is the apolitical doctrine that defeat can turn itself, by the twist of tragedy, into victory.[7] The tragic hero is the scapegoat who takes our punishment. By his suffering he performs a ritual of expiation, and as we watch in sympathy our emotions are purged, as Aristotle noted, through the operations of pity and terror. We leave the theater or close the book

> with new acquist
> Of true experience from this great event,
> With peace and consolation . . .
> And calm of mind, all passion spent.

Religious tragedy reconciles us to the inscrutable dispensation by giving a meaning to suffering and defeat. As tragic art it also confers immortality: Oedipus and Lear may be destroyed by the gods, but we resurrect them ritually on our stage. An annual Shakespeare festival is as ritually appropriate as Easter.

But necessity is blind, says Marx, only insofar as it is not understood. With Zola the novel becomes a laboratory in which man is the subject of the experiments and in which the new Marxian and Darwinian laws of fatality are traced. The laws of heredity and environment that send Clyde Griffiths to the electric chair are unfolded in an experimental novel by Theodore Dreiser called *An American Tragedy*. Clyde's fall still awakens tragic pity and terror in us, but it also awakens righteous anger and turns it upon society.[8] To this extent naturalism politicizes tragedy.

There is a second major transformation of tragedy in modern times. In the drama of crime detection the inscrutable order of the gods has become a remote but benign temporal order ruled over by the police, the upstart hero has become the criminal challenger of the law, and the intelligence of the tragedian (the oracle, the Tiresias-figure) has been embodied in the detective investigator who sniffs out the tragic error (clue) and thence unravels the line of the criminal hero's tragic fate. This authoritarian moral inversion (the hero now evil, the gods good) holds our sympathy by an equivocation: the investigator is presented as a private eye or lone agent nominally distinct from the police gods, the criminal is invested with the trappings of diabolical power (minions, infernal machines, an underworld empire).

What religious tragedy, naturalistic tragedy, and the crime story have in common are the idea of a reigning order and the idea of fatality. What religious tragedy and naturalistic tragedy have further in common is the evocation of pity and terror. What is unique to religious tragedy is ritual catharsis. What is unique to naturalistic tragedy is its rebelliousness. What is unique to the crime story is its evocation of not pity and terror but exultation at the fate of the transgressor. The crime story has a reactionary political form; religious tragedy is apolitical or quietistic. The predominant example of religious tragedy in South Africa is Alan Paton's *Cry, the Beloved Country*. A young African comes to the city, falls among bad companions, kills a white, and is hanged. The fathers of the dead men console and learn to respect each other. The hero who bears the blows of fate is here doubled in the persons of the two fathers; we share their suffering as they share each other's suffering, in pity and terror. The gods are secularized as the pitiless justice of the law. Nevertheless, Paton's fable bears the invariant content of religious tragedy: that the dispensation under which man suffers is unshakable, but that our pity for the hero-victim and our terror at his fate can be purged by the ritual of reenactment.[9]

A Walk in the Night

A Walk in the Night is a tragic story, but in what way?

A young black, Michael Adonis, is sacked for talking back to his white foreman. Angry, drunk, and barely responsible for the act, he kills a harmless old white. He sneaks away, seen only by a couple of loitering gangsters. A second young black, a smalltime thug named Willieboy, enters the dead man's room, is surprised there, loses his head, and runs away. A sadistic white police officer, Raalt, gets on his trail and guns him down. Adonis is blackmailed into joining the underworld.

The mainspring of the plot is retribution. The death of the old white is literally fatal: his room is a fatal nexus, he who enters is doomed. An offense has been committed against the secular divinity of the law, and the law, through its police agents, will exact its penalty. Who pays does not seem to matter—Adonis or his double Willieboy. Willieboy is the unlucky one, the one who is seen and remembered. The agent who goes after him happens to be in a murderous mood. Reading of Willieboy's death we feel the tragic emotions of pity and terror, pity for his youth and ignorance, terror because we too may be black, unlucky, or both.

Thus far the book seems to read like an inversion of the crime story (the hunter is in the wrong), that is, like a second inversion of the original tragic scheme (our sympathies remain with the hero defeated by the now secularized police-gods). If this reading were a complete one, its political meaning would be that man suffers under an inscrutable secular authority, but that the emotional turmoil created by our witnessing his suffering can be purged by the ritual therapy of art. However, the reading is not complete. The core of retributive tragedy is modified by two political criticisms of Adonis/Willieboy visible at the level of the structure of the novel.

1. Modes of life that do not capitulate to authority but are not predatory are portrayed in two peripheral characters. One is Joe, a harmless youth who lives by handouts and by scavenging along the seashore as the aboriginal coast-dwellers of southern Africa had done. Joe stands for an obsolete collectivist, communal ethic; it is he who tries to stop Adonis' drift toward the underworld (74). The second is Franky Lorenzo, a stevedore who lives in the tenement where the killing takes place and who stands up briefly against Raalt's bullying (62–63). Lorenzo's wife falls pregnant annually. He laments this, not realizing, as she obscurely does, that his people's strength lies in numbers and that a new generation may see a new dawn. Lorenzo stands for a proletariat as yet unaware of its powers.

2. Necessity is blind only insofar as it is not understood. The elements of a political explanation of the situation of Adonis/ Willieboy are present in the novel, but the hero is blind to them. There are, for instance, elements of a global political perspective. The novel is set in 1950 or 1951. Adonis meets a man in a bar who refuses to listen to political talk (subject: "Whites act like that because of the capitalis' system"), dismissing it with the catch-phrase "Those bastards all come from Russia" (17). This man refuses to admit any connection between white terrorism (a lynching in the U.S. South) and internecine black violence (a knife fight in the Cape Town ghetto). A few hours later Willieboy makes a drunken attack on three American sailors for crossing the sexual color bar, is beaten off, meets the man from the bar in a dark alley, and mugs him. The clues toward a political interpretation of this ironic sequence are there, but only the god's eye of writer or reader can see them.

We can penetrate further into the political meaning of the book if we ask what forces make for stability or instability in La Guma's ghetto.

The action of the book represents a violent disturbance, lasting about twelve hours, of a precariously stable social system. At the end of the action the system returns to an equilibrium perhaps marginally more precarious than before. This equilibrium is, however, of a peculiar kind, a stability only of the ghetto vis-à-vis the rest of the city, and maintained only by shutting the ghetto off from the city. The ghetto itself seethes with internal violence.

Raalt's police companion clearly advocates the principle of closure: "I don't like any trouble . . . Let these hottentots kill each other off" (39).

What detonates the action is the victimization of Adonis by his foreman. He is enraged and takes out his rage on the old white. The killing occurs inside the ghetto, which thus fulfills its stabilizing function of absorbing the consequences of unequal black-white contact. There is an unsettling feature of the killing, however: the old man is a white living in the ghetto, where he should not be, as the normative second police officer again notes (61). He mixes the categories *white* and *ghetto-dweller*, thereby drawing Raalt into a confusion of roles: he becomes both godlike avenger of the law (white) and practitioner of street warfare (black). This alarms his orthodox companion, who sees him as a dysfunctional psychotic *macho* who will "do something violent to one of those black bastards and as a result our superiority will suffer" (39). His fears are well-founded. When Raalt shoots down Willieboy, the watching crowd threatens to unite and attack. To the police this is a moment of anarchy, to the crowd a moment during which the anarchy of the ghetto is overthrown. But the moment passes, the *status quo ante* returns: "They wavered for a while and then surged forward, then rolled back, muttering before the cold dark muzzle of the pistol" (86). The crowd disperses, the police drive away with the dying Willieboy. The book comes to a close on three night images: a cockroach emerges to lap up the vomit (victory for the predatory ways of the ghetto); the scavenger Joe makes his way to the sea and the "beckoning hands" of the seaweed (end of the old communal fellow-feeling); and Lorenzo's pregnant wife lies waiting for dawn feeling "the knot of life within her" (promise of the future) (96).

There is nothing tragic in the system of punishments we see here: it is simply oppression. Only when we get down to the level of individual lives does the question of fate reappear: why does an innocent man have to open a door on a corpse and then run into a cop with a grudge? Is there not an arbitrariness in the sequence that must either seem incredible to us or lead us back to the sources of a tragic view of life?

The old man dies because Adonis is sacked. Adonis is sacked with impunity because he is black and may not belong to a trade union. Willieboy dies because a black must die because Raalt's unfaithful wife cannot be punished with impunity because she is white. These are two of the causal chains we find in the book. A notable feature of such chains is asymmetry: a chain of violence may begin in the white city or the black ghetto, but it must end in the ghetto and its last victim must be black. Thus when a black woman is unfaithful, a black man kills a black man (the anecdote on 17–19); when a white woman is unfaithful, a white man takes out his gun and kills a black man (Raalt and Willieboy). Causal chains like these are visible to writer and reader but not to the ghetto. When two chains of causes converge on Willieboy and claim him as their double victim, what looks to the reader like a specific case of bad luck (the improbable but clearly definable convergence) looks to the crowd and to Willieboy himself like inscrutable bad luck, the way things are in the ghetto. That is, whereas the ghetto is still at a prepolitical stage in its conception of fate, writer and reader can see laws of fatality at work, can conceive of fate naturalistically. As to the question of the arbitrariness of the convergence, we should recognize that by calling a plot arbitrary we mean that it is conceived in the interests of neatness, imposing on the subject an aesthetic shape that does not fit. (If by calling a plot arbitrary we mean simply that it has a low statistical probability of occurring in "real life," we stand for a degraded standard of the real.) But the plot of Willieboy's doom, action as meaning, follows only too closely the contours of political reality. The plot is not arbitrary but, in Georg Lukács' term, "extreme." To Lukács the great achievement of nineteenth-century Russian realism was the discovery of

> that extreme expression of clearly revealed social determinants which makes possible a true typicality, far beyond the mere average . . . The primary, essential means of transcending the average is to create extreme situations in the midst of humdrum reality, situations which yet do not burst through the narrow framework of this reality as far as social content is concerned, and which, by their extreme character, sharpen rather than dull the edge of social contradictions.[10]

What distinguishes the realism of *A Walk in the Night* from the "critical realism" of Lukács' great tradition (Stendhal, Balzac, Tolstoy, Thomas Mann) is that at the end of the book we are back nearly where we started. The realist assumes "change and development to be the proper subject of literature," whereas a "basically static approach to reality" belongs to the naturalistic novel.[11] This useful distinction allows us to pinpoint the major technical difficulty La Guma must have faced composing his novel, one which, it seems to me, he resolved inadequately. On the one hand, the urban Colored population of South Africa in the early 1950s, a time of rampant reaction, was politically fragmented, cancered with crime, and lacking in consciousness of the mechanisms of oppression operating against it. Any fictional account of the ghetto closing ranks against the police would have been a falsification of reality. On the other hand, the chaos of Willieboy's last day on earth rendered unmediated through Willieboy's eyes would have missed Lukács' "change and development" and issued in little more than the diffuse pathos of low tragedy. La Guma's solution, technical and epistemological, is to locate change and development not in the world of his characters but in his reader's synthesizing intelligence, as it puts together the elements of a pattern too scattered for the characters to perceive: the characters call it bad luck; the reader sees not fate but oppression.

An alternative La Guma may have contemplated would have been to develop Lorenzo, the man who tries to unify the tenement against the police and whose unborn child is linked with the dawn, as a central intelligence within the novel. For reasons of his own he did not. He chose a narrative point of view above the world of his characters, the point of view of a spectator watching people act out their lives ("I am my father's spirit, doomed for a certain time to walk the night," recites the old man, an actor, to Adonis before he dies) (28) and savoring the bitter ironies of crime and punishment in a state in which Law and Crime overlap. For irony is all he can inject to compensate for the dullness of a world without consciousness, aptly imaged in the roach eating vomit in the dead of night. Toward his world La Guma feels much like the Flaubert who wrote, "I execrate ordinary life. I have always withdrawn from it as much as I could. But aesthetically I wanted . . . to get hold of it to the very bottom."[12] Paragraphs of *A Walk in the Night* are given over to fascinated catalogues of "ordinary life"— "massed smells of stagnant water, cooking, rotting vegetables, oil, fish, damp plaster and timber, unwashed curtains, bodies and stairways, cheap perfume and incense, spices and half-washed kitchenware, urine, animals and dusty corners" (48)—as though by inventorizing the world he could dispose of it. La Guma's first novel, despite its insight into the dynamics of power and its concern to unmask fate, displays a fastidiousness toward the material world that accords with the gulf it establishes between life and the intelligence that makes order of life. "A class can acquire class consciousness only if it sees itself from within and without at the same time," says Sartre, writing about the relation between the writer and his class of origin.[13] In his second novel La Guma confronts the task of apprehending life from the inside.

And a Threefold Cord

In *And a Threefold Cord* the Lorenzo figure is developed into the central character. He is named Charlie Pauls, a casual laborer with parents and brothers to support in a desolate shantytown on the outskirts of Cape Town. In the course of a few days Pauls takes three heavy blows: his father dies, his teenage brother kills a girl, and the children of the young widow he loves are burned alive. As he tries to make sense of his fate, his mind keeps turning to the words of the fellow worker who gave him his first political lesson: "If all the stuff in the world was shared out among everybody, all would have enough to live nice . . . People got to stick together and get this stuff." Pauls's frightened auditor responds with the lesson of the master: "Sound almost like a sin, that. Bible says you mustn't covet other people's things . . . That's communis' things. Talking against the government" (83). But Pauls is now well on his way out of the dead end of every-man-for-himself, and the act of knocking down a white police officer is a further great step in his psychic liberation, setting free a humiliated rage that in the normal course of events would have been turned upon himself and the black community. The police wage the psychological warfare of the double bind; the black man must either stand silent while his woman is insulted or stand up for himself and be punished. Pauls cuts the knot by hitting the officer and escaping in the dark. His brother, on the other hand, is still caught in the labyrinth of introverted violence. Believing that his girlfriend has broken the taboo and slept with a white man, he kills her.

The white man in question is named Mostert, and as Pauls is a development of Lorenzo, he is a development of the murdered old actor. He runs a service station and junkyard across the highway from the shantytown—most of the shanties are in fact built with junk from his yard. He spends lonely days staring toward the shanties "past the petrol pumps which gazed like petrified sentries across the concrete no-man's-land of the road," but remains "trapped in his glass office by his own loneliness and a wretched pride in a false racial superiority" (67). Pauls suggests that he come over one evening, hinting that he can find him a girl. He wavers, makes tangential contact on the outskirts of the shanty-town with the girl who is killed, and retreats.

Both boundary-crossings—by the actor in *A Walk in the Night* and by Mostert here—eventuate in crime and punishment. In nei-ther case does the white cause the crime; but, willy-nilly, his alien presence precipitates the release of destructive rages that are part of the emotional structure of oppression. Both set in disequili-brium the finely balanced system of oppression and introverted black violence, and balance is restored only when Justice follows the chains of causes to their ends and executes Willieboy and Ronnie Pauls.

Throughout the novel it rains. Rain dominates the lives of the characters. Pauls visits Mostert to beg scrap to patch a leaky roof; his visit eventuates in his brother's death. The children are incin-erated when they upset a stove that burns all day to dry out their shanty. Rain, and rain falling on dereliction, are the structural equivalent in this novel to the squalor of *A Walk in the Night*. The rain is a condition of life that exerts its oppressive weight equally on all the poor. It is a condition which has not lifted by the time the book ends but which, in the natural course of things, will. This allows the image of hope with which the book closes: "Charlie Pauls stood there and looked into the driving rain . . . He saw, to his surprise, a bird dart suddenly from among the patchwork roofs of the shanties and head straight, straight into the sky" (169).

The Stone Country

In *The Stone Country* the Lorenzo-Pauls figure is further developed. His name is now George Adams, he is politically active, and he has just been picked up in a Security Police trap. We follow him through his first few days in the "stone country" of jail awaiting trial. Here he rediscovers the law of the jungle, which he hates because it reminds him of his slum childhood, and which he fights because of the anarchic individualism it fosters. By standing up to the prison guards and by sharing his food and cigarettes he manages to pierce the defensive cynicism of the prisoners, one of whom defends him against the prison bully, another of whom, a teenage killer, is moved from inhuman fatalism to the first stirrings of affection. Thus in his quiet way Adams introduces fellow feeling among this forgotten criminal population. Where La Guma's earlier protagonists were still learning, Adams is teaching.

Adams has two kinds of enemies: the thugs who run the network of terror in the prison, and the guards. The guards, though sadistic by temperament (124), remain aloof from the prisoners in day-to-day contacts. Only in the excitement of recapturing an escapee do they let themselves go in an orgy of violence. Custodial violence erupts at the borders of the stone country, where prisoners try to cross into freedom. As long as the borders are protected, the prisoners' introverted violence will do the guards' work for them. Thus the guards wink at the activities of the prison bullies but mark down Adams, who tries to channel the prisoners' emotion in an outward direction, as a troublemaker. Toward violence Adams' attitude is ambivalent. When he arrives the prisoners invest him with the spurious glamor of the saboteur and promote him to the prison aristocracy as "an equal, an expert from the upper echelons of crime" (39). But in his own eyes he is only an organizer, someone who has read and thought and gone to meetings and now "did what you decided was the right thing" (74). He is grateful to the prisoner who fights on his behalf, but also saddened: "What a waste; here they got us fighting each other like dogs" (74).

While Adams tries to bring unity, three prisoners in an isolation cell are sawing through their window bars. During the night they climb onto the roof. Here their precarious treaty breaks down and each makes his individual break for freedom. Two succumb to panic and vertigo and are retaken; the runt of the group escapes. "A threefold cord is not quickly broken," runs the epigraph to La Guma's second novel.

In the Fog of the Seasons' End

The theme of La Guma's oeuvre clarifies itself further: the growth of resistance from the aimless revolt of individuals without allies or ideology (anarchy, crime) to the fraternal revolt of men who understand and combat oppression, psychological and physical. *And a Threefold Cord* reflected the dawn of a man's conception of himself as a political creature; in *The Stone Country* the first cracks in the chaotic, defensive individualism of the oppressed appeared and alliances began to sprout; *In the Fog of the Seasons' End* presents both the political conception of man's fate and the fraternal alliance as accomplished facts. The alliance is a proletarian one, though it has sympathizers among the bourgeoisie and intelligentsia; its ideology is an eclectic Marxism. Thus, although the novel has a main character who is continuous with figures from the earlier novels, it is, at the level of structure at which ideas and their embodiments enter into conflict, more appropriate to speak of a nascent collective resistance as the new protagonist.

Beukes is the name of the new Lorenzo-Pauls-Adams figure. He is a cell leader in the underground of the late 1960s, but old enough to have had experience of trade unionism and passive resistance. The novel follows him through a long day during which he distributes illegal strike leaflets. The following day, at a rendezvous with his immediate superior, Elias Tekwane, he is betrayed by an unknown informer. He escapes, wounded; Tekwane is captured and dies under police torture. Some days later we find Beukes engaged in organizing transport for guerrilla recruits. One of the volunteers, he discovers happily, is Isaac, a young man from his cell, also betrayed and also on the run.

The structure of oppositions among the three personages within the collective protagonist is complex. Tekwane has his faith put to the ultimate test; Beukes escapes, preserves his anonymity, but is threatened by loss of faith in himself and the movement. Tekwane dies, Isaac takes up the struggle. Isaac looks forward to armed resistance, Beukes backward to the old politics of rallies and speeches. But in their collectivity they have found a response to the humiliations of their personal life stories. Introverted rage and violence have been transformed into organized struggle. The street warfare of the ghetto exists only mutedly in the image of children holding up passersby with toy guns (61). The white enemy, on the other hand, has grown to live vicariously on the violence of news reports and gossip, and these reveal in particular the murderous contradictions of the introverted nuclear family. While the whites feed on fantasy, Beukes, up against the police, undergoes a reverse movement: "The torture chambers and the third degree [are] transferred from celluloid strips in segregated cinemas to the real world" (25). His very worst fantasies are realized; the fairy-godmother fantasy of the triumph of the weak and oppressed through the force of their faith has to be discarded. Chief among the virtues demanded of the revolutionary, he discovers, is the "granite" of the life and death of Tekwane. "These days one could not depend only on faith: the apparatus of the Security Police scraped away faith like strata of soil until they came to what was below. If they reached crumbly sandstone, it was splendid for them. It was the hard granite on which they foundered" (131).

The action of the novel catches Beukes, Tekwane, and Isaac at a time when danger forces them to confront their own fears. Thus Beukes, into whose soul the iron has not yet entered, undergoes nightmares of defeat in which his pregnant wife is disemboweled (children in La Guma stand for the future: the novel closes on an image of children in the sunlight). But the nature of the collective is to bring out the best in the weak. Beukes is fortified by his relation with the granite of Tekwane. Isaac suffers a whim of chance—his betrayal—but finds an avenue that enables him to turn it to positive action. Tekwane is taken to the limits of resistance under torture but there finds fortitude in hallucinated visions of the long history of African resistance. (And Beukes, passing a cast of a Bushman in an ethnographic museum, also recognizes an ancestor, "the first to fight" [14].)

Beneath this new optimistic writing the old fatal pattern can still be made out on the palimpsest. The young Tekwane comes out of Paton's *Cry, the Beloved Country* and Doris Lessing's "Hunger," and is thereby saddled with a freight of tragic connotation, religious and naturalistic. The disaster of the collective sprouts from a mysterious canker, the traitor in its body. Beukes is saved from capture by luck (a stranger with a wound much like his is picked up). Nevertheless, Tekwane is finally not the tennis ball of the stars but a hero who engages his death in full consciousness of its meaning, and his killers are agents not of an inscrutable order but of a desperate regime whose end he sees: "You are reaching the end of the road and going downhill towards a great darkness, so you must take a lot of people with you" (6), he tells his torturers. Tekwane's suffering and death are unrolled in chapters that form a high point in La Guma's writing and whose achievement it is to demystify the torture chamber, inner sanctum of the terroristic state.

Achievement

La Guma's achievement is to present a particularly lucid description of the resultants of white oppression in self-destructive black violence and to embody his novels a growing political understanding of the process in the consciousness of a developing protagonist. His four novels do not cohere closely enough to form a tetralogy, but read in sequence their political meaning is quite plain. They portray a Colored working class that initially has little consciousness of how its energies are redirected against it by its rulers as the anarchic force of crime. The representative of its best qualities grows from a puzzled stevedore to a laborer who has begun his psychic liberation, to a declassed activist, at first cautious, then freed for armed struggle by a heroic African example. Plotting and characterization are deliberate enough to leave the uncommitted reader perhaps resentful of La Guma's palpable design, but as social taxonomy the characterization must be acknowledged to be rich in insight.

However, style is the great betrayer. La Guma is the inheritor of the worst excesses of realism. In a paragraph like the following from *A Walk in the Night*—and hardly a page of this book passes without indulgence in the like—we see him straining after an effect no other than literariness itself.

> The room was as hot and airless as a newly opened tomb, and there was an old iron bed against one wall, covered with unwashed bedding, and next to it a backless chair that served as a table on which stood a chipped ashtray full of cigarette butts and

burnt matches, and a thick tumbler, sticky with the dregs of heavy red wine. A battered cupboard stood in a corner with a cracked, flyspotted mirror over it, and a small stack of dog-eared books gathering dust. In another corner an accumulation of empty wine bottles stood like packed skittles.   (25–26)

This is not only the interior of a certain room but an interior with the fingerprints of Literature all over it, an interior heavy with affect. The slums of *A Walk in the Night,* the shanties of *And a Threefold Cord,* the cells of *The Stone Country,* the depressed suburbs of *In the Fog of the Seasons' End,* are all rendered in this style. The style has a double signification. First, it is La Guma's Writer's Union card.[14] But also, more specifically, it is a style in which a single emphatic gesture is repeated over and over; " . . . an *old* iron bed . . . *unwashed* bedding . . . a *backless* chair . . . a *chipped* ashtray . . . cigarette *butts* . . . *burnt* matches . . ."— everything named is named with its own gesture of repudiation. The signification of the passage is not a room and its details, but rather a room plus horror of the room. Similarly for the slums, the shanties, the cells, the suburbs. La Guma's world, so overflowing with things, is nonetheless not an objective world, for the things themselves are overflowing with the writer's subjectivity.

The same holds true for people. Four of the prison officials in *The Stone Country* are described in individual detail. Here are extracts from the descriptions. "His pink face was thin and hard as the edge of a pot-lid, and the eyes revealed no expression" (18). "He had . . . a puckered mouth that was merely a pink orifice, and little blue eyes, flat as pieces of glass" (22). "He had a plump, smooth, healthy pink face . . . the eyes were pale and washed-out and silvery, much like imitation pearls, and cold as quicksilver" (61). "He had a dry, brittle face like crumpled pink tissue-paper with holes torn in it for eyes" (68). Such repetition gives the guards away as not four distinct alien men but a single threatening figure. The threat is not in the figure, for the figure is threat. In the same way the slum, the shanties, the cells, the suburbs are La Guma's horror of them. Here there is no evolutionary development in La Guma. Each of his novels exposes us to a long-sustained shudder of revulsion—a revulsion that must confess in places to being merely fastidious. It is this posture of rejection, emblematized at the moment when George Adams pushes aside his prison food (56), that brings La Guma closest to the Flaubert who confessed his execration of "ordinary life." The less interesting side of this posture is its expression of alienation from the material world. The more interesting side is a repetitiousness that becomes excessive and even obsessive, the testament of one man's horror of a degraded world.

Into the Dark Chamber:
The Writer and the South African State
(1986)

When a colony is founded, wrote Nathaniel Hawthorne, "among [the] earliest practical necessities [is] to allot a portion of the virgin soil as a cemetery, and another portion as the site of a prison." Prisons, those "black flowers of civilized society," burgeon all over the face of South Africa. They may not be sketched or photographed, under threat of severe penalty. I have no idea whether laws against the representation of prisons exist in other countries. Very likely they do. But in South Africa such laws have a particular symbolic appropriateness, as though it is decreed that the camera lens must shatter at the moment it is trained on certain sites; as though the passerby shall have no means of confirming that what he saw, those buildings rising out of the sands in all their sprawl of gray monotony, was not a mirage or a bad dream.

The true explanation is, of course, simpler. The response of South Africa's legislators to what disturbs their white electorate is usually to order it out of sight. If people are starving, let them starve far away in the bush, where their thin bodies will not be a reproach. If they have no work, if they migrate to the cities, let there be roadblocks, let there be curfews, let there be laws against vagrancy, begging, and squatting, and let offenders be locked away so that no one has to hear or see them. If the black townships are in flames, let cameras be banned from them. (At which the great white electorate heaves a sigh of relief: how much more bearable the newscasts have become!) Is apartheid about segregation of blacks or segregation of the poor? Perhaps not an important question, when blacks and the poor are so nearly the same. Certainly there are many lands where prisons are used as dumping-places for people who smell wrong and look unsightly and do not have the decency to hide themselves away. In South Africa the law sees to it as far as it can that not only such people but also the prisons in which they are held become invisible.

The headquarters of the Security Police in Johannesburg, in a square fittingly named after Balthazar John Vorster, onetime prime minister of the Republic and patron under whom the security police grew to their present bad eminence, is another site that may not be photographed. Into this building untold scores of political prisoners have been taken for interrogation. Not all have returned alive. In a poem titled "In Detention," Christopher van Wyk has written as follows:

> He fell from the ninth floor
> He hanged himself
> He slipped on a piece of soap while washing
> He hanged himself
> He slipped on a piece of soap while washing
> He fell from the ninth floor
> He hanged himself while washing
> He slipped from the ninth floor
> He hung from the ninth floor
> He slipped on the ninth floor while washing
> He fell from a piece of soap while slipping
> He hung from the ninth floor
> He washed from the ninth floor while slipping
> He hung from a piece of soap while washing

Behind the so-called suicides and accidental deaths to which van Wyk alludes here, behind the cursory postmortems by government functionaries, the bland, unlikely inquest findings, lie the realities of fear, exhaustion, pain, cruelty. One can go about one's daily business in Johannesburg within calling distance (except that the rooms are soundproofed) of people undergoing the utmost suffering. "It is no different from walking past a child-brothel. It is no different from walking past an abattoir. These things happen. These things are done." Perhaps. Perhaps these things are done all the time, all over the place. But there is a certain shamelessness in doing them in the heart of a great city, a shameless characteristic of all the security operations of a state which asserts that its own survival takes precedence over the law and ultimately over justice. Van Wyk's poem plays with fire, tap-dances at the portals of hell. It comes off because it is not a poem about death but a parody of the barely serious stock of explanations that the Security Police keep on hand for the media.

In 1980 I published a novel *(Waiting for the Barbarians)* about the impact of the torture chamber on the life of a man of conscience. Torture has exerted a dark fascination on many other South African writers. Why should this be so? There are, it seems to me, two reasons. The first is that relations in the torture room provide a metaphor, bare and extreme, for relations between authoritarianism and its victims. In the torture room unlimited force is exerted upon the physical being of an individual in a twilight of legal illegality, with the purpose, if not of destroying him, then at least of destroying the kernel of resistance within him.

Let us be clear about the situation of the prisoner who falls under suspicion of a crime against the state.

What happens in Vorster Square is nominally illegal. Articles of the law forbid the police from exercising violence upon the bodies of detainees except in self-defense. But other articles of the law, invoking reasons of state, place a protective ring around the activities of the security police; and the rigmarole of due process, which requires the prisoner to accuse his torturers and produce witnesses, makes it futile to proceed against the police unless the latter have been exceptionally careless. What the prisoner in effect knows, what the police know he knows, is that he is helpless against whatever they choose to do to him. The torture room thus becomes like the bedchamber of the pornographer's fantasy, where, insulated from moral or physical restraint, one human being is free to exercise his imagination to the limits in the performance of vileness upon the body of another.

The fact that the torture room is a site of extreme human experience, accessible to no one save the participants, is a second reason why the novelist in particular should be fascinated by it. Of the character of the novelist, John T. Irwin, in his book on Faulkner, writes: "It is precisely because [he] stands outside the dark door, wanting to enter the dark room but unable to, that he *is* a novelist, that he must imagine what takes place beyond the door. Indeed, it is just that tension toward the dark room that he cannot enter that makes that room the source of all his imaginings—the womb of art." To Irwin (following Freud but also Henry

James), the novelist is a person who, camped before a closed door, facing an insufferable ban, creates, in place of the scene he is forbidden to see, a representation of that scene, and a story of the actors in it and how they come to be there. Therefore, my question should not have been phrased: Why are writers *in South Africa* drawn to the torture room? The dark, forbidden chamber is the origin of novelistic fantasy per se; in creating an obscenity, in enveloping it in mystery, the state unwittingly creates the preconditions for the novel to set about its work of representation.

Yet there is something tawdry about *following* the state in this way, making its vile mysteries the occasion of fantasy. For the writer the deeper problem is *not* to allow himself to be impaled on the dilemma proposed by the state, namely, either to ignore its obscenities or else to produce representations of them. The true challenge is: how not to play the game by the rules of the state, how to establish one's own authority, how to imagine torture and death on one's own terms.

The writer faces a second dilemma, of a no less subtle nature, concerning the person of the torturer. The Nuremberg trials and, later, the trial of Adolf Eichmann in Jerusalem presented us with a paradox in morality: a stupefying disproportion between the pigmy stature of the men on trial and the enormity of the crimes they had committed. Hints of the same paradox have surfaced at the two inquests in South Africa (those on Steve Biko and Neil Aggett) at which members of the security police have briefly emerged from their native darkness into the public gaze.

How is the writer to represent the torturer? If he intends to avoid the clichés of spy fiction, to make the torturer neither a figure of satanic evil, nor an actor in a black comedy, nor a faceless functionary, nor a tragically divided man doing a job he does not believe in, what openings are left?

The approaches to the torture chamber are thus riddled with pitfalls, and more than one writer has fallen into them. For example, in *A Ride on the Whirlwind*, a novel dealing with the 1976 uprisings, Sipho Sepamla writes: "Bongi's frayed bodice was ripped off exposing the fullness of her turgid breasts and pointed teats to the beastliness of the two cops . . . Cold-bloodedly, the cop undid the pliers on the one nipple and placed it on the other. Bongi screamed, tears pouring down her soft brown skin." Sepamla clearly succumbs here to erotic fascination. He also makes his torturers both all too satanic ("demonic" is his word) and all too easily human: "The young cop was sick . . . He lived with subterranean streams in his makeup . . . He suffered from dual personality. The nature of his work was such that to survive he developed a split personality."

A considerably stronger book about the same historical events is Mongane Serote's *To Every Birth Its Blood*. Serote declines the false issue of whether the torturer is man or devil. He limits himself to the physical experience of torture and, more important, takes on the challenge of finding words adequate to represent the terrible space of the torture chamber itself.

> A mixture of deodorant smells and paper, tobacco, old furniture, turned into a single smell, which characterizes all the places whose functions are proclaimed by notices, where warnings burden walls, counters and filing cabinets, where the sweat, tears, vomit and blood of many many people, who came and went, who never made it out of the doors, leave their spirits hanging in the air, which can never ever be cleaned.

There is a certain dark lyricism to this writing, a lyricism even more strongly evident in Alex La Guma's *In the Fog of the Seasons' End*, another novel about resistance and torture. Since the time of Flaubert, the novel of realism has been vulnerable to criticism of the motives behind its preoccupation with the mean, the low, the ugly. If the novelist finds in squalor the occasion for his most soaring poetic eloquence, might he not be guilty of seeking out his squalid subject matter for perversely literary reasons? From the beginning of his career, La Guma—a neglected writer who died in 1985 in exile in Cuba—ran the risk of immortalizing a Cape Town of seedy slums and dripping rain in a prose of somewhat lugubrious grandeur. In his presentation of the world of the security police, no matter how much he insists on its banality, its lack of depth, there is a tendency to lyrical inflation. It is as though, in avoiding the trap of ascribing an evil grandeur to the police, La Guma finds it necessary to displace that grandeur, in an equivalent but negative form, onto their surroundings, lending to the very flatness of their world hints of a metaphysical depth: "Behind the polished windows, the gratings and the Government paintwork, was another dimension of terror. . . . Behind the picture of normality the cobwebs and grime of a spider reality lay hidden."

Presenting the world of the interrogator with a false portentousness, a questionable dark lyricism, is not a fault limited to South African novelists: the same criticism might be leveled against the torture scenes in Gillo Pontecorvo's film *The Battle of Algiers.*

I am not arguing that the world of the torturer should be ignored or minimized. I would not wish that we did not have Breyten Breytenbach's *True Confessions of an Albino Terrorist*, which contains some searching explorations, based on personal experience, of the spiritual sphere in which the police live, human beings who find it possible to leave the breakfast table in the morning, kiss their children goodbye, and drive off to the office to commit obscenities. But Breytenbach's book is a memoir. It does not matter if at one moment Breytenbach exhibits a canny suspiciousness about the wish to get *behind* the security police (get behind the walls, get behind the dark glasses, find out their innermost secrets), yet at other times literally lets his poetic imagination go, to fly deeper and deeper into the labyrinth of the security system, toward "the inner sanctum . . . where the altar of the State [the scaffold] is erected [in] the final heart of loneliness." Because it is an interim report, a partial biography of a phase of Breytenbach's life, *True Confessions* does not have to solve the problem that troubles the novelist: how to justify a concern with morally dubious people involved in a contemptible activity; how to find an appropriately minor place for the petty secrets of the security system; how to treat something that, in truth, because it is offered like the Gorgon's head to terrorize the populace and paralyze resistance, deserves to be ignored.

Although the work of Nadine Gordimer is never without a political dimension, it contains no direct treatment of the secret world of security. But there is one episode in particular that, in an indirect way, addresses the same moral problems I have been trying to put my finger on. I refer to the episode of the flogging in *Burger's Daughter*, an episode that harks back to the famous episode of the flogging of the horse in Dostoevsky's *Crime and Punishment.*

Rosa Burger is driving around, half lost, on the outskirts of the black townships of Johannesburg, when she comes upon a family of three in a donkey cart, the man flogging the donkey in a drunken fury. In a frozen instant she beholds

the infliction of pain broken away from the will that creates it; broken loose, a force existing of itself, ravishment without the ravisher, torture without the torturer, rampage, pure cruelty gone beyond the control of the humans who have spent thousands of years devising it. The entire ingenuity from thumbscrew and rack to electric shock, the infinite variety and gradation of suffering, by lash, by fear, by hunger, by solitary confinement—the camps, concentration, labor, resettlement, the Siberias of snow or sun, the lives of Mandela, Sisulu, Mbeki, Kathrada, Kgosana, gull-picked on the Island . . .

How is Rosa Burger to react? She can put a halt to the beating, bring her authority to bear on the driver, even have him arrested and prosecuted. But does this man—"black, poor, brutalized"—know how to live other than by brutality, doing unto others as has been done unto him? On the other hand she can drive past, allowing the torture to continue. But then she may have to live with the suspicion that she passed by out of no better motive than a self-regarding reluctance to be thought "one of those whites who care more for animals than people."

She drives on. And a few days later leaves South Africa, unable to live in a country that poses such impossible problems in day-to-day living.

It is important not to read the episode in a narrowly symbolic way. The driver and the donkey do not stand respectively for torturer and tortured. "Torture without the torturer" is the key phrase. Forever and ever, in Rosa's memory, the blows will rain down and the beast shudder in pain. The spectacle comes from the inner reaches of Dante's hell, beyond the scope of morality. For morality is human, whereas the two figures locked to the cart belong to a damned, dehumanized world. They put Rosa Burger in her place: they define her as within the sphere of humanity. What she flees from, in fleeing South Africa, is the negative illumination they bring: that there exists another world parallel to hers, no further away than a half-hour's drive, a world of blind force and mute suffering, debased, beneath good and evil.

How to proceed *beyond* this dark moment of the soul is the question that Gordimer tackles in the second half of her novel. Rosa Burger returns to the land of her birth to join in its suffering and await the day of liberation. There is no false optimism, on her part or on Gordimer's. Revolution will put an end neither to cruelty and suffering, nor perhaps even to torture. What Rosa suffers and waits for is a time when humanity will be restored across the face of society, and therefore when all human acts, including the flogging of an animal, will be returned to the ambit of moral judgment. In such a society it will once again be *meaningful* for the gaze of the author, the gaze of authority and authoritative judgment, to be turned upon scenes of torture. When the choice is no longer limited to *either* looking on in horrified fascination as the blows fall *or* turning one's eyes away, then the novel can once again take as its province the whole of life, and even the torture chamber can be accorded a place in the design.

Athol Fugard, *Notebooks, 1960–1977* (1984)

Athol Fugard's *Notebooks* are the record of eighteen years of creative life, covering a period from the early 1960s, when Fugard first tried his hand at a novel, gave it up, and decided "I am a playwright," to the late 1970s, when he had established himself as a playwright of international stature.[1] They trace the impact of day-to-day events upon him, the slow process by which kernels of truth crystallize from memories, and the sometimes halting and painful growth of his plays out of these kernels. As a record of the inner experiences of a self-aware and articulate creative consciousness, they are of absorbing interest, and we should be grateful to Fugard and his editor, Mary Benson, for making them public.

The *Notebooks* are, however, more than this. They are also the autobiography of a man of intelligence and conscience who chose to remain in South Africa at a time when many fellow writers were opting for (or being forced into) exile. Fugard's choice meant, among other things, that he would make his life among those juxtaposed scenes of placid comfort and desperate poverty that belong to present-day South Africa, and continually be brought face to face with the question of his relationship with a ruling order characterized by a remarkably loveless attitude toward its subjects (or some of them), an attitude of lovelessness that sometimes extends to atrocious callousness. Fugard's pleasure in the beauty of South Africa, and particularly of the Eastern Cape coast, where he lives—a pleasure that he communicates in passages of glitteringly precise description of its sights and sounds and smells—is therefore repeatedly subverted by "the nausea brought on by reading the newspapers," by bouts of "dumb and despairing rage at what we are doing." This revulsion leads in turn to doubts about the value of his art, which seems to be founded on material privilege, to be personal in its nature, to be only ambivalently committed to tangible political goals. How to commit himself without losing his integrity as an artist becomes a central preoccupation of the notebook entries of the mid-1960s. "The horror of what this government and its policies have done to people . . . has built up such an abyss of hatred that at times . . . I [have] been quite prepared to take the jump and destroy—but, so far . . . the company of executioners remains loathsome," he writes in 1968. "I can't think of any moral dilemma more crucifying than this one."

Yet fidelity to his subject matter—which we may broadly define as the attempts of people to retain their self-respect in a degraded social order—makes him suspicious of an art yoked too closely to a political program. In *Boesman and Lena*, he asserts, what engages him is the "metaphysical" predicament of the couple rather than a "political [or] social" one. He reserves his judgment on *Sizwe Bansi Is Dead* because he feels that it "[walks] the tightrope between poetry and propaganda."

The route he follows out of his crisis of conscience is to take upon himself (following Sartre) the task of *bearing witness*. "The truth [must] be told . . . I must not bear false witness." "My life has been given its order: love the little grey bushes," by which he means, love the insignificant, the forgotten, the unloved. Against a system whose own degradation he measures by the degradations it imposes on others (at one point he goes further and suggests that the ultimate and unwitting victims of a regime of degradation are its perpetrators), Fugard opposes an ethic of love. "South Africa's tragedy is the small, meager portions of love in the hearts of the men who walk this beautiful land." "People must be loved." "I love man for his carnality, his mortality. It is a hard love—a big love—and I must still grow." "What is Beauty? The result of love. The ugliness of the unloved thing."

This program of witness and love is carried out from a position which Fugard explicitly—at least in the early 1960s—identifies with that of Camus's Stranger, or Outsider. He records a "climacteric" in his life: sitting in a courtroom one day witnessing the processes of South African law, he realizes that what is taking place before him has little to do with justice, that (more significantly) all human law has its origin in a position of compromise;

his own position, he decides, must henceforth be founded on a rejection of compromise, and therefore on a rejection of the moral claims of the law. Although the outsider status that he hereby assumes comes under considerable stress as pressure mounts upon him from the left to engage himself politically (or rather, since Fugard's art *is* an engaged art, to allow the terms of his engagement to be determined for him by the political struggle), he never really deserts it, partly because it allows him the autonomy he needs as a writer, partly because it gives definition to his persistent sense of himself as "not 'really' belonging, of being a 'stranger,'" no matter how much he sometimes wishes to become a "subscriber."

During 1962 and 1963 Fugard in fact undertook a systematic reading of Camus, and the formative influence of Camus on his own thought is clear. "Would be happy to spend the next ten years deepening my understanding and appreciation of this man," he writes. "Overwhelmed by Camus." The stance of what he calls "Heroic Pessimism," by which he characterizes his own work, comes to him from this reading, as well as such injunctions to himself as "Live prepared for death."

But Camus is only the chief in a long roll of intellectual influences charted in the *Notebooks*. From his cottage at Schoenmakerskop, Fugard kept well abreast of intellectual currents: there are notes on Faulkner and Kazantzakis and Robbe-Grillet, Brecht and Genet, Pound and Lowell and Pasternak, Jung and Laing and the Zen thinkers, all of whom can be shown either to have helped him define his own position or to have pointed him in new directions.

The most absorbing pages of the *Notebooks* are those in which Fugard explores the currents of his own creativity and the genesis and unfolding of his plays. "I've always known that in my writing it is the dark troubled sea [of the unconscious], of which I know nothing, save its presence, that [has] carried me," he writes. Later he contemplates a project of writing a notebook parallel to one of his plays in which he hopes to trace every stage of its creation—a project, in other words, for a more systematic version of the *Notebooks* we have—and then wryly dismisses it for its "naïveté": he is too much "adrift" in the "deep and dark currents" of his creative unconscious, he realizes, to be able to chart their depths.

This confidence in his own unconscious processes leads to an untroubled acceptance of periods in his creative life that appear from the outside to be infertile, as well as to a certain intellectual passivity.

> Nothing, ever, in my life seems to stem from my asking a question and needing an answer. My consciousness of self and the world around me is, most times, the best times . . . as smooth and solid as the sea tonight . . . I don't think I live negatively—the impulse to write is a vigorous, affirmative one, but it never has its origins in the need for answers.
>
> So often the paradox in writing: discover your beginning when you reach the end.

Insofar as the *Notebooks* make clear a method or pattern in Fugard's playwriting, it is one of worrying for months and some-times years at a subject, often a subject suggested by a real-life encounter, until the image, the kernel out of which the play will eventually grow, emerges with "a life of its own, a truth bigger than itself." Much of the book is devoted to recording the quest for these images of "truth . . . [which] when it comes, flashes back like lightning, through all that [has] preceded it."

Of his poetics, Fugard writes: "I strive quite consciously and deliberately for ambiguity of expression . . . My whole tempera-ment inclines me to be very unequivocal indeed. That is not dif-ficult—but it would be at the cost of truth." "Darkness is . . . an essential help to the truly poetic image." Made in 1969–1970, these statements serve to remind us of how strenuously Fugard has striven to deploy the poetics of modernism over a field that might seem to belong only to social realism; this deployment, when it is successfully achieved, is what gives his work its uniqueness.

Out of his orientation toward the hidden and irrational comes the succinct and powerful formulation by which in 1976 he char-acterizes his art: "A man must have a Secret, and as a result of that an Act which takes others by surprise."

There is less about theater, and about Fugard's experience in theater in Britain and the United States, than admirers of his plays might expect. The main reason is that the *Notebooks* were written in South Africa during spells of privacy; gaps in the chro-nology mark his absences abroad. But the *Notebooks* do record the excitement and disappointments of his work with black theater groups in the Port Elizabeth townships, thoughts on the staging of his plays, records of conversations with the actors John Kani and Yvonne Bryceland, and comments on the nature of theater that illuminate his own creative practice. Thus: "One of the reasons . . . why I write for the stage . . . [is] the Carnal Reality of the actor in space and time. Only a fraction of my truth is in the words."

We must presume that Fugard did some editing of his own before he passed the notebooks over to Mary Benson in 1979. Nevertheless, there remains much that is autobiographical in a personal way—criticism of his own "self-indulgence, self-pity, romanticism," of his evasive and confused treatment of the beggars who haunt all good liberals, of his "incurable inability to say 'No,'" of the "anarchistic, destructive core to [his] being." There are dark intervals when he records "almost total loss of all sense of value" or, on the last page of the *Notebooks*, "inner agony . . . death in life . . . the total extinction of my creativity . . . I have feared for my sanity." There are also glimpses of Fugard poring for hours over rock pools, experiencing the "electric, orgiastic" pleasures of spearfishing, angling along the coast. ("Zen and the art of angling. Every cast a cast into your soul.")

Mary Benson has supplemented the *Notebooks* with several pages of useful notes and a glossary of South African terms. By and large these are adequate, though Benson is mistaken in thinking that the Afrikaans verb *moer* has anything to do with murder. There also seem to have been misreadings of Fugard's text. Eliot did not write a poem called "The Rack," nor is it likely that Fugard called Beckett and Ionesco "absurdities."

One is hardly entitled to criticize a writer for what he has chosen to write or not write about in his private notebooks. Nevertheless, there are points at which one wishes Fugard had pushed his thinking an inch or two further. The notion of the natural dignity of all life, most of all human life, is a keystone of Fugard's thought. At the heart of the evil of white *baasskap* or *Herrschaft* in South Africa, in Fugard's view, is its desire not only to use the black man as a tool for its own material gain, but to strip him of all dignity in the process. The ruling order has thus literally become an *order of degradation*: no black man finds a place in society till he has passed the rite of being "taught a lesson" and abased.

I have no quarrel with such an analysis, as far as it goes. But Fugard, not an Afrikaner, is close enough to the Afrikaner to know that the humiliation of the weak by the strong has been a characteristic practice of the Afrikaner within his own culture, a practice underpinned by a perhaps perverted reading of scripture that inordinately emphasizes authority and its converse, abasement. The humbling of children by parents, of students by teachers, and generally of the younger by the older (the uninitiated by the initiated)—humbling that does not cease till face has been lost—is part of the life experience of most Afrikaners, and is kept alive, against liberalizing counterforces, by such institutions as the armed forces, which reach into most white households. There are many authoritarian societies on earth, but Afrikanerdom strikes one as a society in which castration is allotted a particularly blatant role. Fugard knows the castrating urge behind South African *baasskap*, knows that the castrated, the unloved, usually takes his place at the forefront of the castrators. Does he guess, too, that in probing the apparently peripheral phenomenon of humiliation he is coming close to the heart of the beast? It would be interesting to know.

From the fact that the *Notebooks* begin to tail off after 1973 we may infer that Fugard's impulse to keep this form of diary has waned, and that there will be no second volume. We must therefore take what we have as a record of a phase in Fugard's life that has closed, a phase in which, in a spirit of total engagement, he searched in daily experience and in books for the germs of truth. Even the reader only sketchily familiar with Fugard's plays will find it an absorbing experience to follow him on his search.

Breyten Breytenbach, *True Confessions of an Albino Terrorist* and *Mouroir* (1985)

South of the city of Cape Town lies a tranquil, almost rural, suburb named (after the wine) Tokai, and zoned for white occupation only. Driving through Tokai you pass, on your right, forest and vineyard, on your left comfortable houses with spacious lawns and gardens. Then at a certain point the suburban idyll ends, giving way to a monotonous gray wall ten feet high, behind which you can glimpse watchtowers and blank-faced buildings. This is Pollsmoor, a maximum-security prison, the home at one time of Breyten Breytenbach, poet, painter, and convicted "terrorist." *The True Confessions of an Albino Terrorist* is the story of how Breytenbach came to be in Pollsmoor, what he did there, and how he departed.[1]

Breyten Breytenbach was born in 1939 into an ordinary small-town Afrikaner family. One of his brothers became an officer in the South African armed forces, another a well-known journalist. Breytenbach's comments on his brothers give an idea of how far he has moved from his origins. The first he calls "a trained (and enthusiastic) killer," the other "a fellow traveller of the [security police], with decidedly fascist sympathies." Breyten, the maverick of the family, early made a name for himself in literary circles, and came to be seen as the leading poetic talent of his generation. Even after he left South Africa, took up residence in Paris, married a woman who would be called in Afrikaans *anderskleurig*, "of another color" (meaning of a color other than white), and involved himself in the antiapartheid movement, he remained the idol of much of the Afrikaans literary world. In 1973 he obtained official dispensation to visit his homeland. Audiences at poetry readings gave him and his wife a rapturous welcome. The word in the air was "reconciliation." The prodigal son would yet return, the breach would be healed, and all would be well.

The next time Breytenbach visited South Africa, circumstances were different. He had shaved off his beard, and he carried a passport identifying him as Christian Galaska, citizen of France. His mission was to recruit members to Okhela, a resistance organization that had already embarrassed the West German government by stealing classified documents and revealing details of military cooperation between Bonn and Pretoria. Tipped off by an informer in Europe, the South African security police kept "Galaska" under surveillance for a while, then closed in and arrested him. At the end of a trial conducted in surprisingly subdued terms, Breytenbach was given a stiff nine-year sentence. (In *True Confessions* he claims that the authorities reneged on a deal to let him off lightly in return for not conducting a political defense.) He spent two years in isolation in Pretoria Central Prison, a spell from which he emerged with his sanity miraculously unimpaired, followed by five years in Pollsmoor. In 1982 he was released and flown off to France.

The Breytenbach case has troubled and continues to trouble Afrikaners. Breytenbach took the position from the beginning that he had gone into exile, that the reasons for his exile were political, and that only changes that would bring all political exiles home would bring him home. Afrikaner public opinion, on the other hand, particularly liberal opinion, preferred to see his defection as a family matter, a generational quarrel within the greater Afrikaner family, to be sorted out within the family. To those who hold this view it remains possible for Breytenbach to be a great Afrikaans writer while still adopting the stance of a rebel. But in *True Confessions* Breytenbach spells out his position anew. He is not a rebel but a revolutionary, in will if not in deed. And he is no longer one of the family.

> To be an Afrikaner is a political definition. It is a blight and a provocation to humanity . . . I do not consider myself to be an Afrikaner. To be an Afrikaner in the way they define it is to be a living insult to whatever better instincts we human beings may possess.

Given his unequivocal rejection of his Afrikaner birthright, why should Breytenbach have received from the police and prison authorities the odd touches of indulgence, mixed in with the usual harshness and cruelty, that we find described in this book? Breytenbach suggests that Red Cross and other international observers exerted a cautionary influence on his jailers. His own deliberately unheroic attitude ("Be pliant and weak when you have to. Cry if you must") may have contributed, too.

But I think there is a deeper reason. Prisoners in South Africa are not permitted to conduct economic activities from within jail. Breytenbach is a professional painter and writer. The letter of the law would have been on the side of the authorities if they had prohibited him from painting or writing in prison. In fact he was given permission to write, though not to paint. The works he wrote in prison, *Mouroir* among them, were taken into custody as they were completed and returned to him on his release. The censors have allowed the publication of these works in South Africa. The public buys and reads them. They are honored with literary prizes. Why? Breytenbach writes:

> People who absolutely rejected me and my ideas and what my life stood for but who, perhaps from an obscure sense of uncomfortableness, if not guilt, and also, surely, because of a true concern for my work, applied to the minister to allow me to continue writing. "For the sake of Afrikaans literature." Was it a way for some of them to establish in their own minds their evenhandedness?

Perhaps. The fact is that, by the standards of the Afrikaans literary tradition, Breytenbach is a great poet. He is a poet, moreover, whose emotional makeup includes feelings of passionate intimacy with the South African landscape that, Afrikaners like to think, can be expressed only in Afrikaans, and therefore (here comes the sinister turn in the reasoning) can be experienced only by the Afrikaner. Closeness of fit between land and language is—so the reasoning goes—proof of the Afrikaner's *natural* ownership of the land. (Ideas like these are not new: *natural* congruence between a people, a language, and an ancestral landscape is a commonplace of German Romanticism.) There is a considerable communal investment in presenting the Afrikaans literary tradition—a tradition, let it not be forgotten, that is the occasion for a vast echoing ideological discourse in classrooms and cultural organs—as speaking with a single voice on the subject of the land. There is a certain interest, even for official, establishment Afrikaans culture, in seeing Breytenbach as the bearer of a talent that he cannot, despite himself, betray; and to view his politics as an aberration that does not touch his poetic soul. There is an interest in not acknowledging that there can coexist in a single breast both a belief in a unitary democratic South Africa and a profound Afrikaans *digterskap*, poetness.

Hence the notion that the "terrorist" in Breytenbach can be incarcerated and punished while the poet in him can be left free. By acting as though Breytenbach must be a radically divided personality, one self a poet to be saved, the other self a traitor to be condemned, the greater Afrikaner family preserves its belief (and perhaps does so sincerely and in good faith) that the language, the mystical nation-essence, is greater than the fallible vessels who bear it.

The embrace of the Afrikaner, stony yet loving, finds its expression in the insufferable intimacy forced on Breytenbach by his security police interrogators, in which compassion and cruelty seem at times pathologically intertwined ("I am convinced that some of the people they have killed in detention probably died when the interrogator was in a paroxysm of unresolved frustrations, even that the interrogator killed in an awkward expression of love and sympathy"). The interrogators feed upon, and therefore depend upon, their prisoners. But Breytenbach extends the scope of the Hegelian master-slave dyad. What is the difference, he asks himself, between the "true confession" he utters into a microphone in Palermo in 1983 (eventually to become this book) and the "true confession" his interrogators demanded in Pretoria in 1975? Are not both of them answers to the question "What is the truth of your mission to South Africa?"? Before the interrogator, before the microphone, before the blank page, Breytenbach finds himself in the same position, staring at himself. So he develops the mirror as the master metaphor of his book; and the most interesting passages are the dialogues he conducts with the figure in the mirror, which is variously the cruel interrogator, the "true" Breytenbach, and the dark brother-African: "I see you now as my dark mirror-brother. We need to talk, brother I. I must tell you what it was like to be an albino in a white land. We are forever united by the ultimate knowledge of the depravity man will stoop to. Son of Africa. Azanians."

To his "dark mirror-brother" Breytenbach expresses his misgivings about the postrevolutionary South Africa of the future, which he foresees will fall under a no less totalitarian regime than the present one, and his bitterness against the "fat, institutionalized friends in the liberation movement" who sent him off on his fool-hardy mission in the first place. Bitterness emerges even more strongly in his judgments on white South Africa: "Let that bloated village of civil servants and barbarians [Pretoria] be erased from the face of the earth." As he observes, one of the effects of prolonged isolation is to kill off parts of you, "and these parts will never again be revived."

What will survive of Breytenbach's *True Confessions*, I think, is not the narrative of capture, interrogation, and imprisonment, ab-sorbing enough though that is, nor the apologia he gives for his quixotic foray into the fortress of the enemy, valuable though that is for its analysis of the appeal of direct political action to the intel-lectual. A feature of Breytenbach's poetry is that it *stops at nothing:* there is no limit that cannot be exceeded, no obstacle that cannot be leaped, no commandment that cannot be questioned. His writ-ing characteristically *goes beyond*, in more senses than one, what one had thought could be said in Afrikaans. The pages of *True Confessions* that stand out, that could have been written by no one else, are those in which he tries to feel his way into the experience of the condemned man, into the experience of death itself, and then into the moral world of the men who order deaths, build prisons, carry out tortures, and then into the very interior of the mad think-ing of "security" itself.

Mouroir was written during Breytenbach's prison years. It is a more substantial work than *True Confessions*, but more difficult, and probably of less general appeal. In quality it is variable. Subti-tled "Mirrornotes of a Novel," it consists of thirty-eight pieces, some short, some long. Some are no more than jottings. Others are profoundly impressive in their evocation of a terminal landscape, a landscape from beyond the war, where children go about giving birdcalls to lure the fled birds back to the earth. Though certain fragments are linked closely enough for us to follow an erratic, dreamlike narrative line through them, we would be hard put to form the pieces into the skeleton of any conceivable novel. We are better advised to read the book as an assemblage of stories, para-bles, meditations, and fragments, some of them centering on the themes of imprisonment, death, and freedom, others linked by the recurrent figures of the mirror and the labyrinth (the title of course plays on *mourir*, to die, and *miroir*, mirror). It is not too fanciful to conceive of the text that Breytenbach has left us as a kind of Ariadne's thread that he spins behind him as he advances through the labyrinth of his fictions (and his dreams) toward a meeting with the monstrous Other who is also both the self in the mirror and death.

But a merging with the mirror-self is not achieved, the heart of the labyrinth is not attained. Instead, as in Jean Cocteau's Orpheus films, the surface of the mirror becomes a hole of entry into another world, into yet another branch of the labyrinth. Thus we find Breytenbach's text moving forward by a continual process of metamorphosis, particularly a metamorphosis of landscape. Though the process seems dreamlike, the forward movement is purposeful, the motivations are not obscure, the connections are present on the surface or not too far beneath it. It is a form of writing that pays its respects to Kafka and Nabokov (one of Breytenbach's alter egos is called Gregor Samsa). In technique it owes much to the *nouveau roman*, though its focus is less on surfaces, as in Robbe-Grillet and Claude Simon, more on interiors and the properties of interiors: darkness, softness, wetness. Nevertheless, Breytenbach's voice is clearly his own.

The weakest sections are those in which Breytenbach works in the mode of the parable. When he deprives himself of the generative, metamorphosing powers of language and follows the more linear path of irony, the end results are thin. His irony gains bite only when he turns it on himself, as in his story about the radical writer who gives a press conference at the Rome airport before flying off to join the liberation struggle in South Africa: "Not in salons and ivory towers will revolutions be made. Purification in the struggle. Self-sacrifice. Freedom! *(Liberté!)* . . . Fierce fire in the pupils before the lashes are lowered."

How to write a revolutionary literature is a question to which *Mouroir* returns several times. One story deals with a writer who gives in to the pleas of friends and commences a conventional bourgeois tale of suburban adultery. Soon he discovers how hard it is to carry on writing when one's pants are soaked in horse blood. Nevertheless he plods on, in gathering darkness, till the fictional world he has created turns nasty, takes on a life of its own, and rends him.

The bloody horse alluded to here becomes a complex, ambivalent, and recurrent symbol in *Mouroir* as a whole. In the richly meaningful cover Breytenbach designed for the Afrikaans edition, a naked pink (albino?) figure (the artist?) passes by a barred window, his head covered (replaced?) by the huge eyeless severed head of a horse: stalking horse, Trojan horse; also Minotaur, mirror-taurus, figure of death from the dead center of the labyrinth; also the ludicrous counterimage of the warlike, passionate centaur.

A word must be said about the translation. There exists no Afrikaans edition of *True Confessions*. The edition we have must be accepted as a work written in English by Breytenbach. However, telltale solecisms indicate that Breytenbach is translating, and sometimes mistranslating, from an Afrikaans original. *Mouroir*, on the other hand, appeared in South Africa in 1983 in an edition partly in English but mainly in Afrikaans. Since no translator is named in the preliminaries to the American edition, we are justified in inferring that Breytenbach again did some or all of the translation; and the recurrence of idiosyncratic mistranslations tends to confirm this conclusion.

While the translation of parts of *Mouroir* is little short of masterly, in other parts it is nothing short of inept. Examples: "And then he went away with the cancer" (instead of "And then he died of cancer"); "wire obstacle" (instead of "barbed-wire entanglement"); "sucking black" (instead of "pitch-black"); "a sentence of grass" (instead of "a strip of grass"). These mistranslations emerge from a cursory check of a few odd-sounding passages. A careful check would, I am sure, produce hundreds more. Should the author's response be that what I call mistranslations are in fact creative reworkings, I would have to reply that what we have been given to read remains a poor substitute for the original.

Nadine Gordimer, *The Essential Gesture* (1989)

This collection of writings by Nadine Gordimer includes an autobiographical memoir, travel pieces, polemics on censorship, reflections on significant South African figures, and a variety of writings on the place of the writer in South Africa.[1] Among this last-mentioned group are several major interventions in the cultural life of South Africa; my attention will be devoted almost exclusively to them.

As Stephen Clingman emphasizes, in his editorial introduction here and in his book on Gordimer's novels (*The Novels of Nadine Gordimer*, 1986), Gordimer must be read against the background of her times. (I would qualify this by suggesting that, since Gordimer is uncannily prescient about shifts in historical mood, we should also read her against the background of what is/was *on the point* of happening.) Thus, for example, the first of her major essays, "A Writer's Freedom," dating from 1975, seems to foresee 1976 and the pressure for commitment that post-1976 South Africa would bring to bear on the writer.

What is a writer's freedom? It is "his right to maintain and publish to the world a deep, intense, private view of the situation in which he finds his society . . . He must take, and be granted, freedom from the public conformity of political interpretation, morals and tastes." And what does a "private view" mean? Gordimer is clear: "The truth as he sees it."

The most obvious threat to this freedom is official censorship. But a "more insidious" threat comes from the writer's "very awareness of what is expected of him": "conformity to an orthodoxy of opposition." This is the particular problem, as Gordimer sees it, of black South African writers. On these writers the pressure toward conformity extends down to the level of language, demanding that they write in "the jargon of struggle."

Though Gordimer takes her analysis of the demands of the South African situation no further here, she has sketched the contending demands—of art and politics, of Europe and Africa—that are more fully explored in the later essays (as indeed they are in her novels).

But, as if responding to the revolutionary writer impatient with *ars longa* and the kind of practice her own work represents, she does put forward the example of Ivan Turgenev, the (to her) exemplary realist who was able to subordinate his personal political beliefs to the demands of his art to such a degree that his readers could not tell whether his sympathies lay with the progressive characters in his novels or with the reactionaries. "His friends, admirers and fellow progressives stopped short, in their understanding of his genius, of the very thing that made him [a genius]— his scrupulous reserve of the writer's freedom to reproduce truth and the reality of life even if this truth does not coincide with his own sympathies."

An admirable ideal. But, however much inspiration the lonely figure of Turgenev could provide for a writer of Gordimer's generation, he was not, perhaps, the most appropriate figure—a cosmopolite, a romantic, and, in the best 1840s sense of the word, a liberal—to hold up as an exemplar to impatient young black writers post-1976. Gordimer does not make that move again.

The next major essay in the book, and the most closely argued, is "Relevance and Commitment" (1979). Gordimer returns to the subject of commitment. For the black artist, she writes, "relevance . . . is the supreme criterion." "Struggle is the state of the black collective consciousness and art is its weapon." When the writer gives in to pressure to use this weapon within an orthodoxy, the result is usually agitprop, "a phony sub-art." But hope enters when a second commitment is joined to the commitment to relevance: a commitment to create a new language and a new art for the people.

But what of the white writer? The fact that blacks now no longer offer whites the promise of a shared and equal future (one should remember that this essay was written during the ascendancy of

Black Consciousness thinking among black intellectuals) creates new inner difficulties for him.

> Exploitation, which the blacks *experience as their reality*, is something the white artist repudiates, refuses to be the agent of . . . The black creation of new selfhood is [therefore] based on a reality he, as a white, cannot claim and that could not serve him if he did since it is not of his order of experience. If he is to find his true consciousness, express in his work the realities of his place and time, if he is to reach the stage where commitment rises within him to a new set of values based on those realities, he has to admit openly the order of his experience as a white as differing completely from the order of black experience.

Once he has come to this realization, the white writer will have to find his own way to reconnect his art to "the total reality of the disintegrating present." In rethinking his own attitudes and conceptions he must aspire to the same relevance and the same commitment as the black writer to a future common indigenous culture. In that process he must find something to replace "the daemonic forces of disintegration which both drove him into alienation and were his subject."

The best-known and most controversial of the essays is "Living in the Interregnum" (1982). Here Gordimer starts by defining unambiguously her historical and social position: she belongs to a "segment" of the white population preoccupied neither with running away nor merely surviving, but on the contrary hoping to have "something to offer the future." Specifically, the question for her is: "How to offer one's self."

The interregnum, she says, quoting Antonio Gramsci, is a time when "the old is dying and the new cannot be born; in this interregnum there arises a great diversity of morbid symptoms." The interregnum is "not only between two social orders but between two identities, one known and discarded, the other unknown and undetermined . . . The white who has declared himself or herself for that future . . . does not know whether he will find his home at last."

During the interregnum, literary standards, like everything else, are confused. Gordimer admits she finds it hard to accept the reigning compulsory egalitarianism of black art ("All blacks are brothers; all brothers are equal; therefore you cannot be a better writer than I am"). She cannot accept that the truly gifted writer should have to deny his gifts, or that he should have to bow to an orthodoxy of agitprop. But, she goes on,

> the problem is that agitprop . . . has become the first contemporary art form that many black South Africans feel they can call their own. It fits their anger . . . I know that agitprop binds the artist with the means by which it aims to free the minds of the people . . . But how can my black fellow writer agree with me . . . ? There are those who secretly believe, but few who would assert publicly, with Gabriel García Márquez: "the writer's duty—his revolutionary duty, if you like—is to write well." The black writer in South Africa feels he has to accept the criteria of his people because in no other but the community of black deprivation is he in possession of selfhood . . . The black writer is "in history" and its values threaten to force out the transcendent ones of art. The white, as writer and South African, does not know his place "in history" at this stage, in this time.

In the most personal declaration in the book, she continues: "There are two absolutes in my life. One is that racism is evil . . . The other is that a writer is a being in whose sensibility is fused [a certain duality of the inward and outer reality], and he must never be asked to sunder this union. *The coexistence of these absolutes often seems irreconcilable within one life, for me* . . . The morality of life and the morality of art have broken out of their categories in social flux. If you cannot reconcile them, they cannot be kept from one another's throats, within you" (emphasis added).

Simply to embrace the role of dissident is no longer enough, for thereby the white writer remains "*negatively* within the white order." He has to "declare himself positively as answerable to the order struggling to be born."

Gordimer believes herself to have entered into this commitment, and believes that her writing since 1975 or so reflects it. Yet, while committed to finding a place "in history," she asserts her allegiance to "values that are beyond history. I shall never give them up."

As to her politics in a broader sense, she nails her colors to the mast. She can no longer believe in the capacity of Western capitalism to bring social justice to Africa. She recognizes how cruelly communism has betrayed its promise, but asserts nevertheless that there is socialism and socialism; she pins her hopes on the kind of politics represented by Poland's Solidarity.

The last essay in the group on which I concentrate is "The Essential Gesture" (1984). After taking swipes at "self-appointed cultural commissars" abroad who decide for the writer what his duties are at home, and at interviewers suspicious of anyone who is not in jail, Gordimer returns to the question of "black writers [being] expected to prove their blacknesss *as a revolutionary condition* by submitting to an unwritten orthodoxy of interpretation and representation in their work," and is happy to report that "many black writers of quality . . . have [now] begun to negotiate the right to their own, inner interpretation of the essential gesture by which they are part of the black struggle."

I have emphasized a single concern—the place of the writer in South Africa—in a single group of Gordimer's essays. Besides these, *The Essential Gesture* includes travel essays, a valuable memoir of her youth, "A Bolter and the Invincible Summer," and many minor pieces interesting in their own right, including the well-known early essay, "Where Do Whites Fit In?" (1959), where she writes: "I myself fluctuate between the desire to be gone—to find a society for myself where my white skin will have no bearing on my place in the community—and a terrible, obstinate and fearful desire to stay"—how much she has changed in thirty years, and how much remained the same!

This is a book about writing and the duties of the writer but not really a book of criticism. Gordimer is not interested in criticism as such: though her roots as a writer are in European realism and modernism, I am not aware of any extended discussion by her of writers from this tradition. Her critical writing is, in a specific sense of the word, occasional: most of the pieces dating from after 1970 started their lives as lectures or addresses. Without necessarily being egocentric, she is more interested in herself than in other writers: in herself as the site of a struggle between a towering European tradition and the whirlwind of the new Africa. Her intelligence is practical rather than theoretical, her interest in other writers a practical interest in what she can learn from them and use for her own purposes.

Nevertheless, Gordimer is a formidable presence on the South African intellectual scene, combining as she does a wide field of reference, an acute, no-nonsense mind, and a Shelleyan feeling for the stirrings of historical currents. My sense is that she is not much read in the Afrikaans community, in part perhaps because she has never demonstrated much sympathy for the Afrikaner. (There are other ways of putting this. One would be that she has from the beginning seen through the more genial and engaging forms of self-presentation employed by the Afrikaner.) If this sense is accurate, it is time that Afrikaans readers woke up: not only because Gordimer has behind her an oeuvre that constitutes a major piece of historical witness, an oeuvre greater than the sum of its parts, one that will be read years after the interregnum out of which it has emerged has passed into dust, but because the road that intellectuals of conscience in the Afrikaans community are at this moment traveling is a road that Gordimer herself passed along years ago. Anna Akhmatova speaks of the artist as "a visitor from the future" (Gordimer quotes her at the end of one of her essays). Gordimer, in the South Africa of the 1970s and 1980s, has been such a visitor from the future. It is a stature that she has created for herself by year after year of close listening and intense work: silence and cunning without exile.

That stature has come, of course, at personal cost, though no word of regret or self-pity breathes from the pages of this collection. The gifted young social satirist of *Friday's Footprint* had before her the prospect of quite a different and more attractive life than the life in the belly of the whale that the historical Gordimer has chosen for herself. Thus, for instance, though some of the pieces reprinted here are polemical—against the South African censors and more generally against apartheid—they provide no evidence that Gordimer has an appetite for polemic. I suspect that she sees this kind of writing as a job someone has to do: since there is no one better fitted than she to do it, she does it, and does it well (everything she does she does properly, thoroughly: her standards are never less than professional). But she does not thrive on strife. She is not even, in a fundamental sense, a political writer. Rather, she is an ethical writer, a writer of conscience, who finds herself in an age when any transcendental basis for ethics (as for aesthetics) is being denied in the name of politics. "The morality of life and the morality of art have broken out of their categories," she wrote in 1982. "If you cannot reconcile them, they cannot be kept from one another's throats, within you." It is a struggle for the reconciliation of public and private that this book charts.

= Retrospect

Interview

DA: We began these conversations by talking about autobiography, and it seems appropriate to return to that point in this final exchange. You spoke then of the open-endedness of autobiography and brought it into line with other forms of writing. At this stage, as you look back over the whole project, I want to ask you to reflect on where it has taken you: what are the moments of crystallization, the breaks or continuities, that the dialogue has enabled you to address, and what additional thoughts do you have on the nature of autobiography itself?

JMC: Let me return to what I was saying about autobiography as a biographical activity. Biography is a kind of storytelling in which you select material from a lived past and fashion it into a narrative that leads into a living present in a more or less seamless way. The premise of biography is continuity between past and present. Even the biography of crisis—for instance, so-called conversion narrative—doesn't deny this continuity. Conversion narrative may present the reborn self as having utterly superseded the past self; but it *thematizes* the discontinuity as something that could not have come about naturally, that could be the result only of divine intervention.

What sets autobiography apart from other biography is, on the one hand, that the writer has privileged access to information and, on the other, that because tracing the line from past to present is such a self-interested enterprise (self-interested in every sense), selective vision, even a degree of blindness, becomes inevitable—blindness to what may be obvious to any passing observer.

All autobiography is storytelling, all writing is autobiography. In these dialogues you have asked what I, in my blind way, have seen as I look back over the past twenty years of writing; and now you ask what I see when I look back over the dialogues themselves.

I must reply that more and more I see the essay on Tolstoy, Rousseau, and Dostoevsky emerging as pivotal. Why? For two reasons. One, that

391

there I see myself confronting in a different genre—the essay—the very question that you have faced me with in these dialogues: how to tell the truth in autobiography. Two, that I find the story I tell about myself has a certain definiteness of outline up to the time of that essay; after that it becomes hazier, lays itself open to harder questioning from the future.

What was going on in the essay? In the present retrospect I see in it a submerged dialogue between two persons. One is a person I desired to be and was feeling my way toward. The other is more shadowy: let us call him the person I then was, though he may be the person I still am. The field of their debate is truth in autobiography. The second person takes the position I have sketched above, but in a more extreme version: there is no ultimate truth about oneself, there is no point in trying to reach it, what we call the truth is only a shifting self-reappraisal whose function is to make one feel good, or as good as possible under the circumstances, given that the genre doesn't allow one to create free-floating fictions. Autobiography is dominated by self-interest (continues this second person); in an abstract way one may be aware of that self-interest, but ultimately one cannot bring it into full focus. The only sure truth in autobiography is that one's self-interest will be located at one's blind spot.

In the terms brought into prominence in the essay, the debate is between cynicism and grace. Cynicism: the denial of any ultimate basis for values. Grace: a condition in which the truth can be told clearly, without blindness. The debate is staged by Dostoevsky; the interlocutors are called Stavrogin and Tikhon.

Standing on the hillock or island created by our present dialogue, let me tell you, in the retrospect it provides, what the story of the past twenty years looks like when I make that story pivot on the essay on confession, written in 1982–83.

In the first half of this story—a story spoken in a wavering voice, for the speaker is not only blind but, written as he is as a white South African into the latter half of the twentieth century, disabled, disqualified—a man-who-writes reacts to the situation he finds himself in of being without authority, writing without authority. In this first half he reacts: he does not engage with his situation at a philosophical level.

The realization that he is disabled comes early, or so the evidence seems to say, when he looks back over his life, filling in the story. As a teenager, this person, this subject, the subject of this story, this I, though he more or less surreptitiously *writes*, decides to become, if at all possible, a scientist, and doggedly pursues a career in mathematics, though his talent there is no more than modest. How do I read this resolve? I say: he is trying to find a capsule in which he can live, a capsule in which he need not breathe the air of the world.

All his life he has lacked interest in his environment, physical or social. He lives wherever he finds himself, turned inward. In his juvenile writings he follows in the steps of Anglo-American modernism at its most hermetic. He immerses himself in Pound's *Cantos*. He admires Hugh Kenner above other critics. He admires Kenner's range of knowledge, his wit (which he is, alas, too plodding to imitate), but also the sangfroid with which Kenner ignores a whole range of experience: as for living, let the servants do that for us.

At the age of twenty-one he departs South Africa, very much in the spirit of shaking the dust of the country from his feet. When in the mid-1960s he quits computers in favor of an academic life—a life-saving decision on his part—it is to literature very narrowly conceived as an object of study that he turns. He writes a formalistic analysis of Beckett, concentrating on texts from a period in Beckett's life when Beckett too was obsessed with form, with language as self-enclosed game.

Does he grow homesick for South Africa? Though he feels at home neither in Britain nor in the United States, he is not homesick, nor even particularly unhappy. He merely feels alien.

Let me ("me") trace this feeling (of alienness, not alienation) further back in time. A sense of being alien goes back far in his memories. But to certain intensifications of that sense I, writing in 1991, can put a date. His years in rural Worcester (1948–1951) as a child from an Afrikaans background attending English-medium classes, at a time of raging Afrikaner nationalism, a time when laws were being concocted to prevent people of Afrikaans descent from bringing up their children to speak English, provoke in him uneasy dreams of being hunted down and accused; by the age of twelve he has a well-developed sense of social marginality. (People of his parents' kind are thundered at from the pulpit as *volksverraaiers*, traitors to the people. The truth is, his parents aren't traitors, they aren't even particularly deracinated; they are merely, to their eternal credit, indifferent to the *volk* and its fate.)

His years in Worcester are followed by adolescence in Cape Town, as a Protestant enrolled in a Catholic high school, with Jewish and Greek friends. For a variety of reasons he ceases visiting the family farm, the place on earth he has defined, imagined, constructed, as his place of origin. All of this confirms his (quite accurate) sense of being outside a culture that at this moment in history is confidently setting about enforcing itself as the core culture of the land.

Sociologically, it helps, perhaps, to think of him in his late teens as a *raznochinets*, in the line of Turgenev's Bazarov and those hordes of young men in Dostoevsky's novels with their pallid faces and burning eyes and schemes to change the world—as a socially disadvantaged, socially marginal young intellectual of the late British empire. Disadvantaged? Well, perhaps not disadvantaged. But by the standards of the white middle class, unadvantaged. His parents have no foothold in either Afrikaans or English social circles. They have unending financial troubles. He pays his own way through university doing odd jobs, if only because he is too squeamish to witness his mother's sacrifices.

Politically the *raznochinets* can go either way. But during his student years he, this person, this subject, my subject, steers clear of the right. As a child in Worcester he has seen enough of the Afrikaner right, enough of its rant, its self-righteousness, its cruelty, to last him a lifetime. In fact, even before Worcester he has perhaps seen more of cruelty and violence than should have been allowed to a child. So as a student he moves on the fringes of the left without being part of the left. Sympathetic to the human concerns of the left, he is alienated, when the crunch comes, by its language—by all political language, in fact. As far back as he can see he has been ill at ease with language that lays down the law, that is not provisional, that does not as one of its habitual motions glance back skeptically at its premises. Masses of people wake in him something close to panic. He cannot or will not, cannot and will not, join, shout, sing: his throat tenses up, he revolts.

This is the person who, in a slightly maturer version, goes to Texas to resume his studies in literature. I don't want to disparage the formalistic, linguistically based regimen he prescribed for himself for the fifteen years thereafter. The discipline within which he (and *he* now begins to feel closer to *I: autre*biography shades back into autobiography) had trained himself/myself to think brought illuminations that I can't imagine him or me reaching by any other route. But the essay on confession, as I reread it now, marks the beginning of a more broadly philosophical engagement with a situation in the world, his situation and perhaps still mine. It is best read, I think, side by side with *Waiting for the Barbarians*. The novel asks the question: Why does one choose the side of justice when it is not in one's material interest to do so? The Magistrate gives the rather

Platonic answer: because we are born with the idea of justice. The essay, if only implicitly, asks the question: Why should I be interested in the truth about myself when the truth may not be in my interest? To which, I suppose, I continue to give a Platonic answer: because we are born with the idea of the truth.

That is Part One, as I see it today, in the light of all that has passed between us. I'll stop there.

=

Notes

Editor's Introduction

1. John Leonard, "Beckett Safe from Computers." *The New York Times Book Review* 19 August 1973: p. 27. My thanks to Lindsay Waters, Shaun Irlam and Derek Attridge for their comments on earlier versions of this introduction.
2. J. M. Coetzee, "Samuel Beckett's *Lessness:* An Exercise in Decomposition," *Computers and the Humanities* 7, no. 4 (1973), 195–198.
3. A measure of Coetzee's success is the awards his fiction has received. Internationally, he has won the Geoffrey Faber and James Tait Black Memorial prizes (for *Waiting for the Barbarians*), the Booker-McConnell and Jerusalem prizes and the Prix Femina Etranger (for *Life & Times of Michael K*), and the *Sunday Express* Book of the Year award (for *Age of Iron*). In South Africa, he has won the Mofolo-Plomer prize (for *Dusklands*) and the CNA prize (for *In the Heart of the Country, Barbarians,* and *Michael K*). Coetzee is a fellow of the Royal Society of Literature, an honorary fellow of the Modern Languages Association of America, and a Nobel nominee.
4. J. M. Coetzee, *Foe* (Johannesburg: Ravan Press, 1986), pp. 135–136.
5. This account might be compared with Coetzee's own, "Retrospect." A complete bibliography of Coetzee's writing is to be found in K. Goddard and J. Read, eds., *J. M. Coetzee: A Bibliography*, National English Literary Museum Bibliographic Series no. 3. (Grahamstown: National English Literary Museum, 1990).
6. Nadine Gordimer, "Living in the Interregnum," in *The Essential Gesture: Writing, Politics, and Places* (London: Penguin, 1989), pp. 261–284. The phrase is from Gramsci's *Prison Notebooks*, which Gordimer cites in her epigraph to *July's People:* "The old is dying and the new cannot be born; in this interregnum there arises a great diversity of morbid symptoms" (Harmondsworth: Penguin, 1982).
7. Jean-Paul Sartre, Introduction to Léopold Sédar Senghor, *Anthologie de la nouvelle poésie nègre et malgache de langue française* (Paris: Presses universitaires de France, 1948); reprinted in *What Is Litera-*

ture? and Other Writings (Cambridge, Mass.: Harvard University Press, 1988).

8. J. M. Coetzee, *In the Heart of the Country* (Johannesburg: Ravan Press, 1977), p. 138.

9. C. P. Cavafy, *Collected Poems*, ed. George Savidis, trans. Edmund Keeley and Philip Sherrard (Princeton: Princeton University Press, 1975), pp. 17–18.

10. Michel Foucault, *The Archaeology of Knowledge*, trans. A. M. Sheridan Smith (London: Tavistock, 1972), p. 12.

11. J. M. Coetzee, *Waiting for the Barbarians* (Johannesburg: Ravan Press, 1981), p. 133.

12. J. M. Coetzee, *Life & Times of Michael K* (Johannesburg: Ravan Press, 1983), p. 160.

13. Gayatri Chakravorty Spivak, "Theory in the Margin: Coetzee's *Foe* Reading Defoe's *Crusoe/Roxana*," in *Consequences of Theory: Selected Papers from the English Institute, 1987–1988*, ed. Jonathan Arac and Barbara Johnson (Baltimore: Johns Hopkins University Press, 1991); reprinted in *English in Africa* 17, no. 2 (October 1990), 1–23.

14. Coetzee, *Foe*, p. 157.

15. J. M. Coetzee, *Age of Iron* (London: Secker & Warburg, 1990), p. 137.

16. Theodor Adorno, "Commitment," in Ernst Bloch, Georg Lukács, Bertolt Brecht, Walter Benjamin, and Theodor Adorno, *Aesthetics and Politics*, trans. and ed. Ronald Taylor (London: New Left Books, 1977), p. 194.

Interview

1. J. M. Coetzee, "Statistical Indices of 'Difficulty,'" *Language and Style* 2, no. 3 (1969), 226–232.

2. J. M. Coetzee, Review of Wilhelm Fucks, *Nach allen Regeln der Kunst*, *Style* 5, no. 1 (1971), 92–94.

3. J. M. Coetzee, "Samuel Beckett's *Lessness:* An Exercise in Decomposition," *Computers and the Humanities* 7, no. 4 (1973), 195–198.

4. J. M. Coetzee, "Surreal Metaphors and Random Processes," *Journal of Literary Semantics* 8, no. 1 (1979), 22–30.

5. Hugh Kenner, *Samuel Beckett: A Critical Study* (Berkeley: University of California Press, 1968), p. 132.

6. J. M. Coetzee, "Nabokov's *Pale Fire* and the Primacy of Art," *University of Cape Town Studies in English* 6 (1974), 1–7.

7. Rainer Maria Rilke, *Letters*, trans. Jane B. Greene and M. D. Herter (New York: Norton, 1945–1948), vol. 2, pp. 373–374.

The Comedy of Point of View in Beckett's Murphy

1. Samuel Beckett, *Murphy* (New York: Grove Press, 1957), p. 38.
2. A convenient way of selecting 100 sentences randomly is to use five-digit random numbers to give page number and sentence number. For obvious reasons, we should exclude from consideration Suk's prophecy (32–33) and the chess game (243–244).
3. Samuel Beckett, *Watt* (New York: Grove Press, 1959), p. 126.
4. Samuel Beckett, "Bram van Velde," in *Proust/Three Dialogues* (London: Calder, 1965), p. 125.
5. Samuel Beckett, *The Unnamable*, in *Three Novels* (New York: Grove Press, 1965), p. 291.
6. Fyodor Dostoevsky, *Notes from Underground*, trans. Ralph E. Matlaw (New York: Dutton, 1960), p. 16.

The Manuscript Revisions of Beckett's Watt

1. There are several changes between the Olympia Press edition of 1953 and the Grove Press edition of 1959 (which I use here), most notably the omission of Arsene's pet duck: compare pp. 49–50 of the former with p. 45 of the latter. The revisions are not particularly thorough—there remains an unexplained reference to the duck in the 1959 edition (p. 80), finally disposed of only in the French translation—but I have taken the 1959 edition as Beckett's final word in English.
2. Samuel Beckett, *Watt* (Paris: Editions de Minuit, 1968). The translation is by Ludovic and Agnes Janvier "in collaboration with the author." This was Beckett's first collaborative translation of a major work since he and Patrick Bowles had translated *Molloy* in 1955.
3. On "being properly born," see Addenda, p. 248. The story of Larry Nixon's birth, purely digressive in *Watt* (12–15), is an amplification of the story of the birth of Knott in the first draft. The recurring decimal in the song in *Watt* (34) represents the number of weeks in 2080, the year in which *A Clean Old Man* will first raise a laugh. The title Beckett gave to draft A was *Poor Johnny Watt*.
4. See "The Comedy of Point of View in Beckett's *Murphy*." The quotation is from *Murphy* (New York: Grove Press, 1957), p. 122.

Samuel Beckett and the Temptations of Style

1. Samuel Beckett, "Imagination Dead Imagine" (1965), in *No's Knife* (London: Calder, 1967), p. 161. All the translations quoted from in this essay are Beckett's own.

2. Samuel Beckett, *The Unnamable*, in *Three Novels* (New York: Grove Press, 1965), p. 291.
3. Samuel Beckett, *Ping*, in *No's Knife*, p. 168.
4. Samuel Beckett, *Lessness* (London: Calder & Boyars, 1970), p. 21.
5. Samuel Beckett, *Watt* (New York: Grove Press, 1959), p. 120.
6. Beckett, quoted in Lawrence E. Harvey, "Samuel Beckett on Life, Art, and Criticism," *Modern Language Notes* 80 (1965), 555.
7. Gustave Flaubert, letter to Louis Bonenfant, 12 December 1856, in *Correspondance*, ed. Jean Bruneau (Paris: Gallimard, 1980), vol. 2, p. 652.
8. Flaubert, letter to Louise Colet, 16 January 1852, ibid., p. 31.
9. Beckett, quoted in Niklaus Gessner, *Die Unzulänglichkeit der Sprache* (Zurich: Juris, 1957), p. 32n.
10. Richard N. Coe, *Beckett* (London and Edinburgh: Oliver & Boyd, 1964), p. 14.
11. Samuel Beckett, "Three Dialogues," in *Proust/Three Dialogues* (London: Calder, 1965), p. 103.
12. Of his friend Bram van Velde, Beckett writes that he is "the first to admit that to be an artist is to fail, as no other dare fail, that failure is his world"; "Three Dialogues," p. 125.

Interview

1. Marcellus Emants, *A Posthumous Confession*, Library of Netherlandic Literature, vol. 7, ed. Egbert Krispyn (Boston: Twayne, 1975; reprint, London: Quartet, 1986).
2. Besides Achterberg's "Ballade van de gasfitter," the translations are: Hans Faverey, seven poems from *Chrysanthen, roeiers* (Amsterdam: De Bezige Bij, 1977), in *Writing in Holland and Flanders* 38 (1981), 35–38; three poems from the same volume, together with Sybren Polet, "Zelfrepeterend gedicht," and Leo Vroman, "Gras Hooi," in *Dimension: Contemporary German Arts and Letters*, special issue, 11, 1 (1978), 46–51, 130–141, 178–181.

Achterberg's "Ballade van de gasfitter"

1. Gerrit Achterberg, "Ballade van de gasfitter," in *Verzamelde gedichten* (Amsterdam: Querido, 1967), pp. 833–847. Achterberg (1906–1962) is generally recognized as the most influential poet of his generation in the Netherlands. First published in 1953, the "Ballade" reiterates a theme that dominates Achterberg's poetry from the 1930s to the early 1950s: the death of the beloved and her recall through the power of the poetic word. The "Ballade" is the most ambitious work of a poet

who otherwise specialized in short, tightly constructed poems collected in successive volumes of *Cryptogramen*.

2. See particularly Anthonie Donker, "Het experiment van de gasfitter," *Critisch Bulletin* 21 (1954), 160–167; Andries Middeldorp, "De tragedie van de gasfitter," in *Nieuw commentaar op Achterberg*, ed. Bert Bakker and Andries Middeldorp (The Hague: Bakker, 1963), pp. 175–188; Kees Fens, "De onoverwinnelijke gasfitter," *Raster* 2 (1968), 157–170 and *Raster* 3 (1969), 197–208 (hereafter cited as Fens); K. Meeuwesse, "Bij Achterbergs ballade van de gasfitter," *Ons Erfdeel* 13 (1970), 19–23 (hereafter cited as Meeuwesse); Stanley M. Wiersma, "Gerrit Achterberg, Gasfitter," *Christian Scholar's Review* 1 (1971), 306–317 (including a translation) (hereafter cited as Wiersma). There is a detailed exegesis of the "Ballade" in A. F. Ruitenberg–de Wit, *Formule in den morgenstond* (Amsterdam: Querido, 1968), pp. 113–135. Sharing no common ground with this reading, I have made no use of it, nor have I consistently tried to carry across in my translation that polysemy which, read systematically, opens the poem to a Jungian interpretation.

3. Roman Jakobson, *Shifters, Verbal Categories, and the Russian Verb* (Cambridge, Mass.: Harvard University Russian Language Project, 1957), p. 2; Emile Benveniste, "La Nature des pronoms," in *Problèmes de linguistique générale* (Paris: Gallimard, 1966), pp. 254, 256.

4. See Meeuwesse, p. 19; Wiersma, p. 307.

5. See Meeuwesse, p. 178.

6. Benveniste, "La Nature de pronoms," p. 252.

7. Wallace Stevens, "Notes toward a Supreme Fiction," in *Collected Poems* (New York: Knopf, 1955), pp. 395–396.

8. Martin Buber, *I and Thou*, trans. R. G. Smith, 2d ed. (Edinburgh: Clark, 1959), pp. 3, 24, 21, 16, 34; idem, *Between Man and Man*, trans. R. G. Smith (London: Fontana, 1961), p. 246. I call Buber's *I–Thou* a myth advisedly (Buber does not use the term). It is an "in the beginning" myth, both ontogenetic and phylogenetic, a myth of the fall into the quotidian from an original state of relation, as pp. 18–22 and 24–28 of *I and Thou* make clear.

9. Buber, *I and Thou*, p. 3.

10. These characteristics of the *You* emerge from linguistic analysis of the occurrences of the pronoun "you" (Achterberg's *gij/u*, properly "thou," here translated as "You") in the poem. These occurrences include two where "you" is part of "we." (The notation 9/6 stands for sonnet 9, line 6; and so forth.)

a. "You must have made your entries from the rear" (1/1). The verb is marked for inferential modality. (The Dutch says literally, "You have reached the houses from behind," but this is an *a posteriori* inference from the appearance of You in each windowframe.)

b. "You appear and reappear" (1/4), "You vanish" (1/5). The relation between the sentence pairs

> You appear [to me]
> I see you

and

> You vanish [to me]
> I do not see you

is *ergative:* the second is in each case a causally transformed version of the first. The *You* is the object of the gaze of the *I*.

c. "As if You could escape me" (2/8). That is, "You cannot escape me."

d. "The apple-hawker lures You" (1/11). The modality of the sentence is hypothetical, and *being lured* is by definition involuntary.

e. "Indoors with You" (2/1). The *I* and the *You* are in a relation of locativity.

f. "I . . . see You standing" (2/2–3). The pseudoactivity (in fact the mere locativity) of the *You* is attested only by the gaze of the *I*. (This emphasis is even stronger in the original, literally "my eyes . . . see you stand.")

g. "We grow murky" (2/5). The relation between the sentences

> We grow murky [to each other]
> We see each other murkily [that is, do not see each other clearly]

is again ergative. There is reciprocity, but it is a reciprocity of incapacity.

h. "You and I can keep our incognito" (2/9). "Keep" (= continue) is a dummy verb (that is, a verb absent from the deep structure) carrying a progressive aspect marker. The underlying sentence is "We do not know each other."

i. "You are gone" (4/7). The *You* is absent. In the original, lines 6–7 read literally, "I turn with an explanatory gesture toward You, but You are no longer there." The (absent) *You* marks the direction of orientation of the *I*.

j. "The higher I ascend, the wider space/yawns between You and me" (9/1–2). The spatial relation between *I* and *You* is defined by the activity of the *I*.

11. Jean-Paul Sartre, *Being and Nothingness*, trans. Hazel E. Barnes (New

York: Washington Square Press, 1966), p. 59. See also p. xxxviii of the translator's introduction. Imagery of the leak in being occurs elsewhere in Achterberg's oeuvre. "Gehenna" (1953) begins: "I am the weak spot in the universe[,]/ the hidden leak" (*Verzamelde gedichten*, p. 789). The gasfitter's crisis is literally an experience of nothing, "a vacuum" (11/5).

12. The following seven parallels are notable:
The blessing of Jesus by God (Matthew 3:17); the blessing of the gasfitter by his supervisor (sonnet 5)
The inner torment of Jesus, followed by resignation to the will of God, and sleep of the disciples (Matthew 26:38–46); evasiveness of the gasfitter before his supervisor's commands, followed by flirtation with escape, and sleep of the concierge (sonnets 5–7)
The mocking of Jesus and the ascent of Calvary; the mocking of the gasfitter by the maid and his ascent in the elevator (sonnet 8)
Jesus' moment of doubt on the cross (Matthew 27:46); the gasfitter's admission of failure (sonnet 9)
Acclamation of the Lamb by a host "of all nations, and kindreds, and people, and tongues" (Revelations 7:9–10); scorning of the gasfitter by a host "of every nation, race, and tongue" (sonnet 10)
The descent from the cross and the burial of Jesus (Matthew 27:58–60); the descent of the gasfitter in the elevator and his journey "underground" (sonnet 10)
The ascent of Jesus to the right hand of God (Mark 16:19); the return of the gasfitter to his supervisor and his dismissal (sonnet 11)

13. Sören Kierkegaard, *Concluding Unscientific Postscript*, trans. David F. Swenson and Walter Lowrie (Princeton: Princeton University Press, 1944), p. 187; idem, *Training in Christianity*, trans. Walter Lowrie (Princeton: Princeton University Press, 1944), pp. 127, 131.

14. Rudolf Bultmann, "What Does It Mean to Speak of God?" in *Faith and Understanding*, vol. 1, trans. Louise P. Smith (London: SCM Press, 1966), p. 53.

15. Gabriel Marcel, "I and Thou," in *The Philosophy of Martin Buber*, ed. Paul A. Schilpp and Maurice Friedman (London: Cambridge University Press, 1967), p. 44. Buber's reply to Marcel—that there is a distinction between the *Thou* that I "mean" and the word that I say—misses Marcel's point, which is that language does not preserve the stress of intention. See Buber, "Replies to My Critics," ibid., pp. 705–706.

16. Eugene Ianesco, quoted in George Steiner, *After Babel* (London: Oxford University Press, 1975), p. 185.

17. Kierkegaard, *Concluding Unscientific Postscript*, p. 412.

18. "The women say . . . the language you [women] speak is made up of signs that rightly speaking designate what men have appropriated. Whatever they have not laid hands on . . . does not appear in the language you speak. This is apparent precisely in the intervals that your masters have not been able to fill with their words of proprietors and possessors, this can be found in the gaps, in all that which is not a continuation of their discourse, in the zero, the 0, the perfect circle that you invent to imprison them and to overthrow them"; Monique Wittig, *The Guérillères*, trans. D. Le Vay (London: Pan, 1972), p. 123. The 0, the circle, the hole are symbols of that which male authoritarian language cannot appropriate.

19. See Fens, pt. I, 162–165, and pt. II, 198–199.

20. In chapter 3 of Lewis Carroll's *Through the Looking-Glass*, Alice and the fawn walk lovingly together through "the wood where things have no names." At the edge of the wood the two beings recover their lost names "fawn" and "human child." "A sudden look of alarm came into [the fawn's] beautiful brown eyes, and in another moment it had darted away at full speed."

21. "The cords of all link back," wrote Joyce, back along all the genealogies of names to Adam, who issues out of the black hole of the void with God's maieutic help; *Ulysses* (New York: Random House, 1961), p. 38.

22. Herman Melville, *Moby-Dick*, chap. 36.

23. The puzzling question of why this sonnet alone, of the sequence 1–12, is dominated by the past tense, is debated in the essays cited in note 2 above. I find none of the explanations I have read convincing, but have none of my own to offer.

24. Gustave Flaubert, letter to Louise Colet, 16 January 1852, in *Correspondence*, ed. Jean Bruneau (Paris: Gallimard, 1980), vol. 2, p. 31.

25. Samuel Beckett, "Three Dialogues," in *Proust/Three Dialogues* (London: Calder, 1965), p. 103.

26. S. Dresden, "Horizontale poëzie," in Bakker and Middeldorp, *Nieuw commentaar of Achterberg*, p. 21.

27. Wiersma, p. 315. The original reads:

Hoe hoger of ik stijg hoe groter wordt
de ruimte tussen u en mij. Het leven
voelt zich door nikkel en door staal omgeven.
Het bouwsel komt geen klinknagel te kort.

Hier zit geen gas. God is het gat en stort
zijn diepten op mij uit om te beleven
aan een verwaten fitter hoe verheven
hijzelf bij iedere étage wordt.

Verdieping na verdieping valt omlaag.
Ik weet niet waar of wat ik moet beginnen.
Misschien schiet me een laatste woord te binnen
als ik hem naar de eerste oorzaak vraag.
Een schok gaat door mij heen. Ik moet er uit
en geef het over aan zijn raadsbesluit.

Quoted by permission of Stichting Willem Kloos Fonds, The Hague.
28. Wiersma, p. 309.

The First Sentence of Yvonne Burgess' *The Strike*

1. Jorge Luis Borges, "Pierre Menard, Author of the *Quixote*," trans. James E. Irby, in *Labyrinths*, ed. Donald A. Yates and James E. Irby (New York: New Directions, 1962), p. 43.

A Note on Writing

1. Roland Barthes, "To Write: An Intransitive Verb?" in *The Languages of Criticism and the Sciences of Man*, ed. Richard Macksey and Eugenio Donato (Baltimore: Johns Hopkins University Press, 1970), pp. 134–156.
2. Ibid., p. 142.

Interview

1. J. M. Coetzee, "The Great South African Novel," *Leadership SA* 4 (1983), 74–79; idem, "The White Tribe," *Vogue*, March 1986, pp. 490–491, 543–544; idem, "Tales of Afrikaners," *New York Times Magazine*, 9 March 1986, pp. 19–22, 74–75, reprinted in *Reader's Digest*, August 1986, pp. 19–26, and in *Fair Lady*, 28 May 1986, pp. 66–69, 130, 132–133.
2. In "The Burden of Consciousness in Africa."

Captain America in American Mythology

1. *Captain America and the Falcon*, published in New York by Marvel Comics Group, a division of Cadence Industries Corporation. The period of Captain America's life dealt with in this essay is 1972–1974, when the script was written by Steve Englehart and the artwork done by Sal Buscema (occasionally by Alan Lee Weiss). Inking, lettering, and coloring were done by house personnel. References of the form 164/12 are to issue 164, page 12.
2. Freud: "The ego is first and foremost a bodily ego; it is not merely a

surface entity, but is itself the projection of a surface"; *The Ego and the Id*, trans. Joan Riviere, ed. James Strachey (New York: Norton, 1962), p. 16. In a footnote to the 1927 English translation, Freud adds: "I.e., the ego . . . may be regarded as a mental projection of the surface of the body" (ibid).

3. "Performance principle: the prevailing historical form of [Freud's] reality principle . . . Libido is diverted for socially useful performances in which the individual works for himself only in so far as he works for the apparatus"; Herbert Marcuse, *Eros and Civilization* (London: Abacus, 1972), pp. 42, 48.

4. Issue 179 (November 1974) deals with Captain America's reactions to the Watergate scandal.

The Burden of Consciousness in Africa

1. The film *The Guest* (1977) was directed by Ross Devenish and starred Athol Fugard.

2. Leon Rousseau, Die *groot verlange* (Cape Town: Human & Rousseau, 1974), p. 384.

3. Ibid., p. 380.

Four Notes on Rugby

1. Johan Huizinga, *Homo Ludens*, trans. R. F. C. Hull (London: Routledge & Kegan Paul, 1949), p. 7.

Triangular Structures of Desire in Advertising

1. René Girard, *Deceit, Desire, and the Novel* (1961), trans. Yvonne Freccero (Baltimore: Johns Hopkins University Press, 1965); hereafter cited as *DDN*.

2. René Girard, *Violence and the Sacred* (1972), trans. Patrick Gregory (Baltimore: Johns Hopkins University Press, 1977).

3. René Girard, *To Double Business Bound* (Baltimore: Johns Hopkins University Press, 1978), p. 66; hereafter cited as *DB*.

4. Alexis de Tocqueville, *Democracy in America* (1840), trans. Henry Reeve, ed. Richard D. Heffner (New York: New American Library, 1956), p. 194.

5. Max Scheler, *Ressentiment* (1915), trans. B. Holdheim (New York: Free Press, 1961), pp. 60–77.

6. Fred Inglis, *The Imagery of Power: A Critique of Advertising* (London: Heinemann, 1972).

The Rhetoric of the Passive in English

1. Richard Ohmann, "Prolegomena to the Analysis of Prose Style" (1959), in *Essays on the Language of Literature*, ed. Seymour Chatman and Samuel R. Levin (Boston: Houghton Mifflin, 1967), p. 405.
2. In this early essay Ohmann is still working in the tradition of European *Stilforschung*. Behind the certainty that a continuous path can be traced back from syntactic pattern to epistemology lies an organicist conception of the literary work such as we find in Leo Spitzer: "The lifeblood of the poetic creation is everywhere the same, whether we tap the organism at 'language' or 'ideas,' at 'plot' or at 'composition'"; *Linguistics and Literary History* (Princeton: Princeton University Press, 1948), p. 18.
3. Ernest Hemingway, "Che ti dice la patria?" in *Men without Women* (New York: Scribner's, 1927), pp. 109–110.
4. We may later revise our reading and see Hemingway's narrator as someone holding back powerful emotions, particularly a sense of the pity of it all. A tension between these two conceptions of the narrator, tough and tender, may be what Hemingway wants us to experience. But this dual sense arises out of a full reading of the stories and can only be read back afterward into the affectlessness of the sentences quoted.
5. Aristotle, *Rhetoric*, trans. W. Rhys Roberts (New York: Modern Library, 1924), I.1. E. M. Cope comments that by a science Aristotle understands "a systematic and rational procedure, governed by the general rules derived from experience, but distinguished from mere practical skill . . . by the apprehension of *cause* . . . and the recognition of *general* principles"; *An Introduction to Aristotle's Rhetoric* (London, 1867), p. 135n.
6. Ian Watt, "The First Paragraph of *The Ambassadors*," in Henry James, *The Ambassadors* (1903), ed. S. P. Rosenbaum (New York: Norton, 1963), p. 470.
7. Roger Fowler, "Style and the Concept of Deep Structure," *Journal of Literary Semantics* 1 (1972), 17.
8. Richard Ohmann, "Mentalism in the Study of Literature," in *Proceedings of the Conference on Language and Language Behavior*, ed. Eric M. Zale (New York: Appleton-Century-Crofts, 1968), p. 194.
9. Walker Gibson, *Tough, Sweet, and Stuffy: An Essay on Modern American Prose Styles* (Bloomington: Indiana University Press, 1966), p. 123. Julia P. Stanley expands on this observation: "Either we choose the active voice because it places the speaker in a position of having to accept responsibility for her assertions, or we choose the

passive voice because it is more 'objective,' placing the responsibility for the validity of our assertions on some unspecified 'generic' person"; "Passive motivation," *Foundations of Language* 13 (1975), 37.

10. See Roman Jakobson, "Quest for the Essence of Language," *Diogenes* 51 (1965), 28.

11. Aldo Scaglione, *The Classical Theory of Composition* (Chapel Hill: North Carolina University Press, 1972), pp. 3–4; R. H. Robins, *Ancient and Mediaeval Grammatical Theory in Europe* (London: Bell, 1951), pp. 34, 40, 66.

12. Quintilian, *Institutio oratoria*, trans. H. E. Butler, 4 vols. (London: Heinemann; New York: Dutton, 1920), vol. 1, I.iv.28–29.

13. Robins, *Grammatical Theory*, pp. 40n, 66.

14. The basic classification of devices in classical rhetoric is into tropes and figures. The precise line of demarcation between the two is vexed and has always been; see Richard Lanham, *A Handlist of Rhetorical Terms* (Berkeley: University of California Press, 1968), p. 101, for discussion. It makes no difference to my argument which class hyperbaton is taken to fall into. Quintilian, the most encyclopedic of the rhetoricians, is hesitant in his classification of the device: see *Institutio oratoria*, vol. 3, VIII.vi.62–67 and IX.iii.24.

15. See Scaglione, *Classical Theory of Composition*, pp. 76–86.

16. Paul de Man, "Semiology and Rhetoric," *Diacritics* 3, no. 3 (1973), 28.

17. Noam Chomsky, *Aspects of the Theory of Syntax* (Cambridge, Mass.: MIT Press, 1965), pp. 103–106.

18. K. Hasegawa, "The Passive Construction in English," *Language* 44 (1968), 230-243.

19. Robert Friedin, "The Analysis of Passives," *Language* 51 (1975), 384–405.

20. J. R. Hust, "The Syntax of the Unpassive Construction," *Linguistic Analysis* 3 (1977), 31–63; Joan Bresnan, "A Realistic Transformational Grammar," in *Linguistic Theory and Psychological Reality*, ed. Morris Halle, Joan Bresnan, and G. A. Miller (Cambridge, Mass.: MIT Press, 1978).

21. C. L. Baker, "Syntactic Theory and the Projection Problem," *Linguistic Inquiry* 10 (1979), 533–581.

22. *Oxford English Dictionary*, s.v. *with*, 38b, 40.

23. V. S. Khrakovsky, "Passive Constructions," in *Trends in Soviet Theoretical Linguistics*, ed. Ferenc Kiefer (Dordrecht: Reidel, 1973).

24. For an attempt to define the passive along these lines, see Vilem Mathesius, *A Functional Analysis of Present-Day English on a General Linguistic Basis* (1961), ed. Josef Vachek (The Hague: Mouton, 1975), pp. 107–114, and particularly Mathesius' range of examples.

25. Bresnan, "Realistic Transformational Grammar," pp. 14–23.

26. Noam Chomsky, "Remarks on Nominalization," in *Studies on Semantics in Generative Grammar* (The Hague: Mouton, 1970).

27. George O. Curme, *Syntax* (Boston: D. C. Heath, 1931), p. 446.

28. Dwight Bolinger, "Syntactic Blends and Other Matters," *Language* 37 (1961), 366–381; Jan Svartvik, *On Voice in the English Verb* (The Hague: Mouton, 1966), pp. 159–163.

29. Jerrold J. Katz and Paul Postal, *An Integrated Theory of Linguistic Descriptions* (Cambridge, Mass.: MIT Press, 1964), p. 80.

30. Joseph E. Emonds, *A Transformational Approach to English Syntax* (New York: Academic Press, 1976), pp. 69–74.

31. Khrakovsky, "Passive Constructions"; Irene Warburton, "The Passive in English and Greek," *Foundations of Language* 13 (1975), 563–578; John Haiman, "Agentless Sentences," *Foundations of Language* 14 (1976), 19–53.

32. J. Wackernagel, *Vorlesungen über Syntax* (Basle, 1926); Khrakovsky, "Passive Constructions."

33. The evidence for 3 is summarized in Bresnan, "Realistic Transformational Grammar," pp. 44–45.

34. Charles N. Li and Sandra A. Thompson, "Subject and Topic: A New Typology of Language," in *Subject and Topic*, ed. Charles N. Li (New York: Academic Press, 1976).

35. *Basic* here is used in the strict sense of E. L. Keenan in "Towards a Universal Definition of 'Subject,'" in Li, *Subject and Topic*, p. 307.

36. Charles Fillmore, "The Case for Case," in *Universals in Linguistic Theory*, ed. Emmon Bach and Robert T. Harms (New York: Holt, Rinehart and Winston, 1968), p. 58.

37. Vilem Mathesius, "On Linguistic Characterology" (1928), in *A Prague School Reader in Linguistics*, ed. Josef Vachek (Bloomington: Indiana University Press, 1964), p. 66.

38. J. Firbas, "Non-Thematic subjects in Contemporary English," *Travaux linguistiques de Prague* 2 (1966), 244–245; Wallace L. Chafe, *Meaning and the Structure of Language* (Chicago: University of Chicago Press, 1970), pp. 219–222.

39. Leslie Butters, "Thematization and Topicalization: Their Functioning in Movement Tranformations in English," *Cahiers linguistiques d'Ottawa* 5 (1977), 80–83.

40. Ian Watt argues that Augustan irony insists on differences of social rank by dividing its readers into an elite who can decode it and a mob who are mystified by it. It is thus a defense erected by aristocratic sensibilities against middle-class encroachments; "The Ironic Tradition in Augustan Prose from Swift to Johnson," in *Restoration*

and Augustan Prose, ed. James R. Sutherland and Ian Watt (Los Angeles: University of California Press, 1956).

The outstanding exception to my generalization about novelists is Henry James. See, for example, *The Ambassadors*, pp. 307–308.

41. Ohmann is explicit on the psychological reality he attributes to syntactic structures: "Quite literally the structures and forms in a literary work can only be forms—be realized as forms—in some mind. It follows that literary criticism is a study of mental structures"; "Mentalism," p. 209.

42. Edward Gibbon, *Decline and Fall of the Roman Empire* (1781), ed. J. B. Bury, 7 vols. (London and New York: Dent, n.d.), II, 28.

43. David Hume, *An Inquiry concerning Human Understanding* (1758) (New York: Liberal Arts Press, 1955), p. 140.

44. Gibbon, *Decline and Fall*, III, 205.

45. Since *with* can govern an agentive in Hume's English, we have a kind of structural pun here: as an agentive phrase, *with miracles* forms a pair with *by any reasonable person;* as an adverbial phrase it forms a pair with *without one.*

46. On the interpretation of parallelism, see the important observations of Roman Jakobson in "Linguistics and Poetics" (1958), in *Essays on the Language of Literature*, ed. Seymour Chatman and Samuel R Levin (Boston: Houghton Mifflin, 1967), as well as Jakobson's numerous essays on poetic texts.

47. Jonathan Swift, *A Modest Proposal* (1729), in *Satires and Personal Writings of Jonathan Swift*, ed. W. A. Eddy (London: Oxford University Press, 1932), p. 26.

48. Henry Fielding, *Jonathan Wild* (1743) (London: Cass, 1967), p. 9.

49. David Hume, *The History of England* (1762) (London, 1789), p. 368.

50. According to Svartvik, the number of passives per 1,000 words averages 23 for science writing, 13 for writing in the humanities, 9 for everyday speech, and 8 for fiction; *On Voice in the English Verb*, p. 152.

51. See, for instance, A. E. Darbyshire, *A Grammar of Style* (London: Deutsch, 1971), pp. 87–88.

52. G. W. Turner, "The Passive Construction in English Scientific Writing," *AUMLA* 18 (1962), 181–197.

53. R. S. Westfall, *Force in Newton's Physics* (New York: Elsevier, 1971), p. 336.

54. Isaac Newton, *De mundi systemate liber* (London, 1728), p. 3; *A Treatise of the System of the World* (1731) (London: Dawson, 1969), p. 5.

55. The sources for these lists are as follows. (1) L. Kellner, *Historical Outlines of English Syntax* (London: Macmillan, 1892), p. 224; Otto Jespersen, *The Philosophy of Grammar* (London: Allen and Unwin,

1924), p. 167; Khrakovsky, "Passive Constructions," p. 72; Mathesius, *A Functional Analysis*, p. 107; Chafe, *Meaning and Structure*, p. 219; Haiman, "Agentless Sentences," p. 50. (2) Kellner, p. 224; Jespersen, p. 167; Mathesius, "On Linguistic Characterology," p. 62; Fillmore, "The Case for Case," p. 58; A. C. Partridge, *Tudor and Augustan English* (London: Deutsch, 1969), p. 134; Chafe, p. 221; R. W. Langacker and P. Munro, "Passives and Their meaning," *Language* 51 (1975), 820; Li and Thompson, "Subject and Topic," p. 463; Warburton, "The Passive in English and Greek," p. 571; Robert S. Kirsner, "On the Subjectless 'Pseudo-Passive' in Standard Dutch," in Li, *Subject and Topic*, p. 389; Haiman, p. 50. (3) Kellner, p. 224; Jespersen, p. 168; Mathesius, *A Functional Analysis*, p. 107. Note that in the case of (2) I combine "topicalize" and "give prominence to" under "thematize."

The Agentless Sentence as Rhetorical Device

1. Daniel Defoe, *Robinson Crusoe* (1719), ed. Michael Shinagel (New York: Norton, 1975), p. 6. I have modernized the spelling.
2. Thus statal predicates as well as actional passives may fall into my class of passives, as long as they can plausibly take an agentive phrase. For justification of this treatment, see Jan Svartvik, *On Voice in the English Verb* (The Hague: Mouton, 1966), pp. 159–163.
3. See Maximilian E. Novak, *Defoe and the Nature of Man* (London: Oxford University Press, 1963).
4. See Jerrold J. Katz and Paul Postal, *An Integrated Theory of Linguistic Descriptions* (Cambridge, Mass.: MIT Press, 1964), pp. 79–80.
5. See Joseph E. Emonds, *A Transformational Approach to English Syntax* (New York: Academic Press, 1976), pp. 69–74; Katz and Postal, *Integrated Theory*, p. 80.
6. See V. Khrakovsky, "Passive Constructions," in *Trends in Soviet Theoretical Linguistics*, ed. Ferenc Kiefer (Dordrecht: Reidel, 1973); John Haiman, "Agentless Sentences," *Foundations of Language* 14 (1976), 19–53. The psychological evidence is summarized in Joan Bresnan, "A Realistic Transformational Grammar," in *Linguistic Theory and Psychological Reality*, ed. Morris Halle, Joan Bresnan, and G. A. Miller (Cambridge, Mass.: MIT Press, 1978). On the relative frequency of short and long passives, see Khrakovsky, p. 24.
7. Samuel Beckett, *Three Novels* (New York: Grove Press, 1965), p. 12.
8. Henry James, *The Ambassadors*, ed. S. P. Rosenbaum (New York: Norton, 1963), p. 307.
9. The basis of the distinction I draw between a stylistic device and a

rhetorical device is that, whereas the former may be peculiar to a single text, the latter has general application and can be said to form part of a rhetorical system. The notion of system is fundamental to the Aristotelian conception of rhetoric: see *Rhetoric* I.i.

10. Of the 74 passives in a text of some 6,000 words, only 6 have an expressed agent. Two do not fall into any of the groups I have defined. For the four groups the counts are, respectively, 40, 15, 4, 7.

11. Jonathan Swift, *An Argument against the Abolishing of Christianity*, in *Satires and Personal Writings of Jonathan Swift*, ed. W. A. Eddy (London: Oxford University Press, 1932), p. 11. I have modernized the spelling.

12. See Paul de Man, "Semiology and Rhetoric," *Diacritics* 3, no. 3 (1973), 27–33.

13. Edward Gibbon, *Decline and Fall of the Roman Empire*, ed. J. B. Bury, 7 vols. (London and New York: Dent, n.d.), III, 213.

14. Gibbon's footnote to the sentence glosses his meaning: "At Minorca, the relics of St. Stephen converted in eight days 540 Jews; with the help, indeed, of some wholesome severities, such as burning the synagogues, driving the obstinate infidels to starve among the rocks, etc."

15. Richard Ohmann, "Mentalism in the Study of Literature," in *Proceedings of the Conference on Language and Language Behavior*, ed. Eric M. Zale (New York: Appleton-Century-Crofts, 1968). Some of the details of Ohmann's analysis have been rendered obsolete by developments in grammatical theory, but the argument as a whole retains its force.

16. See Harold Bond, *The Literary Art of Edward Gibbon* (Oxford: Oxford University Press, 1960), p. 126.

17. See Walker Gibson, *Tough, Sweet, and Stuffy: An Essay on Modern American Prose Styles* (Bloomington: Indiana University Press, 1966), p. 123; A. E. Darbyshire, *A Grammar of Style* (London: Deutsch, 1971), pp. 87–88; Julia P. Stanley, "Passive Motivation," *Foundations of Language* 13 (1975), 37.

18. In my essay "The Rhetoric of the Passive" I argue that, particularly in the prose of Newton, we see agentless sentences used as means for representing physical processes in regard to which the question of agency or cause is to be held in abeyance, outside the terms of the discussion. See also G. W. Turner, "The Passive Construction in English Scientific Writing," *AUMLA* 18 (1962), 181–97.

19. See Ian Watt, "The Ironic Tradition in Augustan Prose from Swift to Johnson," in *Restoration and Augustan Prose*, ed. James R. Sutherland and Ian Watt (Los Angeles: University of California, 1956).

Isaac Newton and the Ideal of a Transparent Scientific Language

1. Wilhelm von Humboldt, "On the Differentiation of the Structure of Human Language and Its Effect on the Spiritual Development of the Human Race" (1830–1835), in *Werke*, vol. 3: *Schriften zur Sprachphilosophie*, ed. Andreas Flitner and Klaus Giel (Stuttgart: Cotta, 1963), pp. 433–434.
2. Wilhelm von Humboldt, "On Comparative Philology in Relation to the Various Epochs of Linguistic Evolution" (1820), ibid., p. 19.
3. See Robert L. Miller, *The Linguistic Relativity Principle and Humboldtian Ethnolinguistics* (The Hague: Mouton, 1968), pp. 103–120.
4. Benjamin L. Whorf, *Language, Thought, and Reality: Selected Writings*, ed. John B. Carroll (Cambridge, Mass.: MIT Press, 1956), pp. 240–244.
5. E. J. Dijksterhuis, *The Mechanization of the World Picture*, trans. C. Dikshoorn (Oxford: Oxford University Press, 1961), p. 479. I am indebted to this work for my sketch of the seventeenth-century background.
6. Quoted in ibid., p. 480; my translation.
7. Gottfried Wilhelm von Leibniz, letter of 1711, quoted in Alexander Koyré, *Newtonian Studies* (Chicago: University of Chicago Press, 1965), p. 141.
8. "Hypotheses non fingo." On the sense of *hypotheses,* and for an argument that *fingo* is better translated "feign," see ibid., pp. 36–39.
9. Isaac Newton, *Mathematical Principles of Natural Philosophy*, 3d ed., trans. Andrew Motte, translation rev. Florian Cajori (Berkeley: University of California Press, 1934), pp. 546–547; hereafter cited as Motte–Cajori.
10. Isaac Newton, *Optics* (New York: Dover, 1952), Book III, query 31 (p. 401).
11. Isaac Newton, letter of 1692, quoted in Dijksterhuis, *Mechanization*, p. 488.
12. Koyré, *Newtonian Studies*, p. 163.
13. Motte–Cajori, p. 397.
14. Newton, quoted in Rolf-Dieter Herrmann, "Newton's Positivism and the A Priori Constitution of the World," *International Philosophical Quarterly* 15 (1975), 207.
15. Motte–Cajori, p. 10.
16. Isaac Newton, *Principia*, Book III, prop. IV, scholium (Motte–Cajori, p. 409).
17. Ibid., prop. IV (Motte–Cajori, p. 407).

18. Isaac Newton, *De mundi systemate* (London, 1728), sec. 3; Motte–Cajori, p. 551. Newton's Latin reads: "viribus centripetis Planetas in orbibus certis retineri posse" (p. 3).
19. Newton, *Optics*, Book III, query 31 (pp. 389, 401).
20. Charles Fillmore, "The Case for Case," in *Universals in Linguistic Theory*, ed. Emmon Bach and Robert T. Harms (New York: Holt, Rinehart and Winston, 1968), p. 24.
21. The growth in the use of the passive is discussed in G. W. Turner, "The Passive Construction in English Scientific Writing," *AUMLA* 18 (1962), 181–197. Turner points to the evolution from the solitary scientific investigator to the team of investigators, and the resulting anonymity of the investigating agent, as an additional reason for the proliferation of agentless sentences.
22. Roman Jakobson, "Poetry of Grammar and Grammar of Poetry," *Lingua* 21 (1968), 597–609.
23. Richard Boyd, "Metaphor and Theory Change," in *Metaphor and Thought*, ed. Andrew Ortony (Cambridge: Cambridge University Press, 1979), p. 360.
24. See, for example, Ian G. Barbour, *Myths, Models and Paradigms* (London: S.C.M. Press, 1974), p. 44.
25. This is the *Aufhebung* of metaphor proposed by Hegel in *The Philosophy of Fine Arts*. See Jacques Derrida, "White Mythology," *New Literary History* 6 (1974), 5–74, particularly 24–25.

Interview

1. Walter Benjamin, *Illuminations* (1955), ed. Hannah Arendt, trans. Harry Zohn (New York: Schocken Books, 1969), p. 126.
2. Theodor Adorno, "Commitment," in Ernst Bloch, Georg Lukács, Bertolt Brecht, Walter Benjamin, and Theodor Adorno, *Aesthetics and Politics*, trans. and ed. Ronald Taylor (London: New Left Books, 1977), p. 180.
3. Neil Lazarus, "Modernism and Modernity: T. W. Adorno and Contemporary White South African Literature," *Cultural Critique* 5 (1987), 131–155.
4. J. M. Coetzee, *Life & Times of Michael K* (Johannesburg: Ravan Press, 1983), p. 228.
5. Nadine Gordimer, "The Idea of Gardening," *New York Review of Books*, 2 February 1984, pp. 3, 6.
6. Paul Ricoeur, *Time and Narrative*, trans. Kathleen McLaughlin and David Pellauer, 2 vols. (Chicago: University of Chicago Press, 1985).

7. J. M. Coetzee, *In the Heart of the Country* (Johannesburg: Ravan Press, 1978), pp. 79,80.

8. J. M. Coetzee, *Waiting for the Barbarians* (Johannesburg: Ravan Press, 1981), p. 133.

9. Coetzee, *Life & Times of Michael K*, p. 216.

Time, Tense, and Aspect in Kafka's "The Burrow"

1. Franz Kafka, *The Complete Stories*, trans. Willa Muir and Edwin Muir, ed. Nathan Glatzer (New York: Schocken Books, 1946), p. 325. Because the Muir translation is the standard one, I use it throughout in this essay except at points where the Muirs, perhaps baffled by Kafka's unusual tense sequences, attempt to smooth out the time structure by silent emendation. I have indicated in notes all departures from the Muir translation, in most cases through reference to the German text edited by J. M. S. Pasley in *Der Heizer. In der Strafkolonie. Der Bau* (Cambridge: Cambridge University Press, 1966). Pasley's text is based on a fresh reading of Kafka's manuscript and improves on the text given by Max Brod in Franz Kafka, *Gesammelte Schriften*, vol. 5 (New York: Schocken, 1946). For a cautionary word about Pasley's text, however, see Heinrich Henel, "Das Ende von Kafkas *Der Bau*," *Germanisch-Romanische Monatsschrift* 22 (1972), 22–23.

2. The Muir translation reads: " . . . while I was inside it."

3. I follow the Brod text here. The Pasley text is in error; see Henel, "Das Ende," p. 23.

4. See Henel, "Das Ende," p. 7.

5. Although the Muirs translate the next few verbs as preterites, they are present in form in the German.

6. For example: "In such cases as the present it is usually the technical problem [of tracking down the noise] that attracts me" (344); "often already I have fallen asleep at my work" (348); (when he begins to shovel soil) "this time everything seems difficult" (350).

7. Dorrit Cohn, "Kafka's Eternal Present: Narrative Tense in 'Ein Landarzt' and other First-Person Stories," *PMLA* 83 (1968), 144–150; idem, *Transparent Minds* (Princeton: Princeton University Press, 1978).

8. Cohn, *Transparent Minds*, pp. 195–197.

9. Henel, "Das Ende," p. 6, 5.

10. Ibid., pp. 5–6.

11. The cases I cite in note 6 above are enough to indicate that Henel's conclusions are generalizations rather than laws, in the sense in which I use the terms. His generalizations are further weakened by

a habit of selective quotation. For example, he writes of a "wholly new, hitherto never before grasped resolution" at which the creature arrives, "nämlich von dem Leben im Freien 'Abschied zu nehmen,' 'niemals mehr zurückzukommen,' und der 'sinnlosen Freiheit' auf immer den Rücken zu kehren" (p. 6). The paradox Henel does not face here is that even this decisive-sounding resolution is given in a form wholly compatible with an iterative time, as fuller quotation reveals: "Und ich habe Lust, Abschied zu nehmen . . . und niemals mehr zurückzukommen . . . Gewiß, ein solcher Entschluß wäre eine völlige Narrheit, hervorgerufen nur durch allzu langes Leben in der sinnlosen Freiheit" (pp. 121–122 in Pasley; pp. 335–336 in the Muir translation). It is the *content* of the phrases Henel quotes that leads him to think of the resolution as making a break in the cycle; but the paradox is precisely that in this story every irruption into the cycles of time is so ambiguously presented in temporal *form* that it seems at least capable of being absorbed into the cycles.

12. Henel, "Das Ende," p. 4. "As present proper, it describes an occurrence achieving itself in the *now;* as historic present an earlier occurrence; as iterative present a present occurrence that has happened in the same way or a similar way fairly often; as progressive present likewise a present occurrence which extends into an indefinite, perhaps endless future; and finally the present can serve as a form of inner monologue" (ibid.).

13. Gustave Guillaume, *Temps et verbe* (Paris: Champion, 1929); idem, *Leçons de linguistique*, vol. 1, ed. Roch Valin (Quebec: Laval, 1975); W. H. Hirtle, *Time, Aspect, and the Verb* (Quebec: Laval, 1975).

14. For discussion of this point see Bernard Comrie, *Aspect* (Cambridge: Cambridge University Press, 1976), pp. 42–43.

15. Henry Sussman, "The All-Embracing Metaphor: Reflections on Kafka's 'The Burrow,'" *Glyph* 1 (1977), 104, 106.

16. In the same part of his essay from which I quote, Sussman, however, gives a characterization of narrated time in the story that ignores the complexities of time and aspect I have tried to outline, in particular the "dissolve" from (B, E) to (B$_i$, E$_i$), followed by reversion. Thus Sussman's following argument, central to his reading of the story, is so much the weaker: "In having recourse only to the here circumscribed by the construction and the now in which the work of construction goes on, or at least is contemplated, the voice of the text abolishes the 'subject' which is presumably its source and master. Although the ruminations of the animal are always in 'self'-interest, in the absence of any subject, the self becomes the self of language, whose existence, like the concept of the animal, defines the negation

of the (human) self" (104–105). It is irrelevant for the moment whether the self is "the self of language" (Sussman's thesis) or the self of narration (as I would prefer): all that concerns me here is that Sussman's argument is not well founded.

17. In the postscript to his edition of the story, Max Brod, on the authority of Dora Dymant, writes that Kafka completed "The Burrow," and that in the pages lost from the end the creature met his death in a fight with his enemy. However, Heinz Politzer argues cogently that there is no good reason to depend on Dora Dymant's word and that the evidence points more strongly to the conclusion that Kafka himself destroyed the final pages, finding them unsatisfactory. See Max Brod, "Nachwort," in Kafka, *Gesammelte Schriften* (New York: Schocken, 1946), vol. 5, p. 314; Heinz Politzer, *Franz Kafka: Parable and Paradox* (Ithaca: Cornell University Press, 1962), p. 330; Henel, "Das Ende," pp. 15–16. Kafka did not prepare the manuscript for publication. We may therefore suppose that it never underwent a final revision.

18. See the notebook entry for 11 December 1917, in which Kafka writes of the moment of expulsion from paradise as a moment eternally repeated, yet as belonging to a time that "cannot exist in temporal relation" to human time; *Gesammelte Werke: Hochzeitsvorbereitungen auf dem Lande,* ed. Max Brod (New York: Fischer/Schocken, 1953), p. 94.

19. I take the description of the derivational relationship of past to present from Roman Ingarden, *Time and Modes of Being,* trans. Helen R. Michejda (Springfield, Ill.: Thomas, 1964), p. 117. On the experience of the present in Kafka, see further Max Bense, *Die Theorie Kafkas* (Cologne and Berlin: Kiepenheuer & Witsch, 1952), p. 62; Jörg Beat Honegger, *Das Phänomen der Angst bei Franz Kafka* (Berlin: Schmidt, 1975), pp. 29–31.

20. See, for example, Roman Jakobson: "It is the predominance of metonymy which underlies and actually predetermines the so-called 'realistic' trend"; Roman Jakobson and Morris Halle, *Fundamentals of Language* (The Hague: Mouton, 1956), p. 78. See also Victor Erlich, *Russian Formalism* (The Hague: Mouton, 1969), p. 195.

21. Cohn, *Transparent Minds,* p. 197.

22. Kafka, *Hochzeitsvorbereitungen,* pp. 73–74. Quite aside from the literary-biographical problem of relating the journal entry to a story written some six years later, we should be wary of erecting large interpretive edifices upon journal entries that may be no more than fleeting, partial insights developed in greater precision by the fiction. Cohn perhaps places too much reliance on this particular entry in her reading of "The Burrow." For a caveat against abstracting the

thoughts Kafka notes down in his journals from the particular density of the experiences they arise from, see Maurice Blanchot's essay "La Lecture de Kafka," in *La Part du feu* (Paris: Gallimard, 1949), pp. 9–19. Blanchot writes: "The Journal is full of remarks that seem connected to theoretical knowledge . . . But these thoughts . . . relapse into an equivocal mode that does not allow them to be understood either as the expression of a unique happening or as the explication of a universal truth" (p. 10).

23. Cohn's paraphrase would fit more comfortably over Kafka's meditations, in the same notebook, on the eternal return of the expulsion from paradise (*Hochzeitsvorbereitungen*, p. 94); that is, they describe a mythic present. I would suggest parenthetically that part of the reason for Cohn's failure to push her conclusions far enough may lie in her reliance on the treatment of the present in Harald Weinrich's *Tempus*. Weinrich treats the "historic present" as an "als ob" for a past time and as a component of a "Metaphorik der Tempora." It is, however, precisely the metaphoricity of the narrative present that Kafka is bringing into doubt in this story. See Weinrich, *Tempus: Besprochene und erzählte Welt* (Stuttgart: Kohlhammer, 1964), pp. 125–129; Cohn, "Kafka's Eternal Present," p. 149.

Robert Musil's Stories of Women

1. Quotations are from Robert Musil, *Five Women*, trans. Eithne Wilkins and Ernst Kaiser (1966; reprint, Boston: Nonpareil Books, 1986). This volume incorporates two stories by Musil not included in the 1924 collection, *Three Women;* hence the different title.

Interview

1. J. M. Coetzee, *Truth in Autobiography*, 3 October 1984, University of Cape Town (pamphlet).
2. J. M. Coetzee, *Foe* (Johannesburg: Ravan Press, 1986), p. 157.
3. J. M. Coetzee, *Age of Iron* (London: Secker Warburg, 1990), p. 91.

Confession and Double Thoughts

1. St. Augustine, *Confessions*, trans. Albert C. Outler (London: SCM Press, 1955), II.iv,ix; pp. 54–55, 59; hereafter cited in the text.
2. In a useful essay in definition, Francis R. Hart describes confession as "personal history that seeks to communicate or express the essential nature, the truth, of the self," apology as "personal history that

seeks to demonstrate or realize the integrity of the self," and memoir as "personal history that seeks to articulate or repossess the historicity of the self." Thus "confession is ontological; apology ethical; memoir historical or cultural"; "Notes for an Anatomy of Modern Autobiography," in *New Directions in Literary History*, ed. Ralph Cohen (Baltimore: Johns Hopkins University Press, 1974), p. 227.

3. For example, in the essays "Of Exercise or Practice" (Book II, chap. vi) and "Of Presumption" (Book II, chap. xvii). Montaigne expresses his intention to "see and search myself into my very bowels" in Book III, chap. v. Michel de Montaigne, *Essays*, trans. John Florio (London, 1891), p. 430.

4. See Peter M. Axthelm, *The Modern Confessional Novel* (New Haven: Yale University Press, 1967).

5. I use the term *confessor* to denote the one to whom the confession is addressed and the term *confessant* for the one who confesses. It is worth noting that Oswald Spengler, quoting Goethe's lament over the end of auricular confession brought about by Protestantism, suggests that it was inevitable that after the Reformation the confessional impulse should find an outlet in the arts, but also that, in the absence of a confessor, it is inevitable that such confession should tend to be "unbounded"; *The Decline of the West*, trans. Charles F. Atkinson (London, 1932), II, 295.

6. Leo Tolstoy, *The Kreutzer Sonata and Other Stories*, trans. Louise and Aylmer Maude (Oxford: Oxford University Press, 1924), p. 233. Where I give the Russian, I quote from "Kreitserova sonata," in L. N. Tolstoi, *Sochineniya*, IV (Berlin, 1921), pp. 160–293. Subsequent references appear in the text.

7. Leo Tolstoy, "An Afterword to *The Kreutzer Sonata*," in *Essays and Letters*, trans. Aylmer Maude (London, 1903), pp. 36, 38.

8. Donald Davie, "Tolstoy, Lermontov, and Others," in *Russian Literature and Modern English Fiction*, ed. Donald Davie (Chicago: University of Chicago Press, 1965), p. 164.

9. T. G. S. Cain, *Tolstoy* (London: Elek, 1977), pp. 148–149.

10. On becoming engaged, Pozdnyshev (like Levin in *Anna Karenina*) hands over his intimate diaries to his future wife, who reads them with horror. Tolstoy draws in both novels on the episode in his own life when he gave his intimate diaries to his fiancée, Sonya Behrs. In his biography of Tolstoy, Henri Troyat describes the part the diaries played in the marriage. Quoting an entry from 1863 ("Nearly every word in his notebook is prevarication and hypocrisy. The thought that she [Sonya] is still here now, reading over my shoulder, stifles and perverts my sincerity"), Troyat comments that the "private

confessions" the couple made in their diaries "unconsciously turned into arguments of prosecution and defense" against each other. As Tolstoy's fame grew and it became clear that his diaries would one day become public, the question of what he might write in them became a matter of strife, his wife on occasion denouncing him in her diary for insulting her in his diary. In the last year of his life Tolstoy kept a secret diary, which he hid in his boot (his wife ferreted it out while he was asleep); Troyat, *Tolstoy*, trans. Nancy Amphoux (Harmondsworth: Penguin, 1970), pp. 371, 397, 366, 718–719, 902, 917.

Countess Tolstoy regarded *The Kreutzer Sonata* as neither a free-floating fiction nor a sermon but a personal attack "directed against me, [mutilating] me and [humiliating] me in the eyes of the whole world." She wrote a novel in response, denouncing Tolstoy, the preacher of celibacy, as a sexual brute, and was barely restrained from publishing it (Troyat, pp. 665–668).

11. Rainer Maria Rilke, letter of 21 October 1924, in Henry Gifford, ed., *Tolstoy: A Critical Anthology* (Harmondsworth: Penguin, 1971), p. 187.

12. William C. Spengemann, *The Forms of Autobiography* (New Haven: Yale University Press, 1980), p. 15.

13. Leo Tolstoy, *My Confession*, in *My Confession and The Spirit of Christ's Teaching*, trans. N. H. Dole (London, n.d.), p. 77; hereafter cited in the text. Where I give the Russian, I quote from *Ispoved'* (Letchworth: Prideaux Press, 1963). The title can be rendered *Confession* or *A Confession* (there is no article in Russian).

14. Leo Tolstoy, *Anna Karenina*, trans. Rosemary Edmonds (Harmondsworth: Penguin, 1954), p. 829.

15. Man "*knows* himself in consequence of and in accordance with the nature of his will, instead of *willing* in consequence of and in accordance with his knowing"; Arthur Schopenhauer, *The World as Will and Idea*, trans. R. B. Haldane and J. Kemp, 4th ed. (London, 1896), I, 378.

16. Matthew Arnold, "Count Leo Tolstoi," in *Essays in Criticism*, 2d series (London, 1888), p. 283.

17. Leo Tolstoy, *Life*, trans. Isabel F. Hapgood (London, 1889), p. 70.

18. V. V. Zenkovsky, *A History of Russian Philosophy*, trans. George L. Kline (London: Routledge, 1953), I, 391.

19. Quoted in Cain, *Tolstoy*, p. 9; Maxim Gorky, *Reminiscences of Tolstoy, Chekhov and Andreev*, trans. Katherine Mansfield, S. S. Koteliansky, and Leonard Woolf (London: Hogarth Press, 1968), p. 30.

20. Jean-Jacques Rousseau, *Confessions*, anonymous translation, 2 vols. (London: Dent, 1931), I, 1; hereafter cited in the text. Where I give

the French, I quote from *Oeuvres complètes*, ed. Bernard Gagnebin and Marcel Raymond (Paris: Gallimard, 1959), vol. 1.

21. Paul de Man, *Allegories of Reading: Figural Language in Rousseau, Nietzsche, Rilke, and Proust* (New Haven: Yale University Press, 1979), p. 280.

22. This strategy is common in Rousseau. For example: "Far from having been silent about anything or suppressed anything that might have been laid at my door, I often found myself tending to lie in the contrary sense, and accusing myself with too much severity rather than excusing myself with too much indulgence; and my conscience answers me that one day I will be judged less severely than I have judged myself"; "Quatrième Promenade," in *Oeuvres complètes*, p. 1035; my translation.

23. De Man, *Allegories of Reading*, pp. 285–286.

24. See, for example, Wordsworth's second "Essay upon Epitaphs" (1810): "Where [the] charm of sincerity lurks in the language of a tombstone and secretly pervades it, there are no errors of style or manner for which it will not be, in some degree, a recompense"; *Prose Works*, ed. W. J. B. Owen and J. W. Smyser (Oxford: Clarendon Press, 1974), II, 70.

25. See, for example, T. S. Eliot, "The Metaphysical Poets" (1921): "A philosophical theory which has entered into poetry is established, for its truth or falsity in one sense ceases to matter, and its truth in another sense is proved"; *Selected Prose*, ed. John Hayward (Harmondsworth: Penguin, 1953), p. 118.

26. Jean Starobinski, *Jean-Jacques Rousseau: La Transparence et l'obstacle* (Paris: Plon, 1957), pp. 214–215.

27. Ibid., pp. 228, 240.

28. *Annales*, quoted in ibid., p. 243.

29. Starobinski, *Rousseau*, p. 248.

30. Though it is an easy eloquence that betrays Rousseau here, the language of the Other from which he more often strives to free himself is the language of La Rochefoucauld, La Bruyère, and Pascal. "The great prose writers of seventeenth-century France," writes Margery Sabin, "established an authoritative language of psychological description which drew strength precisely from the public character of language." Rousseau carries his protest against this language of feeling, says Sabin, down to "every level of the work, even to the implications of syntax and the meanings of individual words." She goes on to give an exemplary analysis of Rousseau's style in his description of his feelings for Mme. de Warens, where phrases "circle" the elusive feeling rather than pinning it down. "If his emotion remains elusive,

confusing, paradoxical—well, the style argues, that is the true nature of his inner life"; *English Romanticism and the French Tradition* (Cambridge, Mass.: Harvard University Press, 1976), pp. 19, 29.

31. The episode is recounted in Book VII (I, 261, 292–294).

32. Starobinski comments that Rousseau first uses "the principle of immediacy" to clarify his psychology, but that almost at once this principle "takes on the value of a superior justification, of a moral imperative" of higher validity than "ordinary rules of right and wrong" (*Rousseau*, p. 132). In fact the principle is not given a moral coloring in the passage I am considering.

33. For example, in the discussion of his "miserliness" during his time with Mme. de Warens, or of his dislike of giving money for sex (Books V, VII; I, 188, 261).

34. Jacques Derrida, *Of Grammatology*, trans. Gayatri Chakravorty Spivak (Baltimore: Johns Hopkins University Press, 1976), pp. 157, 163–164, 245.

35. It might be objected that I draw too sharp a line between being aware and not being aware of the "deeper" truth, ignoring the gradations and subtleties of self-deception that stretch between the extremes of innocence and mendacity. But, as Michel Leiris for one recognizes, the autobiographer takes on himself in the same way that the *torero* takes on the bull: there are no excuses for defeat; *Manhood*, trans. Richard Howard (London: Cape, 1968), p. 20.

36. For this account of the mechanism of self-deception I im indebted to Herbert Fingarette, *Self-Deception* (London: Routledge, 1969), pp. 86–87.

37. David Hume, *A Treatise of Human Nature*, ed. Ernest Mossner (Harmondsworth: Penguin, 1969), p. 300.

38. Fyodor Dostoevsky, *The Insulted and Injured*, trans. Constance Garnett (London, 1915), pp. 240–251.

39. This is in essence the position taken by Alex de Jonge in *Dostoevsky and the Age of Intensity* (London: Secker and Warburg, 1975). De Jonge's thesis is that many of Dostoevsky's confessants—Valkovsky, Marmeladov, and Svidrigailov among them—are adherents of a "cult of intensity" founded by Rousseau, who exploit the masoschistic pleasures of self-abasement. De Jonge sees Dostoevsky as a psychologist of confession exploring the ways in which people with no sense of self, no sense of guilt, no interest in the truth, use self-revelation as an instrument of power and pleasure (pp. 175–176, 181, 186–187).

40. Mikhail Bakhtin argues that the Dostoevskian novel is a form of Menippean satire, a mixture of fictional narrative with philosophical

dialogue, confession, hagiography, fantasy, and other usually incompatible elements. In addition, says Bakhtin, Dostoevsky exploits the old European tradition of the carnival, where customary social restraints may be dropped and utter frankness may reign in human contacts; *Problems of Dostoevsky's Poetics,* trans. Caryl Emerson (Manchester: Manchester University Press, 1984), chap. 4. To Bakhtin the confession is thus in the first place a structural element of Dostoevsky's fiction, though he goes on to explore a "dialogic" attitude toward the self in Dostoevsky's first-person narrators, the self becoming its own interlocutor (chap. 5).

41. Fyodor Dostoevsky, *Notes from Underground,* in *Notes from Underground and The Grand Inquisitor,* ed. and trans. Ralph E. Matlaw (New York: Dutton, 1960), pp. 6, 8, 9, 16, 8; hereafter cited in the text. The metaphor of self-consciousness as a disease is a commonplace in Europe by the 1860s. "Self-contemplation . . . is infallibly the symptom of disease," wrote Thomas Carlyle in 1831: only when "the fever of Scepticism" is burned out will there be "clearness, health"; "Characteristics," in *Critical and Miscellaneous Essays* (London, 1899), vol. 3, pp. 7, 40. See also Geoffrey H. Hartman, "Romanticism and 'Anti-Self-Consciousness,'" in *Romanticism and Consciousness,* ed. Harold Bloom (New York: Norton, 1970), pp. 46–56.

42. On Part I of *Notes from Underground* as a critique of the Nihilism of the the 1860s, see Joseph Frank, "Nihilism and Notes from Underground," *Sewanee Review* 69 (1961), 1–33.

43. "I wish to declare . . . that if I write as though I were addressing readers, that is simply because it is easier for me to write in that way . . . I shall never have readers" (35).

44. "Metaphysical concern for the end of Man is realized in the most formal attributes of the structure of [Dostoevsky's] novels, the narrative shape. And this is so because he was among the first to recognize that what a man might be could not be separated from the question of what might constitute an authentic history"; Michael Holquist, *Dostoevsky and the Novel* (Princeton: Princeton University Press, 1977), p. 194.

45. Fyodor Dostoevsky, *The Idiot,* trans. David Magarshak (Harmondsworth: Penguin, 1955), pp. 344–346; hereafter cited in the text. Where I give the Russian I quote from *Idiot* (Kishinev, U.S.S.R.: Kartya Moldovenyaske, 1970).

46. I have amended Magarshak's translation slightly, rendering *imenno* as "precisely" rather than "merely."

47. The paradox of the seed probably comes from John 12:24: "Except a

corn of wheat fall into the ground and die, it abideth alone: but if it die, it bringeth forth much fruit." The verse is quoted in *The Brothers Karamazov*, trans. Constance Garnett (London, 1927), I, 320.

48. "There will be full freedom when it will be just the same to live or not to live . . . He who will conquer pain and terror will himself be a god . . . Every one who wants the supreme freedom must dare to kill himself . . . He who dares kill himself is God"; *The Possessed*, trans. Constance Garnett, with a translation of the chapter "At Tikhon's" by Avrahm Yarmolinsky (New York: Modern Library, 1936), pp. 114–115; hereafter cited in the text.

49. René Girard, *Deceit, Desire, and the Novel: Self and Other in Literary Structure*, trans. Yvonne Freccero (Baltimore: Johns Hopkins University Press, 1965), p. 276.

50. However, the paradox inherent in the notion of self-compulsion stands. And, at the moment of stress when Stavrogin confesses "the whole truth," namely that he wants to forgive himself, and asks for "measureless suffering," Dostoevsky returns to a dualistic psychology in which an "inner" self utters itself: Stavrogin speaks "as if the words had again issued from his mouth against his will" (727).

51. Insofar as the metarule of the game is that the rules should not be spelled out—in fact that it should not be spelled out that there are any rules, or any game—the account of the mechanisms of self-deception given by Fingarette neatly describes the game (see note 36 above).

52. Fyodor Dostoevsky, *The Diary of a Writer*, trans. Boris Brasol (London: Cassell, 1949), II, 787–788.

Interview

1. J. M. Coetzee, "Blood, Taint, Flaw, Degeneration: The Novels of Sarah Gertrude Millin," *English Studies in Africa* 23, no. 1 (1980), 41–58; reprinted in Coetzee, *White Writing: On the Culture of Letters in South Africa* (New Haven: Yale University Press, 1988), pp. 136–162.

2. "André Brink and the Censor," *Research in African Literatures* 21, no. 3 (1990), 59–74; "Censorship and Polemic: The Solzhenitsyn Affair," *Pretexts* 2, no. 2 (1990), 3–36; "Breytenbach and the Censor," *Raritan* 10, no. 4 (1991), 58–84.

The Taint of the Pornographic

1. C. H. Rolph, ed. *The Trial of Lady Chatterley* (London: privately printed, 1961), pp. 70–72, 89–90, 159.

2. D. H. Lawrence, *Lady Chatterley's Lover* (New York: Modern Library, 1957), p. 252; hereafter cited as *LCL*.
3. D. H. Lawrence, *A Propos of Lady Chatterley's Lover* (London: Mandrake Press, 1930), pp. 9–10.
4. Tylor, quoted in Mary Douglas, *Purity and Danger: An Analysis of Concepts of Pollution and Taboo*, rev. ed. (London: Routledge & Kegan Paul, 1969), p. 13.
5. Rolph, *Trial*, p. 98.
6. Ibid., pp. 253, 255.
7. Ibid., p. 265.
8. The force of "bad language" that the gamekeeper exerts on Connie is clearest in the first version of the story. In one episode, Parkin/Mellors derides Connie's word "lover" and confronts her with himself as her "fucker." "'Fucker!' he said, and his eyes darted a flash at her, as if he shot her"; *The First Lady Chatterley* (London: Heinemann, 1972), p. 108. This aggressive verbal act is directed not only by Parkin at Connie: as Evelyn J. Hinz points out, the baring of obscene words is also a baring of the teeth by Lawrence at his (British) readers; "Pornography, Novel, Mythic Narration: The Three Versions of *Lady Chatterley's Lover*," *Modernist Studies* 3 (1979), 41.
9. D. H. Lawrence, *Selected Letters*, ed. Diana Trilling (New York: Farrar, Straus, Cudahy, 1958), p. 275.
10. For the first three, see D. H. Lawrence, *Selected Literary Criticism*, ed. Anthony Beal (New York: Viking, 1966), pp. 26–30, 32–51, 52–67; hereafter cited as *SLC*.
11. Jonathan Swift, "The Lady's Dressing Room," "Cassinus and Peter," "A Beautiful Young Nymph Going to Bed," and "Strephon and Chloe"; *Complete Poems*, ed. Pat Rogers (New Haven: Yale University Press, 1983), pp. 448–466.
12. For a detailed reading along these lines, see T. B. Gilmore, "The Comedy of Swift's Scatological Poems," *PMLA* 91 (1976), 33–41.
13. Lawrence writes: "There is a poem of Swift's . . . written to Celia, his Celia—and every verse ends with the mad, maddened refrain: 'But—Celia, Celia, Celia shits!'" (*SLC*, p. 29). Huxley published his essay on Swift in 1929. See Aldous Huxley, *On Art and Artists*, ed. Morris Philipson (New York: Harper, 1960), pp. 168–176.
14. D. H. Lawrence, letter to Lady Ottoline Morrell, 28 December 1928, *SLC*, p. 26; Introduction to *Pansies*, *SLC*, p. 29; *A Propos of Lady Chatterley's Lover*, p. 14.
15. See David Burnley, *A Guide to Chaucer's Language* (Norman: University of Oklahoma Press, 1983), chap. 8.
16. At this point Lawrence writes most clearly under the influence of

Frazer. To Frazer, what characterizes the savage is a failure to distinguish between *unholiness* and *uncleanness*. As Mary Douglas points out (*Purity and Danger*, pp. 10–11), by relegating uncleanness to the kitchen and bathroom, Christianity makes it a matter of (secular) hygiene, leaving holiness as a purely moral/spiritual category. From this point of view—which Lawrence, with his nonconformist Christian background, seems to share—to revive what ought to be a matter of simple hygiene as a taboo with the force of religion (or superstition) behind it, is precisely a throwback to savagery.

17. Rolph, *Trial*, pp. 221–224. At least one observer came away convinced that the jury failed to understand the prosecution's innuendos. John Sparrow, "Regina vs. Penguin Books Limited," *Encounter* 18, no. 2 (February 1962), 35–43.

18. Georges Bataille: "Organized transgression together with the taboo make social life what it is. The frequency—and the regularity—of transgressions do not affect the intangible stability of the prohibition since they are its expected complement . . . just as explosion follows upon compression. The compression is not subservient to the explosion, far from it; it gives it increased force." Bataille quotes Sade: "The best way of enlarging and multiplying one's desires is to try to limit them"; *Death and Sensuality*, anonymous translation (New York: Walker, 1962), pp. 65, 48.

19. This verdict essentially repeats Henry Miller's. Reading *Lady Chatterley* as an obscene book, rejecting the notion that any justification of obscenity can or should be given, Miller concludes that it is "a pity . . . that Lawrence ever wrote anything *about* obscenity, because in doing so he temporarily nullified everything he had created"; *The World of D. H. Lawrence* (Santa Barbara: Capra Press, 1980), pp. 175–177.

Censorship in South Africa

1. J. C. W. van Rooyen, *Censorship in South Africa* (Cape Town: Juta, 1987), p. 7; hereafter cited as *CSA*.

2. As van Rooyen presents the story, Mulder's intervention had nothing to do with his own feelings. As responsible minister, "he does not choose sides, but simply refers the book to the Appeal Board when uncertainty arises as to whether the decision of the [relevant] committee was right [*juis*]"; *Publikasiebeheer in Suid-Afrika* (Cape Town: Juta, 1978), pp. 13–14; hereafter cited as *Publikasiebeheer*.

3. *CSA*, 7. In calling its language vague, van Rooyen by no means intends criticism of the Act.

4. Publications Control Board, "Die tweede beslissing oor *Magersfontein, O Magersfontein!*" *Standpunte* 33/4 (no. 148) (1980), 11.

5. "Even though [the average man] might, in an unguarded moment, laugh at or become interested in the [reading] matter in question, his actions very often differ from his ideals of what should be allowed to be published and distributed"; *Publikasiebeheer*, 64.

6. D. N. MacCormick, "Privacy and Obscenity," in *Censorship and Obscenity*, ed. Rajeev Dhavan and Christie Davies (London: Martin Robertson, 1978), pp. 83–93.

7. Patrick Devlin, *The Enforcement of Morals* (Oxford: Oxford University Press, 1965); H. L. A. Hart, *Law, Liberty and Morality*, rev. ed. (Oxford: Oxford University Press, 1981); Ronald Dworkin, *Taking Rights Seriously* (Cambridge, Mass.: Harvard University Press, 1977).

   Dworkin points out that what appears to be a single argument in Devlin is in fact two arguments. The first is that society has a moral right to protect itself by imposing its standards on those who dissent, particularly when the public persistently voices feelings of "intolerance, indignation and disgust" on the issue. Dworkin labels this argument "intellectual sleight of hand": since "nothing more than passionate public disapproval is necessary" before the organs of the state are called into action, we are not in the area of morals at all but of politics (pp. 242–245). For this reason he dismisses it.

   The second argument Dworkin identifies in Devlin states that a society has a right to protect its central social institutions against acts that the vast bulk of its members disapprove on moral principle. One premise of this argument is that legislators must follow "any consensus of moral position which the community at large has reached" because this is a matter of "democratic principle" (Devlin, p. 17). But in fact this argument fails too, says Dworkin, because Devlin uses the notion "moral position" in a merely "anthropological sense." "It remains possible that this common opinion is a compound of prejudice . . . rationalization . . . and personal aversion (representing no conviction but merely blind hate . . .)" (Dworkin, pp. 253–254).

8. Dworkin, *Taking Rights Seriously*, p. 254.

9. Hart, *Law, Liberty and Morality*, pp. 48–49.

10. Ibid., p. 58.

11. Dworkin, *Taking Rights Seriously*, p. 24.

12. Ibid., p. 258.

13. In making inner conviction one criterion of true moral belief, Dworkin diverges from Mill, who identifies unreasoned inner conviction with mere opinion: "The contest between the morality which appeals to an external standard, and that which grounds itself on internal con-

viction, is the contest of progressive morality against stationary—of reason and argument against the deification of mere opinion and habit"; quoted in John C. Rees, *John Stuart Mill's On Liberty* (Oxford: Clarendon Press, 1985), p. 45.

Alexander Welsh argues powerfully that the political philosophy of J. S. Mill, and in particular his belief that conflict results from inadequate knowledge, was a determining influence on Freud's conception of censorship. Like Mill, Freud saw social rather than political constraint as the enemy. In *The Interpretation of Dreams*, the topics subjected to censorship are much the same as those not addressed freely in social intercourse: sex, aggression, ambition, negative judgments; John Stuart Mill, *On Liberty*, ed. Gertrude Himmelfarb (Harmondsworth: Penguin, 1974), p. 63; Alexander Welsh, *George Eliot and Blackmail* (Cambridge, Mass.: Harvard University Press, 1985), pp. 352–353.

14. Gilbert Marcus, "Reasonable Censorship?" in *Essays on Law and Social Practice in South Africa*, ed. Hugh Corder (Cape Town: Juta, 1988), pp. 353, 356.
15. Van Rooyen writes of a "tide of conservative reaction" that had by that time subsided in Britain and the United States but, by implication, had not yet subsided in South Africa (*CSA*, 14–15).
16. "A sickly [*sieklike*] treatment of sex." An instance of digital manipulation of a woman's sex organs is "perverse," part of "a sickly and morbid treatment of the sexual." Of a novel in which a murderer castrates his victim and leaves his testicles in his mouth: "Something of this kind belongs in a book about psychiatry. To give these revolting descriptions in fiction amounts to a dehumanization and bestialization of man" (*Publikasiebeheer*, 17, 18, 81). *Sickness/health* is a well-established metaphor in South African legal discourse as it seeks an object on to which to displace the undesirable. In 1972, for instance, the chief justice identified as his moral touchstone "the average modern reader with a healthy mind" (*CSA*, 56).
17. For Gordimer's own comment on these charges, see Nadine Gordimer et al., *What Happened to Burger's Daughter* (Johannesburg: Taurus, 1980), pp. 22–23.
18. Marcus, "Reasonable Censorship?" p. 352.
19. Sigmund Freud, "Psychoanalytic Notes on an Autobiographical Account of a Case of Paranoia" (1911), in *Pelican Freud Library*, vol. 9, ed. James Strachey and Angela Richards (Harmondsworth: Penguin, 1979), p. 218; hereafter cited as "Paranoia."
20. Ibid., pp. 213–214.
21. *CSA*, 147. As an instance of the extension of this metarule to the day-

to-day operations of the censorship itself, I cite an extraordinary judgment dating to 1971, which van Rooyen quotes in no spirit of criticism. The court prohibited a play in which interracial sex was favorably presented, not on the grounds that the play itself represented indecent/obscene/offensive/harmful acts but on the grounds that it brought the law against *performing* certain acts (namely interracial sexual acts) into contempt (*Publikasiebeheer*, 124). On the entire question of the authority of moral judgments, see R. W. Beardsmore, who argues persuasively that "in morality the notion of being in a better position to judge lacks sense"; "The Censorship of Works of Art," in *Philosophy and Fiction*, ed. Peter Lamarque (Aberdeen: Aberdeen University Press, 1983), p. 102.

22. "Paranoia," pp. 200–201. Far from taking Freud's little table of transformations lightly, Jacques Lacan argues that it is a powerful explanatory account; *De la psychose paranoiaque dans ses rapports avec la personnalité* (1932) (Paris: Seuil, 1975), pp. 261–262.
23. See Kenneth M. Colby, *Artificial Paranoia: A Computer Simulation of Paranoid Processes* (New York: Pergamon, 1975); Margaret A Boden, "Freudian Mechanisms of Defense: A Programming Perspective," in *Freud: A Collection of Critical Essays*, ed. Richard Wollheim (New York: Anchor Doubleday, 1974), particularly pp. 252–253, 263–264; William S. Faught, *Motivation and Intentionality in a Computer Simulation Model of Paranoia* (Basel: Birkhauser, 1978).
24. Lacan, *De la psychose paranoiaque*, p. 293.
25. Sigmund Freud, "Negation" (1925), in *Standard Edition*, vol. 19, ed. and trans. James Strachey (London: Hogarth Press, 1961), p. 239.
26. Freud, in a 1937 paper quoted by J. Laplanche, and J.-B. Pontalis, *The Language of Psycho-Analysis*, trans. Donald Nicholson-Smith (New York: Norton, 1973), pp. 262–263.
27. Ibid., pp. 139.
28. Jeremy Bentham, *An Introduction to the Principles of Morals and Legislation* (1823) (Oxford: Clarendon Press, 1907), pp. 205, 3, 23.

Man's Fate in the Novels of Alex la Guma

1. Wole Soyinka, "The Writer in the African State," *Transition*, no. 31 (1967), 12.
2. Lewis Nkosi, "Fiction by Black South Africans," in *Introduction to African Literature*, ed. Ulli Beier (Evanston: Northwestern University Press, 1967), p. 211.
3. Ibid., p. 212.

4. Jean-Paul Sartre, *What Is Literature?* trans. Bernard Frechtman (London: Methuen, 1967), p. 14.
5. The editions used in this essay are: *A Walk in the Night* (Evanston: Northwestern University Press, 1967); *And a Threefold Cord* (Berlin: Seven Seas, 1964); *The Stone Country* (Berlin: Seven Seas, 1967); *In the Fog of the Seasons' End* (London: Heinemann, 1972). La Guma published one more novel before his death in 1985: *The Time of the Butcherbird* (London: Heinemann, 1979).
6. Lewis Nkosi develops the same metaphor in the story "The Prisoner," reprinted in *African Writing Today*, ed. Ezekiel Mphahlele (Harmondsworth: Penguin, 1967). Comparing the two treatments, one can see that La Guma's allegiance belongs to an earlier literary generation than Nkosi's does.
7. See Alain Robbe-Grillet, "Nature, Humanism, Tragedy," in *For a New Novel*, trans. Richard Howard (New York: Grove Press, 1965), pp. 49–75. Robbe-Grillet's epigraph is from Roland Barthes: "Nothing is more insidious than tragedy."
8. "Pity is the feeling which arrests the mind in the presence of whatsoever is grave and constant in human suffering and unites it with the human sufferer. Terror is the feeling which arrests the mind in the presence of whatsoever is grave and constant in human suffering and unites it with the secret cause"; Stephen Dedalus in *Portrait of the Artist as a Young Man*, pt. 5.
9. The doubling of the hero complicates the structure. Each of the hero-victims acts as audience to the other, each is purged in and by the process of the other's suffering, and the reading audience is disenfranchised by having its catharsis embodied in the drama. This development is at least consistent with the nonparticipatory nature of book-reading.
10. Georg Lukács, *Studies in European Realism*, trans. Edith Bone (London: Hillway, 1950), pp. 170, 171.
11. Georg Lukács, *The Meaning of Contemporary Realism*, trans. John & Necke Mander (London: Merlin, 1962), pp. 34, 35.
12. Gustave Flaubert, letter of October 2, 1856. *Correspondance*, ed. Jean Bruneau (Paris: Gallimard, 1980), II, 635.
13. Sartre, *What Is Literature?* p. 75.
14. Roland Barthes describes how the style of nineteenth-century French realism, with its "spectacular signs of fabrication," came to be adopted first by the petit bourgeoisie as a favored style for their reading matter and later by socialist realist writers. See "Writing and Revolution," in *Writing Degree Zero*, trans. Annette Lavers and Colin Smith (New York: Hill & Wang, 1968), pp. 67–73.

Athol Fugard, *Notebooks, 1960–1977*

1. Athol Fugard, *Notebooks, 1960–1977*, ed. Mary Benson (New York: Knopf, 1984).

Breyten Breytenbach, *The Confessions of an Albino Terrorist* and *Mouroir*

1. Breyten Breytenbach, *The True Confessions of an Albino Terrorist* (New York: Farrar, Straus and Giroux, 1985) and *Mouroir* (New York: Farrar, Straus and Giroux, 1984).

Nadine Gordimer, *The Essential Gesture*

1. Nadine Gordimer, *The Essential Gesture*, ed. Stephen Clingman (Johannesburg: Taurus; Cape Town: David Philip, 1988).

=

Sources and Credits

"The Comedy of Point of View in Beckett's *Murphy*." First published in *Critique* 12 (1970).

"The Manuscript Revisions of Beckett's *Watt*." An abridged version of an article first published in *Journal of Modern Literature* 2 (1972). Copyright Temple University. Quotations courtesy of the Harry Ransom Humanities Research Center, The University of Texas at Austin.

"Samuel Beckett and the Temptations of Style." First published in *Theoria*, no. 41 (1973).

"Remembering Texas." First published as "How I Learned about America—and Africa—in Texas" in the *New York Times Book Review*, 15 April 1984. The original text has been restored.

"Achterberg's 'Ballade van de gasfitter': The Mystery of I and You." First published in *PMLA* 92 (1977). Copyright Modern Language Association of America.

"The First Sentence of Yvonne Burgess' *The Strike*." First published in *English in Africa* 3 (1976).

"A Note on Writing." First published in *Momentum: On Recent South African Writing*, ed. M. J. Daymond, J. U. Jacobs, and Margaret Lenta (Pietermaritzburg: University of Natal Press, 1984).

Jerusalem Prize Acceptance Speech. Delivered in Jerusalem in April 1987 on the occasion of receiving the Jerusalem Prize.

"Captain America in American Mythology." First published in *University of Cape Town Studies in English*, no. 6 (1976).

"The Burden of Consciousness in Africa." First published in *Speak* (Cape Town) 1, no. 1 (1977).

"Four Notes on Rugby." First published in *Speak* 1, no. 4 (1978).

"Triangular Structures of Desire in Advertising." First published in *Critical Arts* (University of the Witwatersrand) 1 (1980).

"The Rhetoric of the Passive in English." First published in *Linguistics* 18 (1980).

"The Agentless Sentence as Rhetorical Device." First published in *Language & Style* 13, no. 1 (1980).

"Isaac Newton and the Ideal of a Transparent Scientific Language." First published in *Journal of Literary Semantics* 11 (1982).

"Time, Tense, and Aspect in Kafka's 'The Burrow.'" First published as

"Time, Tense, and Aspect in Kafka's 'Der Bau'" in *Modern Language Notes* 96 (1981).

"Robert Musil's Stories of Women." A review of Robert Musil's *Five Women* first published in the *New York Review of Books*, 18 December 1986. Copyright © Nyrev, Inc.

"Confession and Double Thoughts: Tolstoy, Rousseau, Dostoevsky." First published in *Comparative Literature* 37 (1985).

"The Taint of the Pornographic: Defending (against) *Lady Chatterley*." First published in *Mosaic* 21, no. 1 (1988).

"Censorship in South Africa." First published in *English in Africa* 17 (1990).

"Man's Fate in the Novels of Alex La Guma." First published in its present version in *Studies in Black Literature* 5 (1974).

"Into the Dark Chamber: The Writer and the South African State." First published in shorter form in the *New York Times Book Review*, 12 January 1986.

Review of Athol Fugard, *Notebooks, 1960–1977*. First published in *New Republic*, 9 April 1984.

Review of Breyten Breytenbach, *True Confessions of an Albino Terrorist* and *Mouroir*. First published in *New Republic*, 11 March 1985.

Review of Nadine Gordimer, *The Essential Gesture*. First published in *Die Suid-Afrikaan*, no. 24 (December 1989).

Index